WINNING HEARTS AND

British Governments, the Media and Colonial Counter-insurgency 1944–1960

WINNING HEARTS AND MINDS

British Governments, the Media and Colonial Counter-insurgency 1944–1960

SUSAN L. CARRUTHERS

Leicester University Press
London and New York

First published 1995 by
Leicester University Press, *A Cassell imprint*
Wellington House, 125 Strand, London WC2R 0BB, England
215 Park Avenue South, New York, New York 10003, USA

British Library Cataloguing-in-Publication Data
Carruthers, Susan L.
  Winning Hearts and Minds: British
  Governments, the Media and Colonial
  Counter-insurgency, 1944–60
  I. Title
  322.42

ISBN 0-7185-0027-X (hardback)
    0-7185-0028-8 (paperback)

Library of Congress Cataloging-in-Publication Data
Carruthers, Susan L. (Susan Lisa)
    Winning hearts and minds : British governments, the media and colonial counter-
  insurgency 1944–1960 / Susan L. Carruthers.
      p.   cm.
    Includes bibliographical references and index.
    ISBN 0-7185-0027-X (hb), — ISBN 0-7185-0028-8 (pb)
    1. Great Britain—Colonies—History—20th century.
  2. Counter insurgency—Great Britain—Colonies—History—20th century. 3. Public
  opinion—Great Britain—Colonies—History—20th century. 4. Insurgency—Great
  Britain—Colonies—History—20th century. 5. Mass media—Great Britain—Colonies—
  History—20th century. 6. Terrorism—Great Britain—Colonies—History—20th century.
  7 Propaganda, British.   I. Title
  DA16.C34   1995
  325'.3141—dc20

                                                                                    95-7954
                                                                                    CIP

Printed and bound in Great Britain by Biddles Ltd, Guildford and
King's Lynn

Contents

Contents

Acknowledgements

In any project of this size, gratitude is owed to more people and institutions than can be thanked individually. Those whom I have listed below deserve special credit.

To begin with institutions: The Public Record Office at Kew formed the major archival source of this book, and I am indebted to the many members of staff who both supplied documents and answered queries. Crown-copyright material in the Public Record Office is quoted with the permission of the Controller of Her Majesty's Stationery Office. I would also like to thank the Librarian of Rhodes House Library, Oxford, for allowing me access to, and permission to cite, a number of collections of private papers housed therein. Similarly, I must thank the Department of Documents at the Imperial War Museum, for allowing me to use private papers and letters. More particularly, I acknowledge the permission of the family of General Erskine to quote from his letters. The family of Field Marshal Templer have also kindly allowed me to use material from Templer's papers, which are housed within the National Army Museum. I am grateful to Jacqueline Kavanagh and the staff of the BBC Written Archives Centre, Caversham, for their assistance on my research trips there, and for allowing me to use material from BBC scripts and policy documents. Times Newspapers Limited must also be thanked for permission to use collections of papers housed in *The Times* Archive. While many libraries have been used in the writing of this book, I wish to thank in particular the staff of the British Library (including the Colindale Newspaper Library); the Brotherton Library, University of Leeds; the Hugh Owen Library, University of Wales, Aberystwyth; and the National Library of Wales, Aberystwyth. I was also fortunate to be able to view archive newsreel material at the Visnews, British Movietone and Pathé archives. The staff of the last named, especially, must be thanked for giving freely of their time and expertise.

As for individuals to whom I owe particular thanks: Dr Philip Taylor, at the Institute of Communications Studies, University of Leeds, supervised my doctoral thesis (which this book took its life from) since its inception. The British Academy provided me with the financial wherewithal to undertake a prolonged period of postgraduate research. Professor Charles Townshend of the University of Keele, as examiner of the thesis, supplied a number of perceptive reflections on my work. On a more day-to-day basis, my colleagues in the Department of International Politics, University of Wales, Aberystwyth, have provided me not only with a stimulating intellectual environment in which to complete this book, but also with much good humour and friendship. In the completion of the manuscript, Conor McGrath devoted a very considerable amount of his time to assist me, and was an invaluable weeder-out of my inconsistencies. Finally, I wish to thank my parents, who have over the years provided me with so much. I dedicate this book to them with love and gratitude.

Abbreviations

AAC	Anglo-American Commission on Palestine
AKEL	Cypriot Communist Party
ANC	African National Congress
BBC	British Broadcasting Corporation
BIS	British Information Service
CAB	Cabinet (Papers)
CC	Cabinet Committee
CCP	Chinese Communist Party
CIC	Cyprus Intelligence Committee
CID	Criminal Investigation Department
CIGS	Chief of the Imperial General Staff
CO	Colonial Office
COI	Central Office of Information
COID	Colonial Office Information Department
COS	Chief of Staff
CP	Cabinet Paper
CP	Communist Party
CPGB	Communist Party of Great Britain
CPSU	Communist Party of the Soviet Union
CRO	Commonwealth Relations Office
CT	Communist Terrorist
dir	Directed by
DO	Dominions Office
EOKA	National Organization of Cypriot Fighters
ETA	Basque Homeland and Liberty
ETU	Electrical Trades Union
FO	Foreign Office
GHQ	General Headquarters
GOC	General Officer Commanding
H.C. Debs	House of Commons Debates (Hansard)
HQ	Headquarters
HMG	His/Her Majesty's Government
HMSO	His/Her Majesty's Stationery Office
HO	Home Office
IPD	Information Policy Department
IRA	Irish Republican Army
IRD	Information Research Department
ISD	Information Services Department

Abbreviations

ITV	Independent Television
IWM	Imperial War Museum, London
JIC	Joint Intelligence Committee
JIPC	Joint Information and Propaganda Committee
KAU	Kenya African Union
KCA	Kikuyu Central Association
MCP	Malayan Communist Party
MELF	Middle East Land Forces
MFU	Malayan Films Unit
M-O	Mass-Observation
MOI	Ministry of Information
MP	Member of Parliament
MPAJA	Malayan Peoples' Anti-Japanese Army
MRLA	Malayan Races Liberation Army
MSS	Malayan Security Service
NAM	National Army Museum, London
NATO	North Atlantic Treaty Organization
NCO	Non-commissioned officer
NFA	National Film Archive, London
NY	New York
OAG	Officer Administering the Government
PEAK	Pan-Hellenic Committee for Self-Determination for Cyprus
PEON	Pan-Cyprian Youth Organization
PIO	Palestine Information Officer
PM	Prime Minister
POW	Prisoner of War
PPS	Paliamentary Private Secretary
PQ	Parliamentary Question
PRC	People's Republic of China
PREM	Prime Minister's Papers
PRO	Public Record Office, Kew
PRO	Public Relations Officer
PWE	Political Warfare Executive
RAF	Royal Air Force
RIC	Royal Irish Constabulary
RIO	Regional Information Office
RN	Royal Navy
SEP	Surrendered Enemy Personnel
S.S.Cols	Secretary of State for the Colonies
TUC	Trades Union Congress
UK	United Kingdom
UMNO	United Malays National Organization
UN	United Nations
UNO	United Nations Organization
UNSCOP	United Nations Special Commission on Palestine

USA	United States of America
USSR	Union of Soviet Socialist Republics
WAC	BBC Written Archives Centre, Caversham
WFTU	World Federation of Trade Unions
WO	War Office

Introduction

FOR YOUR CLICHÉ ALBUM

In what can no man tell the future has for us?
Store.
With what do certain belligerents make their military disposi-
tions?
Typical Teutonic thoroughness.
In what manner do wishful thinkers imagine that the war will
be over this year?
Fondly.
Take the word, 'relegate'. To what must a person be relegated?
That obscurity from which he should never have been permitted
to emerge.
What may one do with a guess, provided one is permitted?
Hazard.
And what is comment?
Superfluous.

Myles na Gopaleen (Flann O'Brien)[1]

O'Brien might have added: 'Which part of people's anatomies do politicians aspire to win besides their minds? Hearts.' The phrase 'winning
hearts and minds' is now routinely invoked by those attempting to
appeal to public opinion, whether as agents of the state or challengers
to it. The coinage was apparently General Templer's (although his title
is not undisputed) during his reign as High Commissioner in Malaya,
and to Templer's apparent chagrin it has rarely been out of currency
ever since.[2] While the prospect of a third 'total war' recedes, considerable scholarly and military attention has over the past decade been
devoted to what is (sometimes rather euphemistically) termed 'low-
intensity conflict'. Britain's colonial counter-insurgency campaigns have
received their share of attention, as one of the associated phenomena.
The genre encompasses both monographs on particular colonial 'Emergencies' such as David Charters's, *The British Army and Jewish Insurgency
in Palestine, 1945–7* and Richard Stubbs's *Hearts and Minds in Guerrilla Warfare: The Malayan Emergency 1948–60*, as well as overarching treatments
of Britain's counter-insurgency experience as a whole, most notably
Thomas Mockaitis's *British Counterinsurgency, 1919–60*.[3] Yet what such

1

studies tend to lack, perhaps rather surprisingly, is due attention to what 'winning hearts and minds' actually meant. In particular, there has been insufficient recognition that the 'hearts and minds' at stake for British governments were not confined to the contested colonial territories, but were to be found among the electorate of the United Kingdom itself. It is to this issue that the present volume is addressed.

The book examines British governmental attempts to influence opinion about challenges to colonial rule in four counter-insurgency campaigns which occurred largely after World War II.[4] They are the Zionist insurgency in Palestine (1944–47), the Malayan Emergency (1948–60), Mau Mau in Kenya (1952–60) and the EOKA campaign in Cyprus (1955–59). In elucidating how successive governments laboured to shape public opinion a number of contested terms will unavoidably appear, foremost among them 'terrorism' and 'propaganda'. During each insurgency, those who took up arms against British rule were deemed 'terrorists' – though not always immediately, for reasons that will be examined below. Much of this study is, in effect, an examination of how particular uses of violence were interpreted by governments, militaries and colonial servants; of both what 'terrorism' was taken to mean, and of how it was projected to wider audiences. It has long been realized that the label 'terrorism' is frequently (arguably, always) applied as a stigmatizing label to violent acts of which the commentator disapproves, thus the cliché 'one man's freedom fighter is another man's terrorist' – a truism which dates back to the French Revolution, according to E.V. Walter, since when '"terrorist" has been an epithet to fasten on a political enemy'.[5] A more sophisticated formulation of the 'common-sense' view is the argument, first proposed by Greisman in 1977, that terrorism can only have a socially constructed meaning.[6] In Jennifer Hocking's words:

> Replete with implied moral opprobrium, a socially assigned value and meaning, an imputation of illegitimacy and outrage, 'terrorism' can never fit the apparently value-neutral typologies much used in the social sciences.[7]

Each chapter of this book explores how governments (and their agents) attempted to construct 'terrorism' in a distinct setting. The task of assigning meaning to the term, and thus of mediating public perceptions of the enemy, was carried out partly through official channels: press releases, speeches in the Houses of Parliament and Parliamentary Questions, material produced by the Central Office of Information (COI) or similar offices in the colonies themselves, and so on. Through these means and other more informal channels, successive governments attempted to persuade the mass communications media to share their values and interpretations of events in the colonies: a process now (if not at the time) dubbed 'news management'. Both activities are referred to broadly herein as 'propaganda'. Like terrorism, the word propaganda is frequently regarded as carrying pejorative overtones – tarnished by its association with manufactured atrocity stories in World War I and with Goebbels's supposed fondness for the 'Big Lie' in World War II. As used in this book, however, 'propaganda' is not intended to convey a negative meaning; rather it is used to signify the self-interested nature of the process by which governments (or indeed their opponents) communicate with their audiences. Thus while the term 'propaganda' is, in this usage, neutral in the sense that it conveys no value judge-ment on the message being propagated, its use suggests that political communication is itself *not* neutral. That both the incumbents of power and their challengers may well have believed that the version of events which they promoted was 'the truth' is immaterial. Propaganda is not defined by its untruthfulness, and few writers on the subject would now agree with Leonard Doob's proposition that propaganda is necessarily directed 'towards ends considered unscientific or of doubtful value in a society at a particular time'.[8] 'Propaganda' thus denotes a process of communication, and there seems little meaningful distinction to be drawn between 'information' or 'publicity', the terms governments prefer for their own efforts at persuasive communication, and 'propaganda', the label invariably given to their opponents' attempts at the same.

This emphasis on governmental propaganda, and on government–media relations, is the reverse to that more normally found in writ-ings on terrorism and counter-insurgency. Traditionally, it has been the terrorists or insurgents who are seen as engaged in a propagandistic strategy, through which they attempt to gain publicity by manipulating the media's fascination with violence. Even before mass media existed, the linkage between terrorism and propaganda had been made, with certain nineteenth-century Russian revolutionaries and other European anarchists, who are often seen as the progenitors of modern terrorism, describing their activities as 'propaganda of the deed'. They viewed vio-lence as not only functional in its own right – by removing key state office-holders or destroying buildings – but as serving a wider, symbolic purpose: that of rousing onlookers to action.[9] A similar function is often attributed to contemporary terrorist 'atrocities'. Insurgent terrorism, as Schmid and de Graaf were among the first to argue, is a 'violent communication' strategy, in which there are at least two targets: those who are selected for physical attack, and the psychological targets – namely the wider audience. In the latter respect, terrorists may be attempting to evoke several responses simultaneously, by aiming at different audiences. Schmid and de Graaf distinguish between the 'target of attention' and the 'target of demands'.[10] For example, the protagonists may wish to arouse in some a terror that will generate political pressure on policy-makers to accede to their organization's demands, or sufficient fear that the target audience will not actively support counter-terrorist measures. In a different segment of the audience, however, they may wish to arouse the sympathy which will sustain them. As Mao famously remarked, the terrorist 'fish' require 'water' in which to swim.

Terrorism, in short, may be viewed as a propagandistic strategy, in the sense that it is largely psychological, as opposed to purely physical. Definitions of propaganda and of terrorism can be strikingly similar. For example, Qualter's definition of propaganda as 'the deliberate attempt by the few to influence the behaviour and attitudes of the many by the manipulation of symbolic communication'[11] reads very much like T.P. Thornton's understanding of terrorism as 'a symbolic act designed to influence political behaviour by extra-normal means'.[12] As Schmid and de Graaf conclude:

Terrorism cannot be understood only in terms of violence. It has to be understood primarily in terms of propaganda. Violence and propaganda have much in common. Violence aims at behaviour modification by coercion. Propaganda aims at the same through persuasion. Terrorism is a combination of the two.[13]

Not only are terrorism and propaganda intimately connected, but also (as has again been frequently pointed out) terrorists often accompany their violent actions with more conventional propaganda of the word – with leaflets, pamphlets, communiqués, and even clandestine radio broadcasts.[14] The use of propaganda by terrorist organizations has been the subject of a growing number of studies. In particular, Maurice Tugwell has undertaken considerable research in the area, and a recent monograph by Joanne Wright has added substantially to the growing body of literature on the Provisional IRA's propaganda.[15]

If terrorism relies on the transmission of various messages to audiences who may be remote from the location of violent acts, then it follows that the media have a role to play in transmitting those messages. The notion that terrorists are essentially publicity-seekers has become commonplace. In Britain the belief that terrorists seek the media's attention and that by denying them publicity one can help defeat terrorism became entrenched in legislation during the 1980s. Margaret Thatcher's view of publicity as the 'oxygen of terrorism' (a formulation which she borrowed, with permission, from the former Chief Rabbi, Lord Jakobovits[16]) resulted in limitations on broadcasts featuring members of proscribed organizations in Northern Ireland.[17] The lifting of the ban – widely viewed as having been counter-productive, even among a majority of Conservative Cabinet ministers – was one of the Major administration's first symbolic responses to the Provisional IRA's ceasefire in September 1994.

The seeming complicity of the media in terrorism also prompted a wider moral panic outside the United Kingdom, resulting in a rush of literature during the 1980s and early 1990s probing this relationship.[18] Many of these works (often the offshoot of conferences) sought to elucidate how far the media had a responsibility to aid state counter-terrorist initiatives, and whether broadcasters and journalists should consequently submit to voluntary 'restraint' or involuntary censorship when reporting terrorism. Some critics of the orthodoxy, however, have elucidated the utility to the state (as well as the media) of an exaggerated terrorist threat: for the media, terror attracts audiences; for the state, fear of terrorism encourages a largely uncritical acceptance of counter-terrorist measures which may often be injurious to civil liberties, if not of dubious international legality.[19] From this perspective, it is questionable whether terrorists – by generating newsworthy events – automatically turn the media into unwitting accomplices, since the media have their own uses for terrorism. Nor would critics such as Schlesinger, Elliott and Murdock accept A.H. Miller's contention that 'for terrorists, it is not really important if the self-portrayal is publicly approved or disapproved'.[20] They, indeed, would dispute whether terrorism *is* necessarily always publicity-seeking:

Political violence is not reducible to communicative behaviour alone, even though certain acts have made prime-time viewing of late. This thesis assumes that violent acts take place only, or primarily, because they will achieve media coverage.[21]

Like Eric Hobsbawm, they would argue that acts labelled terrorism are frequently a violent enactment by the disenfranchised of the familiar phrase 'Don't just stand there, do something.'[22] Publicity is not the only objective of terrorists: their real aim is to alter political structures, to which end publicity may be but a first step.

Certainly the emphasis on terrorism's symbiotic relationship with the media has helped foster a certain historical myopia. Several writers on 'international terrorism' have suggested that this was a new hybrid which was only born in 1968 – the year in which the first skyjacking (of an El Al airliner by the Popular Front for the Liberation of Palestine) occurred.[23] The rationale behind seeing international terrorism as an entirely new departure lay in the fact that terrorists exploited new technology – from jet aircraft to lightweight explosives – and that, in particular, *international* terrorists needed the media (with their new satellite communications capabilities) to ensure that target audiences across the world learnt of their technologically innovative actions. Accordingly, Chaliand argued that the explosion of terrorism after 1968 could be 'attributed almost exclusively to the development of the mass media'.[24] Nor was he alone in being seduced into regarding 1968 as a watershed year. Many writers appear ignorant of terrorism's existence before 1968, or think that it was qualitatively so different as not really to constitute 'terrorism' at all, just as Chaliand claims that 'today's terrorism ... has virtually nothing in common with the conventional terrorism long used by such political movements with a specialist armed wing, such as Irgun and the Stern Gang'.[25] The Royal United Services Institute, for example, published a collection in 1979 entitled *Ten Years of Terrorism*.[26] Likewise, Conor Gearty, writing in 1991, set out to answer the question whether '"terrorist" and "terrorism" have any coherent meaning today, twenty-three years after they first began to seep into our vocabulary'.[27]

Terrorism has, of course, existed for much longer than the past twenty-five years, although for precisely how much longer depends on what one considers terrorism.[28] The term terrorism first came into currency after the French Revolution to describe the reign of terror visited on the French aristocracy by the Jacobins.[29] The Jacobins practised what Thornton describes as 'enforcement' terror: violence from above to achieve compliance with the state.[30] 'Agitational' terror – a 'siege' rather than a 'reign' of terror, enacted by those challenging the incumbents of power – followed not far behind.[31] Indeed, Noel O'Sullivan has argued that the French Revolution gave birth to a form of ideological politics (the 'can-do' ethos of the Enlightenment) of which terrorism was but the most extreme form:

> ever since 1789, there has existed at the very heart of the Western political tradition a fundamental ambiguity which has not only left it – and continues to leave it – exposed to extremist interpretations of the terrorist sort, but has also ensured widespread sympathy in Western states for acts of violence perpetrated in the name of political causes.[32]

Britain has a particularly long history of dealing with what has been perceived, at least in Whitehall and Westminster, as terrorism. Throughout the nineteenth century, small oath-bound groups of Irish tenants formed organizations which attacked the land tenancy system, using terror to compel compliance. 'Whiteboyism', as Charles Townshend has remarked, was 'of course labelled "terrorism" by the government' – with some justification.[33] 'Agitational' terror, which seeks to rouse onlookers to action rather than to ensure passive co-operation, also has a long, though sporadic, history in Ireland. While Narodnaya Volya was developing a theory of terrorism (propaganda of the deed) in Russia, certain Irish organizations were also beginning to think along similar lines.

Some of the most notorious Irish 'atrocities' of the nineteenth century, the Clerkenwell and Manchester explosions of 1867, were not, however, intentional acts of terrorism at all. Both the explosions were meant to release Irish Republican Brotherhood prisoners rather than to kill their guards, but the unforeseen panic which the bombs caused in England, resulting in 'Fenian fever', doubtless convinced other Irish rebels that terror could have useful political effects. Gladstone himself credited the 'Fenian conspiracy' with drawing Ireland to public attention in England,

and placing it on the political agenda. His words, in turn, were roundly condemned by John Devoy (an opponent of terrorism), who argued that they 'proved a stronger argument in favour of physical force – and even of Terrorism – on the part of Ireland . . . than any Irishman ever made'.[34]

In the 1880s three separate Republican groups did espouse varieties of terrorism, more or less self-consciously. The notorious Phoenix Park murders of 1882 were carried out by the Irish National Invincibles, who saw the killings of Lord Frederick Cavendish, the new Chief Secretary for Ireland, and the Permanent Under-Secretary, Thomas Burke, as a form of propaganda: 'light thrown in terrible handfuls' into the eyes of the masses.[35] The years 1880–87 also saw a bombing campaign in Britain carried out by two Irish-American organizations: Clan na Gael and Jeremiah O'Donovan Rossa's Skirmishers. These groups both rejected assassination in favour of dynamite 'outrages', which would, in Ken Short's phrase, hold London to ransom.[36] Pressure was to be applied directly to English public opinion, with *The Times* conveying the belief, in January 1885, that the dynamiters aimed 'to strike terror into the souls of Englishmen, whether by the indiscriminate slaughter of holiday makers and working people, or by the destruction of precious historical monuments'.[37]

The Easter Rising of 1916 made more conventional use of physical force. Although there was a propaganda dimension to the violence of the Rising – Townshend suggests that it amounted to '"demonstration politics", the armed propaganda of a self-selected vanguard which claimed the power to interpret the general will' – its architects did not seek terror so much as an outright seizure of power.[38] However, in the aftermath of the failed coup, the Irish Republican Brotherhood (which transmogrified into the Irish Republican Army) began to elaborate guerrilla principles which were put into operation in the 'war' of 1919–21. While historians have tended to regard the IRA's campaign as essentially a guerrilla one, it was nevertheless one in which 'the use of terror played an important part in removing dangerous enemies, weakening British morale and deterring civilians from helping the government forces'.[39] Furthermore, Lloyd George's administration regarded its opponents as employing 'terrorism'; as Walter Long informed the Cabinet on 21 November 1918: 'We were face to face with an organised movement to overthrow the Government of Ireland and to reassert the authority of a terrorist Sinn Fein minority.'[40] Periodically since 1921, British governments have faced fresh onslaughts from the IRA in its various reincarnations: a brief bombing campaign in England between 1938 and 1939; sporadic violence (largely within Northern Ireland and the Republic) in the late 1950s and early 1960s; and the 'Troubles' which began in 1969.

Successive British governments have additionally seen 'terrorist' challenges to their imperial authority in a wide variety of settings, predating those which we will analyse. Terrorism was a recurring problem in

India's North West Frontier province and Bengal.[41] A report on Indian terrorism in 1933 suggested that terrorists in Chittagong had employed methods which 'bore a marked resemblance to those of Sinn Feiners'.[42] If terrorist organizations copied from one another (and it is generally assumed that they did and still do[43]), British governments similarly transferred the techniques of 'imperial policing' developed to deal with Indian terrorism, such as the use of air power to bomb rebellious areas and the employment of tear gas, to terrorist insurgencies elsewhere, in particular the Arab Rebellion in Palestine between 1936 and 1938.[44]

In the 1930s the designation 'terrorism' was also applied by British (and other) governments to the spate of assassinations of leaders and statesmen. Following the assassination of M. Barthou, the French Foreign Minister, and King Alexander of Yugoslavia in 1934, terrorism appeared an international problem of such dimensions that the League of Nations attempted to legislate against it.[45] As the United Nations subsequently found in its attempts to frame legislation on international terrorism, the first problem is to reach inter-governmental agreement on what constitutes terrorism. The League sought to differentiate between 'a mere act of private vengeance or hostility' and an act 'intended or likely to create a state of terror or panic, either in the mind of the individual or in the minds of a restricted number of persons or in the public mind'.[46] Needless to say, the League's attempt to outlaw terrorism was as unsuccessful as the League itself. World War II, whose outbreak hammered the last nail in the coffin of that attempt at collective security, is also sometimes 'blamed' for the prevalence of terrorism in the post-war era. Michael Walzer, for example, in the course of his argument for justice in warfare, ascribes the profusion of post-1945 terrorism to the indiscriminacy with which World War II was fought:

> terrorism in the strict sense, the random murder of innocent people, emerged as a strategy of revolutionary struggle only in the period after World War Two, that is, after it had become a feature of conventional war.[47]

Walzer appears slightly wide of the mark here, on several counts. Terrorism is not necessarily 'random'. It may have the appearance of being indiscriminate while actually being quite selective, as Thornton pointed out, though he (less convincingly) insisted that all terrorists must aim for the appearance of indiscriminacy.[48] Walzer's phrase 'innocent people' is similarly problematic, for it begs the question 'innocent according to whom?'. If one considers the most persistent 'terrorist organization' of the modern period, the Provisional IRA, it is obvious that it has targeted both the unarmed, who in conventional warfare would not be considered legitimate targets, and members of the security forces, who would. Are both civilians and members of the security forces 'innocent people' because the IRA is not strictly speaking at war with Great Britain, or is the IRA only 'terrorist' when it murders civilians 'randomly'? What, then, of the selective murder of civilians? We must recognize that there are competing standards of legitimacy in operation: the Provisional IRA would claim, as did the IRA in 1919–21, that 'legitimate targets' – the guilty – include those who aid the state or the security forces in tangential ways.[49] Indeed, Townshend argues that the enforcement terror practised by 'the Fenians and their successors' has relied on cultivation of the 'myth of infallible vengeance against "spies and informers"'[50]: in other words, that it has been both discriminate and predictable. In fact, most organizations which have been labelled 'terrorist' both before and after World War II – including those with which this study is specifically concerned – have engaged in violence which *did* discriminate to some degree, although the categories discriminated against may have been so broad (or so 'illegitimate' in most observers' eyes) as to appear random, where randomness was taken as the particular evil of terrorism.

The four particular counter-insurgencies examined herein all occurred in the wake of World War II: the Zionist campaign of violence in Palestine began before hostilities ended, though only after it had become clear which side would ultimately triumph. Although these case studies form part of a lengthier history of terrorism in its pre-1968 incarnation, there are also several aspects of the wider post-war context which require elucidation. First, these counter-insurgency campaigns formed part of a broader process of decolonization which occurred with varying degrees of rapidity after the war. World War II weakened Britain's grip over its colonies both morally and materially.[51] In moral terms, 'Empire' increasingly appeared to be an idea whose time had expired – the war having left the two most vocally 'anti-imperialist' powers pre-eminent (though both the USA and the USSR clearly made honourable exceptions of their own imperialistic tendencies). In many, if not all, parts of the Empire, the war had stoked anti-colonial sentiment, and in Asia particularly, the Japanese occupation of British territories vividly illustrated the vulnerability of an imperial power which had hitherto looked wellnigh invincible. Stephen Howe's recent research has also shed light upon how the ideal of colonial freedom gained ground in the United Kingdom during the war, as British anti-colonialists developed closer links with their counterparts in the colonial territories themselves.[52] Paradoxically, however, Britain's economic necessity for retaining its Empire had never been stronger. During the war, the colonies underwrote much of the war effort, and the British government emerged from it indebted not only to the United States but also effectively to the Empire-Commonwealth. Britain's dependency relationships with both continued in peacetime; indeed, precisely because it urgently needed to rectify its balance of payments deficit with the USA, the British government looked to the colonies to help produce much-needed dollars. How catastrophic, then, for Attlee's post-war administration that some of those territories which were precisely the most lucrative for this purpose were also those over which Britain's physical grip had most weakened during war. There is surely no better example of this than Malaya, where Communists, who had formed the main wartime resistance to Japan's occupation, presented a formidable post-war challenge to renewed imperial rule. In each of the case studies, the onset of violent resistance to colonialism portended the end of British rule, though the ultimate beneficiaries were not always those who had mounted the 'terrorist' campaign. The events described herein thus also constitute part of the fabric of decolonization, and can be read as addressing – in however incomplete a fashion – a deficiency which Stephen Howe has highlighted in the surrounding literature: namely its lack of attention to how the British media, and public opinion, perceived the process of losing an Empire.[53]

A second wider context into which these case studies fit is the history of governmental propaganda, as it was employed to meet the exigencies of the post-war era. Again, some reference to wartime developments is germane. World War II saw a more intense mobilization of the psychological weapons of war than any previous conflict. The British government spawned various organizations to prosecute what are often regarded as the shadowier aspects of warfare, in response to Goebbels's extensive Reich Ministry for Enlightenment and Propaganda. (Ironically, British propagandists were competing with an organization Goebbels had partially modelled on Britain's World War I propaganda set-up, which was regarded in Germany as immensely successful in destroying home front morale.) Within the United Kingdom, the Ministry of Information (MOI) dealt essentially with domestic propaganda: lifting and maintaining domestic morale, dealing with the mass communications media (of which the BBC was seen as crucially important), with responsibilities for both releasing and censoring news.[54] Propaganda for overseas audiences, whether they lay in Germany, the occupied territories or the Empire-Commonwealth, took rather longer to organize coherently. It was not until August 1941 that the Political Warfare Executive (PWE) was established to oversee both external propaganda and psychological warfare – that branch of propaganda which was specifically devoted to destroying the enemy's will to fight.[55] The PWE made extensive use of black propaganda techniques, especially radio stations, though certainly far from all of its activities fell into this category.[56] Indeed, its black and white activities were carefully kept at a distance: an important part of the PWE's work involved liaison with the BBC overseas services, which were most anxious to carry as accurate news broadcasts as wartime security dictates permitted, and absolutely refused any connection with black radio broadcasting.

At the end of the war, both the MOI and PWE were rapidly disbanded. Governments in democratic states prefer to maintain that propaganda is resorted to as a wartime expedient only – a claim which should be treated with due scepticism. World War II propaganda and intelligence organizations did not all die quietly at the war's end, though there is no precise parallel in the United Kingdom for the lobbying work which the Office of Strategic Services in the United States carried out on its own behalf, leading ultimately to the creation of the USA's first centralized intelligence agency.[57] In Britain, the MOI was replaced with the Central Office of Information (COI), which bore little resemblance to its predecessor, functioning merely as a service department which produced publicity material for government ministries.[58] Likewise, the PWE was disbanded, though some of its staff went on functioning under auspices of the Foreign Office Political Intelligence Department, which had been used as a cover to fund the PWE's secret wartime existence. Initially, one of the most pressing tasks for post-war propaganda was de-Nazification, both of German POWs in British hands and of occupied Germany more broadly.[59] One legacy of the war was thus that propaganda and psychological warfare were seen in Westminster as immensely important – though precisely how effective was a subject of some debate. The impact of propaganda is notoriously difficult to assess; thus, to derive an example from World War II, it was not easy to disentangle the work which had been done by propaganda, as opposed to strategic bombing, in destroying German morale. In the absence of any scientific means of measuring propaganda's impact, there were naturally disagreements over the limits of what propaganda could achieve. Such differences of opinion can be seen played out in the case studies.

The onset of the Cold War generated a remobilization of many propaganda and psychological warfare 'experts' who had learnt their trade between 1939 and 1945. The period under study coincides with arguably the most intense period of Cold War (only surpassed, in the estimation of some, by the 'Second Cold War' of the early 1980s).[60] The global Cold War intrudes in each of the counter-insurgencies selected for scrutiny, permeating governmental responses to violence, which was consistently greeted as a manifestation – potential or actual – of international Communist intrigue. By 1947, Attlee's Cabinet, urged in this direction by the Foreign Office, had become convinced that the Soviet Union had embarked on a global expansionist crusade, competing not only for physical but also for psychological territory – 'men's minds'.[61] Accordingly, the processes of decolonization and Cold War were intertwined, not least in the minds of Whitehall observers, who feared that the Soviets were fomenting already latent anti-colonial unrest in the colonies. In short, the Cold War was perceived as a global battle of ideas, in which Britain had to make redoubled efforts to sell the Empire-Commonwealth as 'a world-wide community of peoples associated for mutual benefit and not for the exploitation of one by another'.[62] But if the Cold War made Britain vulnerable to the charges of Soviet propaganda (and never more so than when Britain was engaged in quelling colonial unrest), in another sense it did at least ameliorate the USA's attitude to the Empire-Commonwealth. As Lord Inverchapel told Bevin in May 1946, Britain should now seek to convince the United States that the 'critical problem in the contemporary world is to avert the chaos which would inevitably come of any further contraction of Britain's imperial and economic influence'.[63] The Empire could be projected as a necessary line of defence against the encroaching Red hordes, and lengthy counter-insurgency operations could be justified in precisely these terms, as we will see.

The Cold War also had powerful domestic ramifications, which helped dictate which British 'hearts and minds' governments paid most attention to wooing. As Ralph Miliband and Marcel Liebman have pointed out, in many ways the term '"Cold War" is somewhat misleading ... the notion of "international civil war" is closer than "Cold War" to the real nature of the confrontation'.[64] The post-war competition between the Soviet Union and its former wartime Allies unleashed disruptive forces within, as well as between, the states of the major antagonists. Nowhere in the West was this internecine aspect taken to greater extremes than in the United States, with McCarthyism as its principal manifestation. While such excesses were avoided in the United Kingdom, similar tendencies were nevertheless discernible. Peter Weiler's study *British Labour and the Cold War* provides an admirable assessment of how the global battle of ideas was reproduced at the domestic level. Paranoia about the Soviets' external ambitions fused with a longer tradition of fratricidal strife within the labour movement (between its reformist and revolutionary factions), leading to purges of Communists, and indeed some non-Communist leftists, from the trade union movement and the civil service in the late 1940s and early 1950s – by a Labour administration.[65] It thus seems pertinent to bear in mind that while the Emergency was in progress in Malaya, Britain itself briefly underwent a State of Emergency, as Attlee's government drafted in 15,000 servicemen to break a dockworkers' strike (behind which Communist intrigue was perceived) in protest at the 'wage freeze' policy.[66]

Given that British policy-makers viewed the Cold War, both internationally and within Britain, as a battle for ideological allegiance, it is no surprise that considerable initiative went into anti-Communist propaganda. Towards the end of 1947, encouraged in this direction by the Cabinet Russia Committee, Attlee's government decided to create a secret anti-Communist propaganda organization within the Foreign Office. This was the Information Research Department (IRD), whose existence remained a closely guarded secret until its demise in 1977.[67] Initially the IRD set out to present Britain as a 'third force' in international affairs ('neither Washington nor Moscow', so to speak). It also attempted to sell welfare statism as the model to which those in the colonies – looking for a blueprint for their future development – should aspire.[68] These activities, however, were rapidly relegated to the rear burner, while the IRD concentrated on negative themes: the excesses of Soviet Communism, and the imperialist machinations of Beijing and Moscow.[69] As British officials could not divorce events in the colonies from the global Cold War, the IRD was implicated in counter-insurgency operations at a number of levels. During the Malayan Emergency, in particular, the IRD had a substantial role to play on the ground, as a Regional Information Office (RIO) was established in Singapore in 1949 to act as the IRD's South East Asian outpost. The IRD was also involved in the process of representing the colonial insurgents: disseminating material on colonial insurgencies (particularly concerning their actual, or presumed, connection with international Communism) to a wide variety of contacts, in the Empire-Commonwealth and Foreign Office posts around the world, and in the UK itself. Here, the IRD developed particularly close links with the trade union movement and the Labour Party, hoping to counter the effect of Communist publications (most notably the *Daily Worker*) which presented an extremely hostile interpretation of British counter-insurgency operations.[70]

Having considered the background to the colonial insurgencies, it remains to outline in more specific terms what the case studies are being scrutinized for. In each, a number of questions are pursued. First, how did policy-makers, the military and the media respond to violence in the colonies? In particular, how did they arrive at their perception of violence as 'terrorism' in each of these settings? Was the latter seen as a distinctly less moral form of violence, and was it correspondingly important to governments to ensure that those whom they perceived as 'terrorists' were similarly regarded by other audiences? This is not a question of 'mere semantics', as the act of labelling opponents is a profoundly political process. As already suggested, many writers on terrorism have argued that to call one's opponent a terrorist is part of a delegitimizing strategy. Conor Cruise O'Brien, advocating less squeamishness about use of the term 'terrorist', illustrates the point well:

> In political and ideological struggles, words are weapons, not analytical tools. . . . The use of the designation 'terrorism' constitutes a declaration of illegality of the political violence referred to. So whether we use the term, refrain from using it, or hesitate to use it, has a bearing on how long the political violence is likely to continue and how many lives it will cost.[71]

Philip Schlesinger has shown that the BBC has, for some years, had guidelines to help broadcasters distinguish between 'terrorists', 'guerrillas' and 'freedom fighters', with the choice of term used affecting viewers' understanding of where legitimacy lies.[72] Likewise Peter Taylor, in an article assessing whether print journalists operate according to similar instructions from their editors, remarks that each of those terms 'now carries a particular nuance which cannot be divorced from the society in which it is used'.[73] We need, then, to interrogate the nuances of language used to describe violent events in the colonies. Furthermore, we must assess the extent to which, in the 1940s and 1950s, broadcasters and journalists reproduced 'decisions and definitions . . . initiated by the state', as Schlesinger suggests they do now.[74]

British governments have long been in the business of news management both in and out of wartime, and regardless of whether they had any particular 'terrorist threat' to counter. However, it seems pertinent to question how far policy-makers (civil servants, as well as politicians) regarded terrorism, in the chosen case studies, as a propagandistic strategy, which sought publicity, and therefore required countering *especially* through propaganda and manipulation of terrorists' channels of communication. As far as possible, I have also tried (more briefly) to assess whether the 'terrorists' in question did have the objectives attributed to them.

The difficulty of ascertaining how those deemed 'terrorists' actually conceived their strategy is one reason why, in looking broadly at terrorism and propaganda, the focus is primarily on *governments'* use of propaganda as a tool of counter-terrorism. To look inside insurgent organizations is clearly problematic: for one thing, they tend not to generate paperwork in the same way that governments and bureaucracies do. Those which did have a penchant for policy documents and written records – particularly EOKA and the Malayan Communist Party (MCP) – soon realized the costs when such documents fell into security force hands. Such captured documents, plus the organizations' own printed material (which is not necessarily a good guide to thoughts or intentions), as colonial administrators, government departments and the military did amass now form the principal source material available in Britain on the organizations in question. Not only is the material limited to what British authorities gathered from their opponents in the course of fighting them (much of which, of course, then had to be translated into English), but the quantity which has found its way into the public domain doubtless represents only a fraction of what was collected during each campaign. Nor can one rely on written material to reveal a comprehensive picture of an organization such as Mau Mau which contained a substantial number of illiterate members.[75]

An alternative window into insurgent organizations is provided by memoirs. Memoirs written by former 'terrorists' suffer from various drawbacks.[76] Although they apparently take us closer to the mind of the organization, memoirs are self-serving at the best of times, and the mixed fortunes suffered by the Irgun and Lehi, the MCP, Mau Mau and EOKA once their campaigns of violence were terminated, coupled with the ambivalence with which such 'liberation movements' have been retrospectively viewed within their newly independent states, may make such volumes a poor guide as to how their authors thought at the time. While the Irgun and Stern Gang, Mau Mau and EOKA were all arguably successful in hastening the end of colonial rule in the territories concerned, former members and leaders have nonetheless been reluctant to lay bare precisely what they hoped their particular violent strategy would achieve, and, in their eagerness to illustrate that they fought justly for a just cause, loath to concur that it was 'terrorism'. The least successful organization studied, though that which held down the security forces longest, the MCP, slipped into obscurity following the Emergency, and has generated no English-language retrospective accounts of the campaign.

Easier access to sources is not the only reason why the propa-ganda of governments is privileged over that of insurgents. Studies of how governments have used propaganda – by which is meant both the production of 'official' material (such as pamphlets, posters and films) promoting the governmental viewpoint, and the process of news management – to counter terrorism are inadequate when one looks at terrorism in its pre-1968 form. To some extent, this gap in the literature is surprising. After all, as Jennifer Hocking has remarked, the inevitable outcome of the perceived symbiosis between the media and terrorism is a 'prescription of counterterrorism measures by the state that includes at its heart a controlling of the alleged media–terrorism symbiosis'.[77] Britain's case certainly bears this out. In the United Kingdom some attention has recently been paid to how the government has used propaganda and news management techniques to counter terrorism in Ireland – as one would expect when, in the 1980s, the reporting of Northern Ireland almost certainly formed the most troubled area of government–media relations.[78]

Why, then, has no one sought to test the historical validity of Hocking's assertion with regard to earlier terrorisms? Is it because terrorism – and indeed the media – prior to 1968 (or another date of preference) are thought to have been qualitatively different, with neither terrorists seeking publicity nor the media in a position to accord them instant global gratification? Yet terrorism *has* been perceived as attention-seeking for much longer than is frequently supposed. Charles Townshend writes:

> Since the development of a full-scale 'psychological warfare execu-tive' and apparatus in the Second World War, propaganda has become an obsession of media-saturated western societies. The belief that terrorism is fuelled by publicity has become an *idée fixe*, although it has no historical basis.[79]

The belief that terrorism is fuelled by publicity is to be found in each of the case studies, albeit in varying degrees. In one sense, then, the prevalent view in the 1980s that publicity was terrorism's oxygen *did* have a historical basis, derived from the cumulative weight of Britain's counter-insurgency experience. However, Townshend is correct in so far as the recurring perception that terrorists sought attention was not grounded in anything other than subjective estimation. The *idée fixe* may thus in fact be based on a misperception, although its underlying proposition is scarcely one that lends itself to empirical verification.

A relatively small amount of attention has been accorded to the use of propaganda as a tool of counter-insurgency. In this respect, rather more heed has been paid to the Malayan Emergency than to the other campaigns examined in this book, perhaps for the simple reason that Templer made so much of winning 'hearts and minds'. The first generation of counter-insurgency theorists – in particular, Richard Clutterbuck, Robert Thompson, Anthony Burton, Frank Kitson and Julian Paget, some of whom were actually involved in the military prosecution of the campaigns studied herein – all state the importance of getting the media on-side and stress the role of propaganda in encouraging terrorist surrenders and winning neutral (or outrightly hostile) 'hearts and minds'. However, such remarks are often made as prescriptions for future handling of terrorism rather than as revelations of how propaganda was employed in specific campaigns. David Charters has suggested that the military are not well placed to tell this story:

> Although propaganda had played a major role in World War II on the home front and against the enemy, and an even more significant part in post-war conflicts, the British Army has dealt with psychological operations only sporadically and tangentially. The reason is simple: 'Political Warfare', as it was called in World War II, was a civilian task, and remained so after the war; the Army played a relatively small role in most psychological campaigns.[80]

On the evidence of the case studies, this remark appears of only limited usefulness. In two counter-insurgencies, Malaya and Cyprus, a military man was placed in overall charge of the colony for at least a part of the Emergency, and both Templer and Harding left a very personal imprint on the conduct of propaganda and psychological warfare in the campaign. And in all four campaigns the commanders of the security forces played a considerable role in shaping how terrorism was presented to the outside world, as well as in the operational employment of propaganda. The Army may not, however, have been fully aware of the extent to which efforts were taken to influence public opinion away from the site of the conflict, although it was sensitive to shifts in public opinion within the United Kingdom and the perceived consequences for the troops' morale.

Examination of the efforts taken to mould *British* public perceptions of terrorism form the core of this book. There appears to be an unspoken assumption in much counter-insurgency literature that British opinion was unimportant in counter-insurgency campaigning, although both Vietnam and the Falklands war gave the lie to any generalization that governments are unconcerned with domestic opinion when fighting low (or relatively low) intensity wars in faraway places. It is certainly harder to establish from official records what steps were taken to influence opinion at home than it is for overseas opinion, or that of the disputed colony's population. In peacetime, the extent to which a government should employ propaganda to mobilize opinion on an 'Emergency' in a colony is obviously less clear-cut than the need for propaganda in time of total war, and a certain discretion has clearly been exercised in the selection of public records for preservation. Thus wherever possible, official records have been supplemented with memoirs, biographies, private papers and letters.

In addition, one faces the perennial difficulty of assessing the impact of propaganda, both on the media and on public opinion. As D.G. Boyce has written,

> The evidence on which to base such an assessment is often piecemeal and circumstantial, and there is no completely reliable method of discovering when public opinion was influenced by propaganda and when it would have arrived at a particular conclusion regardless of attempts to form, control or alter its attitudes.[81]

There is no entirely satisfactory solution to this conundrum. There is circumstantial and anecdotal evidence relating to the sources of public opinion, but, as Boyce asserts, we can never be entirely sure what causes particular attitudes to be held. It is similarly impossible to be categorical about why the media report events in any given way, and how far the tenor of reportage is the product of government efforts at news management. Within the confines of available sources, the output of the media of mass communication has been examined to see how far they reproduced the governmental understanding of terrorism – but one should be wary of assuming that consensual reportage was the product of government pressure alone. Inevitably (though regrettably) there is some imbalance in the media sources studied. While newspapers are freely available, and the newsreel archives are accessible, if costly, the televised presentation of each Emergency is unviewable. The written archives of the BBC are invaluable for scripts of radio and television broadcasts, in addition to policy documents, but it is impossible to view old material, for the simple reason that it has not been preserved for posterity. The only mitigating factor is that British governments appear to have rated Fleet Street more highly as a domestic and international opinion-moulder than other media, even by the end of the period studied, when television in Britain was becoming a truly mass medium.[82]

To conclude, this book is intended as a contribution to existing literature on counter-insurgency, adding the frequently neglected propaganda dimension. In so doing, it will test the historical validity of propositions raised in recent writing on terrorism and the media, by studying, in a historical context, issues such as the importance of language, government–media relations, the use of censorship and so on. It will also assess how far public opinion in Britain was wooed by British governments, and the means employed to this end. It should therefore also add to the growing body of material exploring the peacetime use of propaganda in post-war Britain. Although no post-war British government ever appeared likely to lose an election over the conduct of a counter-insurgency campaign, public opinion was never neglected. Indeed, as we shall see, a surprising amount of effort was devoted to propaganda, both for British and overseas audiences.

Notes

1   Myles na Gopaleen (Flann O'Brien), *The Best of Myles*, ed. Kevin O Nolan (Picador edition, London, 1977), p. 206.

2   As Templer's biographer, John Cloake, remarks, 'How he wished he had never invented that bloody phrase which had become such a cliché'; *Templer, Tiger of Malaya: The Life of Field Marshal Sir Gerald Templer* (Harrap, London, 1985), p. 2.

3   David Charters, *The British Army and Jewish Insurgency in Palestine, 1945–7* (Macmillan, London, 1989); Richard Stubbs, *Hearts and Minds in Guerrilla Warfare: The Malayan Emergency, 1948–60* (Oxford University Press, Oxford, 1989); Thomas R. Mockaitis, *British Counterinsurgency, 1919–60* (Macmillan, Basingstoke, 1990).

4   Strictly speaking, neither Palestine nor Malaya was a British colony as such. The former was ruled by the British government as a Mandated Territory, on behalf of the League of Nations, from 1922. Malaya, particularly before 1939, had a more confusing legal status, as different states within the territory reached different administrative arrangements with Britain.

5   E.V. Walter, *Terror and Resistance: A Study of Political Violence with Case Studies of Some Primitive African Communities* (Oxford University Press, Oxford, 1969), p. 4.

6   H.C. Greisman, 'Social Meanings of Terrorism: Reification, Violence, and Social Control', *Contemporary Crises*, 1 (1977), 303–18.

7   J.J. Hocking, 'Governments' Perspectives' in D.L. Paletz and A.P. Schmid (eds), *Terrorism and the Media* (SAGE Publications, Newbury Park, Calif., 1992), p. 86.

8   Leonard Doob, *Public Opinion and Propaganda* (Holt, New York, 1948), p. 390.

9   A number of the contributors to Wolfgang J. Mommsen and Gerhard Hirschfeld's *Social Protest, Violence and Terror in Nineteenth- and Twentieth-Century Europe* (Macmillan, Basingstoke, 1982) provide useful historical illustrations of this point.

10   A.P. Schmid and J. de Graaf, *Violence as Communication: Insurgent Terrorism and the Western News Media* (SAGE Publications, London, 1982). See also a portion of Schmid and Jongman's comprehensive definition of terrorism in their *Political Terrorism: A New Guide to Actors, Authors, Concepts, Data Bases, Theories and Literature* (North-Holland Publishing, Amsterdam, 2nd ed., 1988): 'The purpose of this indirect method of combat is either to immobilize the target of terror in order to produce disorientation and/or compliance, or to mobilize secondary targets of demands (e.g. a government) or targets of attention (e.g. public opinion) to produce changes of attitude or behaviour favouring the short or long-term interests of the users of this method of combat'; p. 1.

11   T.H. Qualter, *Opinion Control in the Democracies* (Macmillan, London, 1985), p. 124.

12   T.P. Thornton, 'Terror as a Weapon of Political Agitation', in H. Eckstein (ed.),

Internal War: Problems and Approaches (Free Press, New York, 1964), p. 73.

13   Schmid and de Graaf, *Violence as Communication*, p. 14.

14   Paul Wilkinson writes that terrorist organizations engage in propaganda as a preliminary to their violent campaign: 'Every terrorist campaign that is launched in liberal
democratic states entails an intensive propaganda warfare stage directed at defamation
of liberal values and institutions and character assassinations of leaders'; *Terrorism and
the Liberal State* (New York University Press, New York, 2nd ed., 1986), p. 79.

15   Maurice Tugwell, 'Revolutionary Propaganda and Possible Counter-measures' (unpublished PhD thesis, King's College, London, 1979); and 'Terrorism and Propaganda:
Problem and Response', in P. Wilkinson and A.M. Stewart (eds) *Contemporary Research
on Terrorism* (Aberdeen University Press, Aberdeen, 1987); J. Wright, *Terrorist Propaganda* (Macmillan, Basingstoke, 1991).

16   M. Thatcher, *The Downing Street Years* (HarperCollins, London, 1993), p. 408.

17   The popularly (but misleadingly) named 'Sinn Fein Ban' was first announced by
Douglas Hurd in the House of Commons on 19 Oct. 1988, when he issued a notice
under section 29(3) of the Broadcasting Act 1981 and Clause 13(4) of the BBC Licence
Agreement, which restricted interviews with eleven Irish organizations including Sinn
Fein and the Ulster Defence Association. This move bore some resemblance to similar
legislation in the Republic of Ireland, pioneered by Gerry Collins in 1971, and tight-
ened up by Conor Cruise O'Brien while Minister for Posts and Telegraphs in 1976. A
study of the effects of the legislation can be found in the Glasgow University Media
Group's 'Speak No Evil: The British Broadcasting Ban, the Media and the Conflict in
Ireland' (unpublished report, 1990).

18   See, for example, A.H. Miller, *Terrorism, the Media and the Law* (Transnational,
New York, 1982); Y. Alexander and R. Latter (eds), *Terrorism and the Media:
Dilemmas for Government, Journalism and the Media* (Brassey's (US), Washington,
1990); Y. Alexander and R.G. Picard (eds), *In the Camera's Eye: News Coverage
of Terrorist Events* (Brassey's (US), Washington, 1991); Paletz and Schmid (eds),
Terrorism and the Media; A.O. Alali and K.K. Eke (eds), *Media Coverage of Terrorism:
Methods of Diffusion* (SAGE Publications, Newbury Park, Calif., 1991).

19   Bethami Dobkin, for example, has shown how American network television's exaggerated reportage of terrorism, and the threat it represented, resulted in overwhelming
popular support for Reagan's anti-terrorist measures, including the bombing of Tripoli
in April 1986 – despite the fact that few of its supporters thought it would produce
the desired effect; B.A. Dobkin, *Tales of Terror: Television News and the Construction of
the Terrorist Threat* (Praeger, New York, 1992). British television coverage of terrorism has also been the subject of a study sceptical of the orthodoxy: P. Schlesinger,
G. Murdock and P. Elliott, *Televising 'Terrorism': Political Violence in Popular Culture*
(Comedia, London, 1983).

20   Miller, *Terrorism, the Media and the Law*, p. 4.

21   Schlesinger *et al.*, *Televising 'Terrorism'*, p. 158.

22   Eric Hobsbawm cited by G. Fairbairn, *Revolutionary Guerrilla Warfare: The Countryside
Version* (Penguin Books, Harmondsworth, 1974), p. 365.

23   See, for example, G. Chaliand, *Terrorism: From Popular Struggle to Media Spectacle*
(Saqi Books, London, 1987), p. 7.

24   Ibid., p. 13.

25   Ibid., p. 13.

26   J. Shaw, E. Gueritz and A.E. Younger (eds), *Ten Years of Terrorism: Collected Views*
(RUSI, London, 1979).

27   C. Gearty, *Terror* (Faber and Faber, London, 1991), p. 7.

28   Walter Laqueur and Yonah Alexander, for example, argue that terrorism is virtually
as old as 'history itself', citing Plutarch's defence of Brutus's assassination of Caesar as
an argument for discriminatory terrorism; *The Terrorism Reader: A Historical Anthology*
(Meridian, New York, 1987), pp. 18-19. T.P. Thornton, on the other hand, has argued

that assassination cannot be conflated with terrorism: 'If the objective is primarily the removal of a specific thing (or person) with a view toward depriving the enemy of its usefulness, then the act is one of sabotage'; Thornton in Eckstein, *Internal War*, p. 78.

29   This is where the *Oxford English Dictionary* commences its definition of terrorism. For fuller treatment of French revolutionary *terreur* see N. Hampson, 'From Regeneration to Terror: The Ideology of the French Revolution', in N. O'Sullivan (ed.), *Terrorism, Ideology, and Revolution: The Origins of Modern Political Violence* (Wheatsheaf Books, Brighton, 1986).

30   Thornton in Eckstein, *Internal War*, p. 72. Note the similarity between Thornton's distinction between terror dedicated to enforcement and to agitation, and Ellul's separation of 'integration' and 'agitation' propaganda; J. Ellul, *Propaganda: The Formation of Men's Attitudes* (Vintage Books edition, New York, 1973), p. 71.

31   Walter makes this distinction in *Terror and Resistance*, p. 10 and *passim*.

32   N. O'Sullivan, Preface to *Terrorism, Ideology, and Revolution*, p. x.

33   C. Townshend, 'The Process of Terror in Irish Politics' in O'Sullivan, *Terrorism, Ideology, and Revolution*, p. 94.

34   J. Devoy, *Recollections of an Irish Rebel* (New York, 1929, reprinted Irish University Press, Shannon, 1969), p. 250, cited by C. Townshend, *Political Violence in Ireland: Government and Resistance since 1848* (Clarendon Press, Oxford, 1983), p. 37.

35   This rationale, among others, was provided by Patrick Tynan in *The Irish Invincibles and Their Times*; see C. Townshend, 'Terror in Ireland: Observations of Tynan's *The Irish Invincibles and Their Times*', in Wilkinson and Stewart, *Contemporary Research on Terrorism*, p. 184.

36   K.R.M. Short, *The Dynamite War: Irish-American Bombers in Victorian Britain* (Gill and Macmillan, Dublin, 1979), p. 1.

37   *The Times* (26/1/1885).

38   Townshend, *Political Violence in Ireland*, p. 312.

39   M. Laffan, 'Violence and Terror in Twentieth Century Ireland: IRB and IRA', in Mommsen and Hirschfeld, *Social Protest, Violence and Terror*, p. 161.

40   WC(505), 21/11/1918, Cabinet Minutes; CAB 23/8.

41   See S. Nath, *Terrorism in India* (National Publishing House, New Delhi, 1980), and D.J. Clark, The Colonial Police and Anti-terrorism: Bengal 1930-1936, Palestine 1937–1947 and Cyprus 1955–1959 (unpublished PhD thesis, Oxford University, 1978).

42   'Terrorism in India: A Summary of Activities up to March 1933', p. 5; WO 106/5445.

43   Robert Taber, among others, makes this point: 'the struggle that led to the (still conditional) independence of Cyprus was almost blow for blow a repetition of "the troubles" that had freed Catholic Ireland from the English rule more than three decades earlier. The lessons of Ireland were also applied in Israel; leaders of the Irgun and the Stern Group studied the writings of the Irish Republican Army commanders, the better to know their enemy and the means by which he could be driven out of Palestine'; *The War of the Flea: A Study of Guerrilla Warfare Theory and Practice* (Paladin, St Albans, 1970), p. 92.

44   For a comparative study of Ireland and Palestine, see T. Bowden, *The Breakdown of Public Security: The Case of Ireland 1916–1921 and Palestine 1936–1939* (SAGE Publications, London, 1977). Mockaitis argues that Britain's 'success' in the field of counter-insurgency was due to the learning curve of experience, which commenced in Ireland 1919–21; *British Counterinsurgency, passim*.

45   See the records of the International Conference on the Repression of Terrorism in Geneva (1934–36) in HO 189/1-33.

46   'Report by the UK Delegations', p. 2; HO 189/1.

47   M. Walzer, *Just and Unjust Wars: A Moral Argument with Historical Illustrations* (Basic Books, New York, 2nd ed., 1992), p. 198. Noel O'Sullivan has expressed a similar opinion: 'The Second World War . . . did much to eliminate any distinction between

combatant and non-combatant by legitimating the deliberate massacre of civilians. To that extent, the horrific threats and actions by terrorists against innocent passengers which are now a familiar part of aircraft hijacks are symptomatic of attitudes towards violence which the West itself has sanctioned, in principle at least'; in O'Sullivan, *Terrorism, Ideology, and Revolution*, p. 16.

48 Thornton suggests that 'terror is most effective when it is indiscriminate in appearance but highly discriminate in fact'; in Eckstein, *Internal War*, p. 82. Townshend, however, has rightly taken issue with Thornton's insistence that 'terror must always have at least some element of indiscrimination, else it becomes predictable', which conflates 'discriminate' with 'predictable'. Townshend suggests that terrorists may need to be 'unpredictable' (in timing and method) rather than indiscriminate; Townshend in O'Sullivan, *Terrorism, Ideology, and Revolution*, p. 92.

49 (At the time of writing, the IRA ceasefire was three months old.) Townshend cites Ernest Blythe's call in *An tOglach*, the Irish Volunteer journal, for the killing (if conscription were introduced in Ireland) of 'anyone, civilian or soldier, who assists directly, or by connivance in this crime against us', which had a profound effect on the future development of Republican strategy; *Political Violence in Ireland*, p. 320.

50 Townshend, *Political Violence in Ireland*, p. 412.

51 For a lengthier treatment of this theme, see John Darwin, *Britain and Decolonisation: The Retreat from Empire in the Post-war World* (Macmillan, Basingstoke, 1988), Chapters 2 and 3.

52 Stephen Howe, *Anticolonialism in British Politics: The Left and the End of Empire, 1918–1964* (Clarendon Press, Oxford, 1993), ch. 3.

53 Ibid., p. 318.

54 For a good comparative treatment of Britain's and Germany's wartime propaganda organizations, see Michael Balfour, *Propaganda in War, 1939–45* (Routledge and Kegan Paul, London, 1979). The fullest account of the MOI's domestic activities is found in Ian McLaine's *Ministry of Morale: Home Front Morale and the Ministry of Information in World War II* (George Allen and Unwin, London, 1979). On the MOI's relations with the news media, see N. Pronay, 'The news media at war', in N. Pronay and D. Spring (eds), *Propaganda, Politics and Film, 1918–45* (Macmillan, London, 1982), pp. 173–208.

55 For an account of PWE's activities see Charles Cruickshank, *The Fourth Arm: Psychological Warfare 1938–45* (Oxford University Press, Oxford, 1977).

56 The best account of black radio broadcasting is to be found in Sefton Delmer's memoir, *Black Boomerang* (Secker and Warburg, London, 1962). See also Ellic Howe, *The Black Game: British Subversive Operations against the Germans during the Second World War* (Queen Anne Press/Futura, London, 1982).

57 See Bradley Smith, *The Shadow Warriors: OSS and the Origins of the CIA* (André Deutsch, London, 1983). On the afterlife of Britain's equivalent organization for subversion overseas, see Richard Aldrich, 'Unquiet in Death: The Post-War Survival of the "Special Operations Executive", 1945–51', in A. Gorst, L. Johnman and W.S. Lucas (eds), *Contemporary British History 1931–1961: Politics and the Limits of Policy* (Pinter, London, 1991), pp. 193–217.

58 For fuller accounts of the COI's work see Sir Fife Clark, *The Central Office of Information* (George Allen and Unwin, London, 1970), and Marjorie Ogilvie-Webb, *The Government Explains: A Study of the Information Services* (George Allen and Unwin, London, 1965).

59 See N. Pronay and K. Wilson (eds), *The Political Re-education of Germany and Her Allies after World War II* (Croom Helm, London, 1985).

60 See, for example, Fred Halliday, *The Making of the Second Cold War* (Verso, London, 2nd ed., 1986).

61 On the reorientation of Foreign Office policy towards the Soviet Union see Raymond Smith, 'A Climate of Opinion: British Officials and the Development of British Soviet

Policy, 1945–7', *International Affairs*, 64 (1988), 631–47, and Ray Merrick, 'The Russia Committee of the British Foreign Office and the Cold War, 1946–47', *Journal of Contemporary History*, 20 (1985), 453–68.

62   'Projection of Britain Overseas': proposed statement as revised by Herbert Morrison for Committee on Overseas Information Services (OI(46)10); CAB 124/1007.

63   Inverchapel (British Ambassador to the USA) to Bevin, 13/5/46; FO 37/47857/N15072; cited by P. Weiler, *British Labour and the Cold War* (Stanford University Press, Stanford, Calif., 1988), p. 193 and footnote 30, p. 357. For a fuller treatment of the Attlee government's wooing of America, see Caroline Anstey, 'The Projection of British Socialism: Foreign Office Publicity and American Opinion, 1945–50', *Journal of Contemporary History*, 19 (1984), 417–51.

64   Ralph Miliband and Marcel Liebman, 'Reflections on Anti-Communism', *Socialist Register* (1984), pp. 11–12, cited by Peter Weiler, *British Labour and the Cold War*, p. 13.

65   Weiler, *British Labour and the Cold War*, *passim*. See also Reg Whitaker, 'Fighting the Cold War on the Home Front: America, Britain, Australia and Canada', *Socialist Register* (1984), 23–67.

66   See Keith Jeffery and Peter Hennessy, *States of Emergency: British Governments and Strikebreaking since 1919* (Routledge and Kegan Paul, London, 1983), ch. 7.

67   As the records of the IRD remain closed to inspection, it is difficult to provide an adequate account of its activities. However, a number of articles have outlined its origins and *modus operandi*: R. Fletcher, 'British Propaganda since World War Two: A Case Study', *Media, Culture and Society*, 4 (1982), 97–109; L. Smith, 'Covert British Propaganda: The Information Research Department, 1947–77', *Millennium: Journal of International Studies*, 9, i (1980), 67–83; W. Wark, 'Coming In from the Cold: British Propaganda and Red Army Defectors, 1945–52', *International History Review*, 9, i (Feb. 1987), 48–72; W. Scott Lucas and C.J. Morris, 'A Very British Crusade: The Information Research Department and the Beginning of the Cold War', in R. Aldrich (ed.), *British Intelligence, Strategy and the Cold War* (Routledge, London, 1992).

68   Weiler, *British Labour and the Cold War*, p. 205.

69   See Lucas and Morris, 'A Very British Crusade', pp. 99–106.

70   On the IRD's relationship with the labour movement see Weiler, *British Labour and the Cold War*, ch. 6.

71   C.C. O'Brien, 'Terrorism under Democratic Conditions: The Case of the IRA', in M. Crenshaw (ed.), *Terrorism, Legitimacy, and Power: The Consequences of Political Violence* (Wesleyan University Press, Middletown, Conn., 1983), pp. 93–4. Similarly, Maurice Tugwell concluded in his doctoral thesis that: 'Activists [i.e., terrorists] must if possible be denied the sure belief that they are on firm moral ground. If journalists refrain from describing rebels as "freedom fighters", or "guerrilla soldiers" and their acts as "daring attacks" or "shootings", and if the full facts of terrorism are exposed, some of the certainty may weaken'; *Revolutionary Propaganda*, p. 331.

72   P. Schlesinger, *Putting 'Reality' Together: BBC News* (Methuen, London, 2nd ed., 1987), pp. 229–30.

73   P. Taylor, 'The Semantics of Political Violence' in P. Golding, G. Murdock and P. Schlesinger (eds), *Communicating Politics: Mass Communications and the Political Process* (Leicester University Press, Leicester, 1986), p. 212.

74   Schlesinger, *Putting 'Reality' Together*, p. 229.

75   Donald Barnett and Karari Njama's account of Mau Mau reveals that the literate and non-literate wings of the organization grew increasingly hostile to one another, with the latter resenting the former's arrogation of leadership to itself; D. Barnett and K. Njama, *Mau Mau from Within: Autobiography and Analysis of Kenya's Peasant Revolt* (MacGibbon and Kee, London, 1966).

76   This problem is addressed by David Rapoport in 'The International World as Some Terrorists Have Seen It: A Look at a Century of Memoirs', *Journal of Strategic Studies*,

10 (1987), 32–58. For an attempt to use terrorists' memoirs to ascertain the 'place of publicity in the terrorist strategy', see Robin Gerrits, 'Terrorists' Perspectives: Memoirs', in Paletz and Schmid, *Terrorism and the Media*, pp. 29–61.

77   Hocking in Paletz and Schmid, *Terrorism and the Media*, p. 87.

78   The lengthiest treatment is Liz Curtis's, *Ireland: The Propaganda War. The British Media and the Battle for Hearts and Minds* (Pluto Press, London, 1984). The Glasgow University Media Group has also undertaken research in this area; in addition to its work on the Broadcasting Ban, see D. Miller, 'The Northern Ireland Information Service and the Media: Aims, Strategy, Tactics', in John Eldridge (ed.), *Getting the Message: News, Truth and Power* (Routledge, London, 1993), pp. 73–103.

79   C. Townshend, *Britain's Civil Wars: Counterinsurgency in the Twentieth Century* (Faber and Faber, London, 1986), p. 36.

80   D.A. Charters, 'From Palestine to Northern Ireland: British Adaptation to Low-Intensity Operations', in D.A. Charters and M. Tugwell (eds), *Armies in Low-Intensity Conflict: A Comparative Analysis* (Brassey's, London, 1989), p. 223.

81   D.G. Boyce, *Englishmen and Irish Troubles: British Public Opinion and the Making of Irish Policy, 1918–22* (Jonathan Cape, London, 1972), p. 88.

82   Whereas in 1947 there were 15,000 television licence holders in Britain, by 1959 this figure had risen to 9,255,000; C. Seymour-Ure, *The British Press and Broadcasting since 1945* (Basil Blackwell, Oxford, 1991), p. 76.

1 'A Wordy Warfare':[1] Terrorism in Palestine, 1944–47

The Background to the Jewish Insurgency in Palestine

The historical background to the Palestine question is so well known that it hardly needs to be rehearsed here at undue length. From 1922 until her withdrawal in 1948, Britain administered Palestine as a Mandated Territory on behalf of the League of Nations. Under the League's terms of reference, Britain was obliged to confirm the right of the Jewish people to establish a national home there, provided that 'nothing should be done which might prejudice the civil and religious rights of existing non-Jewish communities in Palestine'.[2] These two duties proved to be mutually exclusive, for as Jewish immigration into Palestine increased, the Arab population felt a threat to precisely those rights which the British were supposed to safeguard. While the British were mindful of Arab fears of being overwhelmed by Jews, and of the need not to antagonize Arab and wider Muslim feeling in the dangerous international climate of the 1930s, the case for greater Jewish immigration was also less easily countered as Hitler's racial policies took effect.

Arab unrest at increasing Jewish immigration bubbled over into open revolt in 1936, with the Arabs practising what was seen by the authorities in Jerusalem and Westminster as a form of terrorism.[3] The rebels' activities included sniping at Jewish settlements, sabotaging crops and property, mining railways and bombing oil pipelines, ambushing the police and attacking members of the British Mandatory Authorities.[4] By October 1938, the High Commissioner reported to the Colonial Secretary that 'the Rebellion has unquestionably become a national revolt involving all classes of the Arab community in Palestine and enjoying considerable support from the Arabs outside it'.[5] Using imperial policing methods learnt in India, and with the formation of mobile troop units – a technique employed to deal with the IRA's flying columns during the 1919–21 Anglo-Irish war – the Arab insurgency was effectively quelled by 1939.[6] Although the revolt had been put down at considerable cost to Arab life, the British government did, however, announce a new policy for Palestine in May 1939 which was widely regarded as a concession to Arab sensitivity. Under the terms of the 1939 White Paper, Jewish immigration into Palestine would be limited to 75,000 over the next five

24

years, with any subsequent immigration dependent on Arab consent.[7] To militant young Zionists the message was that terrorism clearly paid: only through violence had the Arabs won this concession, and if Zionism was to make headway Jews would have to, as Arthur Koestler put it in his 1946 novel *Thieves in the Night*, reply in 'the only language which, anno domini 1939, the world understood'.[8]

Even before the Arab rebellion ended, Chamberlain's government had been disturbed by reports from Palestine of Jewish retaliation to Arab attacks. Initially such incidents appeared to be the work of frenzied individuals who could no longer restrain themselves from repaying Arab attacks in kind. In late 1937 a young Jew, Shlomo Ben Yosef, was sentenced to death for firing at a bus full of Arab passengers.[9] Jewish retaliation escalated in 1938: on 6 July a powerful bomb was thrown into the Arab melon market in Haifa, which produced panic and indiscriminate shooting, resulting in the deaths of twenty-one Arabs and six Jews. This sparked a month of Jewish–Arab clashes and bombings, culminating in a repeat bombing of the Haifa market on 25 July, which killed forty-six Arabs and wounded a further forty-four, of whom seven later died.[10]

It soon became apparent, however, that what had seemed to be individual acts of retaliation in fact heralded the emergence of Jewish 'terrorist organizations'. In 1939 the Colonial Office opened a file on an organization known as the Irgun Zvai Leumi (National Military Organization). Its information as to the Irgun's aims and activities was confined to one pamphlet, printed by the 'Irgun Press' and entitled *Bulletin of the Irgun Zwai Leumi*. The Irgun announced its presence as an organized Jewish fighting force to retaliate against Arab onslaughts and to promote the foundation of a National Home:

> The flood of memoranda published by the Jewish Agency is of no interest for anybody; paper protests with no action behind them are ridiculous. All these ways lead nowhere. The actual historical period of extraordinary trials and exceptional catastrophes claims a fighting spirit and revolutionary methods.[11]

Among the organization's listed activities was propaganda. In particular the Irgun stressed the role of its secret broadcasting station (transmitting in Hebrew as well as English) as 'the most forceful weapon against the British Administration which suppresses free speech and press in the country'. The Colonial Office reaction to the Irgun's announcement was characteristically restrained. S.E.V. Luke minuted that Britain could afford to take this organization 'fairly lightly in peacetime', although it would be 'much more menacing in time of war'.[12]

These words were written on 2 September 1939. The following day Britain and France declared war on Nazi Germany. The turmoil which

25

the outbreak of war entailed extended to Palestine and brought about new strategic alignments. The Arab Higher Committee spent the better part of the war years flirting with Nazi Germany, despite Britain's best efforts not to antagonize it. Meanwhile, the Jewish Agency, which represented Palestine's Jews, decided to restrict its opposition to the White Paper to protests against restrictions on Jewish immigration and land purchase, while entreating HMG that Jews be recruited to serve in the British armed forces to hasten the defeat of Nazi Germany. The Irgun, under David Raziel's military command, followed the political lead of Jabotinsky (head of the right-wing Revisionist Party) and accepted the Agency's wartime policy. But even a temporary accommodation with Britain was rejected by the Irgun's political head, Abraham Stern, who argued in effect that Britain's misfortune represented Zionism's opportunity, and attacks against the White Paper should therefore be intensified rather than postponed.[13] This schism led to the creation of a splinter organization, the so-called Stern Gang or Fighters for the Freedom of Israel (Lehi). The challenge which it represented to the Mandatory Authorities was insufficient to prevent Britain responding positively to the Agency's calls for the setting up of Jewish combative organizations and the arming of the *Yishuv* (the Jewish community in Palestine). Thus, shortly after the outbreak of war, those members of the Irgun who had been placed in the Latrun detention camp were released and some were subsequently enlisted to play their part in covert operations in the Middle East theatre. As in Malaya, Britain helped train in resistance operations some of those who, after the war, would use the same techniques against the British themselves. Moreover, the fact that Britain and the Allies clearly approved of certain activities, such as sabotage, selective assassination and so on, which constituted legitimate 'resistance' when directed against Axis powers, but 'terrorism' when targeted against Britain, provided the Irgun and Lehi with fertile propaganda material.

Terrorism, which had been all but quiescent during the first three years of war (the Stern Gang having lapsed into a temporary abeyance after a number of failed bank robberies and explosions in 1941 and the shooting of Stern in February 1942), reappeared in Palestine well before victory in Europe and the Pacific had been secured. In 1943 a propaganda policy document from the Ministry of Information (MOI) Overseas Planning Committee outlined British fears of imminent 'civil war' in Palestine, 'either immediately on or before the end of hostilities in Europe'. The reasons posited included both communities' conviction that the war was nearly over and that they could now safely 'give play to internal politics'; the ebullient self-confidence and nationalism of the Jewish community after El Alamein; the impending termination of Jewish immigration under the terms of the White Paper; and the massacre of the Jews in Europe, which had produced an intensification of pro-Jewish feeling.[14] The MOI felt that it could do little to avert civil war through propaganda, as this would mean openly acknowledging its fears, but credited itself and the government generally with admirable discretion in having 'purposely not hastened a climax by disclosing to the people of Palestine that [we] know of the danger, or to the rest of the world that the danger exists'.[15]

The Ministry of Information's forecast was only partially correct. Already the Stern Gang's actions had shown that the British, rather than the Arabs, could expect to be the chief target in the recrudescence of Jewish terrorism – at least in the short term. As the war in Europe drew to a close, the Jewish insurgents were able to profit from Britain's economic indebtedness to the United States. Britain's inability to survive without an American loan, coupled with the dependence of American politicians on winning the Jewish vote in large cities (especially New York), afforded unprecedented opportunities for Zionists to press their case. The Irgun and Lehi sought to draw American attention to the impending termination of Jewish immigration into Palestine under the 1939 White Paper stipulations, and to gain financial and moral support for their activities aiding Jewish refugees in (illegally) passing from occupied Europe to Palestine. The American government was to be drawn into a struggle which would not remain submerged from world attention for long.

In 1944 the re-emergence of terrorism in Palestine was loudly trumpeted by the assassination on 6 November of Lord Moyne, Minister Resident in Cairo, by two Lehi gunmen. Together with that organization's attempted murder of Sir Harold MacMichael, High Commissioner of Palestine, the previous August there could have been no clearer announcement that a determined campaign of opposition to the Mandatory regime was under way. As a disgruntled Palestine policeman put it to the *Sunday Express*: 'Perhaps now they've had a go at a big shot, someone will tell the truth about this country. When they only bomb and shoot up British policemen no one is interested.'[16] Certainly the fact that Lehi had been carrying out a campaign of assassination against the Palestine Police had not received undue prominence in the British press until the spectacular events of August and November.[17] Nor had much attention been paid to the Irgun's 'declaration of war' on the British administration in Palestine in January 1944.[18] These organizations initially largely confined their attacks to the police and targets connected with immigration. Acts such as the blowing up of immigration offices in Jerusalem, Tel Aviv and Haifa in February 1944 were calculated to achieve powerful symbolic resonance, drawing attention to the despised White Paper and demonstrating the insurgents' claim to legitimacy as true upholder of the *Yishuv*'s interests.[19] The Irgun's early activities also included diamond thefts, general attacks on government offices and much propaganda.[20] The latter was aimed not only at the *Yishuv* but also at Palestine's Arab population, and contained a considerable element of enforcement terror against those who were more likely to prove willing collaborators with the British against Zionist terrorism.[21]

After a brief flurry of violent activity, the Irgun and Lehi were temporarily halted in late 1944 and early 1945. Following the assassination of Lord Moyne, the Jewish Agency sought to recapture the initiative for non-violent Zionism by responding positively to the Mandatory Authorities' calls for assistance in rooting out the terrorists. For some months, in what was known as 'the season', the Agency co-operated with the administration and provided hitherto unforthcoming intelligence enabling the arrest of a substantial number of both the Irgun and Lehi's members.[22] The Agency's armed wing, the Haganah, meanwhile carried out its own anti-terrorist operations, chiefly kidnappings.[23] The period of collaboration was to be short-lived. When violent attacks against the British resumed in October 1945, these were the work of a very different, and somewhat surprising, alliance of the Irgun, Lehi and the Haganah. What had changed was principally a growing realization within all these organizations, particularly the Haganah, that the election of Attlee's Labour government in May 1945 was not going to bring any closer the establishment of a Jewish state in Palestine – the objective to which all three were committed, despite differences over the territorial extent of the proposed state. Labour in government appeared to be retreating rapidly from its earlier pro-Zionist stance. When this became clear, the Haganah abruptly terminated its co-operation with the authorities, and for a period of some nine months formed the 'United Resistance Movement' together with the Irgun and Lehi.

This phase was ushered in on 31 October 1945 with a series of attacks throughout Israel: widespread damage was caused to railway lines, a lesser amount to oil refineries, and some security force members were injured.[24] Although this was the only period in which all three organizations co-ordinated their activities, and indeed after August 1946 the Haganah restricted its activities to aiding illegal immigration, violence against British targets continued at a high level until Britain's withdrawal in 1948. The Irgun and Lehi's actions fell into a number of distinct categories: thefts of arms, chemicals and explosives, and bank robberies; attacks on Palestine's communications infrastructure; assaults on government offices, particularly targets associated with immigration, including coastguard stations and police launches; attacks on members of the security forces, either individually or in groups (both on and off duty), and on their quarters and *matériel*; and assassinations of government officials.

Tactics altered as the campaign progressed. Both organizations attempted on a number of occasions to internationalize the campaign of violence. Targets in Italy were attacked and an assault planned on the Colonial Office itself.[25] Within Palestine, from 1946, an increasing number of actions involved the mining of roads or railways and vehicles. The Irgun also took to mimicking the Mandatory Authorities' measures, to some effect: thus when in December 1946 two young Irgun members were administered a flogging as their punishment for participation in terrorism, the Irgun kidnapped four British soldiers and subjected them to the same treatment.[26] Flogging was consequently abandoned by the administration.[27] The Irgun also made increasing use of kidnapping as a weapon, taking British troops, and a number of civilians (with the justification that they were agents of the state in some way), to gain another form of leverage over the administration. Thus when the Authorities announced the execution of members of the Irgun, the latter responded by holding British soldiers or civilians to ransom.[28] If the executions went ahead, the Irgun held their own 'trials' of their captives and sentenced them to a similar fate. The most notorious example of this was the Irgun's hanging on 29 July 1947 of Sergeants Paice and Martin, whose bodies were found booby-trapped in an orange grove in Nathanya. This was the climactic act of the Irgun's campaign against the British rule in Palestine; the announcement that the future of Palestine would be turned over to United Nations jurisdiction came only days afterwards. The outrage which the hanging caused in Britain was the culmination of feeling built up after a number of well-publicized atrocities in Palestine. Of these the most notorious were the killing of seven soldiers in Tel Aviv on 25 April 1946; the bombing of the King David Hotel (headquarters of the British military in Palestine) on 22 July 1946, in which ninety-one people were killed; and the Irgun's attack on the Goldsmith Officers' Club in Jerusalem on 1 March 1947, resulting in twenty-nine casualties.[29]

Naming the Enemy: British Interpretations of Terrorism

It has to be remembered that for British politicians and officials the Palestine problem was, in Richard Crossman's apt metaphor, 'just something extra on an overcrowded plate'. While he and his fellow members of the Anglo-American Commission (appointed in October 1945 to investigate the twin problems of Palestine and the 'displaced persons' who survived the Holocaust) had the luxury of three full months in which to ponder the Palestine problem in its entirety, most busy ministers were 'lucky if they had 100 consecutive minutes to think about Palestine'.[30] Furthermore, the groping towards a clear understanding of what the violence in Palestine *meant* – what its aims were, and how best to deal with it – took place in the charged atmosphere of the war's end and the Cold War's commencement. Attempts to counter terrorism in Palestine had to run alongside diplomatic initiatives to resolve the undeniable (and intractable) political problems of the region. In particular, the question of immigration had to be addressed to find a new post-White Paper formula. Along with the crisis in Greece and the end of British rule in India, domestic crises (fuelled by the ruinous cost to Britain of her part in the war) were also heaped in generous portions on Attlee's plate and these all constituted competing claims to the government's attention.

Whatever else was uncertain about the violence in Palestine, both policy-makers and colonial officials on the scene were in no doubt – from the outset – that the violent strategy espoused was both the product of propaganda and a form of it.[31] When the Irgun Zvai Leumi bombed the Immigration Department's offices in February 1944, *The Times* opined that 'propaganda by terrorism is becoming increasingly common with a section of the Jewish community which is campaigning against the White Paper and for the immediate establishment of a Jewish commonwealth'.[32] The view that terrorism was essentially a means of gaining publicity was shared by the High Commissioner. Sir Harold MacMichael reported a growing belief that 'extremism is an effective method of drawing attention to Zionist demands'.[33] Even responsible Jewish leaders, who feared that public opinion in America and the United Kingdom would not be able 'to discriminate between Jews and Jews', could not 'resist the idea that publicity for these crimes tends also to bring into the limelight the claims of Jewry, and the urgency of solving the problem of Palestine in a way favourable to themselves'.[34] Besides this publicity-generating function, terrorism was also intended, MacMichael believed, to 'intimidate HMG into further measures of appeasement and to stimulate their official leaders [i.e. the Jewish Agency] into decisive action'.[35]

The relationship between propaganda and political violence was thus circular rather than simply causal. Zionist propaganda fuelled terrorism, which generated further publicity (of both the word and the deed), and in turn drew new recruits to the ranks of the Irgun and Lehi. Propaganda provided the germs of the 'gangster virus'.[36] The activities of the Irgun and the Stern group placed an unmistakable emphasis on propaganda. The Irgun, Lehi and the Haganah all made use of secret radio transmissions, the latter organization through the Kol Israel (Voice of Israel) transmitter, sometimes with the Agency's connivance.[37] Additionally each organization had its own newspaper, which was supplemented by such a profusion of pamphleteering that on occasion the situation in Palestine was characterized as a 'pamphlet war'.[38] Pamphlets were distributed in various ways, including the use of 'pamphlet bombs' as well as more traditional bill-posting methods. Perhaps the most innovative propaganda technique employed in this period was the 'hijacking' of cinemas to project slides bearing political slogans or insignia of the underground organizations.[39] Besides this wealth of propaganda activity, in the latter part of the campaign the Irgun also attempted to cultivate good relations with visiting journalists (usually American) – this despite the considerable disadvantage of being an underground organization.[40] Among less well-disposed reporters and cameramen, the Irgun spread a message of fear.[41] As far as the Mandatory Authorities were concerned, cultivation of the media was wont to pay off.[42]

As in later counter-insurgencies, the British authorities within the territories concerned (and their Whitehall counterparts) generated psychological profiles of their terrorist opponents. Thus MacMichael tended to regard certain types of Jews – distinguished by their cultural background and/or psychological traits – as more likely to be infected by the 'gangster virus'. Soon after terrorism intensified in Palestine in 1944 MacMichael reported to Oliver Stanley (the Colonial Secretary):

> In recent years, Palestine has been entered by a large number of Jews from Central Europe whose background is anarchist. These have derived continuous encouragement and instigation from provocative and insidious propaganda directed through organised channels by political extremists already in Palestine. . . . Their natural tendency to violence is further accelerated by a vengeance complex aroused by the repressive measures which the police have been compelled with the fullest justification, to take against their fellow terrorists.[43]

Likewise, Sir John Shaw, who assumed command of the Palestine administration for some months in late 1944 and early 1945, stressed the different political culture from which many of Palestine's recently arrived Jews came. For this reason, and on account of what he (and many others) appear to have perceived as innate racial differences between Jews and Gentiles, they could not be expected to behave like the British:

> Reiterated innuendoes that countless Jewish lives were sacrificed in the abattoirs of Europe to deliberate obstructionism of [the British government] has rendered youthful minds receptive to the inflammatory nonsense of illegal newspapers and anarchist pamphlets of Irgun Zwai Leumi and the Stern Group. [The] Public towards whom all this effort is focused, is not phlegmatic, sensibly critical and good humoured like a British crowd: it is emotional, sentimental and excitable; a large proportion of the people come from countries where popular conceptions of law and order, constitutional methods and the spheres of police in the body politic, differ radically from our own.[44]

A further explanation for terrorism lay in a rather different sort of psychological proposition: the notion that terrorism was a form of fascism which had rubbed off on Jews as a result of contact with the Nazis. This idea was widely repeated. It was one to which the Palestine Information

31

Officer in Jerusalem, Christopher Holme, certainly subscribed, which may partially explain the frequency with which the British press and politicians echoed what must have appeared as an officially sanctioned interpretation of terrorism. In a talk on British publicity in Palestine in March 1945, Holme stated with complete assurance that terrorism was 'of course a manifestation of Nazism'.[45] A particularly striking elaboration of this theme was made by Herbert Morrison in his statement to the House of Commons after the King David Hotel explosion in July 1946:

> The shock of the King David Hotel explosion has surely aroused us to a fuller understanding, if that were needed, of the horrible and monstrous nature of those 'evil things' – to borrow a phrase used on a famous occasion – against which we are fighting. The curse of Hitler is not yet fully removed. Some of the victims fleeing from the ravaged ghettoes of Europe have carried with them the germs of those very plagues from which they sought escape – intolerance, racial pride, intimidation, terrorism and that worship of force. . . . Sane and healthy nationalism has inspired many of the finest achievements of mankind; its perversion spells only degradation and depravity.[46]

Indeed, as will be seen at greater length below, both sides regularly levelled accusations of Nazism at their opponent. While British officials used this interpretation as a way of both explaining and condemning terrorism, the Irgun and Lehi frequently likened the British Mandate to Nazi Germany. As Gerald Cromer has pointed out, Lehi propaganda portrayed the British as worse than Hitler: 'not only did they fail to prevent German atrocities and commit many of their own; they were also occupying the Jewish homeland'.[47]

One of the most critical issues facing the British government and the military in each counter-insurgency examined was to gauge the level of popular support enjoyed by the insurgents. This was a question of far more than academic interest, for whether the terrorists represented few but themselves or a wide constituency determined both the shape of counter-insurgency operations and how the political disputes which had given rise to violence were tackled. In Palestine, as elsewhere, the answer shifted over time. As violence spread, the Mandatory Authorities advised Westminster that a growing proportion of Jews were culpable. Initially, MacMichael had believed that the *Yishuv* as a whole were hostile to terrorism; he reported in April 1944 that the general population were becoming increasingly nervous of the effect of 'this cancer in their midst'.[48] Counter-insurgency operations and propaganda policy thus proceeded on the basis of attempting to widen the schism between moderate, non-violent Zionists and the terrorist groups.[49] This in effect meant the reappearance of a 'murder gang' mentality, as in Ireland between 1919 and 1921 – a development Richard Crossman, for one, cautioned against.[50]

However, the belief, as held by Crossman, that there were 'just a handful of wicked men in Palestine' who were causing all the trouble, gave way to a tendency to hold the *Yishuv* collectively responsible for acts of terrorism. Partly this may have derived from the growing prevalence of racial theories to explain terrorism and the failure of the *Yishuv* to root out those infected, which blurred distinctions between active and passive supporters of the Irgun and Lehi. Collective punishments, arrests of Jewish Agency officials and searches of Agency premises – in short, the attribution of wider responsibility for terrorism than hitherto – were measures which the military had urged on the civil authorities for some months before the latter concurred. Indeed, the Chief of the Imperial General Staff, Field Marshal Montgomery, had disagreed vehemently with Sir Alan Cunningham's handling of the counter-insurgency, until the Cabinet (with the High Commissioner's approbation) sanctioned a search operation against the Jewish Agency in June 1946.[51] Although by November 1946, Cunningham still rejected Monty's verdict that 'terrorism is accepted by all and sundry',[52] he recognized that there was a fundamental difference of perception, if not of terrorism itself, then of where legitimacy lay on emotive issues such as immigration, especially the controversial British policy of sending shiploads of illegal immigrants back to their ports of embarkation, or to temporary camps in Cyprus. As Cunningham found during a conversation with Moshe Shertok (Head of the Jewish Agency's Political Department), 'although the *Yishuv* considered terrorism an outrage, they also thought the deportation of refugees an outrage'.[53] While the Mandatory Authorities never entirely abandoned their effort to win over 'moderate' Zionists, they became increasingly pessimistic as to its chances of success.

The debate as to the level of popular support enjoyed by the terrorists, and the appropriate politico-military response, also affected the language used to describe the enemy. As has already been noted, in battles for legitimacy 'words are weapons'. Accusations of Nazism formed one component of the verbal battle between government and insurgents, and application of the label 'terrorist' was another means of delegitimizing the enemy which both sides employed for at least some of the campaign. Government and insurgents alike demonstrated considerable self-consciousness in their use of terminology, and an awareness of the way in which language shaped meaning, and consequently affected perceptions. In July 1946, Trafford Smith remarked on 'the narrow meaning which it is now fashionable to give to "terrorism"', as evidenced by a recent House of Commons debate, which showed that 'in Members' minds terrorism is what Irgun and Stern do, while Hagana [sic] activities are presumably to be described in some less drastic phraseology'.[54] This suggests that the word 'terrorist' did carry more pejorative overtones than other labels which might be applied to exponents of politically motivated violence. Can one, then, speak of a conscious policy of describing members of the Irgun and Lehi as 'terrorists'? Certainly there had been a preferred designation of the Arab rebels during the 1936–39 Rebellion, even if by March 1945 the Palestine Information Officer felt that the label had been inappropriate:

> It was part of our news policy to represent the many Arabs who took active part in the rebellion at that time as bandits. Some of them probably were, but a good proportion of them were intellectuals, inspired by a genuine, if misguided idealism.[55]

There was no such sympathy (even *ex post facto*) for the Jewish insurgents. There was some debate in 1944 as to whether the political objectives of the insurgents should be openly acknowledged, and this had repercussions for their labelling. In discussing a forthcoming government communiqué, which was to condemn recent 'bomb outrages' in Palestine, Lord Moyne argued strongly that the effect 'would be weakened by allowing it to be supposed that we regard [the] authors of these outrages primarily as "Gangsters" rather than as political revolutionaries'. He was thus adamant that the communiqué 'bring out the fact that [the] terrorists openly avow they are acting for political aims'.[56] For most of the campaign, 'terrorist' was the label applied to members of the Irgun and Lehi, as it conveyed the stigma attached to proponents of this type of violence, while not carrying the implication of apolitical violent crime which attached to the terms 'bandit' and 'gangster'.

However, as the military assumed a larger role in the counter-insurgency, and their view of the general responsibility of the *Yishuv* for terrorism became more prevalent, so too did the term 'terrorist' appear (to some at least) unsatisfactory. In March 1947, following the bombing of the Tel Aviv Goldsmith Officers' Club, the Middle East Land Forces rejected the term 'terrorism':

> It is no longer possible to differentiate between passive onlookers and active armed members of the Jewish population, and the word 'terrorist' is no longer being applied to differentiate one from the other. All suffer from the martyr complex and instability of temperament, which makes their reactions in circumstances of any political stress both violent and unpredictable.[57]

That avoidance of the term 'terrorist' represented both a private analysis and a propaganda ploy for public consumption was made plain in the order enshrining the alteration in terminology:

> It has been the habit in the past to refer generically to members of the Stern and Irgun and other Jews involved in outrages and

sabotage as 'terrorists'. This invests the individuals concerned with a certain amount of glamour, and raises them on a pedestal all by themselves, thus drawing publicity to them . . .

The so called terrorists are in fact members of the Jewish community of Palestine. Nor could any terrorist organisation exist in any country where the local inhabitants were on the side of the security forces and where they were prepared to give information about them, they would soon be rooted out.

The word 'terrorist' will therefore not be used; when referring to such persons terms such as armed Jews, Jews, thugs, murderers will be used or they may be referred to as members of the Irgun and Stern as may be appropriate.[58]

Even among British observers, then, there was disagreement as to the nuanced meaning signified by certain words. While Trafford Smith had spoken of 'terrorism' as a 'drastic phraseology' – used to tarnish its proponents – the military in Palestine, by the spring of 1947, felt that its use was glamorizing, and created an unwarranted distinction between active and passive supporters of violence. Even within the military different connotations were attributed to the term. To Major R. Dare Wilson, who served with the Sixth Airborne Division in Palestine, 'terrorism' should be avoided because:

The word implies that those who were engaged with them had cause to be terrified by them. This, of course, could not have been further from the truth – the perpetual regret of all ranks was that there were so few opportunities of getting to grips with them. The term was an unfortunate journalistic choice which, despite the efforts of the Army, persisted until the end in general use by the press and BBC.[59]

That journalists in fact took their lead from the discourse of the civil and military authorities, and not vice versa, is suggested by the surely not co-incidental frequency with which – for a short time after the 'order' appeared - British journalists referred to members of the Irgun and Lehi as 'thugs' or 'gangsters'. The day after the *Daily Telegraph*, for example, reported that 'terrorist' was to be replaced in the Army's vocabulary with the terms 'murderers, felons and common thugs', the paper scrupulously used the word 'gangsters' whenever referring to members of the under-ground organizations – even if it did shortly resume use of 'terrorists'.[60] As Brigadier Bernard Fergusson observed, with greater realism than Wilson, the word 'thugs' was 'so obviously inappropriate that in fact everybody continued to talk about "terrorists"'.[61] This provided Begin, the Irgun's leader, with an opportunity for retrospective gloating: 'The British press and the British troops continued to call us by the name which, in their General's opinion, suggested bravery on our part and fear on theirs. They called us "terrorists" to the end.'[62]

The Irgun, Lehi and the Interpretation of Terrorism

During the campaign, however, the Irgun and Lehi were less keen on that description. In 1943, Lehi had defended its adoption of terrorism (which it defined as 'exercising influence by illegal means'), stating in its newspaper, *Hehazit*, that strategically it was 'the only way':

> It proclaims in a clear and audible language to the world and to our brethren in exile why we are fighting the real terrorist – the invader – and the laws he tries to impose on us. Our terrorism is not directed against individuals but against the leaders and therefore it must succeed. If, at the same time, it awakens the *Yishuv* from its sleep, the better.[63]

While Lehi maintained its attempt to brand the British authorities as the 'real terrorist' until they withdrew, it became more sensitive to that label when applied to itself. Interviewed for the American publication *Liberty* in October 1946, Lehi leader Friedman Yelin claimed that they were 'not terrorists. Terrorism is an attempt to intimidate one into acting counter to justice or morality' – a definition which differed markedly from that offered in 1943.[64] The organization also objected to being termed the 'Stern Gang', writing to newspaper representatives in Palestine in April 1947 that this appellation smacked of misrepresentation: the 'enemy quite naturally seek to misrepresent our legal and legitimate fight for freedom as gangster activities, exactly as the Germans did with regard to the French maquis or the Balkan partisans'.[65]

Similarly, the Irgun leader (and later Prime Minister of Israel) Menachem Begin – while gratified that to the British 'terrorist' meant one who created terror, and that this was their perception of his organization – sought to distance himself from the label:

> the term 'terror' became current in political terminology during the French Revolution. The revolutionaries began cutting off heads with the guillotine in order to instil fear. Thenceforward the word 'terror' came to define acts of revolutionaries or counter-revolutionaries, of fighters for freedom and oppressors. It all depends on who uses the term . . .
> The historical and linguistic origins of the political term 'terror' prove that it cannot be applied to a revolutionary war of liberation. . . . A revolution, or a revolutionary war, does not aim at instilling fear. Its object is to overthrow a regime and to set up a new regime in its place.[66]

Justificatory rhetoric such as this makes it difficult to determine exactly how the Irgun and Lehi intended their particular uses of violence and propaganda to achieve the desired political outcome. Members of both organizations have proved reluctant, retrospectively, to acknowledge the creation of fear as a tactical objective. They are more willing to attest the gaining of publicity as an end. The memoirs of 'Avner', an anonymous Lehi member, hint at this when he relates that 'with the feeble reserves at the disposal of Lehi, a continual bluff was necessary in the game of poker that we were playing' – in other words, the publicity attaching to acts of violence would create the impression that a more substantial organization was behind them.[67]

On the subject of publicity, Begin famously claimed that the revolt made Palestine resemble 'a glass house', and that, largely as a consequence of the world looking in 'with ever increasing interest', the Irgun was able to pursue its struggle to a 'successful climax'.[68] His memoirs also imply that the international audience's attention prevented the British from responding too rigorously to the insurgency (although security force measures were always presented as over-reactions at the time), with the remark that public interest 'created a lifebelt around the population'.[69] Yet Begin also claims that his organization did not place any reliance on the moral restraints of the enemy – a tacit rejection of the oft-made point that terrorists consciously exploit the liberal sensibilities of the states they attack.[70] The question of whether the Irgun's strategy was to provoke reprisals from the security forces, conscious of the latter's frustration at the constraints placed upon their response to terrorism by the civil authorities, is similarly left unanswered, as is the issue of how far the Irgun saw negative publicity as serving its end.[71]

What then was the Irgun and Lehi's violence meant to achieve? Charters writes that their strategies rested on the simultaneous undermining of 'the British right, will, and ability to govern Palestine'.[72] The two did in fact employ distinct tactics, although the Army in Palestine did not seem always conscious of this. Having initially concentrated on assassinating key individuals, Lehi, according to Nathan Yelin-Mor, began to see attacks as more successful the more apparently indiscriminate they were:

> There are advantages in killing individually selected people. You eradicate some of the people responsible for the policy you are fighting. But it was a big empire and these people could easily be replaced. More effective perhaps were our attacks on the rank and file, ordinary soldiers and policemen.[73]

Such acts undermined both the will and ability of the British to maintain its presence in Palestine. In addition, sabotage (the cutting of oil pipelines, and arson attacks on refineries) and the disruption of communications in Palestine made the territory appear less attractive economically and as a military base. Not only, then, did the Irgun and Lehi aim to raise the physical stakes of staying in Palestine for the British, but also the financial ones. As for undermining Britain's right to be in Palestine, this was the task of both words and deeds. As Begin put it:

> The very existence of an underground, which oppression, hangings, torture and deportations, fail to crush or to weaken must, in the end, undermine the prestige of a colonial regime that lives by the legend of its omnipotence. . . . Politically every attack was an achievement.[74]

Britain's inability to terminate the Irgun's existence eventually led British politicians and newspapers to call for the government to 'rule or quit', as the *Sunday Express* had it.[75] The Irgun's actions were a gesture of defiance and an inducement to British public opinion to press for 'quitting' – as the less painful alternative to ruling.

British Opinion and the Palestine Problem

Before turning our attention to the matter of *how* the government attempted to influence the presentation of terrorism, some appreciation is needed of *why* public opinion (particularly in Britain) mattered. In one respect the answer seems obvious: both the incumbents and the insurgents in Palestine agreed that a primary function of violence was to attract attention. With the spotlight on Palestine, the government could reasonably be expected to take some pains as to the presentation of its own activities and those of its opponent. Yet there are also compelling reasons why Attlee's government might *not* have expended too much energy on influencing the presentation of terrorism in Palestine. As Crossman pointed out in *Palestine Mission*, 'no election would ever be decided on the merits of the Government's handling of Palestine'.[76] According to Crossman, the press showed little interest in the Palestine problem (or the wider question of the displaced persons' fate). When the Palestine situation was reported, the bias tended to be pro-Arab, in marked contrast to the tenor of the American press:

> Public opinion tends to accept facts which suit its mood and to reject those which do not; and its newspapers, sensitive to reader reaction, provide news which confirms these prejudices. The American press, in reporting the Middle East, is strongly pro-Jewish, while British newspapers give relatively more space to items which illustrate the Arab point of view. This is due not, as most Englishmen imagine, to a conspiracy among Jewish proprietors, but to the intimate relations between the newspaper

and its readers. . . . In England, where the Jewish community is relatively unimportant, the Jewish case is fully presented only in the small Jewish Press, and in a few Liberal papers, such as the *Manchester Guardian*.[77]

British Jewry at the time was 300,000 strong, and represented by twenty-five Jewish Labour MPs.[78] But while the Jewish population had perhaps a disproportionately high level of political representation, Zionist propaganda was unlikely to make a serious impact on the thinking of the non-Jewish British public.

If Fleet Street did not devote too much attention to the Palestine problem up to mid-1946, as Crossman suggested, elucidation of the reasons requires no great deductive skill. When terrorism re-emerged in Palestine, the war in Europe was still being fought, and this understandably received far more coverage than the occasional bouts of violent Jewish opposition to the White Paper. Also during the war the stringent Middle East censorship (regarded at the time as one of the most severe) tended to limit the amount of dissidence which could be reported from that strategically critical theatre. Certainly major 'outrages', such as the Moyne murder and subsequent trial, received generous coverage but the lesser incidents were frequently left unreported or were tucked away in small columns off the front pages. Even after the war was over the rationing of newsprint meant that, as censorship was relaxed, British papers (often only four to six pages long) still had to devise strict criteria for reporting the news of most interest to the British public.

There was plenty closer to home to interest the newspaper-reading public other than terrorism in Palestine: the shortage of housing and problem of squatting; demobilization of the armed forces and remobilization in peacetime industry; the balance of payments crisis and the exports drive; and the continuation of food rationing, extended to bread for the first time in 1946. If Crossman's metaphorical plate was overcrowded, in reality plates for many British people were alarmingly empty in the immediate post-war years, and this (unsurprisingly) was a matter of greater moment than what was going on in Palestine. A Gallup opinion poll conducted in January 1947, when terrorism was approaching its climax, found that only 4 per cent of respondents thought Palestine to be the government's most urgent problem – housing forming the most pressing concern.[79] The public's preoccupation with domestic matters found a telling illustration in the editorial decision of the *Daily Mirror*, the day on which the King David Hotel bombing broke in Britain, to lead with the story of a riot at Harringay Stadium over a greyhound race, before reporting (in less column space) '60 Dead, 200 Hurt in HQ Wreck; Still Digging'.[80]

A general lack of interest in Palestine is amply borne out in surveys conducted by Mass-Observation on the subject. For example, in October

1946 a *Note on Popular Attitudes to Palestine and Arab Countries* reported that:

> Even at the peak point of interest in Palestine, there is little evidence of more than a most rudimentary knowledge of the situation amongst the majority of the people. The Arabs come up well largely by default rather than from any positive interest or understanding of their cause.[81]

In September 1947 a further survey revealed that one in every three people questioned had either never heard the word 'Zionism' or had an entirely erroneous conception of what it was. Half of those asked had never heard of the Balfour Declaration – this at a time when the Palestine situation was almost daily on British front pages after some of the most intensive terrorist activity.[82]

Did popular ignorance and apathy militate against government intervention in the presentation of terrorism? Charters suggests that the government saw little need for mediating the reportage of events in Palestine:

> Propaganda counter-measures directed at the British audience showed even less drive or imagination than efforts in America. It may be fair to suggest that once British soldiers were being killed such measures were unnecessary because the British population tended to sympathise with the army in such difficult circumstances.[83]

We will return to the criticisms of British counter-propaganda later, but whatever the flair (or otherwise) of the measures undertaken, the Foreign and Colonial Offices were certainly very much concerned with the presentation of Jewish political violence. Far from feeling that the reportage of terrorism could be left to look after itself (since the immorality of the violence would be understood by all 'right-thinking' people), the government repeatedly intervened in the process. One point which emerged clearly as the campaign developed was that public sympathy with the Army did not necessarily translate into political support for the government, especially when the reasons for Britain's military presence in Palestine were not felt to outweigh the loss of British lives. The need for propaganda was thus not obviated – indeed, was increased – by the deaths of British boys in Palestine.

Although Mass-Observation recorded a general lack of interest in Palestine, the one aspect of the situation which did concern the British public was terrorism and the attendant British casualties.[84] Popular sympathy for the difficult task facing the Army was all too likely to manifest itself in calls for Britain to leave Palestine with undue haste, or to employ a ruthlessness in stamping out terrorism which the government was reluctant to sanction. Even if they were reluctant to admit it themselves, for the Irgun and Lehi it was British outrage – not sympathy with Zionism – which mattered, as *The Times* explained in August 1947:

> Recalling acts of savagery which shocked the world, it is essential to make a point often overlooked – that it was precisely the terrorists' intention to shock the world. The harder the impact of the gruesome details on the British public, the better the terrorists' cause is served. They believe that the cry is then raised by many in Britain that the British should leave Palestine. It is the fundamental objective of the terrorists to see the British leave the country, after which, if the Jews were left to themselves, they would be free to organise the expansion of the Jewish state.[85]

The need for official intervention in the presentation of terrorism was not because there was a danger of the British switching their allegiance to the terrorist side. Indeed the effect of terrorism on large numbers of British people was quite the reverse: a startling rise in anti-Semitism. The initial aim of government propaganda was rather to ensure that the British public *appeared* to be sufficiently anti-terrorist to interested onlookers in Palestine and the United States. In addition, the government needed to ensure that domestic support continued for the counter-terrorist campaign, even after the announcement that the Palestine problem would be examined by the UN. Had this commitment been lacking, Attlee's administration would have been exposed to the charge of reneging on its frequent pledges of 'no surrender' to terrorism.

Aims and Methods of British Publicity: Propaganda by News

From an early date it was apparent that propaganda was a necessary component of Britain's counter-terrorist activities. The propaganda campaign had to be waged on several fronts simultaneously: in Palestine, to persuade the *Yishuv* of the dangers inherent in supporting terrorism, and to calm Arab fears and antagonism; in America, to counter the influential Zionist lobby, which was encouraging Truman to intervene in HMG's handling of the Palestine problem (particularly over the immediate admittance of 100,000 Jewish immigrants), in addition to providing psychological and material aid to the terrorists themselves; and in Britain itself, where public expressions of opposition to terrorism and hostile press and BBC coverage of political violence provided useful ammunition to fire back at the other target audiences abroad.

The British effort in this sphere has found few champions. Most critics have argued that British propaganda on (and in) Palestine was doomed to failure on account of an absence of policy in Westminster concerning the territory's future. Thus Tugwell writes:

> The British response in the war of words and ideas was flawed throughout by the lack of a forward political policy on Palestine. Answers to revolutionary propaganda can be effective if based on a defence of a political status quo, provided that the political situation to be defended has positive virtues, or they can be effective if related to the introduction of new policies, in the manner of counter-revolution. Britain's search for a Palestine settlement demonstrated that she was dissatisfied with the existing arrangements: her failure to find an acceptable compromise deprived her of any new ideal. Both the security campaign and the propaganda war were therefore defensive or negative in character, and thus gravely handicapped.[86]

Similarly Mockaitis considers that Britain was effectively prevented from waging a battle for hearts and minds. The absence of an effective campaign of this sort was not the result of ineptitude or a failure to recognize its necessity to successful counter-insurgency, but a product of the intractability of the political problem in Palestine: Britain found herself 'in the unenviable position of being unable either to offer the carrot or to wield the stick'.[87] In these difficult circumstances, then, what did British propaganda attempt to achieve, and through what channels?

World War II had seen Britain rely heavily on a 'propaganda by news' strategy. During the war, the Ministry of Information interposed itself between the Departments of State and the news media. While the latter were allowed to comment freely upon current events, the flow of information which they received was regulated by the MOI.[88] Likewise in Palestine news – as regulated by the authorities – was to form the 'shocktroops of propaganda'.[89] Partly because of the war, and partly because Palestine was, as the MOI's Mr Grubb put it, 'a particularly ticklish part of the world', the MOI had a large information office when the Zionist insurgency began.[90] Thus, whereas in other Emergencies, the outbreak of terrorism found disorganized, or virtually non-existent, information teams in the territories concerned, the Palestine Information Office had a staff of around 100 in 1945.[91] Propaganda both in and about Palestine was complicated not only by the number of internal and international audiences to which any message had to be directed, but by the number of agencies involved in publicizing events there. Until its demise in March 1946, the MOI was primarily responsible for the dissemination of news on Palestine, and the Palestine Information Office acted as its regional office. Yet the MOI at its London headquarters,

Senate House, felt that it did not always receive sufficient information from the Colonial Office, which was in direct contact with the High Commissioner and Secretariat in Jersualem, to enable it to expedite its news-disseminating function. As the MOI's Arabic specialist, J.H. Driberg, complained to the Colonial Office's J.G. Eastwood:

> If anything, we should have more information made available to us at times of crisis, and not less, if our activities are to be effective. . . . One *cannot* tell journalists nothing, particularly American journalists: if we do, they will merely invent something.[92]

Such tensions were eased somewhat by the termination of the MOI and creation of a Central Office of Information (COI), which had a very much reduced role – acting merely as a service department to the information sections of other Departments of State.[93] However, strains still existed between the Foreign and Colonial Offices over the handling of publicity on Palestine. Although there was a division of labour between the two, their information activities nevertheless had a degree of overlap, and, in any case, had to be co-ordinated as it had been decided that separate propaganda lines on Palestine should not be pushed.[94] The Colonial Office sphere of responsibility included publicity on Palestine in Britain, the workings of the Palestine Information Office and the Censor's office, and relationships with foreign correspondents covering events on the spot. From Church House, the Colonial Office kept a close watch over the reportage of events in Palestine in the British press. The Foreign Office concerned itself with the international aspects of the Palestine problem and with propaganda in and for the USA, liaising closely with the British Information Service (BIS) in that country. Although there was always an element of friction between Church House and the Foreign Office, over Palestine their relations were given added piquancy as a result of the Colonial Office perception that the Foreign Office was less than neutral. As Sir John Martin (Colonial Office Under-Secretary of State) later recalled: 'The Foreign Office attitude was quite definitely pro-Arab in its bias. Though it may sound priggish to say so, I think we did in the Colonial Office try to be pro-nobody in particular.'[95]

At the centre of this complex web of relationships was that between the Whitehall Departments, the government in Westminster and the civil and military authorities in Palestine on the one hand and the British press on the other. Most of the objectives of British publicity on Palestine involved managing the presentation of news by the press, and other news media to a lesser degree. Fleet Street occupied a position centre stage not simply because of its importance in influencing the domestic perception of terrorism, but also on account of the weight that British newspapers carried overseas. As Charters has remarked, British propaganda initiatives seemed to be aimed primarily at audiences beyond Palestine.[96] Another commentator has suggested that 'compared with American or Arab opinion, public opinion in Britain was less important for policy-makers and publicists', but this is perhaps to underestimate the role envisaged for British opinion and the London press in the publicity strategy.[97]

Mediating the Presentation of Terrorism

The overriding aim of British propaganda on Palestine appears to have been to encourage the Jewish Agency and international Zionist organizations to take a sufficiently hard line against the terrorist activities of the Irgun, Lehi and the Haganah such that these groups would either abandon their violent strategy or find themselves unable to continue through absence of moral and material assistance (as happened briefly during 'the season'). In short, propaganda, along with military operations, was designed to deprive the fish of their water, to use Mao's analogy. To this end, Britain's information organizations needed to provide adequate publicity for terrorist activities, and attempt to encourage condemnation of them. Indeed, when terrorist activities became more widespread in Palestine in 1944, the Foreign Office, which was firmly set against a Zionist solution to the Palestine problem, initially hoped that terrorism might prove functional to its cause.

By early 1944 the Foreign Office was exploring means of bringing home to American Zionists 'the connection between Zionist agitation in the USA and this outbreak of violence in Palestine'.[98] In this connection, the Eastern Department's Hankey suggested that the best propaganda line for the USA would be 'to use the huge publicity machine we have to blacken the faces of *all* Jews with these incidents, then the Jews themselves will quickly stop them'.[99] Hankey had already floated a less strongly worded version of this idea to the Colonial Office a month earlier:

> One of the best ways in which Zionists in the United States could be prevented from gaining an embarrassing degree of public support and influence would be for careful publicity to be given to harmful activities of extreme Zionists in Palestine. . . . There is every possible advantage in the American public being given as much information as possible about incidents of this sort [assassinations of British police officers, bombs at the Immigration Office, and so on] and arrangements should be made for such information to be given to numerous American correspondents in the Middle East.[100]

He insisted that news relating to terrorist incidents should be released at source, as 'news' rather than 'official handouts' from London, and that MacMichael must be persuaded to give out fuller information on incidents of this sort, improving on the present 'rather scanty press releases'.[101]

There were obvious drawbacks with Hankey's scheme. The first was that, as Hankey recognized in a dig at Churchill's pro-Zionism, 'the PM is unlikely to allow it for his own reasons';[102] the second, that it wilfully misrepresented the general Zionist attitude to terrorism. As the Colonial Office's Battershill had pointed out to the British Embassy in Washington:

> Nothing would create greater resentment in responsible circles of the Zionist organisation than an attempt by the Palestine Government and British authorities in Washington to represent that these excesses of extremist factions are symptomatic of the Zionist attitude as a whole to British authority.[103]

Nevertheless, Hankey's proposal was not completely abandoned, with the Foreign Office concluding that, without accusing 'Zionist organisations of responsibility for terrorism', the British Information Service could 'point out that a continued campaign of abuse against HMG and vilification of the Palestine Administration is bound to encourage violence'.[104] What mattered, Hankey concluded, with a nod at Colonial Office scruples, was that the 'facts' should be made known in America.[105] In other words, far from being denied the oxygen of publicity, the Jewish terrorists were to be administered an overdose.

There were various mechanisms for encouraging a steadier flow of news concerning terrorist activity. Hankey had recommended that the Palestine government simply release more information at source. However, the Mandatory Authorities generally wanted to direct reportage in a more heavy-handed way - to ensure that terrorism was not simply reported but suitably condemned. This attitude led to attempts to use official communiqués as the channel via which the Palestine adminstration communicated with the news media.

Shortly after the attempt on the life of Sir Harold MacMichael (the retiring High Commissioner), John Shaw (the Officer Administering the Government in Palestine) cabled Oliver Stanley on the need for more condemnatory propaganda:

> Far more effective in discouraging terrorism would be a clear indication that the people of Britain and America are united in condemning it. . . . if they really believed that terrorism is likely to prejudice that public opinion against them, the Jewish community would have a clear case for active participation in the attempt to eradicate terrorism as inimical to their interests.[106]

His most immediate proposal was for a communiqué to be issued by him in Palestine, which would stress the collective responsibility of the Jewish people in Palestine to counter terrorism. The ensuing arrangements for publicizing the communiqué mark the real start of a concerted attempt to intervene in press coverage of terrorist activity in Palestine. As Shaw's remarks and the ensuing discussion between Foreign and Colonial Office staff suggest, British opinion was to be deployed as a weapon against extreme Zionists in Palestine and the United States. Stanley's summary of Colonial Office conclusions on Palestine publicity set the tone for much future activity:

1. Our object is that Jewish leaders and community in Palestine may be convinced that terrorism is doing harm to their cause by prejudicing public opinion against them in this country and America.
2. We do not want big headlines in popular papers so much as leading articles in papers whose opinion responsible Jews respect such as the *Manchester Guardian* and *The Times*.
3. The first essential is that the public be fully informed of the facts. There must be an adequate flow of news from the Middle East and I suggest some easing up of censorship may be desirable.
   . . .
5. Contact is being made here with certain influential newspapermen. The way will be prepared for favourable reception of news arriving from Palestine and they will be given background news which they can make use of as occasion serves.
6. Arrangements will be made for public reaction to news from Palestine to be telegraphed back to Palestine as fully as possible.[107]

As in later counter-insurgencies, the Colonial Office advocated getting the presentation of news right at source. This meant that Middle East censorship (as Hankey had already suggested) needed to be eased, or it would 'be much more difficult to put across to the Press our special points' – editors trusting their local correspondents more than Whitehall Departments or the MOI. As Stanley pointed out, the 'Middle East has at present a reputation for holding news back which inevitably is likely to make the Press suspicious of official attempts to get them to play up certain items of news'.[108] To increase the amount of news available, Shaw instituted a system of sending weekly newsletters to the MOI summarizing the 'events and tendencies' of the terrorist campaign - although these do not appear always to have found their way to Senate House.[109]

Besides attempting to influence what news was reported from Palestine, and in what tone, the British authorities also made some effort to influence *who* reported that news. As far as the authorities in Palestine were concerned, an obstacle to their 'factual' approach to propaganda lay in the failure of large segments of the American press to interpret the facts in the same way as the British government. Shaw offered the following explanation for why government press handouts were failing to have the desired effect:

> the local correspondents of American newspapers are all or nearly all Jews and this naturally limits the scope for action. . . . Opportunities for the right kind of publicity on Palestine occur with the help of visiting correspondents if these are well-disposed and receptive but generally such visitors only come here when there is something sensational occurring, for example the arms trial or terrorist activities. On such occasions the handouts which we give are of course liable to be stigmatized by Jews as anti-Semitic propaganda.[110]

Shaw concluded that 'no amount of the most objectively presented explanation' would 'influence the output of a journalist who comes here with his mind made up and assimilates only what fits in with his preconceived ideas'.[111] While he was perhaps misguided to assume that all Jews were Zionists, and therefore hostile to the government, his belief that little could be done to counter incorrigible opponents seems reasonable. Although government propaganda measures have been attacked, particularly by Tugwell, for failing even to attempt to win over hardline Zionists, Shaw's conclusion (shared by many in the Colonial and Foreign Offices and the BIS) was surely realistic. And while Charters has claimed that during this insurgency Britain 'violated every principle of effective propaganda', to recognize the limitations of persuasion actually accords with one of Jacques Ellul's key observations about propaganda: that it cannot reverse ingrained prejudice.[112] More questionable was Shaw's attempted remedy to the problem of incorrigible reporters – namely to dispatch 'corrective telegrams' to the MOI after any 'particularly mischievous or untruthful' report by an American journalist.[113] Although the Palestine authorities tried to correct unhelpful reports, they increasingly recognized their insufficiency, and, as we shall see, put greater emphasis on issuing speedy and accurate accounts of events before tendentious reports took root.

There was also another way of dealing with unhelpful reporters: to get rid of them. Clearly, pressure could not be put on American editors, but closer to home (and British correspondents too were suspected of Zionist sympathies) the MOI was able to exert its influence. An article in *The Economist* in November 1944 strongly echoed Sir John Shaw's fears about Jewish reporters' objectivity:

> All recent visitors from the Middle East are astonished at our ignorance [on Palestine]. The reasons for it are two: first, the smallness of our newspapers and their absorption with war news;

second, the fact that the trouble-makers of 1944 have been the Jews, that every British daily but one employs, for lack of other journalistic talent in Palestine, a Jewish correspondent, and that these have tended to play down the degree of tension that prevails.[114]

Ignoring the combative reply sent to *The Economist* by six British papers, which pointed out that terrorism was not underplayed but that in wartime news was censored as well as rationed, the Foreign Office was moved to take action.[115] The Eastern Department first attempted to ascertain the truth of *The Economist*'s initial claim and decided that the Palestine correspondents of the *Daily Express*, *Daily Herald*, *News Chronicle*, *Daily Telegraph* and *Exchange Telegraph* were 'certainly Jews' and the United Press correspondent was 'also probably a Jew' – a list identical to the respondents who complained about the piece. This caused some alarm: 'in view of the situation developing in the Middle East, it is of some importance that we should have as far as possible impartial British correspondents in these parts'.[116] The Colonial Office, encouraged by the Foreign Office, consequently requested the MOI to contact newspaper editors, 'to bring it tactfully to the notice of the papers that next time they are appointing a correspondent it would be better to have someone who is not a Jew or an Arab'.[117] Pollock duly referred the matter to Francis Williams (of the MOI Press Division, later Attlee's press secretary) who 'agreed to put in a diplomatic word in the right quarter', despite thinking it primarily a 'manpower' problem.[118]

There were other mechanisms besides communiqués and hand-outs, and less drastic means than having reporters replaced, for increasing the volume of negative publicity given to terrorism. These included statements by prominent politicians in Westminster, either in speeches in the course of Parliamentary debates, or, if there were particular points the Palestine authorities wished to emphasize, through the medium of inspired Parliamentary Questions. The assassination of Lord Moyne in November 1944, for example, provided an opportunity not only to load the press with official statements for verbatim reporting, but for Churchill himself to make an outspoken condemnation of terrorism:

This shameful crime has shocked the world. It has affected none more strongly than those, like myself, who in the past, have been consistent friends of the Jews and constant architects of their future. If our dreams for Zionism are to end in the smoke of assassins' pistols and our labours for its future to produce only a new set of gangsters worthy of Nazi Germany, many like myself will have to reconsider the position we have maintained so consistently, and for so long, in the past.[119]

It was this sort of speech, from one whose opinion mattered to Zionists, that Attlee's government hoped – without success – to extract from Truman, upon publication of the Anglo-American Commission on Palestine's report in April 1946.[120] Even when Truman did condemn terrorism after the King David Hotel bomb, he coupled his remarks with a further appeal for 100,000 Jews to be let into Palestine immediately – nullifying any positive effects which his indictment of terrorism might have had on American Zionists.[121]

Other British propaganda initiatives aimed at pressurizing the Jewish Agency into co-operating with the Palestine Police against terrorism – or to cut off the terrorists' external support – were similarly unsuccessful. Shortly after 'Operation Agatha' (during which the Agency offices were searched, and staff arrested), a White Paper on terrorism was published, which reproduced documents found in the Agency headquarters, presumably in the hope that moderates could yet be appealed to – a similar strategy to that employed by Sir John Harding in Cyprus in his efforts to establish the Orthodox Church's complicity in EOKA terrorism. In Palestine, the attempt was not particularly fruitful. Implying, however obliquely, that all Jews were responsible for terrorism had its dangers. This was seen in July 1946, after the operation against the Agency, when the American Secretary of State, James Byrnes, suggested to Bevin that American opinion wanted reassurance that the recent action had been forced on Britain 'by the terroristic activities of illegal Jewish armed forces' and that Britain had 'no prejudice against the Jews as such' – easier said than done, when Bevin's own words were consistently portrayed in the USA as anti-Semitic.[122] The same month that Byrnes made his remarks, the BIS in Washington decided that – rather than continuing to publicize terrorist activity to the full – the most sensible path might be to remove Palestine from the headlines by whatever means possible.[123] No more successful were attempts to persuade the US government to prohibit Zionist organizations from placing emotive advertisements in American newspapers, soliciting funds for the Irgun and Lehi or for the trade in illegal Jewish immigration.[124]

Defending the Security Forces

After the initial enthusiasm for taking the propaganda offensive (by actually using terrorism to denigrate political Zionism as a movement), the government found itself increasingly on the defensive in 1945 and thereafter. As in other campaigns, the presentation of counter-terrorist measures was no less important than intervention in the portrayal of terrorism itself, not least as the insurgents sought to discredit the measures taken by civil and military authorities against them. Allegations of atrocities against the security forces could not be ignored, partly because charges made in Irgun and Lehi propaganda were widely repeated by the international press. Also, there may have been a sense in Westminster that security force misbehaviour – if people believed it was occurring – was more likely to be condemned than terrorist activity because states were expected to have higher standards of behaviour. This was certainly what had happened during the 1919–21 Anglo-Irish war, with the *Westminster Gazette* encouraging its readers to denounce the excesses of the counter-insurgency:

> Englishmen, unfortunately, cannot control Sinn Fein outrages, and they can do nothing but denounce them, but they can and they ought to control the acts of their own Executive, and they have a duty to insist that it shall not engage in a competition of murder and sabotage with its assailants.[125]

It was unfortunate for Attlee's government that the Irish experience – in which the balance of censure had tipped towards Westminster for its failure to control the notorious auxiliary police unit, the 'Black and Tans' – should have been so frequently before it in dealing with Zionist terrorism. Accusations of 'black and tannery' levelled against the Palestine Police, however, were more than a mere rhetorical flourish, for the force's upper echelons contained a substantial number of Royal Irish Constabulary auxiliaries, who had sought employment in Palestine after 1922.[126]

Before turning to the methods employed to dispel allegations of security force misbehaviour, let us examine the forms such accusations took. Irgun and Lehi propaganda, and a growing number of (particularly American) journalists, made numerous indictments of security force behaviour, and, more broadly, British counter-insurgency measures. With respect to the latter, the Emergency regulations which the Palestine authorities instituted were an easy target, which even some colonial officials in Whitehall thought 'particularly drastic'.[127] Regulations introduced after the murder of Lord Moyne allowed 'persons suspected of being terrorists or of complicity in terrorism' to be detained indefinitely (for a period of up to a year), with no requirement that the detainee be informed of their right of appeal, or even be told of the reason for their detention.[128] Not only were the Mandatory Authorities' draconian powers attacked, but so too were the conditions in which the detainees were kept – a complaint later voiced in both Kenya and Cyprus during their Emergencies. The detention centres, watched over by armed soldiers and surrounded by barbed wire, were easily represented in Zionist propaganda as 'concentration camps'. The Jewish Agency, which in July 1946 established its own Information Office (to supplement the Jewish news agencies Palcor and the Jewish Telegraphic Agency, already in existence[129]), also repeated atrocity allegations. At an Agency press conference that month, for example, the speaker detailed 'medieval torture' methods used on detainees in the Athlit camp, some of whom would be crippled for life.[130]

Many of the indictments of the security forces coupled accusations of brutality with comparisons to the Nazis and charges of anti-Semitism. Fairly typical of the type of reportage Britain had to counter with growing frequency was an article by Meyer Levin in the *New York Post* of 20 November 1945, which accused British troops of having deliberately shot at children during disturbances in Tel Aviv: 'during the hours I spent with the British troops, I heard scores of soldiers express the desire to "pop off" the youngsters'. Moreover, they had taken their pot-shots while singing the Nazi 'Horst Wessel' song (a claim already broadcast on the underground Kol Israel station).[131] In addition, the Jewish news agencies and Irgun and Lehi propaganda represented the security forces' cordon-and-search operations (through which they attempted to uncover terrorist hiding places in the absence of intelligence from the *Yishuv*) as excessive in their brutality. In September 1946, to cite a representative example, Palcor alleged that troops of the Sixth Airborne Division had smashed up a settlement at Ruhama during a search, scribbling 'insulting anti-Jewish expressions' on every piece of paper they found, while one police officer shouted, '"I'm sorry this place cannot be made a second Bergen-Belsen."'[132] Such symbolically charged allegations clearly caused problems for British propagandists, not least as there was evidence that they were not simply trumped up charges born from the hysterical and fevered imagination of the *Yishuv*. As the High Commissioner remarked, there had been 'inevitable' damage to property during search operations in Jewish colonies, although he saw the cause lying in the elaborately constructed hiding places in which arms were secreted.[133]

Cunningham was similarly dismissive of claims concerning Nazi methods or anti-Semitism amongst the troops and police. Asked by George Hall, the Colonial Secretary, to respond to the accusation (about to be broadcast on American radio) that the Palestine Police exhibited 'fascist tendencies', he concluded that 'British policemen have expressed natural disgust and exasperation at all too frequent murders of their comrades by Jews' but there were 'no signs at all of fascist tendencies'.[134] Although this is only what one would expect the High Commissioner to say publicly, there were many indications to suggest that such an attitude was all too sanguine. In December 1945, the Foreign Office received an unsolicited report from a British officer who had spent some considerable time in Palestine, warning that 'Goebbels has many apt pupils wearing British uniform in Palestine' and that 'suspicion and hatred of the Jews is being widely voiced with the bitterest venom'. Throwing off the traditional

British shyness of overt anti-Semitism, officials were now quite outspoken in their racial prejudice:

> A major, whose job would be a responsible one if his character and intellect permitted, once asked me 'Have you ANY sympathy for these Jews?' and then clarified his own position with: 'I'm not for the Jews or against them old boy, but I can't help feeling that Hitler was on the right lines.'[135]

The result was that, as this officer put it, 'the Jews are now The Enemy' – a claim frequently made by critics of the indiscriminacy of the cordon-and-search operations, and of the collective punishments imposed on local Jewish communities that failed to hand over the terrorists believed to be in their midst.[136] The Foreign Office response, like that of the Mandatory Authorities, was complacent: the report concerned 'the Colonial Office and the War Office rather than the Foreign Office, but it hardly seems worth passing it on to them'.[137]

However, publicly expressed anti-Semitism proved to be on occasion a major embarrassment for the Palestine authorities, while providing welcome ammunition to Zionist propagandists in their efforts to de-legitimize the administration. The most notorious case of outspoken anti-Semitism was General Barker's 'non-fraternization' order of 26 July 1946. This forbade contact between British troops and the Jewish community; in Barker's words, 'punishing the Jews in the way the race dislikes as much as any other, namely by striking at their pockets and showing our contempt for them'.[138] Coming a mere four days after the King David Hotel bombing, Barker's order caused the *Yishuv*'s mounting revulsion against the terrorists to be replaced by a sense of outrage against the Palestine administration. A measure of the impact Barker's remarks made on the Jewish population was evidenced in Chaim Weizmann's letter to the Colonial Office, in which he expressed fear that little could be achieved 'so long as General Barker – a self-confessed enemy of our people – remains in command in Palestine'.[139] For his part, Sir Alan Cunningham refused to accept that there was widespread anti-Semitism within the security forces, suggesting that occasional anti-Semitic behaviour was the result of a self-fulfilling prophecy:

> I have received no concrete evidence of troops having indulged in Nazi slogans and inscriptions. It must be remembered, however, that British soldiers and Police are frequently greeted by Jews with provocative slogans likening them to the Nazis. They are also exposed, like others, to relentless and malignant propaganda emanating from Zionist sources. [The] Possibility cannot be excluded that this may have provoked retaliation in kind in a few cases.[140]

Yet the internal records of the Army in Palestine suggest that anti-

Semitism was more widespread than Cunningham would have it. The very language used to describe operations was larded with anti-Semitism; the GOC writing, on one occasion, of 'exterminating' the Irgun and Stern terrorists in a 'Final Solution' of the terrorist problem during 'Operation Agatha'.[141]

A further type of security force behaviour which the authorities were called upon to explain was the taking of unauthorized reprisals. Such actions gave rise to reports of 'black and tannery' re-emerging in Palestine, which were carried by some British newspapers and journals as well as other sources where one would expect reprisals to have featured heavily. In particular *The New Statesman and Nation* made a point of condemning government attempts to whitewash the misdemeanours of the troops in Palestine. In this it echoed the views of those Labour MPs, including the paper's assistant editor, Richard Crossman, who were outspokenly critical of the direction in which the counter-insurgency campaign was heading.[142] Reprisals undoubtedly did occur, though it remains a moot point as to whether or not the civil and military authorities took strenuous enough steps to prevent such incidents. Certainly some of these incidents revealed that the security forces, left to their own devices, had scant regard for the principle of 'minimum force' which supposedly governed counter-insurgency practice. The most serious reprisal occurred after the bodies of the hanged sergeants, Martin and Paice, were discovered; four Jews were killed and fifteen injured when a grenade was thrown into a Tel Aviv cafe from a police armoured car. Earlier in the evening the police car had fired on a crowded Jewish bus and a taxi. When the incident came to be investigated, no punishment was taken because the police officers refused to divulge any information relating to it.[143]

The accusations, then, were all the harder to defend or explain for having considerable substance to them. A number of methods evolved for countering them and defending security force operations. It should, however, be noted that Cunningham did not regard the atrocity allegations as necessarily injurious to the government, or likely to lead to a reappraisal of the counter-insurgency in Britain itself. Indeed, on one occasion after the publication of an article in the *New York Times* quoted above, he suggested that

> the text of Levin's report be made available to English newspapers in order that the British public may be aware of the type of propaganda which is being disseminated about their army which is carrying out in Palestine, with characteristic patience, restraint and good humour, a difficult and distasteful job.[144]

Such a *laissez-faire* attitude could not be adopted with regard to other audiences, and this led to certain revisions to the publicity procedures in and for Palestine. Some accusations were easier to trounce than others. Allegations that the detention centres were 'concentration camps', while they could not be expected to disappear altogether, could be refuted by the simple expedient of allowing correspondents to visit them. Cunningham's decision to let reporters visit the Athlit camp had been 'a very happy thought', George Hall felt, the resulting reports producing an 'excellent effect' in Britain.[145] He recommended that continued latitude be given to the press.

The Mandatory Authorities also saw fit to amend their provisions for the release of news, placing particular emphasis on speed and on 'beating the agencies' – in other words releasing news before Reuters did. Lord Gort (who served briefly as High Commissioner between MacMichael and Cunningham) complained that the agencies, by providing the first news to be published, 'command the greatest attention and nothing that is published subsequently from official sources can repair the damage' – another remark which suggests that colonial officials in Jerusalem had a fairly realistic appreciation of the principles of news management, realizing the inadequacy of remedial briefings.[146] To counter the regrettable tendency of the press, and even the BBC, to base reports on hasty Reuters releases, the High Commissioner proposed to issue informal preliminary 'hand-outs', giving the first news of an incident. He also hoped that the Colonial Office would disseminate these hand-outs at its end, arguing that the informal hand-outs would have a 'sedative effect' rather than acquiring 'undue prominence'.[147] While the Colonial Office declined to use the hand-outs in this way, it did agree to use them (telegraphed *en clair* to Church House) as background, to 'answer the many enquiries received', and undertook to encourage London correspondents and the BBC to check the accuracy of any agency messages received with the Colonial Office on a twenty-four hour basis.[148]

The system, almost inevitably, was not a great success: releasing accurate reports of 'incidents' was hard to achieve quickly. Inaccuracy continued to be rife – the BBC being one of the worst offenders. The BBC Overseas News Service's inaccuracies, complained Richard Stubbs (the Public Information Officer) in December 1946, were 'inclined to upset the very uneasy peace we are doing our best to maintain'; the Corporation had become the laughing stock of the other correspondents who would 'talk about the BBC's "fleet of illegal ships"' which were supposed to be arriving off the coast of Haifa.[149] By the spring of 1947, officials in Jerusalem were questioning whether they could hope to compete with the agencies and press. As one official put it: 'if we wait for accurate details, we are always behind the press, and you will hear the news on the air and see it in your breakfast newspaper before you get it from us'. In the penurious climate of 1947, the 'extra expense' did not 'seem to provide enough advantages'.[150] With or without the system, on some occasions the Colonial Office did not receive any word of serious 'incidents' until press reports had already appeared.[151]

Attempts were also made to improve the security forces' public image, and to oil military–media relations by making the former more accessible. Charters suggests that for the Army 'conducting operations "in the glare of publicity" was a new problem'.[152] Certainly, the Army initially exhibited a tendency to keep the news media at arm's length, finding reporters' presence during operations to be a nuisance and impediment. However, with the volume of complaints about soldiers' behaviour increasing, such prickliness only served to fuel press antagonism to the Army. With the encouragement of the civil authorities, officers therefore urged their men to give assistance to accredited journalists, allowing reporters to accompany the troops on some operations.[153] Public relations officers were appointed to sector, brigade and divisional headquarters to provide more information to the press – again with the emphasis on beating Reuters and forestalling inaccurate (that is to say, unfavourable) reports of their activities. Guidelines were established for operations on which the press accompanied the troops. First, an Army public relations officer (PRO) was always to accompany press parties. If one was not there, *no* rank was allowed to make a statement, as this resulted in 'allegations being made against the troops which [could not] be denied by the command on the spot at the time of the visit'. Second, when the press interviewed civilians, a British interpreter should be present to point out to the PRO or command what had been said. And third, when it was not possible for a PRO to accompany press parties on a large-scale operation, the military command should make a statement to the press, to counter civilian accusations.[154]

In this respect too, however, defensive publicity measures were not uniformly successful. The troops did have a useful ally in the British newsreel companies. Pathé's output on Palestine identified especially closely with the 'British Tommies', who were carrying out 'the dirtiest, most dangerous and most thankless job in the world today' and were 'the hardest-worked ambassadors Britain has ever had'.[155] The newsreels were able to show British soldiers carrying out search operations in an orderly and peaceable manner.[156] The troops' purposefulness in tracking down terrorists was contrasted with the futility and counter-productiveness of their opponents' strategy: all the terrorists got from their bombings, Pathé opined, was 'world condemnation and more graves in the Holy Land', and Movietone was similarly censorious of the 'vain attempts by the Jewish terrorist gang to intimidate authority'.[157] But despite arrangements for the press and cameramen to have greater access to operations, there was no guarantee that the troops, including officers, would always improve the Army's image. On one occasion, during the night of 24 October 1946, after the explosion of a number of bombs near a checkpoint manned by British soldiers (of whom eleven were injured), Lieutenant-Colonel Richard Webb ordered several British and American reporters to be removed from the scene by truck and taken to his HQ. His subsequent tirade was widely reported. In Britain the fullest coverage was found in the *Daily Express*, whose correspondent had been one of those lifted for 'interviewing':

> 'Frankly, we brought you down here because you were distracting the soldiers. The fact is we sometimes have to use the butts of rifles, and you people had, I should say, a rather embarrassing effect on the troops . . .
>
> 'The Jews are all very cocky about the departure of General Barker. But let me tell them – the new GOC (General MacMillan) who used to be my colonel knows how to treat them much better than little Barker. Let them wait until he comes.'[158]

According to the *New York Post*, Webb concluded his performance with the rejoinder, 'Print everything I have said. Use my name. I don't care if I am out of the Army tomorrow.'[159] And so he was. On 29 October, Cunningham related to Creech Jones that as a result of the 'opinions both unauthorised and unofficial' which he had expressed, Webb had been removed from command of his unit.[160] The episode illustrates a recurrent problem in the prosecution of counter-insurgency campaigns: the difficulty experienced by members of the security forces in balancing purely military concerns (their conception of the quickest way to defeat the enemy) with the exigencies of propaganda and the attendant need to remain on good terms with the press.

When it came to handling publicity for incidents in which members of the security forces had clearly done wrong, or made unfortunate statements, there was little to be done to counter them, other than to put them into context – in short, to stress the provocation terrorism wrought. In the case of Webb's remarks, which the British Embassy in Washington felt injurious to Britain's cause, the Foreign Office replied that if his words proved 'substantially true' the Embassy should not 'remain on the defensive': 'while emphasising that we cannot condone remarks of the kind attributed to Colonel Webb, you should try to focus attention on the circumstances in which they are said to have been made'.[161] A similar expedient had been adopted after Barker's non-fraternization order, following which the government felt obliged to disown Barker's 'bitterness of words' but nevertheless emphasized the vexing circumstances in which his order had been written. Stressing the provocation which terrorist atrocities induced among the security forces was, similarly, all that could be done following unauthorized 'reprisals', together with reminding observers that the British forces generally behaved with admirable restraint.[162]

As the insurgency wore on, British propagandists' only real attempt to counter-attack was not so much aimed at rebutting allegations of security force misbehaviour, as at throwing a more jaundiced light over the ongoing passage of illegal immigrant ships to Palestine. Illegal immigration, as already noted, was one of the sorest points for the Palestine authorities, with Irgun and Lehi propaganda on this subject more likely to be accepted by the wider Jewish community. In 1947, the tortuous passage of the illegal immigrant ship the *Exodus* attracted much unfavourable international attention, with Britain coming under attack for sending the ship to Hamburg after the French authorities refused to force the refugees to land.[163] In June and July, the Foreign Office attempted to counter the hostile publicity which the whole question of Jewish immigration was attracting. The Information Policy Department prepared material, or inspired friendly British newspapers to produce articles, on the 'seamy side' of the traffic, the 'profits made by ship-owners and agents out of the distress of Jewish refugees' and the 'ruthless exploitation of these people for political purposes'.[164] The Foreign Office was particularly pleased with a series of articles on illegal immigration published by the *Daily Mail*, which stated that of the $250 it cost to move one concentration camp victim from Europe to Palestine, $50 of each $250 donated went straight to the Irgun. Furthermore, the Haganah, in deciding which Jews should be selected to make the illicit trip from Europe to Palestine, chose strong young people, who would be the best material for building a future Jewish state.[165]

The Recourse to Censorship

The defensiveness of much government publicity work was paralleled by a heavy reliance on censorship within Palestine itself. One of the functions of the Public Information Office was to dissipate, as far as possible, inter-communal friction and ease tension between the authorities and both communities. To calm public unease, the Public Information Office frequently resorted to imposing a drastic local censorship. The Palestine administration had engaged in heavy-handed censorship during the Arab Rebellion; in October 1937, for example, it decided to forbid any mention to be made, or pictures to be circulated, of the Mufti – the chief inspirer of Arab unrest.[166] Subsequently in 1938, the High Commissioner found it necessary to impose censorship on outgoing foreign press telegrams, in view of 'a series of wildly inaccurate and tendentious reports telegraphed to London', many of which had then been reproduced in BBC bulletins and picked up in Berlin.[167] During the war such censorship measures were perhaps more readily accepted by journalists – although a Reuters official told the Colonial Office in 1944 that many reporters in Palestine had resorted to filing their reports in Cairo to avoid the Palestine Censor's scrutiny.[168]

When the war was over, the Jerusalem Information Office did not lightly abandon its reliance on censorship. Although, with the reappearance of terrorism, Whitehall urged that censorship be relaxed so that more could be made of Zionist misdeeds, inside Palestine the local press was subjected to tight control. The High Commissioner always claimed that foreign correspondents' dispatches were not subject to censorship, in answer to occasional accusations that he was trying to create an air of calm by suppressing hostile reports.[169] As for internal censorship, Cunningham claimed that the only articles affected were those which 'might aggravate the local situation or render the task of maintaining order more difficult'.[170] However, the administration interpreted very widely where the boundaries of internal security lay. Not only did it prevent, at different times, the local press from mentioning illegal immigration,[171] and from speculating on whether martial law would be introduced in March 1947, but it considered banning Koestler's novel *Thieves in the Night*.[172] Cunningham objected to it on the grounds that 'a Jewish terrorist organisation identifiable with the National Military Organisation is presented . . . in a sympathetic manner', although Mathieson of the Colonial Office felt that 'in spite of the [author's] contrary intention, it made Jewish terrorism appear hopeless and vaguely ridiculous'.[173] Indeed, banning the novel was more likely to make the Palestine administration seem 'hopeless and vaguely ridiculous'; as one Colonial Office official put it, to ban the book 'might well be, for hostile critics, an answer to Voltaire's prayer, "Oh Lord, make my enemies ridiculous"'.[174]

The 'almighty temper of the Palestine censor' had already been attacked by Fleet Street. The *Evening Standard* had used the occasion of Palestine's contemplated ban on Koestler's novel to complain that:

Newspaper correspondents armed with official Press passes are continually shouted at, held up, searched, and refused admittance to places where, with their passes, they have every right to go – the military authorities' attitude these days to everyone, without exception, is unbearably high-handed and dangerous.[175]

Thus even though Church House dissuaded Cunningham from banning *Thieves in the Night*, the harm had already been done. The Palestine authorities entangled themselves in a vicious circle over the question of censorship. As the campaign progressed, the High Commissioner complained to Whitehall that the only British press comment he received was tendentious material, and reports of atrocities. Although Fleet Street comment was supposed to be helpful in demonstrating the opposition of the British people to terrorism, Cunningham found, by early 1947, that he was having to censor incoming British press reports for being too sensational:

In many cases the British Sunday papers report terrorist incidents in so sensationalist a manner as to constitute what is,
in fact, [an] advertisement for terrorist organisations. Acting in
pursuance of criterion that only such matter should be deleted
from [the] local press as is likely to prejudice public security, it
has on several occasions been necessary for the Press Censor to
exercise his powers of suppression in respect of reproduction in
[the] local press of articles on terrorism appearing in the British
Sunday papers.[176]

This of course attracted further comment in the British press.

Similarly counter-productive had been the attempt to jam the Kol
Israel broadcasts. On 14 November 1945, Shaw (the High Commissioner)
reported that the Kol Israel broadcasts were being jammed, as their
transmissions amounted to an open call for Jews to revolt.[177] This move
was a significant departure from World War II propaganda policy, during
which jamming of enemy broadcasts had been rejected on the grounds
that it would be tantamount to an admission of bad faith, and Begin,
in his memoirs, likened British attempts at jamming to Nazi wartime
interference with BBC broadcasts.[178]

The Absence of Positive Themes

As we have seen, a number of commentators have pointed out that
the problems of British propagandists were compounded by an absence
of policy from Westminster. How justifiable a criticism is this? Certainly,
one can find several instances where those vested with publicizing British activities in Palestine felt themselves to be hampered by an unclear
political lead. In March 1945, for example, the Palestine Information
Officer remarked on the feelings of alienation of youth in Palestine,
which were a well-spring of terrorist activity: 'The dissipation of this
feeling of frustration should be a principal aim of our work; but until the
government declares a policy for the future of Palestine, we can do very
little in this direction.'[179] His attitude was reflected in the MOI's Plan of
Propaganda for Palestine, which concluded that hesitation left the way
open for extremists to allege that Britain had imperialistic designs on
Palestine: 'In the absence of an official policy for the future of Palestine,
propaganda is an uphill task, but it is more than ever necessary.'[180] This
frustration could be found in Whitehall too, with Hankey of the Foreign
Office railing against both Truman's interference in the Palestine problem
and the lack of decisiveness: 'Palestine is *our* responsibility and we must,
I suggest, have the courage of our convictions over it (when we have
decided what those are!).'[181]

It is all too easy to forget that during the period of the insurgency

Britain instigated a number of different diplomatic initiatives to resolve the Palestine problem before relinquishing it to the United Nations. Arguably Britain did not have a clear enough objective for Palestine's future, other than that the Arabs should not be alienated altogether (which effectively ruled out the creation of a Jewish state). As it was, Britain cast about for various alternative solutions. A bi-national state was proposed by the Anglo-American Commission, but co-operation between Washington and London ran adrift over the issue of illegal immigration. Shortly afterwards, a joint scheme for provincial autonomy was put forward, the Morrison–Grady plan, which Truman looked set to accept before being dissuaded by the Zionist lobby.[182] Given the irreconcilability of the parties to the dispute, is it any wonder that Attlee's government did not immediately nail its colours to any one particular mast?

However, the absence of a clear plan for Palestine's future undoubtedly added to the difficulties of creating a positive image for British activities there. It was correspondingly difficult to explain to people at home what British lives were being lost for – a question which some were beginning to ask as the toll of casualties mounted. As one distraught mother of a soldier serving in Palestine wrote to Creech Jones: 'What right have our sons who went bravely to fight for their country . . . [to] be murdered now in such a cause, for this is murder and nothing else.'[183] Major Wilson writes in his history of the Sixth Airborne Division's tour in Palestine that the morale and behaviour of the British Army was so high because the purpose of its presence in Palestine was so clear: 'it was the reverse of war; it was simply "to keep the peace"'.[184] Given that his division had the worst record for misbehaviour, his remarks seem laden with irony, begging the question whether some of the worst excesses of the security forces might have been avoided if they had had a clearer sense of purpose.

Furthermore, the conditions which existed in Palestine during the insurgency were such that British propaganda could not fall back on a staple used in the other campaigns discussed: namely the projection of positive British achievements for the territory. Faced with terrorist challenges to British rule, publicity staff in the affected areas generally tried to present the situation in the territory as being substantially one of peace and progress, with terrorism only affecting, and being carried out by, a minority.[185] In Palestine this was well-nigh impossible. Not only had Palestine been riven by inter-communal and anti-British violence for some years before the Zionist insurgency, but there were very few areas unaffected by the Emergency. The absence of normality was vividly underlined by 'Operation Polly', whereby 'non-essential personnel' – wives and families of British personnel - were evacuated in February 1947.[186] Troops were confined to their barracks and forbidden to venture out alone or unarmed. In an ironic twist, while Zionist propaganda represented the centres in which illegal immigrants and suspected terrorists were detained as 'concentration camps', at least one Briton (a broadcaster) felt that as a result of 'Operation Polly' the expatriate community had become incarcerated in a 'British concentration camp' where life had assumed 'an unreality which is better imagined than experienced'.[187] 'Operation Polly', as a *Daily Telegraph* editorial put it, was 'an admission that terror has made normal civil government impossible and by implication raises the status of Irgun from that of a criminal conspiracy in a civil state to something nearer to an armed revolt.'[188]

Conclusion

Perhaps more reprehensible than the civil and military authorities' failure to mount an effective hearts and minds campaign in Palestine, where conditions hardly allowed for one, was their failure (and Westminster's) to mitigate the anti-Semitic thrust of much British reportage of Zionist terrorism. Indeed, in many ways, advertently or otherwise, the government may have encouraged this trend. It seems that Bevin, for one, contemplated using the spectre of British anti-Semitism as a means of turning Zionist leaders against the terrorist organizations. At a meeting with Dr Silver, a prominent American Zionist, in November 1946 Bevin warned that:

> For the first time in Great Britain a feeling of strong anti-Semitism had been aroused. This had been particularly marked amongst the working classes, where hitherto it had been unknown. We now had a conscript army and the mothers of the soldiers were very reasonably concerned about the safety of their sons, who were being killed while only doing their plain duty. There had therefore been strong resentment against the Jews. The result had been that the general feeling had sprung up which suggested that Palestine was not worth bothering about. The Jews would have to do something about this.[189]

Bevin thus squarely placed the responsibility for the outbreak of anti-Semitism on the Jews themselves. While he was disingenuous to suggest that such prejudices had never tainted the working class before, Bevin was not *manufacturing* the threat, even if he was manipulating it. Mass-Observation conducted research shortly after the King David bombing and found many people expressing opinions in tune with the attitude of one anonymous middle-aged man:

I've always been of the opinion that Hitler's treatment of the

Jewish people was the right one. I mean, I should be glad if the entire Jewish nation was utterly exterminated. . . . The only thing I disapprove of with regard to Hitler's gas chambers was that there were not enough and that they were not efficiently run.[190]

And letters of venomous anti-Semitism arrived on Foreign Office desks with sufficient frequency to suggest a widespread popular revulsion with the entire Jewish people as a result of the terrorist activities of a small number of Zionist extremists.[191]

Press reportage of terrorism certainly helped encourage public opinion along this path. Embellishing government statements which denounced acts of terrorism as worthy of the Nazis, the press made frequent Jewish–Nazi equations.[192] References to the Irgun and Stern group as 'terrorist organizations' were usually prefixed by the word 'Jewish', so that no one would be unsure as to the ethnicity of the terrorists. The *Daily Mirror* went one step further and habitually referred to the 'Jew terror' in Palestine. Following the lead set by the government (in Britain and Palestine) of tending not to stress the political motivation underpinning the terrorist campaign, the press devoted much attention to terrorist atrocities, often without much analysis of why the violence was occurring. In the popular press (if not the quality papers) the simultaneous and complex diplomatic attempts to resolve the Palestine problem received far less coverage. But while the mobilization of British anti-terrorist opinion had initially been a government objective, such press reportage proved damaging in a number of ways: its sensationalism appeared injurious to public order in Palestine (and ultimately in Britain), while opposition to terrorism did not always translate into support for either government policy or the counter-insurgency measures. Some Britons felt that insurgency procedures, and abuses of them, went too far, while a growing number tended to agree with Montgomery's verdict that the troops' hands were tied too tightly. Increasingly the press (both popular and quality) took up the cry that the government must either rule Palestine with a firm hand, or not at all.[193] In short, popular outrage against the Irgun and Lehi appears to have been entirely functional to their cause and injurious to the government's.

Aware that violent anti-Semitism was rising in Britain as a result of Zionist terrorism, and urged by certain Labour and Communist MPs to take action, Attlee's administration refused either to prohibit the flow of anti-Semitic propaganda into Britain, or to clamp down on sensational Fleet Street reporting.[194] But could the government have done anything to curb either the rise of sensational reporting or the growth of anti-Semitism? Certainly it could have tried. Some energy could usefully have been devoted to publicizing the attempts by Haganah and the Jewish community to root out the terrorists in their midst. However, when the matter of publicity for the activities of the Jewish Anti-Terror

League was discussed in the Colonial Office, objections were raised on two counts. The first was that publicity for Jewish 'good deeds' would only attract further unwelcome attention (especially in America) to the manner in which Jewish detainees were dealt with in Palestine: the military courts, lack of appeal and so on. The second objection lay in the view of one official that Jewish counter-terrorist initiatives were probably 'pure socialism', and thus undeserving of publicity.[195] According to Michael Foot the press was similarly negligent in publicizing Jewish attempts to combat, or condemn, terrorism. He drew Parliament's attention to a message received by Silverman (and subsequently circulated through the Press Association) from Jewish displaced persons housed near Belsen, on the day after the discovery of the bodies of Paice and Martin. This read: 'In the German concentration camps our hearts were filled with deep contempt against any form of terrorism. Also, today we oppose all terroristic actions whose pretext is to help us towards our land of promise.' Only the *Daily Worker*, *Manchester Guardian*, and *Daily Herald* had printed it in abbreviated form.[196]

Irgun's hanging of the two British sergeants in July 1947 was in many ways climactic. Not only did it produce the worst 'reprisal' of the campaign in Palestine, but in Britain anti-Semitic riots broke out in some towns and cities, directed primarily against Jewish shops.[197] Mass-Observation questioners on the streets soon after the incident found much public bitterness: its report stated that 'only one in four showed any tendency to qualify their anger with understanding' (of the Jewish case). One in five found nothing objectionable in the anti-Semitic riots, and would doubtless have agreed with the woman who told Mass-Observation, 'Serves them right. It's not fair they should hang our boys like that.'[198] Press reportage of Zionist terrorism was placed under scrutiny. The *Daily Express*, which had run a front-page photograph of the corpses under the caption 'A picture which will shock the world', was censured in Parliament and a direct correlation made between the manner in which terrorism was reported and the rash of anti-Semitic riots in Britain. As Harold Lever MP rhetorically asked:

Was it that sentimental Mr Christiansen, the editor, was anxious to comfort the families by displaying their freshly-hung bodies to public view in an immense photograph on the front page or was it speculative incitement to violence? Was it an intention to speculate on the anti-Semitic feeling which the ignorant were already manifesting because of the brutal murder of those sergeants in Palestine?[199]

The *Express*'s coverage of the outrage was, he concluded, 'the greatest descent from decent journalism and good taste that has appeared in any British newspaper in my life'.[200] The popular outrage which such reporting helped encourage dictated an early announcement by the government of its intention to withdraw from Palestine. Although the Cabinet had been discussing handing the problem to the UN since December 1946, the timing of the announcement made it hard for the government to argue that it had not, indeed, surrendered to terrorism.

Notes

1 In 1923, a Cabinet Palestine Committee paper on the future of Palestine commented that the 'promises and pledges, not always clear and consistent' made over the future of Palestine were such that a 'wordy warfare' could easily be waged; CAB 43(23), 31 July 1923, Appendix CP 351(23); CAB 23/46.

2 Preamble to the Mandate for Palestine, League of Nations, 24/2/22, quoted by Tugwell, 'Revolutionary Propaganda', p. 115.

3 The term is frequently found in reports of the rebels' activities; see for example the dispatches from the High Commissioner to the Secretary of State for the Colonies in CO 935/21.

4 See the account provided in Bowden, *The Breakdown of Public Security*.

5 Telegram from Sir Harold MacMichael (High Commissioner) to Malcolm MacDonald (Secretary of State for the Colonies), 24/10/38; CO 935/21.

6 On the counter-insurgency techniques employed, see Mockaitis, *British Counter-insurgency*, pp. 33–6 and 92–5.

7 R. Ovendale, *The Origins of the Arab–Israeli Wars* (Longman, London, 2nd ed., 1992), pp. 77–9.

8 A. Koestler, *Thieves in the Night* (Hutchinson, London, 1946; Danube ed., 1965), p. 232.

9 OAG to W.G.A. Ormsby-Gore (Secretary of State for the Colonies), 23/11/37; CO 935/21. The first acts recorded as instances of Jewish reprisals were two bomb-throwing incidents occurring in Jerusalem on 11 Nov. Shortly after, the Arab bus was fired on.

10 MacMichael to MacDonald, 13/9/38; CO 935/21.

11 The pamphlet is contained in CO 733/415/4.

12 Minute by S.E.V. Luke, 2/9/39; CO 733/415/4.

13 For a detailed study of the Stern Gang, see Y.S. Brenner, 'The "Stern Gang" 1940–48', *Middle Eastern Studies*, 2, i (Oct. 1965), 2–30.

14 BBC Written Archives Centre, Caversham [hereafter BBC WAC], 'Plan of Propaganda for Palestine. 1st Supplement of the Appreciation', Paper no. 422A, 14/9/43; R34/692/5.

15 Ibid.

16 *Sunday Express* (14/1/45).

17 Brenner, 'Stern Gang', *Middle Eastern Studies*, pp. 5–6.

18 M. Begin, *The Revolt* (Nash Publishing, New York, 1955), p. 43.

19 MacMichael to Oliver Stanley (Secretary of State for the Colonies), 13/2/44, no. 205; CO 733/456/6. See also Clark, 'Colonial Police and Anti-terrorism', p. 183.

20 See the fortnightly District Commissioners' reports in CO 733/456/2.

21 For example, in September 1944 the District Commissioner for Jerusalem reported the appearance of Irgun leaflets in Arabic, threatening Arabs that their hands would be cut off if they co-operated with the authorities in rooting out the insurgents; fortnightly report for 16–30 Sept. 1944; CO 733/456/2.

22 Clark, 'Colonial Police and Anti-terrorism', pp. 189–93; Begin, *The Revolt*, ch. 9.

23 Brenner, 'Stern Gang', *Middle Eastern Studies*, p. 14.

24 Charters, *The British Army and Jewish Insurgency in Palestine*, pp. 53–4.

25 'Avner' (an anonymous former Lehi member) details an attempt to assassinate Ernest Bevin by placing a bomb under the government front bench in the House of Commons, and a letter bomb campaign directed at certain prominent enemies of the Zionist cause; *Memoirs of an Assassin: Confessions of a Stern Gang Killer* (Anthony Blond, London, 1959), *passim*. In November 1946, several British newspapers ran stories on the likely arrival of Stern Gang terrorists in Britain; see, for example, *Daily Mirror* (11/11/46), 'Attlee and Monty Get Death Threats from Terrorists' and *Daily Mail* (12/11/46), 'Stern Gang Girl Sought by Scotland Yard'. The British Army in Palestine responded favourably to this 'big newspaper stunt', which it thought would 'have brought home to the British public something of the meaning and the reality of having terrorists at large in the country'; Intelligence Summary no. 18, 15/11/46; WO 275/58.

26 Telegram from Sir Alan Cunningham (High Commissioner) to George Hall (Secretary of State for the Colonies), 30/12/46, no. 2213; CO 733/456/11.

27 Begin, *The Revolt*, pp. 231–5.

28 See transcript of an Irgun broadcast announcing this policy in WO 275/109.

29 Statistics taken from Charters, *British Army and Jewish Insurgency*, Appendix III, Insurgent Operations in Palestine, pp. 182–96.

30 R.H.S. Crossman, *Palestine Mission: A Personal Record* (Hamish Hamilton, London, 1946), p. 200.

31 On the underground organizations' use of propaganda, see: Charters, *British Army and Jewish Insurgency*, pp. 65–82; Tugwell, 'Revolutionary Propaganda', ch. 4; and G. Cromer, '"In the Mirror of the Past": The Use of History in the Justification of Terrorism', *Terrorism and Political Violence*, 3, iv (1991), 164–78.

32 Cutting from *The Times* (17/2/44) in CO 733/456/6.

33 Telegram from MacMichael to Stanley, 19/2/44, no. 238; CO 733/456/6.

34 Telegram from MacMichael to Stanley, 24/3/44, no. 363; CO 733/456/6.

35 Ibid.

36 Telegram from Sir John Shaw (Officer Administering the Government) to Stanley, 2/10/44, no. 1259; CO733/457/6.

37 The British government revealed Agency co-operation with illegal Haganah broadcasts in the 1946 White Paper, 'Palestine: Statement of Information Relating to Acts of Violence' (Cmd 6873). G. Cohen's *Woman of Violence: Memoirs of a Young Terrorist, 1943–1948* (Rupert Hart-Davis, London, 1966) is a personal account of one member of Lehi involved in underground broadcasting.

38 Report by A.N. Law, District Commissioner for Haifa, 1–16 Jan. 1945; CO 733/456/3.

39 Army Intelligence Summary no. 20, 29/11/46; WO 275/58.

40 Begin, *The Revolt*, pp. 313–14.

41 Ronnie Noble, *Shoot First! Assignments of a Newsreel Cameraman* (Harrap, London, 1955), pp. 134–5.

42 For example, the District Commissioner of Lydda complained in his fortnightly report for 16–31 July 1947 that a correspondent from 'a reasonably reliable British newspaper' had reported an underground interview between the Irgun leader and the Chairman of UNSCOP (the UN Special Commission on Palestine), representing the former as 'a type of Robin Hood'; CO 537/2280.

43 Telegram from MacMichael to Stanley, 24/3/44, no. 363; CO 733/456/6. Note that this analysis was not for publication, with Clarke of the CO Middle Eastern Department minuting that the High Commissioner's report should not be sent to the MOI 'as it could not be used publicly'; minute dated 27/3/44.

44 Telegram from Shaw to Stanley, 2/10/44, no. 1259; CO 733/457/6.

45 'Note of a talk by the P.I.O. Jerusalem (Mr Christopher Holme) on British Publicity

in Palestine and Its Relation to Other Functions of Government', dated 13/3/45; CO 733/465/6.

46 H.C. Debs, vol. 426, Debate on 'Palestine', 31/7/46, col. 963.

47 Cromer, 'In the Mirror of the Past', *Terrorism and Political Violence*, pp. 166–7.

48 Telegram from MacMichael to Stanley, 9/4/44, no. 446; CO 733/456/6.

49 Mockaitis, *British Counterinsurgency*, p. 103.

50 H.C. Debs, vol. 424, Debate on the 'Palestine Situation', 4/7/46, col. 1878.

51 The Cabinet authorized 'Operation Agatha' in June 1946 in the wake of the kidnap of five British officers from the Officers' Club in Tel Aviv; Cab 60(46), 20/6/46, Cabinet Minutes; CAB 128/5. This, however, did not terminate Monty's dispute with Cunningham, details of which can be found in the minutes of a meeting of the Defence Committee held on 20 Nov. 1946, and various telegrams from Cunningham to Arthur Creech Jones (Hall's replacement as Secretary of State for the Colonies) contained in CO 537/1731.

52 Extract from a telegram by the Chief of the Imperial General Staff, contained in a telegram from Cunningham to Creech Jones, 23/11/46, no. 1962; CO 537/1731.

53 Telegram from Cunningham to Creech Jones, 23/11/46, no. 1959; CO 537/1731.

54 Note by Trafford Smith (CO) to Harold Beeley (Foreign Secretary Ernest Bevin's adviser on Palestine), 3/7/46; CO 537/1827.

55 Note of a talk by the PIO, Jerusalem, 13/3/45; CO 733/465/6.

56 Telegram from Lord Moyne (Minister Resident in Cairo) to Stanley, 8/10/44, no. 23; CO 733/457/9.

57 GHQ MELF, Weekly Intelligence Review, for week ending 7/3/47, 'Palestine Outrages'; WO 275/120.

58 Memo by Brigadier J.R. Cochrane, General Staff of the Sixth Airborne Division, to the Sixth Airborne and North Palestine District; WO 275/86. General Macmillan made the same point when interviewed on a Pathé newsreel after the Officers' Club bombing: 'the men responsible for these killings are not terrorists, they're just plain thugs and murderers. The false glamour which grew around the Stern and Irgun bands is gone'; Pathé, issue no. 47-19 (6/3/47), 'Martial Law Declared'.

59 R.D. Wilson, *Cordon and Search: With the Sixth Airborne Division in Palestine* (Gale and Polden, Aldershot, 1949), p. 13.

60 *Daily Telegraph* (4/3/47), 'Word "Terrorist" Banned', p. 6.

61 B. Fergusson, *The Trumpet in the Hall, 1930–58* (Collins, London, 1970), p. 204. Fergusson was appointed in 1946 to form special police undercover units which would prosecute the anti-terrorist campaign in more unorthodox ways.

62 Begin, *The Revolt*, p. 59.

63 Hehazit, *Organ of the Fighters for the Freedom of Yisrael*, no. 2, Aug. 1943; CO 733/466/5.

64 Extract from *Liberty* (12/10/46) contained in E10694/4/31; FO 371/52563.

65 Wilson, *Cordon and Search*, p. 13.

66 Begin, *The Revolt*, p. 59.

67 'Avner', *Memoirs of an Assassin*, pp. 86–7.

68 Begin, *The Revolt*, p. 56.

69 Ibid., p. 55.

70 Ibid., p. 53.

71 While seeming to reject the creation of fear as an objective, Begin does at one point in his memoirs express the view that sensationalist and hostile press reportage in Britain of Irgun deeds may have served his cause; ibid., p. 82.

72 Charters writes that: 'There is nothing in the written record to suggest that the Army – not to mention their political masters – even grasped the nature of the war being waged by the Jewish underground'; 'From Palestine to Northern Ireland: British Adaptation to Low-Intensity Operations', in Charters and Tugwell, *Armies in Low-Intensity Conflict*, p. 191.

73   Quoted by N. Bethell, *The Palestine Triangle: The Struggle between the British, the Jews and the Arabs, 1935–48* (André Deutsch, London, 1979), p. 288. Significantly, he also stressed that Lehi techniques borrowed heavily from the IRA of 1919–21.

74   Begin, *The Revolt*, p. 81.

75   *Sunday Express* (2/2/47).

76   Crossman, *Palestine Mission*, p. 59.

77   Ibid., p. 43.

78   Ibid., p. 60.

79   G.H. Gallup, *The Gallup International Opinion Polls. Great Britain, 1937–1975.* Vol. 1, 1937–64 (Random House, New York, 1976), p. 148.

80   *Daily Mirror* (23/7/46), p. 1.

81   Mass-Observation [hereafter M-O] Archive, Report no. 2431, *Note on Popular Attitudes to Palestine and Arab Countries* (6/11/46), p. 1.

82   M-O Report no. 2515, *Report on Attitudes to Palestine and the Jews* (Sept. 1947), pp. 9 and 24.

83   Charters, *British Army and Jewish Insurgency*, p. 129; see also pp. 163–8.

84   M-O Report no. 2515, op. cit., p. 8.

85   *The Times* (12/8/47).

86   Tugwell, 'Revolutionary Propaganda', p. 159.

87   Mockaitis, *British Counterinsurgency*, p. 101.

88   See Balfour, *Propaganda in War*, ch. 3.

89   The phrase is Lord Reith's; J.C.W. Reith, *Into the Wind* (Hodder and Stoughton, London, 1949), p. 354. This strategy is made explicit in the MOI Overseas Planning Committee's 'Plan of Propaganda for Palestine', 2nd revision, no. 577, 15/5/45; CO 733/465/6.

90   Letter from K.G. Grubb to Noel Sabine (Head of CO Information Department), 18/6/45; CO 733/456/6.

91   Note of a talk by the PIO, Jerusalem, 13/3/45; CO 733/465/6.

92   Letter from Driberg to Eastwood, 16/10/45; CO 733/465/6.

93   Clark, *The Central Office of Information, passim.*

94   Charters, *British Army and Jewish Insurgency*, p. 125; and MOI Overseas Planning Committee Paper 575A, 'Plan of Propaganda for Palestine', 2nd revision, 2/6/45; CO 733/465/6.

95   Sir John Martin interviewed for the Granada TV series *Palestine*; 2nd episode, 'Rebellion', broadcast on 4 July 1978.

96   Charters, *British Army and Jewish Insurgency*, p. 125.

97   C.J. Morris, 'The Labour Government's Policy and Publicity over Palestine 1945-7', in Gorst *et al.* (eds), *Contemporary British History*, p. 170.

98   Minute by H.M. Eyres (FO Eastern Dept.), 29/3/44, E1958/17/31; FO 371/40125.

99   Minute by R.M.A. Hankey, 29/3/44, E1958/17/31; FO 371/40125.

100 Hankey to Battershill (CO), 19/2/44, E910/95/31; FO 371/40133.

101 Ibid.

102 Minute by Hankey, 29/3/44, E1958/17/31; FO 371/40125.

103 Letter from Battershill to Sir Maurice Peterson (Washington), 3/3/44, E1546/95/31; FO 371/40134.

104 Minute by Eyres (FO Eastern Department), 6/4/44, E2088/17/31; FO 371/40125.

105 Minute by Hankey, 6/4/44, E2088/17/31; FO 371/40125.

106 Telegram from Shaw to Stanley, 2/10/44, no. 1259; CO 733/457/6.

107 Telegram from Stanley to Shaw, 13/10/44, no. 1336, E6056/17/31; FO 371/40127.

108 Ibid.

109 Telegram from Shaw to Stanley, 18/10/44, no. 1336; CO 733/457/9.

110 Telegram from Shaw to Boyd, 14/6/44, E5338/95/31; FO 371/40137.

111 Ibid.

112 Ellul, *Propaganda*, pp. 294–302.

113 Shaw to Boyd, 14/6/44, E5338/95/31; FO 371/40137.

114 *The Economist*, CXLVII, no. 5281, (11/11/44), 'Spotlight on Palestine', p. 631.

115 The reply from the *Exchange Telegraph*, United Press, *Daily Express, Daily Herald, News Chronicle* and *Daily Telegraph* was printed on 18 Nov. 1944, *The Economist*, CXLVII, no. 5282.

116 B.A. Burrows to Egyptian Department, 4/1/45, E462/15/31; FO 371/453767.

117 Eastwood to Major A.J.C. Pollock (MOI), 5/3/45, E462/15/31; FO 371/45376.

118 Pollock to Eastwood, 12/3/45, E2019/15/31; FO 371/45377.

119 H.C. Debs, vol. 404, 20/11/44, 'PM's statement on the Moyne murder', col. 2242.

120 Morris, 'The Labour Government's Policy and Publicity over Palestine', in Gort *et al.*, *Contemporary British History*, p. 177.

121 The AAC's recommendation that 100,000 Jews be admitted to Palestine immediately, and the illegal organizations simultaneously be disarmed, formed the major sticking point between the British and American governments. Bethell cites Lehi's Yalin-Mor as saying that, had Attlee's government agreed to the refugees' admission, Lehi would have suspended operations, and argues that a real chance to undercut the ground from the terrorist organizations was thus missed; *Palestine Triangle*, p. 237.

122 Telegram from Bevin to Attlee, 3/7/46, no. 311, E6356/4/31; FO 371/52536. On the ire Bevin's speeches could cause, see Bethell, *Palestine Triangle*, p. 244.

123 Lord Inverchapel (British Ambassador, Washington) to FO, 12/7/46, E6569/4/31; FO 371/52538.

124 Ovendale, *Origins of the Arab–Israeli Wars*, p. 114.

125 Cited by Boyce, *Englishmen and Irish Troubles*, p. 95.

126 Charles Smith states that approximately two-thirds of the Palestine gendarmerie (one branch of the police) raised in 1922 were recruited from the RIC. By 1943, ex-'Black and Tan' men held five of the eight district commander positions in the Palestine Police; 'Communal Conflict and Insurrection in Palestine, 1936–48', in David M. Anderson and David Killingray (eds), *Policing and Decolonisation: Politics, Nationalism and the Police, 1917–65* (Manchester University Press, Manchester, 1992), pp. 63 and 79. See also E. Horne, *A Job Well Done, Being a History of the Palestine Police Force, 1920–1948* (Palestine Police Old Comrades Benevolent Association, Leigh-on-Sea, 1982), p. 76.

127 Minute by W. Clarke (CO), 14/2/45; CO 733/457/7.

128 Minute by K.E. Robinson (CO), 17/2/45; CO 733/457/7.

129 Fortnightly Intelligence Newsletter no. 19 (8–21 July 1946), issued by the HQ British Troops in Palestine and Transjordan; WO 261/562.

130 Telegram from Hall to Cunningham, 3/7/46, no. 1151, E6384; FO 371/52537.

131 Extract from Levin's article, *New York Post* (20/11/45) contained in a telegram from Lord Halifax (British Ambassador to Washington) to FO, 26/11/45; CO 733/456/9.

132 Palcor News Agency Bulletin no. 104, vol. ix, 2/9/46; in CO 537/1789.

133 Telegram from Cunningham to Hall, 22/9/46, no. 1340; CO 537/1789.

134 Telegram from Cunningham to Hall, 4/1/46, no. 21; CO 733/456/10.

135 Elizabeth Hogg (Lord Privy Seal's Office) to Dixon (FO), 26/11/45, contains the text of a note on Palestine by a British officer, E9361/15/31; FO 371/45387.

136 The most widely publicized incident of a collective punishment being imposed as a result of the wider Jewish community being seen as complicit in terrorism occurred in Tel Aviv in April 1946; see telegram from Palestine Press Office to Hall, 27/4/46, E3975/4/31; FO 371/52520.

137 Hogg to Dixon, 26/11/45, E9361/15/31; FO 371/45387.

138 Text of Barker's letter in CO 537/2291.

139 Letter from Chaim Weizmann to Sir John Martin, 16/9/46; CO 537/2317.

140 Telegram from Cunningham to Hall, 7/7/46, no. 111, E6447; FO 371/52537.

141 Note by GOC, 'Military Action to Be Taken to Enforce Law and Order in Palestine', reports on 'Operation Agatha'; WO 275/29.

142 *The New Statesman and Nation* was outspoken on the perceived growth of anti-Semitism among the troops; see for example the letter published on 19 Oct. 1946 (vol. XXXII, no. 817), which reflected the editorial line.

143 Telegram from Cunningham to Creech Jones, 15/11/47; CO 733/477/4.

144 Telegram from Cunningham to Hall, 30/11/45; CO 733/456/9.

145 Telegram from Hall to Cunningham, 4/7/46, no. 1165, E6389; FO 371/52537.

146 Telegram from Lord Gort (High Commissioner) to Hall, 12/10/45, no. 1443, E7865/15/31; FO 371/45381.

147 Telegram from Gort to Hall, 26/10/45, no. 1512, E8256/15/31; FO 371/45383.

148 Telegram from Hall to Gort, 18/10/45, no. 1609, E8256/15/31; FO 371/45383.

149 Letter from Richard Stubbs to Noel Sabine, 5/12/46, BBC WAC, R28/42/3.

150 Letter from Fox Strangways (Chief Secretary's Office, Jerusalem) to Trafford Smith, 5/5/47; CO 733/477/3.

151 For example, Creech Jones (from Oct. 1946, Hall's successor as Colonial Secretary) did not know of the reprisals which followed the discovery of Sergeants Paice and Martin's bodies until he read press reports the following morning; see Cunningham's reply to Creech Jones, 1/8/47, no. 1467; CO 733/477/3.

152 Charters, *British Army and Jewish Insurgency*, p. 125.

153 Ibid., p. 126.

154 These guidelines are contained in a 'Report on Operation "Eel" and "Bream"', 5/9/46; WO 275/42.

155 Pathé, issue no. 46-76 (23/9/46), 'Our Best Ambassadors'. Although this issue was a special tribute, the general tenor of Pathé's coverage was very much along these lines.

156 Movietone's issue no. 47301 of 8/8/46, 'Tension in Tel Aviv', showed the curfew imposed on that town, and the large cache of arms, including dummy pistols – 'useful for intimidation no doubt' – which the troops had uncovered during their search.

157 Movietone, issue no. 47801 (25/11/46), 'Terrorists Blow Up Income Tax Building'.

158 *Daily Express* (26/10/46), 'Lieutenant Colonel Webb Calls in the Reporters', by Eric Grey.

159 *New York Post* (25/10/46), extract contained in telegram from Lord Inverchapel (Washington) to FO, 25/10/46, no. 105, E10606; FO 371/52562.

160 Telegram from Cunningham to Creech Jones, 19/11/46, no. 1923; CO 733/456/11.

161 Telegram from FO to Washington, 26/10/46, no. 10192, E10606; FO 371/52562.

162 For example, after the British press carried reports of 'reprisals' in the night-club quarter of Tel Aviv (e.g. *Daily Mail*, 19/11/46), Cunningham wrote that while the reprisals were most regrettable and could not be condoned, in any announcement mention should be made of the heavy casualties suffered by the police and Army at the hands of Jewish terrorists and the severe strain under which they had operated since 29 Oct., since when ten policemen and seven servicemen had been killed. Telegram from Cunningham to Creech Jones, 19/11/46, no. 1923; CO 733/456/11.

163 Ovendale, *Origins of the Arab–Israeli Wars*, pp. 114–15.

164 Letter from Beith (Eastern Department) to Coulson (British Embassy, Paris), 18/6/47, E4917/48/31; FO 371/61844.

165 The articles were reproduced in the COI Overseas Press Service briefings on 9 and 14 July 1947, E5135/84/31; FO 371/61844.

166 Cab 36(37), 6/10/37, Cabinet Minutes; CAB 23/89.

167 MacMichael to MacDonald, 13/9/38; CO 935/21.

168 Remarks made by Cole (Joint News Manager of Reuters) were passed on by

Sir George Gater (CO) to MacMichael in a letter of 1/5/44; CO 733/466/6.

169 Telegram from Cunningham to Hall, 6/7/46; CO 537/2289.

170 Telegram from Cunningham to Hall, 11/9/46; CO 537/2289.

171 *Daily Mail* (10/8/47), p. 1.

172 Telegram from Cunningham to Creech Jones, 13/12/46, no. 1871; CO 537/2289.

173 Minute by W.A.C. Mathieson, 20/12/46; CO 537/2289.

174 Minute by Fitzgerald to Mathieson, 20/12/46; CO 537/2289.

175 *Evening Standard* (25/11/46), 'Bad-Tempered Censorship'.

176 Telegram from Cunningham to Creech Jones, 10/1/47; CO 537/2289.

177 Telegram from Officer Administering the Government to Hall, 17/11/45, no. 1630, E9642/15/31; FO 371/45429.

178 Begin, *The Revolt*, p. 83.

179 'Note of a Talk by the PIO, Jerusalem', 13/3/45; CO 733/465/6.

180 MOI Overseas Planning Committee, Plan of Propaganda for Palestine, 2nd Revision, no. 577, 15/5/45; CO 733/465/6.

181 Minute by Hankey, 23/3/45, E1725/15/G3; FO 371/45376.

182 Ovendale, *Origins of the Arab–Israeli Wars*, pp. 106–7.

183 Letter from unnamed mother of soldier to Creech Jones, 1/12/46; CO 733/456/11.

184 Wilson, *Cordon and Search*, p. 204.

185 This remains a staple of British government information work on, and in, Northern Ireland; see Roy Greenslade, 'Belfast, Beautiful Belfast', *Guardian* (2nd section, pp. 16–17), 6/12/93, and D. Miller, 'The Northern Ireland Information Service and the Media: Aims, Strategy, Tactics', in J. Eldridge (ed.), *Getting the Message: News, Truth and Power* (Routledge, London, 1993).

186 After a row with the Public Information Officer, journalists managed to persuade the authorities that they did not fall into that category, as had been intended; *Daily Telegraph* (3/2/47).

187 Letter from Rex Keating (Dept. of Broadcasting, Jerusalem) to Cyril Connor (Director of Overseas Programme Services, BBC Broadcasting House), 23/4/47, BBC WAC, E1/1140.

188 *Daily Telegraph* (1/2/47), editorial, p. 4.

189 Record of a conversation between the Secretary of State and Dr Silver on Palestine at the Waldorf Astoria Hotel, 14/11/46; PREM 8/627.

190 M-O Report no. 2515, op. cit., p. 35.

191 See, for example, correspondence from the public in FO 371/52544 and 61783.

192 Such statements were made almost as a matter of routine after a major outrage; see for example the *Daily Herald* report on the official statement after the King David Hotel bombing: 'In the words of the Downing Street statement: "Civil servants serving Palestine no less than Britain, and ordinary quiet citizens going about their peaceful business, have been the victims of outrage more worthy of Nazis than Jewish victims of Nazis." And, it may be added, some of the Jewish propaganda against Britain has been little more scrupulous than the propaganda of the late Goebbels against the Jews', editorial, 14/8/46.

193 The *Daily Telegraph*, having from mid-1946 criticized the government's lack of policy in Palestine, proceeded to take up Churchill's call (after 'Operation Polly'), that the government should withdraw if it was not prepared to take the requisite strong measures to end the 'squalid warfare' in Palestine.

194 See, for example, the way in which Parliamentary Questions asking for anti-Semitic propaganda to be debarred from entry into Britain, and for Fleet Street sensationalism to be curbed, were rejected; PQs by Piratin, 28/11/46 in FO 371/52566 and on 23/1/47 in FO 371/61764; and PQs by Barnet Janner on 20/2/47 in FO 371/61767 and 20/3/47 in FO 371/61770. The government was, however, equally firm in rejecting Tory calls for the Jewish press in UK to be deprived of

newsprint; see PQ by Sir Ernest Graham-Little on 8/5/47 in FO 371/61776.

195 Note by Mathieson on the Anti-Terror League, CO 733/478/3.

196 H.C. Debs, vol. 441, 12/8/47, cols 2367-8.

197 In Liverpool a crowd of several hundred rioted in Myrtle Street, smashing and looting Jewish shops. There were similar mob scenes in Manchester and Eccles; D. Leitch, 'Explosion at the King David Hotel', in M. Sissons and P. French, *The Age of Austerity* (Oxford University Press, Oxford, 1986), p. 59.

198 M-O Report no. 2515, op. cit., p. 65–8. M-O reported that most people were still making a distinction between Jews in general and the terrorists; the figures quoted for how many supported the riots suggest that quite a large number refused to make this distinction. Other circumstantial evidence contradicting M-O's optimistic conclusion includes a strike in Liverpool whereby eighty workers at Stanley abattoir refused to process meat for Jewish consumption, passing a resolution that all Jews were as much responsible for the hanging of the two sergeants as the actual murderers; see Leitch in Sissons and French, *Age of Austerity*, p. 59.

199 H.C. Debs, vol. 441, 12/8/47, 'Palestine', col. 2345.

200 Ibid., col. 2354. In stark contrast to Lever, the editor of an obscure weekly (*The Morecambe and Heysham Visitor*) on 6 Aug. 1967 congratulated the *Daily Express* for publishing the photo. He continued, 'the Jews, indeed, are a plague on Britain. . . . Violence may be the only way to bring them to a sense of their responsibility to the country in which they live.' When the author, James Caunt, was subsequently charged with writing and publishing a seditious libel on the Jewish faith and race in Britain, the jury took only thirteen minutes to decide on a 'Not Guilty' verdict – after the judge had summed up that 'nothing should be done in this court to destroy or weaken the liberty of the Press'. See Leitch, in Sissons and French, *Age of Austerity*, pp. 59–61.

2 'The Forgotten War':[1] Propaganda and the Malayan Emergency, 1948–60

Introduction

In June 1948 a State of Emergency was declared in the Federation of Malaya. It was to be Britain's longest colonial Emergency, not formally ending until 1960 – three years after Malaya had gained its independence. While the insurgency was in progress there were repeated suggestions, often from the beleaguered expatriate community in Malaya, that the situation in the colony would more aptly be described as a war than a mere 'Emergency'. Such a designation would, it was felt, direct greater international attention to the struggle against the Malayan Communist Party (MCP), and put the conflict in Malaya on a more even footing with those concurrently being waged in Korea and Indo-China, which attracted greater publicity.

As it was, the Emergency never received the same level of media coverage as other South East Asian counter-insurgencies. Nor did it provide such sensational copy as Mau Mau, which erupted in Kenya while the Malayan Emergency was in its fifth year. Several features of the campaign help to explain the relative inattention paid to the Emergency. Malaya was, as Trevor Royle points out, a 'long and expensive twenty-two hours' flight away by plane'.[2] Geographical distance, though, does not by itself explain the media neglect of Malaya. Vietnam was even more distant for American reporters and yet the conflict there received abundant (or, as the American military have frequently argued, over-abundant) television and press coverage. Rather the nature of the events themselves was the critical factor. After an initial flurry of interest in Malaya following the declaration of a State of Emergency, it soon became clear that winkling out the Communist insurgents from the dense jungle covering most of Malaya's interior would be a protracted business – not the stuff of daily headlines. Just as the press lost interest in the Korean War when a military stalemate had been reached, so too did their attention wander when the Malayan Emergency dragged on with scant perceptible progress against the MCP.[3]

In other respects too the Emergency was a peculiarly hard conflict to report, whether for print journalists or for the newsreel and television crews. The notoriously impenetrable Malayan jungle in which most of the 'action' (or more often, inaction) occurred hampered reporters just as badly as it did the security forces: there was very little actually to see, let alone to report. The Emergency was thus all too intangible, or, as Graham Greene put it, 'like a mist; it pervaded everything; it sapped the spirits; it wouldn't clear.'[4] More prosaically, the problems of reporting the conflict were summed up by Louis Heren, who reported it for *The Times*, when he wrote in his memoirs that:

> the Malayan emergency was not an exciting war. It was very difficult to report, and only occasionally made the front pages. There was none of the drama of the Vietnam war. The British did not try to defeat the enemy by destroying the country it was defending for the rubber companies. Instead, they fought an intelligent police operation.[5]

Despite Malaya being a somewhat neglected campaign, a detailed examination of the Emergency reveals much about the British government's determination to manage the presentation of terrorism in a fashion which accorded with its own political objectives. In South East Asia the objectives of successive British governments were complex. Obviously the Communist insurgency itself had to be put down, but at the same time Britain was committed to the introduction of self-government in the region at a relatively early date. India had gained its independence shortly before the Malayan Emergency was declared, as had Burma in January 1948.[6] The speed and unexpectedness with which Burma demanded and achieved independence – and her subsequent refusal to become part of the Commonwealth – alarmed British colonial officials and politicians. Efforts to sell the new colonial, and Commonwealth, ideal of 'partnership' were redoubled. This called for much positive propaganda, focusing on the projection of British achievements in the area – not an easy task after the humiliation of the fall of Singapore in 1941, and the overrunning of Britain's South East Asian colonies by the Japanese.

Promoting the new-look Empire-Commonwealth was made all the more necessary by the emergence in South East Asia of Communist movements which offered entirely different models for national development. China – and ultimately Moscow – shone as alternative beacons of allegiance for the peoples of British colonial territories. Events in Malaya were thus not isolated from developments elsewhere, and, as will be seen, the defeat of 'Communist Terrorism' in Malaya was projected (albeit tentatively at times) by the British government as part of the Western powers' global fight against Communism, rather than as a purely colonial insurgency. The campaign to win Malayan 'hearts and minds' merged with the broader aim of persuading Asian audiences that democracy was infinitely preferable to the pernicious ideology of Communism – a task complicated by the Attlee administration's recognition of the People's Republic of China in January 1950. Britain's various objectives in South East Asia, and the Cold War more broadly, demanded a combination of positive (projection of Britain) material and negative (denigration of Communism) propaganda. The need for Britain to enter into the propaganda contest with the Eastern bloc was early recognized by Attlee's Cabinet. Bevin particularly assumed the role of propaganda warrior with some relish, and was influential in the establishment of the Foreign Office's covert anti-Communist propaganda outfit, the Information Research Department (IRD) – whose very existence was unknown to the British public until 1977 when David Owen closed it down.

The Background to the Emergency

In anticipation of the complications which might arise following the resumption of British rule over Malaya on the conclusion of the war in the Pacific, the Ministry of Information launched a special propaganda campaign. It aimed to persuade British (and, to a lesser degree, American) opinion that Britain's record in Malaya was far from shameful, and that a post-war return to the peninsula was necessary both in order to prevent a resumption of aggression in the Far East, and as a prerequisite to world prosperity.[7] Whether it had any such effects or not, the actual re-imposition of colonial rule was an incomplete success. The temporary British Military Administration handed over to a reconstituted Malayan government in 1946. In the same year, an attempt was made to deal with the inequalities in rights between the Malay and Chinese inhabitants (approximately 44 per cent and 38.5 per cent of the population respectively[8]), and to rationalize Malaya's anomalous administrative structure with legislation for a Union of Malaya. However, the plans to give greater rights to the Chinese provoked a swift spoiling operation from the Malays, who effectively quashed the legislation. The assertion of their dominant position within the administration by the Malay sultans and proto-nationalists – who formed the United Malays National Organization (UMNO) – provided something of a fillip to the Malayan Communist Party (MCP). The MCP was largely composed of Chinese Malayans and it sought to strengthen its control over the Chinese population, alienated from the government by its failure to push the Union scheme through. In addition, many of the Chinese lived in so-called 'squatter' settlements, in areas remote from the main administrative centres.[9] Thus in the years prior to the Emergency, the government had never properly regained authority over many of the Malayan Chinese, in whose eyes the MCP had considerable prestige as the main wartime opponent of Japanese occupation.

In the months prior to the declaration of the Emergency the MCP's activities were varied. Infiltration of the nascent trade union movement was one of its main enterprises. There was also some sabotage, particularly of the rubber industry, and a number of murders. Yet until very shortly before the declaration, the colonial administration, on the advice of the Malayan Security Service (MSS), was remarkably sanguine about the political situation in the territory, and quite unaware of the fact that in March 1948 the MCP's politburo had decided to launch a Maoist guerrilla campaign.[10] On 14 June 1948, J. Dalley of the MSS wrote that there was 'no immediate threat to internal security in Malaya'. He felt that although the MCP represented a challenge to the government's authority, and was making substantial inroads into the trade union movement, this danger was latent rather than actual.[11] Only four days later, following the murder of three planters in Perak, Malaya embarked on its twelve-year Emergency. The reaction in Whitehall was that officials on the ground had been caught napping. Many expatriates doubtless experienced momentary *schadenfreude* at the hapless Malayan government's expense, as they had been urging for some time that the MCP represented a dangerous enemy which ought to have been prevented from operating as an open political party.[12] Now they had apparently been vindicated, and in Westminster questions were asked about the alertness of the High Commissioner, Sir Edward Gent, who had apparently allowed a Communist conspiracy to hatch undetected.[13]

Understanding the Enemy: The Interpretation of 'Terrorism'

In May 1950, a Colonial Office report entitled 'The Colonial Empire Today' endorsed the theory that the disturbances caused by the MCP were 'part of the Kremlin's world-wide campaign against the Western powers':

> All available evidence shows that the MCP though small, is a well organised and orthodox communist party implementing an impeccably intransigent Stalinist policy. Evidence of direct links with Moscow or Peking is, not surprisingly, lacking; but unnamed delegates from Malaya attended the Conference of the World Federation of Trade Unions held in Peking last November. These delegates undoubtedly brought back to Malaya advice and instructions based on the war experience of the People's Liberation Army of China. The MCP must thus be recognised as a dangerous and capable enemy which can be overcome only by the methodical destruction of its army and the uprooting of its organisational grip among the workers and peasants of Malaya.[14]

In fact, evidence had always been lacking as to the amount (if any) of external aid given to the MCP by Peking and Moscow, although many accounts of the Emergency's origins have pointed to Zhdanov's statement to the Cominform in 1947 that national liberation movements in South East Asian countries were to operate 'as an important adjunct of the International Communist movement', and the Soviet-sponsored Calcutta conference of Asian and Australian Communists in February 1948, which supposedly catalysed the MCP rebellion.[15]

What emerges from a detailed examination of the relevant Colonial and Foreign Office files is that there was considerable disagreement between the two Departments over the interpretation of terrorism in Malaya – particularly over the issue of external direction. Not only did they dispute the nature of the relationship between the MCP, the Chinese Communist Party (CCP) and the Kremlin, but also they found it most difficult to agree the best propaganda line to adopt on the question of who lay behind the MCP. Frank Furedi asserts that:

> Britain justified the implementation of its emergency in Malaya on the grounds that it had discovered the existence of a plan worked out by Moscow, committing the MCP to an insurrection. This alleged conspiracy has no foundation in reality and all the archival evidence appears to confirm that it was a piece of fiction.[16]

Furedi is correct inasmuch as the Malayan authorities and Whitehall lacked proof of any conspiracy: a report dated May 1948 stated that there was 'no evidence of direct Russian influence', although there were links between the Communist Parties of Malaya, China and even Great Britain.[17] However, in the initial stages of the Emergency the government made little real attempt to insinuate that Moscow was behind events in Malaya, and if anything perhaps underplayed the Communism of the insurgents.

Critics of the Malayan government (or of Attlee's administration) certainly regarded use of the term 'Emergency' rather than 'war', and 'bandit' as opposed to something more pejorative, as evidence that Communism in Malaya was being treated without due seriousness. As Richard Stubbs writes in his study of the 'hearts and minds' technique in Malaya:

> The impression that the Government wasn't fully aware of the true nature of the events which were taking place was accentuated by the use of the term 'bandits' to refer to all 'criminals' or 'bad hats'. . . . The term 'bandit' was essentially an appelation which covered all sorts of evil deeds and its continual use by the Government only served to confuse and mislead people. It appeared not only to deny that the communists could be politically motivated but also to ignore the fact that the MCP had widespread support within certain sections of the population.[18]

However, the reasons why the term 'bandit' was chosen reflect only partially the government's private interpretation of the enemy, and it is misleading to read into the terminology a simple underestimation of the insurgents. Initially 'bandit' was preferable to certain other appelations for predominantly fiscal reasons: if the originators of unrest in Malaya were openly referred to as Britain's 'enemy' then insurance companies might have sought to repudiate their liability under those policies which provided only against 'riot and civil commotion'. In other words, if events in Malaya were described in terms redolent of war, then the government – rather than private insurance companies – would have had to compensate rubber plantations and tin mines for the damage caused by the MCP.[19] In the austere days of the late 1940s, with Britain facing a severe dollar deficit, it is unsurprising that Attlee's government sought (somewhat deviously) to escape part of the financial burden of the Emergency through a semantic sleight of hand.

The insurgents formally remained 'bandits' (or 'terrorists') until 1952, despite frequent criticism from sections of the press and Tory MPs who felt that the term signified a lack of seriousness and lent Emergency operations an unwarranted air of *opera buffa*.[20] The Foreign Office Under-Secretary of State, Robert Scott, wrote in 1950 that,

> The decision to call them 'bandits' or 'terrorists' was taken originally because of the insurance implications of the words 'insurgents' or 'rebels' or 'enemy'.... It was only much later when our propaganda machine began to get going in South East Asia that the propaganda angle of the matter was ever considered.[21]

Yet this does not appear to be wholly true, certainly not from the perspective of other Whitehall Departments. For example, the clear implication of Colonial Office Assistant Secretary of State J.D. Higham's remark to Kenneth Blackburne (Head of CO Information Services) – 'On no account should the term "insurgent", which might suggest a genuine popular uprising, be used' – is that the designation 'bandit' also accorded with Britain's propaganda aims.[22] From early in the Emergency the overriding aim of government publicity was that the MCP should not be regarded as a genuinely nationalist (therefore popular and legitimate) movement.

Westminster showed considerable anxiety that the 'bandits' might be mistaken for patriots. In August 1948, the Colonial Secretary, Arthur Creech Jones, wrote to Malcolm MacDonald (Britain's Commissioner-General for South East Asia, resident at Singapore) informing him that he and Bevin intended to conduct a 'vigorous counter-attack on Communist propaganda both at home and abroad', in order to refute the suggestion that the 'present troubles in Malaya arise from a genuine nationalist movement of the people of the country'. To this end, material was required which would show the (favourable) attitude of the population – 'of all communities and all classes' – to the government of Malaya, and statistics demonstrating that the Communists included 'many alien-born Chinese'.[23] The longer the Emergency lasted the greater the danger of the bandits acquiring, in the Colonial Office's J.B. Williams's phrase, 'a certain glamour'.[24] It was thus important to describe the MCP in a way that did not unduly dignify its members. Accordingly, when, in December 1948, the Central Office of Information failed to adhere to the correct terminology in its publications on the Emergency it was swiftly reprimanded.[25] But while insisting that 'bandit' should be used to designate members of the MCP, the governments in London and Kuala Lumpur did also frequently refer to their opponents as 'terrorists'. Certainly they believed the enemy's strategy to rest on terror. As Malcolm MacDonald stated, their policy was 'to terrorise the population by committing a series of murders and so cause economic chaos from which they hoped to gain political advantage'.[26] In the economic and political chaos following a flight of British capital, the MCP would seize power. While the destruction of Malaya's economic infrastructure was taking place the armed wing of the MCP, in more orthodox Maoist style, would also seek to create 'liberated areas' in the colony's jungle interior. In particular, the MCP was perceived as relying on the support (coerced rather than spontaneous) of Malayan Chinese squatters.

The ethnicity of the 'bandits' was played upon - hence Creech Jones's request for material showing the bandits' ethnic origins. The MCP was thus, by implication, doubly illegitimate: not only did its terrorism place it beyond the pale, but its predominantly Chinese membership meant that it could not possibly represent a Malayan nationalist movement. Moreover, colonial officials regarded the Chinese as peculiarly susceptible to the sort of pressure exerted on them by armed Communist cells. While the Malayan government hesitated to suggest that the Chinese were somehow racially predisposed towards violence (as this might suggest that the 'bandits' enjoyed much spontaneous support, albeit only from their own ethnic constituency[27]), its reports to the Colonial Office – and indeed its public pronouncements on the Emergency – habitually spoke of the Chinese as 'sitting on the fence'.[28] Some in the Colonial Office ascribed Chinese fence-sitting to 'doubts about our ability to protect them'.[29] Others, however, agreed with Sir Henry Gurney's verdict: 'the truth is that the Chinese are accustomed to acquiesce to pressure'.[30]

By the end of 1948, then, it had been recognized that winning the support of the Malayan Chinese would be crucial to the counter-insurgency campaign. The supposedly innate tendency of the Chinese towards vacillation (if not outright collapse) in the face of violence made this task difficult enough. Furthermore, the government wondered how the Malayan Chinese could be persuaded to co-operate with the authorities against the Communist bandits when Communists in China itself had

78

achieved control over that vast nation. Would the natural inclination of the suggestible Malayan Chinese not be simply to support Communism, as the winning side, in whatever guise it appeared? These fears loomed large in the thought of officials in Malaya and in Whitehall's Colonial and Foreign Offices in 1949.

Early in 1949 a protracted wrangle began in Whitehall – primarily between various departments of the Foreign Office and the Colonial Office, with contributions from the Malayan government and Malcolm MacDonald – over the extent to which the government ought to publicize the Communism of the 'bandits'. In formulating a propaganda policy for Malaya they also had to decide whether to emphasize links between the MCP and CCP, or, on the contrary, attempt to drive a wedge between the two. There were two strands to these discussions: one was to decide what support the MCP *actually* received from Moscow and/or Beijing. Clearly, the greater the level of external support enjoyed by the MCP the more protracted the insurgency was likely to be. Additionally, the Colonial and Foreign Offices were concerned with the broader implications of the Malayan situation, wanting to ascertain the strength and cohesiveness of international Communism – a matter on which they substantially disagreed. The second strand of discussions was to decide, regardless of their conclusions on these matters, how best to present to various audiences the MCP's relationship with other Communist parties. Was it preferable to conjure up an international Communist conspiracy, or to paint the MCP as an isolated Communist movement?

The Foreign and Colonial Offices held conflicting views on both the 'reality' of the situation and the best propaganda line to adopt. The former sided with the position adopted by MacDonald and Gurney (Gent's replacement as High Commissioner) early in 1949 that the situation in Malaya was, in MacDonald's words, 'in effect an extension of the Cold War to active terrorism inspired by international communism'.[31] However, proponents of this view were sensible to the pitfalls of propaganda based on a Kremlin conspiracy theory. As Gurney wrote to Creech Jones in October 1949:

> It is sometimes argued that we should present Communism in Malaya as an integral part of [a] Moscow inspired campaign which has been successful in China and as a movement the leaders of which in Malaya have behind them the backing and resources of Russia and [the] China Communist Party. It is claimed for this line that it will bring home to the people of this country the real seriousness of the communist threat with which they are faced.
>
> My own view is that we should aim at driving the largest possible wedge between the two.[32]

As Britain was on the brink of recognizing the People's Republic of

China (PRC), a simplistic lumping together of all Communist Parties as part of the same Soviet threat would have been difficult to sustain. As it was, Gurney suggested that British propaganda should tell the Malayan Chinese that the CCP government of China was a phenomenon altogether different from the MCP. The CCP had the backing of the Chinese people, and was thus tolerated by the United Kingdom, whereas in Malaya the Communists had 'put themselves out of court by adopting a policy of violence against the will of the people'. Thus the MCP could only sustain itself 'on money and supplies extorted by threats and common banditry'. Moreover, stating that the MCP enjoyed CCP patronage would simply encourage the suggestible Malayan Chinese to support the MCP because they would then regard it as a stronger force.

All officials agreed on the desirability of encouraging fissures between Chinese, Soviet and Malayan Communism, with an eye to the long-term goal of effecting a Sino-Soviet split.[33] But while the Colonial and Foreign Offices agreed that to down-play any connection between the MCP and CCP was sensible, they diverged on the issue of how far this line represented propaganda based on truth. These divisions became only too apparent in October and November 1949 when the two Departments endeavoured to draw up a joint statement on propaganda for the Emergency. The Colonial Office tended to concur with the view expressed by J.J. Paskin (CO Assistant Under-Secretary of State) that 'so far as we know, the China Communist Party did nothing to promote, and is doing nothing to perpetuate the present campaign of violence in Malaya'.[34] In short, the Colonial Office believed that the proposed propaganda line was not only correct but also true, while the Foreign Office regarded their colleagues in Church House as dangerously naive in their underestimation of the enemy in Malaya. The Far Eastern Department, on the expert authority of its man Guy Burgess, insisted that there was 'solid evidence that the Malayan Communist Party's campain [sic] of violence is approved and encouraged by the Kremlin and by all Communist Parties in communion with the Kremlin, of which the Chinese Communist Party is one'.[35] They were, however, prepared to forgo publicizing the true nature of links between Moscow, Peking and the MCP for the sake of expediency – to avoid painting 'Communism as so vast an international conspiracy as to represent it by implication as an enormous and successful bandwagon onto which every prudent Chinese should jump'.[36] But to show cleavages between the MCP and CCP was only 'a propaganda policy. It would be fatal if we let ourselves be lulled into *thinking* that the aims of the CCP in S.E. Asia do not coincide with those of the MCP.'[37]

The fear of producing a 'bandwagon effect' in Malaya made portrayal of the MCP as isolated banditry attractive in many ways, but there were also disadvantages to such a line. Thus Malcolm MacDonald argued (with the backing of the IRD, which now had a Regional Information Office at

MacDonald's Singapore residence) that the best policy was to show the MCP as aligned with the Kremlin, not Beijing.[38] This, he argued, was not only true but might also help to encourage Sino-Soviet disaffection and counteract Communist propaganda:

> Our enemies inside and outside Malaya, seek to prove that the Communist terrorist movement in Malaya is a spontaneous local uprising, not (repeat not) fostered by alien forces outside. We shall only help local Communist propaganda if we agree that they have no ... connection with the Moscow-inspired world conspiracy.[39]

MacDonald's views were largely shared by the Foreign Office. Being responsible for propaganda on the Emergency for America and other non-Colonial audiences, the FO was keen that Britain should appear to be fighting an enemy sufficiently threatening to justify the stringent Emergency regulations and prolonged security force operations. Its fears were summed up in J.H. Watson's words:

> it seems to us very dangerous to pretend that the troubles in Malaya are not caused by Communism but only by a kind of local banditry. As we saw in the case of Greece, where the Greek Government were for long anxious to describe the Communists only as bandits, international public opinion in the United States, in Latin American countries with a large vote at UNO, and elsewhere is inclined to take the line that when wholesale military operations are required to suppress mere internal unrest, it is in some way due to bad government. This is especially so in a colony; and instead of receiving sympathy and support from American public opinion in our praiseworthy struggle to combat the wellknown international Communist menace, we shall merely be regarded as a bad colonial power coping with rebellions. It is precisely the aim of the Communists to pretend that what is happening in Malaya is a national liberation movement. It is important to remember that communiqués put out in Malaya are read all round the world and may do considerable harm.[40]

The final draft of the joint statement on propaganda – completed in December 1949, only days before the announcement that Attlee's government was to recognize the PRC – was something of a compromise. It was agreed that a distinction should be drawn between the CCP and MCP, and that there should be no suggestion of any aid from the PRC to the latter, 'unless that Government engages in acts which prove the contrary'.[41] But at the same time British propaganda was to stress that the UK's recognition of Communist China in no way signalled an acceptance of Communism as such. Indeed, Communism was to be depicted as 'the means whereby the Russians seek to expand and to dominate all Asian territories'.[42] Furthermore, the final draft of the joint statement was amended to incorporate the arguments of MacDonald and the IRD:

> While it is desirable for the sake of world opinion to represent the war in Malaya as against the Malayan Communist Party, and not merely against colonial unrest, publicity should avoid writing up international Communism in such terms as to make it seem a powerful bandwagon onto which people would be wise to jump.[43]

Finally, it was to be brought home to the Malayan Chinese (and others) that the Communists in Malaya had 'put themselves out of court' on three grounds: they were a 'small and alien minority'; they were attempting to impose their views on the majority by violent means; and, moreover, their violence was 'of a most morbid type consisting of intimidation, extortion and murder'.[44] Malcolm MacDonald was charged with giving the line 'tactfully to the press and other publicity media'.[45]

However, the Foreign Office soon expressed dissent from the agreed propaganda line. It began to insist that more should be made of the bandits' Communism. The reason was almost certainly that the counter-insurgency campaign, by early 1950, appeared to have taken a turn for the worse, and Gurney was pressing that the bandits should be taken more seriously. Writing to the Secretary of State for the Colonies in January 1950, Gurney stressed that 'the enemy in Malaya is Communism with all its implications, not merely some 3000 bandits. Communism is and has been for many years deeper and more widespread in Malaya than is generally recognised.' He warned that the MCP's military leaders were still at large, and very much in control of their forces, through 'ruthless and rigid discipline' and 'intense and clever propaganda'.[46]

The second half of 1949 had been disastrous for the Malayan government. Although 619 bandits had been killed, 337 captured and 251 surrendered (of a total estimated to be no more than 4,000), there had also been 344 civilian and 229 security force fatalities in the course of the year.[47] The pervading sense of gloom was not alleviated by the disaster of 'Anti-Bandit Month' (January 1950), designed by Gurney as a means of drawing all sections of the Malayan population into the counter-insurgency effort. Rather than reducing bandit atrocities and increasing the flow of information on the MCP to the police, 'Anti-Bandit Month' had precisely the reverse effects. The press was scathing, with Malaya's leading English-language paper, the *Straits Times*, concluding that the Month had 'boomeranged'.[48]

Early 1950 saw major changes to the chain of command in Malaya. Most importantly, Lieutenant-General Sir Harold Briggs was appointed as Director of Operations in March, to co-ordinate the conduct of 'anti-bandit operations' and ensure that the military supported the civilian authorities in a more harmonious fashion than hitherto.[49] Briggs perhaps encouraged Whitehall to re-examine its propaganda policy. His comments at press conferences often contradicted the existing line. On 17 April 1950, for example, Briggs broke two of the agreed 'rules': he referred to a 'War Cabinet' in Malaya – which dignified the bandits as 'belligerents' and implied 'a kind of Civil War in Malaya'[50] – and he identified the terrorists as Communists. This *faux pas* prompted R.H. Scott to muse that perhaps 'in the past we have leaned too far the other way, describing the terrorists as thugs and blood stained ruffians and so forth', when in fact there was 'a hard core of disciplined communists'.[51]

At the same time as such doubts were surfacing, two new committees were inaugurated – the Cabinet Malaya Committee and the Central Office of Information's Far Eastern Publicity Committee – providing inter-departmental fora in which to air the debate anew.[52] Consequently, the months April to July 1950, which saw some of the heaviest casualties of the Emergency, were marked by further vigorous discussion of propaganda policy.

The Foreign Office, encouraged by Malcolm MacDonald and the IRD's Regional Information Office in Singapore, used the Cabinet Malaya Committee to press for a re-examination of the 'ban which has been imposed at the request of the Colonial authorities on describing the real organisation and nature of the MCP and its solidarity with international Communism'.[53] On paper at any rate, there had never been such a ban – only a determination to avoid making international Communism appear an attractive bandwagon. But the Foreign Office was able to exploit the worsening security situation in Malaya to press for an amended policy and a corresponding adjustment to the label applied to the 'bandits'.

At the Cabinet Malaya Committee's fourth meeting, on 8 May 1950, a possible change of terminology to be applied to the enemy was discussed. Although the Minister of Defence (Emanuel Shinwell) advocated that the government should now 'publish to the world the fact that the troubles in Malaya were Communist-inspired', a decision was deferred until after the ministerial visit to Malaya.[54] In May 1950 Jim Griffiths, the new Secretary of State for the Colonies, and John Strachey, Secretary of State for War, visited the colony. In his memoirs, Griffiths suggested that his latent scepticism over the aptness of official terminology was reinforced by first-hand experience:

> Before I left for Malaya I had been advised not to refer to the operations as 'war' but as 'the emergency', and to the Malayan Liberation Army as 'bandits'.
> It did not take John and me long to find out that the so-called bandits were a well-trained, highly disciplined and skilfully led force. Their field commander, known as General Peng, was as

clever a military tactician as he was an astute political leader.[55]

By June, both the Foreign and Colonial Offices had separately come to see 'bandits' as an inappropriate appelation. The Far Eastern Department sought Cabinet permission to describe the Malayan Races' Liberation Army (MRLA), as HMG chose to translate the name of the MCP's fighting wing, openly as 'Communists – or at least Communist bandits'.[56] Similarly, Higham in the Colonial Office wrote to Gurney that, if the name were to be changed, he had 'a soft spot for the phrase "communist bandit" which has a fine minatory ring to it on a par with "imperialist warmonger"'.[57]

In July 1950, the December 1949 joint statement on propaganda was amended. A new secret paper on 'Anti-Communist Propaganda in the Far East' was issued, along with a fresh version of the paper 'Attitude To Be Adopted in Publicity towards Communism in Malaya and China'.[58] With respect to publicity on and for Malaya, the line for channels traceable to British official sources now read: 'It has been agreed that it is no longer necessary to avoid making clear publicly the connection between the Malayan Terrorist Movement and Communism as an internationally organized and centrally controlled force.'[59] In other words, more could be made of the political motivation of the 'bandits' than previously. Indeed, the guidelines suggested that the MCP should be depicted as a party which 'reports direct to Moscow and receives its direction from the Communist Party of the Soviet Union', although the reluctance to suggest too much Chinese government involvement remained, as did the overall goal of weaning Peking away from Moscow.

Although the propaganda policy was thus somewhat altered, there was no change to official terminology. The MRLA remained 'bandits' despite mounting criticism that this label was, as Malaya's Joint Information and Propaganda Committee itself agreed, 'misleadingly inadequate'.[60] One can but hypothesize as to why 'bandit' was not replaced by 'Communist Terrorist' until May 1952. Throughout 1951 there were signs of growing firmness towards the MCP. Briggs continued to insist that Malaya was on a 'war footing'.[61] His bluntness perhaps fuelled backbench dissatisfaction with the vocabulary of the Emergency. Doubtless the assassination of Sir Henry Gurney on 6 October 1951 – the climactic act of MRLA terrorism (although apparently 'accidental', in so far as the ambush was not aimed at the High Commissioner in particular)[62] – lent substance to the arguments of those who felt that 'bandits' was simply an inadequate description. Gurney's death produced a firmer attitude towards the Emergency in both London and Malaya. The hiatus was underscored by the return of Churchill and the Conservatives to power at the end of October. Churchill personally picked out General Sir Gerald Templer as the new High Commissioner, who would possess civil and military control over Malaya. It was only in May 1952, after Templer had been installed and after almost four years of Emergency, that the term 'bandit' was formally dropped. A paper from Malaya's Secretary for Defence then proposed that

> in future . . . the term 'Communist Terrorist' will be the general designation for all members of these organisations, and in the particular context 'Communist Terrorist Army' for the words 'Malayan Races Liberation Army', 'Communist Terrorist Organisation' for the 'Min Yuen'. The designation 'bandit' will not be used in future in official reports and Press releases emanating from the Government.[63]

Noel Barber has said that the change in name reflected the British and Malayan governments' discovery that '"bandits" had been the identical term used by the Japanese and Chiang Kai Shek to describe Communists'. And, Barber continued, 'since neither of these powers had been successful, the use of "bandits" by the British put them on a similar level in the eyes of Malayan Chinese'.[64] Lucien Pye, an American expert on Communist psychology who visited Malaya (with Foreign Office approval) in 1952, made the same point. He wrote that 'the conduct of the MCP' during the early days of the Emergency encouraged the government to label it as 'bandits', which – though appropriate – had unfortunate connotations for the Chinese, who consequently believed 'that the British were simply adopting the same role as other unsuccessful antagonists of Communism in Asia and that they would probably fail to recognise the nature of their enemy'.[65] It would appear, however, that Pye and Barber are both somewhat wide of the mark. The decision was prompted, not by factors internal to Malaya, but by the government's concern over how audiences *outside* Malaya perceived the insurgents - and the need to ensure that they realized the gravity of the situation facing the security forces.

The irony of the timing of this change of terminology was that by May 1952 the 'Communist Terrorists' (CTs) had made a substantial change to their tactics, as a result of which they were arguably no longer terrorists at all. It had been decided in October 1951 that indiscriminate terrorism was to play little or no part in the MCP's campaign. The new policy derived from awareness that terrorism had served only to alienate the Malayan Chinese masses. Activities would now concentrate on sabotage of hard targets, subversion, infiltration of the trade unions and so on.[66] Clearly, it took some time for the rank and file of the MRLA to become aware that a change in tactics had been ordered by the leadership; this could scarcely have been otherwise, given the difficulties of communications in the jungle. Also, by late 1951, the sizeable units of the MRLA which had existed in the earlier stages of the Emergency had splintered in order to render detection by the security forces more difficult. Central control over such a large number of small groups was tenuous, and there were probably units which continued to engage in terrorism long after the directive had been issued.[67]

The Malayan government remained unaware of the directive for some months. In late 1951 and early 1952 reports from Malaya were intermittently optimistic that banditry was decreasing. Vincent del Tufo, the Officer Administering the Government in Malaya after Gurney's assassination, reported to Oliver Lyttelton (the Conservative Secretary of State for the Colonies) in December 1951 that during the previous month the bandits had 'shown little desire to stand and fight or to tackle "hard" targets', although 115,000 rubber trees had been slashed nonetheless.[68] But there was certainly no overwhelming sense that the bandits had abandoned terrorism. Indeed, the Monthly Political Intelligence Report for 15 January–15 February 1952 stated that there had been 'a revival of terrorist activity' with a 'tendency to attack "hard" targets'.[69] British press reports were similarly uncertain as to whether or not the end of terrorism was really in sight, having learnt to treat the Malayan government's unerringly upbeat press releases with considerable scepticism. For example, in August 1952, *The Times*'s Louis Heren reported that a recrudescence of terrorism was quite possible:

> There is no evidence to show that Malaya's Communists are incapable of intensifying and extending their campaign of terrorism. As a body they have generally been remarkably unimaginative, and almost conservative. Fifty ex-members of Irgun Zvei Leumi, whom your Correspondent knew in Palestine, could, if it were possible to disguise them as Asians, bring the country to a standstill and drive the administration to the safety and impotence of barbed-wire enclosures as they did in Jerusalem. Efficiency in terrorism is not a Jewish monopoly . . .
>
> But the Malayan terrorists are learning; they have their own efficiency campaign. Their ambuscades, for instance, are now almost text-book demonstrations, whereas previously they were ragged, ill-planned affrays.[70]

It was not until late September 1952 that the Malayan government actually became aware of the MCP's October directive, although Louis Heren and others have suggested that the document was captured early in 1952.[71] The Malayan authorities had no immediate intention of publicizing the revelation that the CTs were no longer (at least on paper) wedded to terrorism – a decision taken on security grounds, according to Templer's biographer.[72] But the story was leaked in the British press in October, much to the chagrin of Templer and the Malayan administration.[73] Templer was yet more incensed by Heren's 'scoop' in *The Times* on 1 December, in which he précised the directive, having been shown it in confidence by General Lockhart.[74] Heren was subsequently marked out in Government House as 'typical of all communist muck'.[75]

The mutual suspicion and antagonism between *The Times'* correspondent and the High Commissioner should therefore make us rather wary of Heren's suggestion that there was something more duplicitous about the withholding of the directive from the public: namely, that Templer artificially kept the 'terrorist threat' alive in the public imagination to magnify his own reputation and achievements.

To conclude, in late 1951 the MCP made a substantial alteration to its tactics; in May 1952, the insurgents officially became 'Communist Terrorists' and remained such until the end of the Emergency. The new label was not a complete misnomer, as the MCP's October directive took a considerable time to filter down to the rank and file, and terrorism (if one accepts that the term can be used thus) against military targets was not forbidden. Thus periodic ambushes of the security forces still occurred. As the Emergency progressed, though, the Communist insurgents became increasingly elusive.[76] The 'hard core' were confined to the most impenetrable areas of Malaya's jungle interior (known as 'black areas'), while Kuala Lumpur and Malaya's southern provinces were declared Communist-free ('white areas', in the symbolically charged Emergency parlance). The Emergency received fewer and fewer column inches in Britain, the popular perception being that Templer's strategy (itself a continuation of Briggs's plan) would ensure that the insurgents were eventually defeated. By the time Templer left Malaya in May 1954, there was little doubt in most minds as to who would ultimately 'win' the Emergency, despite Templer's cautionary parting shot that he would 'shoot the bastard who says this Emergency is over'.[77]

The Role of Propaganda in the Malayan Emergency

In one sense, the significance of propaganda in the Malayan Emergency is well known. Templer is often credited with having pioneered the 'hearts and minds' approach to counter-insurgency, in which gaining the support of the indigenous populace is regarded as inseparable from inflicting military defeat on the insurgents.[78] 'Winning hearts and minds' thus requires well-publicized policies which will predispose people towards the government. Much has been written about the efforts of High Commissioner Gurney and his Director of Operations, Briggs, and then of Templer (who combined both their roles) to win over the masses of fence-sitting Malayan Chinese on to the government's side, and the US government sought to draw on British expertise to frame its own response to insurgency in South East Asia.[79] While the organization and use of propaganda in Malaya clearly concerns us, the remainder of this chapter will concentrate less on government propaganda *in* Malaya than on how the Emergency was presented beyond the territory. This dimension of British propaganda and news management is less well known.

Perceptions of the Malayan Communist Party's Use of Propaganda

Initially, it is helpful to understand how the British government and Malayan authorities perceived the propaganda of their opponents. With what did government propagandists in London and Kuala Lumpur regard themselves as being confronted? The retrospective literature on the Emergency, which tends to eulogize Templer's 'hearts and minds' technique, has conversely generated a somewhat distorted image of the MCP's propaganda, suggesting that Communist propaganda was ineffectual. In 1967, for example, Julian Paget's *Counter-insurgency Campaigning* implied that Malayan Communist propaganda was doomed to failure because all it offered to the Malays 'was a Communist state and this had little or no appeal'. Furthermore, Paget argued that 'the insurgents lacked any propaganda or political support themselves, such as EOKA had in Cyprus, and this was a great weakness'.[80] The latter assertion is somewhat misleading. The MCP may have had little material support from the People's Republic of China or the USSR, but, as the Foreign Office was well aware, both Communist governments used radio broadcasts as a means of transmitting messages of solidarity with the 'liberation movement' in Malaya. This external psychological support was not as extensive or as well publicized as was the Greek government's support for EOKA in the form of Athens Radio, but the Eastern bloc did engage in one high-profile propaganda stunt in support of the MCP. In February 1953, the Hungarian government offered to release Edgar Saunders (a British businessman imprisoned in Hungary on espionage charges) in exchange for the freeing of Lee Meng (a key courier in the MCP's communications network who was awaiting execution in Malaya). The offer caused Churchill's administration some diplomatic embarrassment, while the Cabinet and Malayan government pondered how to respond to such an offer.[81]

The MCP, then, was not entirely lacking in external propaganda support. In Britain itself the Malayan Communist viewpoint was available in the form of the *Malayan Monitor* – a monthly publication promoted by the *Daily Worker* and written by Lim Hong Bee, an expatriate Malayan Chinese Communist who had assumed residence in London during the Emergency. Moreover, the MCP's own propaganda for various Malayan audiences was both abundant and (so the Malayan government believed) effective. Even before the Emergency was declared the Malayan government was aware that propaganda was very much part of the

88

MCP's arsenal. The MCP's heavy emphasis on propaganda came as no surprise, given that post-war British (and American) governments viewed propaganda as one of the key tools of subversion employed by Communists the world over. Indeed, as already stated, the Cold War itself – not merely the Malayan Emergency – was characterized as a battle for 'hearts and minds' at the level of political ideas. Sir John Sterndale-Bennett elaborated this point in his opening address to the annual Information Officers' Conference at Singapore in 1953: 'We are engaged once more in a struggle against world domination; and it is basically an ideological struggle in which propaganda must play a major part.'[82]

The MCP made extensive use of leaflets – presenting its own political case, and denigrating the Emergency Regulations as a 'white terrorism' against the people of Malaya.[83] The party also produced a newspaper aimed at its supporters, *Freedom News*. Such was the extent of Communist propaganda that, by December 1949, the Malayan government had sufficient material to produce a 60-page booklet, *Anatomy of Communist Propaganda*, which it hoped would expose the tendentious nature of bandit propaganda to those unlikely to be impressed by anti-British and anti-imperialist rhetoric.[84]

Despite the reliance of much of the MCP's written material on what appeared to government analysts to be nothing more than routine Communist claptrap, its non-written propaganda had one outstanding strength: it offered the possibility of participation. It did not simply tell people what to *think*, but told them what they could *do*, if they agreed with the MCP that conditions in Malaya demanded alteration. Lucien Pye found ample evidence of this in the testimony of 'surrendered enemy personnel' (SEPs) interviewed during his fieldwork in Malaya.[85] Among a rural population in which illiteracy was rife, the MCP made much use of verbal and visual propaganda, particularly talks and plays, which dramatically illustrated the MCP's political themes. Many of the Malayan Chinese who joined had little understanding of Marxism-Leninism or Maoism, but were persuaded that the MCP was the best representative of the Chinese community, or that it offered the best opportunity to further the rights of working people. In other words, the MCP was able to tailor its message to various audiences, and its appeal did not lie exclusively (or perhaps even primarily) in its Communist ideology, as both Pye and the Malayan authorities discovered.[86] For example, a Malaya Police Operational Intelligence Summary of March 1950 recounted the case of a bandit who 'says that he does not understand what Communism is, and adds with unconscious humour that he thinks that Communists in this country are all extremists'; he also thought that most other party members knew as little of Communism as he did.[87] Thus Paget wrongly regarded the MCP as having only one message of limited appeal.

Propaganda, then, was intrinsic to the Malayan campaign. Both the insurgents and the authorities sought access to the hearts and minds of the Malayan Chinese.[88] Terrorism – the MCP's 'enforcement terror' enacted on the Malayan Chinese – was very much a psychological weapon, a violent form of communication. Through punishment of actual or suspected traitors (the 'running dog' sympathizers) a powerful message was transmitted to the Malayan Chinese, warning against participation in government schemes. The propaganda of pamphlets and papers fused with the propaganda of the deed. Furthermore, the MCP's terrorism was seen as having a publicity-grabbing function quite apart from its terror-generating effect on the Malayan Chinese. Gurney, for one, believed the MCP to be anxious for international attention. He based his belief, at least in part, on previous experience of Zionist terrorists in Palestine (where he had served as Chief Secretary), whose actions, at Begin's own admission, had aimed at making Palestine a 'glass house' into which the rest of the world would gaze. Complaining about 'misrepresentation of incidents' by the press and BBC, Gurney wrote to Higham in April 1950:

> An unfortunate feature of terrorist campaigns (as distinct from war) is that we do the terrorists' publicity work for them. The BBC is the worst offender in creating the impression that life in Malaya (as in Palestine) consists of a series of incidents. The aim of the grenade thrower is to hit the headlines, and our press and broadcasting do the job for him to his complete satisfaction.[89]

Propaganda as a Tool of Counter-insurgency

It is hard to judge whether the MCP was using terrorism largely as a means of gaining publicity; documents captured by the security forces in the course of counter-insurgency operations fail to elucidate the point. What is significant here, however, is that the High Commissioner *perceived* this to be so. Consequently, for the government, propaganda had several different tasks. News management was required to ensure that, as far as possible, the terrorists received only as much publicity (and of the right sort) as the government saw fit. Additionally, leaflets, posters, films and broadcasts were needed to counter those of the MCP and to win converts to the democratic way of life. Propaganda also had to counter the notion, inside and outside Malaya, that 'Britain cares little for the people of Malaya, only the rubber she produces'.[90] Above and beyond competing at the level of ideas, the Malayan government needed new *policies* to demonstrate that Britain offered something far superior to Communism: hence the promise of independence in 1957 which Templer carried with him on arrival in 1952, and the readjustments to the Federation's electoral system, which provided for Malaya's first direct elections in 1955.[91]

There was also a grimmer side to the 'hearts and minds' approach, for those on the receiving end. It should not be forgotten that the overall objective remained the military and psychological defeat of the CTs. Measures such as forcible resettlement of Malayan Chinese 'squatters' were presented as models of efficient planning, but their real function was to isolate the insurgents from their sources of logistical support.[92] Such measures sought to make it physically impossible for the villagers – surrounded by high perimeter fences, barbed wire and armed guards – to shelter MRLA guerrillas or to provide them with food. Indeed, there was some concern, both at the time of the Emergency and thereafter, that these villages, far from being won over to the government side, were actually teeming with resentment.[93] Purcell, Templer's most trenchant and informed critic, thus makes a convincing (though perhaps rather overstated) case when he argues that political and constitutional reforms were relegated 'to the position of psychological warfare in aid of a military objective'.[94] Far from propaganda considerations always predominating, the essence of the 'hearts and minds' approach was a military strategy to destroy MCP morale and encourage enemy surrenders. Consequently, in addition to 'positive' propaganda through radio, film and so on, much attention was devoted to more conventional psychological warfare techniques: surrender leaflets, voice aircraft (Valettas fitted with loudspeakers) and the production of *New Path News* – a black propaganda paper.

As a result of the diverse types of propaganda required in the Emergency, a complex series of information and psychological warfare organizations gradually evolved. However, it was not until the appointment of Lieutenant-General Sir Harold Briggs (as Director of Operations under Gurney) that a major shake-up of the organization of information and propaganda services was enacted. After a tour of inspection in early 1950, Briggs pronounced that government propaganda was 'non-existent'.[95] This was far from true, but it was a common enough perception.[96] Griffiths pointed out, when the Cabinet Malaya Committee discussed Briggs's remark, that he 'must have been under some misapprehension'. After all, during 1949 some 50 million leaflets had been distributed; there had been continuous radio propaganda, and large numbers of community listening receivers installed; 4 million copies of vernacular newspapers had been circulated; and a mobile public address system established, which reached a quarter of a million people each month.[97] Propaganda and Emergency information were the responsibility of the Department of Public Relations, under J.N. McHugh, who supervised a staff of 200. Thus Briggs was certainly wrong in quantitative terms, and his ill-judged remark (which he retracted in June 1950[98]) provided plenty of ammunition for disgruntled planters in Malaya and

Conservative backbenchers in Westminster, who continued to insist that Britain was lagging badly in the propaganda battle against international Communism.[99] However, in qualitative terms Briggs was perhaps right.

The information services were hamstrung by their sense of alienation and distance from the audience to whom much of their work was addressed: the Malayan Chinese. For the first eighteen months or so of the Emergency, there was a feeling that the Chinese mentality was so antithetical to European psychology that there was little hope of producing effective propaganda. Gurney admitted to a fear that in 'dealing with oriental terrorism armed with modern weapons, our traditional British methods will always be too little and too late'.[100] Similarly, the Colonial Office's Far Eastern specialists who studied MCP propaganda marvelled at the different mentality it revealed. Writing about an MCP one-act satirical play called 'Templer Meeting Gurney', in which the ghost of Gurney – 'with his heart excavated (because he was too cruel), his tongue cut off (because he fabricated lies and calumnies) and his hands chopped away (because he had killed innumerable Malayan people)' – appeared to warn Templer that a similar fate would befall him, T.C. Jerrom was moved to remark: 'I can't really believe that we have the technique to win the hearts and minds of chaps like this.'[101]

One can well believe, as Short suggests, that much of the initial output of McHugh and his team was equally baffling to the Malayan Chinese, not least as literal translations of idiomatic English – particularly the well-worn phrase 'sitting on the fence', used routinely to describe and condemn the Malayan Chinese – produced only a sense of bewilderment.[102] The emphasis on pamphlets and written propaganda was also a weakness, given the high degree of illiteracy among the rural population of Malaya, and though anti-Communist themes were illustrated with relish one wonders, again, what sort of reception they met.[103]

McHugh's Public Relations department certainly did not lack enthusiasm. Nor was external advice in short supply. The Colonial Office and Foreign Office were broadly responsible for the political direction of propaganda policy (particularly on those sensitive areas already examined, such as the insurgents' nomenclature, and the extent to which they should be identified with the CCP). In late 1949, the IRD established a regional outpost in Singapore at the Commissioner-General's Phoenix Park headquarters, under the directorship of John Rayner. The Regional Information Office (RIO) was, in the words of R.H. Scott, a section 'dealing with special counter-communist propaganda', both negative and positive, throughout South East Asia.[104] Clearly Malaya was a prime target for its material, both through geographical proximity and the fact that it faced an actual (as opposed to latent) Communist threat. Singapore also had its own Public Relations Secretary, George Thomson. Both he and Rayner attended the fortnightly meetings of the Joint Information and Propaganda Committee (JIPC), a co-ordinating body set up in February 1950 to manage the proliferation of agencies concerned with propaganda in the region, and to ensure that they should all 'speak with one voice'.[105] The JIPC also kept the heads of the CO Information Services (Kenneth Blackburne) and the IRD (Ralph Murray) fully informed of propaganda measures undertaken in Malaya.

Clearly, though, Briggs did not feel that the existence of a new joint committee was sufficient to meet Malaya's various propaganda needs. His biting criticisms were made two months *after* the JIPC's inauguration. Further changes were instituted. At the beginning of May 1950, Alex Josey was seconded from the Department of Broadcasting to the post of Staff Officer (Emergency Information)[106] and the following month a new department, the Emergency Information Service, was established at the Federal headquarters, with representatives at State level. The process of re-evaluating Malaya's propaganda and psychological warfare needs continued during the visit of the Secretary of State for the Colonies. Griffiths reported back to his Cabinet colleagues that there was still 'room for improvement' in the information services, and that he was urgently investigating the sending over of an anti-Communist expert, who should possess (in Strachey's words) a 'well-trained political mind'.[107] Thus it was that in September 1950, Hugh Carleton Greene – brother of Graham, and later Director-General of the BBC – set out for a year in Malaya, to knock the Emergency propaganda and psychological warfare organizations into shape.

Greene's experience amply qualified him for the nebulous title 'anti-Communist expert'. After his wartime work with the BBC broadcasting to Germany, he had been chosen by Sir Ian Jacob (then Director of the Overseas Service) to head the East European Services broadcasts to the Soviet Union, Romania, Bulgaria, Yugoslavia, Albania and Greece.[108] As Greene's biographer writes, he 'had been brought in to make the East European Service tougher and more aggressive, and tougher and more aggressive it became'.[109] Some of Greene's work was overtly anti-Communist. In particular, BBC broadcasts to Albania in late 1949 were aimed at actively destabilizing the Communist régime, while the IRD and MI6 planned to 'liberate' Albania by smuggling emigrés into the country to organize a coup.[110] In Malaya, Greene had a year to sort out the still unsatisfactory propaganda organization, assuming control from Josey, who had been left, secretary-less, 'to function as a "one man band"'.[111]

Under Greene a stepping up of the propaganda and psychological warfare effort occurred. Greene's three objectives demonstrate how far operational considerations (that is, effecting the surrender of Communists) prevailed:

1. To raise the morale of the civil population and to encourage confidence in Government and resistance to the Communists with a view to increasing the flow of information reaching the Police.

2. To attack the morale of members of the MRLA, the Min Yuen [the MCP's People's Organization] and their supporters and to drive a wedge between the leaders and the rank and file with a view to encouraging defection and undermining the determination of the Communists to continue the struggle.

3. To create an awareness of the values of the democratic way of life which is threatened by International Communism.[112]

His main innovation was the extensive use of SEPs who had turned propagandist for the government's side, and who possessed a keener understanding of the Malayan Chinese than the administration.[113] They subsequently played a prominent role in encouraging disaffection among MRLA ranks.

With respect to winning the 'hearts and minds' of ordinary Malayans, Greene was fairly cynical. Indeed, his approach suggests that (at least in the short term) what the Malayan Chinese actually *thought* was less important than how they *behaved*, and behaviour could best be manipulated by offering financial incentives, rather than by effecting a transformation in attitudes. As Greene wrote in his report: 'the only human emotion which can be expected to be stronger than fear among a terrorised population with very little civic consciousness is greed'.[114] Consequently, he sought and obtained large increases in the size of rewards offered for information leading to the capture of bandits.

But he also initiated a more imaginative attempt to persuade Malayans of the advantages of the 'democratic way of life'. In this area, Greene (as one would expect) promoted the use of both radio and film – two media which had already been identified as crucial before his arrival. Malcolm MacDonald had advised Creech Jones, a year before Greene's secondment, that he and Gurney regarded the Chinese as 'highly susceptible to visual propaganda',[115] and a film expert had been dispatched accordingly to investigate the possibilities for film propaganda in Malaya. In April 1950, Stanley Hawes (formerly Film Commissioner in Australia) sent his report to MacDonald, recommending a strengthening of the Malayan Films Unit (MFU) and appointment of a full-time Films Officer.[116] Noting the tremendous popularity of Tarzan films in Malaya, Hawes also advised that 'a serial film, rather like a Tarzan film, with an anti-bandit hero should be made for showing to the Chinese', and was convinced that 'if such a film were well made, so that it would not cause laughter by its crudity, it would be most valuable in the Emergency'.[117] By the time that Greene wrote his valedictory report, a ten-reel serial film had indeed been produced (*The Adventures of Yaacob*), along with various documentary shorts and newsreels – some of which received a theatrical screening in London during the Emergency.

Greene was also able to report in September 1951 that broadcasting had been 'completely transformed since a year ago'.[118] He concluded that the effectiveness of his alterations could be gauged in the reactions to government propaganda gleaned from captured MCP documents. These revealed that the MCP was now considerably alarmed by the success and cunning of government propaganda.[119]

Such was the situation when Templer (a man for whom both Greene and Josey apparently felt contempt[120]) assumed control. Despite the improvements, Templer nevertheless made substantial changes to the organization of propaganda and psychological warfare. He recruited Alec Peterson (who had been in charge of Force 136's propaganda output[121]) to head the newly merged Department of Information, which combined the old Information Department and the Emergency Information Service.[122] On assuming control, Peterson still found room for criticism: 'the present system suffers from a serious lack of direction, co-ordination and training, from shortage of personnel, from low output and from general distrust in Malaya of "government propaganda"'.[123] Yet in the effort to encourage 'bandit' surrenders, and increase propaganda output, Peterson faced economic stringency measures (a result of the falling rubber price) which Greene had not. If this is borne in mind, in quantitative terms an astonishing amount of psychological warfare material was produced. In 1953, 93 million anti-Communist propaganda pamphlets were distributed, of which 54 million were dropped by the RAF.[124] And in 1956, when (as far as press coverage was concerned, at any rate) the campaign was all but over, in excess of 100 million leaflets were dropped on the Malayan jungle.[125] Sheer volume, of course, does not necessarily equate with a successful campaign. However, in this instance, the efficacy of psychological warfare was so highly rated that an Army report (entitled 'Psychological Warfare Research: Its Role in the Cold War') in 1956 advised that 'in view of the demonstrated effectiveness of psychological warfare operations in Malaya, every effort should be made to begin such operations as soon as possible, in all areas where the Cold War is entering a critical and more active phase'.[126] If the Malayan Emergency is regarded as Britain's greatest success story in counter-insurgency campaigning, then part of that success was undoubtedly due to propaganda and psychological warfare, functioning very much as a 'fourth arm' of the campaign.

The Importance of Opinion in Britain

The foregoing account reveals that considerable time, initiative and expense was devoted to propaganda in Malaya. But what of public opinion outside Malaya? How far did British governments regard it as necessary to persuade those beyond the Federation, and particularly at home, to take a right-thinking view of the Emergency? The role of public opinion on (as opposed to in) Malaya is not an area that has received attention from historians or counter-insurgency strategists, whose writings implicity assume that the minds of Malayans alone mattered. Indeed, this is an attitude which Templer himself professed to share, as evidenced in his remarks to an American doctoral student in 1968:

> I very much doubt whether British public opinion in the United Kingdom had any effect on the outcome [of the Emergency]. Generally speaking, our attempts to settle the matter were well reported in the UK press, except in the few extreme Left Wing papers. However, since any journalist is always looking for some headline which will catch the eye, inevitably in certain cases (such as my personal treatment of the village of Tanjong Malim) the situation was very badly, and I thought, unfairly publicised. Not that it worried me.[127]

Should we, then, conclude that the government was unconcerned with securing public support for a counter-insurgency campaign in a far-flung part of the Empire, about which Britons – certainly during World War II – knew and cared little?[128]

One might have thought that Attlee's government would not have cared to enlighten public opinion on the subject of Malaya to any great degree. The general British ignorance on colonial affairs, which a Colonial Office survey revealed in 1948, and the particular paucity of knowledge about Malaya or fondness for its planting community, might have provided welcome obscurity for the conduct of a counter-insurgency campaign which was, by the very nature of the terrain and the tactics employed on both sides, a largely invisible one.[129] Noel Barber goes so far as to suggest that there was a conspiracy of silence about the Emergency in Whitehall: 'It was almost as though its significance were being deliberately downplayed; not by the newspaper reporters but by Whitehall for its own reasons' – which he fails to elaborate.[130] But if Attlee's administration ever entertained thoughts of allowing ignorance on Malaya to prevail (for which there is no evidence), by the end of 1948 it had already taken active measures to inform British audiences about the Emergency. One of the reasons for the government's eagerness to correct misunderstandings about the nature of the campaign, and to demonstrate the illegitimacy of the 'bandits', was that British Communists were so actively propagating their own view of events in Malaya. The government thus paid special attention to providing trade unions with material which would (it hoped) undo the damage wrought by the *Daily Worker* and Lim Hong Bee's *Malayan Monitor*. From the outset, the *Daily Worker* presented the Emergency as an entirely unwarranted attack by the imperialist British administration in Malaya on the Federation's interlinked nationalist and trade union movements. Legitimate nationalist aspirations were being quashed to keep Malaya safe for big business, under the guise of anti-Communism.[131] Far from threatening the Malayan government, the MCP was depicted as peaceably engaged in 'defence of the living standards of workers and peasants and rights of Trade Union organisations'.[132] The *Daily Worker* also denounced the Malayan government's terminology, particularly objecting to Malcolm MacDonald's reference to the MCP as 'terrorists' – a word used to tarnish 'political opponents, all who criticise the dictatorial colonial regime, all who organise themselves in trade unions or dare to strike for higher wages'.[133]

How much credence did the *Daily Worker*'s interpretation of the Emergency gain? In the early months of the Emergency some left-wing trade unions adopted the paper's stance, and began demanding Britain's withdrawal from Malaya.[134] Here again, the government's *perception* of the situation is as important as the reality. As early as August 1948, Bevin and Creech Jones were certainly alarmed enough at the dent Communist propaganda was making on the attitudes of trade unionists to demand material from MacDonald 'to conduct a vigorous counter-attack on Communist propaganda at home and abroad'.[135] By October 1948, there was more evidence that trade unionists had been 'misled' on Malaya. The Colonial Office Assistant-Secretary, J.D. Higham, recorded 'a mass of correspondence now being received, mainly from trade union branches and shop stewards' committees on the situation in Malaya':

> These letters, forwarding for the most part resolutions passed at local branch meetings, call in general for (a) a cessation of the brutal colonial war being waged against a people struggling for independence and (b) a cessation of the repressive measures against trade unions.[136]

Many of these protests came from the Electrical Trades Union (ETU) and other Communist-dominated unions, and the Colonial Office judged that the main agent of disaffection was the *Malayan Monitor* – the roneoed bulletin which detailed British 'atrocities' in Malaya (often reproduced in the *Daily Worker*). What especially concerned the Department was not only the distorted view of the Emergency which the *Malayan Monitor* projected but the fact that Lim Hong Bee clearly had contacts in the CP, which enabled his material to gain such wide circulation. Thus the Colonial Office's objections to such material were more far-reaching than that it misrepresented the 'bandits' as nationalist heroes; as N.D. Watson, Creech Jones's Private Secretary, remarked, 'If wrong information could be put about in this effective and widespread way on one occasion, the process could be repeated on others as opportunities were afforded by particular events anywhere in the Colonies.'[137]

Several strategies were proposed to counter Communist propaganda. The first was to brief representatives from the left-wing and liberal press, along with Labour Party and TUC public relations officers on the situation in Malaya. Higham suggested that the *Daily Herald, Tribune, New Statesman* and *News Chronicle* were suitable candidates for treatment.[138] On similar lines, the Colonial Office decided to pay special attention to cultivating the trade union movement and the local Labour Party by sending branches specially prepared material on Malaya. This strategy seemed successful: Herbert Tracey, the TUC's Public Relations Officer, was quite amenable, promising N.D. Watson a list of the editors of trade union journals in London. Denis Healey (then of the Labour Party's International Department, shortly to become an MP) also proved most receptive to Colonial Office lobbying, informing Watson over lunch that he would be 'very glad' to receive

> (a) a complete list of the Trade Union branches, Trade Councils etc. who had written to us [the Colonial Office] on the Malayan question, so that he could do everything possible to see that they were fed with proper information in future; and (b) a list of any communist or 'fellow traveller' publications concerned with the Colonies issued in this country, such as the *Malayan Monitor*, so that ... he would know what was to be guarded against.[139]

Watson left lunch certain that 'we can rely on Mr. Healey to help us in tackling any flare-up of this kind which may happen in the future'.[140]

Given the concern with correcting trade unionists' 'misunderstandings', the Colonial Office paid considerable attention to demonstrating that the Malayan authorities were not engaged in a campaign to destroy legitimate (that is, non-Communist) trade unions. Consequently much was made of the visit of two British trade unionists to Malaya in the autumn of 1948 – Mr S.S. Awbery, Labour MP for Central Bristol, and Mr F.W. Dalley, former assistant general secretary of the Railway Clerks' Association – to report on the state of the Federation's unions. Their report detailed the MCP's infiltration into all labour movements and places of employment, setting out how the party had established '"cells" dubbed "Trade Unions" for every type of trade and worker – from miners and rubber workers to cabaret girls' at the end of the war.[141] Awbery and Dalley were emphatic that these organizations were neither representative nor democratic, being simply mouthpieces for the MCP. The report was gratefully hailed in the Colonial Office as 'a smashing indictment of the Communist infiltration of the Malayan Trade Unions, and ... the most effective answer yet to those UK trade unionists who profess to believe that the British have been attempting to smash *legitimate* trade unionism in Malaya'.[142] The IRD saw to it that the report was given a wide distribution overseas: throughout sub-Saharan Africa, in the United States and in Europe under a special arrangement to exchange information on Communism with other signatories of the Brussels Treaty.[143] The main points of the report were also covered extensively in the British press. Significantly, only days before the report was publicized in the press, the TUC's warning against sabotage by the British CP had been fully reported. Anti-Communism was beginning to run high, with the *Daily Herald*'s editor warning:

> Today our trade unionism is challenged by an enemy much more subtle than the reactionary 'boss' and every bit as vicious.
> The Communist wants to break the power of the trade union. He wants to smash the Labour Government and the whole democratic system under which our people are free to think, vote and read according to their instinct and conscience. He wants to turn Britain into a police state where no citizen dare speak his mind. The British Communist wants to make all his countrymen the helpless and blindly obedient vassals of a foreign power.[144]

It seems reasonable to suggest that the Colonial Office intended to draw (or at least hoped to profit from) an implicit parallel in the minds of the British soft Left and moderate trade unionists between the tactics of the British CP and those of the MCP. Once they had grasped the analogy, they would accordingly be more favourably disposed to the efforts of the Malayan government to put down MCP terrorism, recognizing that government's plight as (in large measure) their own.

All these mechanisms to influence British opinion were established early in the Emergency. They were not, however, simply a temporary expedient to be abandoned when opinion became quiescent. A constant check on British (and international) opinion was maintained as the Emergency lengthened. Indeed, opinion in British Communist circles showed no signs of quiescence: the longer the Emergency lasted, the more persuasive their case appeared that the enemy in Malaya was not a mere handful of 'bandits' but a substantial nationalist movement, enjoying wide popular support.[145] Thus the *Daily Worker* maintained its barrage of criticism of the government's conduct of the Emergency, and in 1950, with the outbreak of the Korean War, was able to attack Attlee's South East Asian policy on two fronts.

The year 1950 was a climactic one. Concern about opinion in Britain – thought to be showing signs of growing restiveness about Malaya – was one reason prompting the establishment of the Cabinet Malaya Committee. In the Colonial Office there was some anxiety that propaganda on Malaya was not producing the desired results. We have already seen that in 1950 there was considerable inter-departmental and ministerial debate over the extent to which the international Communist links of the MCP could be played up, and on the most appropriate nomenclature for the insurgents. In addition, the TUC appeared less co-operative in spreading government propaganda than it had been in 1948. The Colonial Office was disappointed, for example, by the TUC's response to the material it was sent on Malaya's Anti-Bandit Month.[146] However, rather than tackle the TUC directly, the CO's Information Department decided on a new tack, one which was also one of the IRD's main *modi operandi* within Britain: the sending of briefing notes to MPs on selected contentious questions about the Emergency. These model answers would enable them to rebut Communist, or fellow-travelling, hecklers more authoritatively at public meetings.

The answers prepared provide a useful index of the issues which the Colonial Office perceived as the government's most vulnerable points. The first anticipated question was 'Are the Communist bandits leading a national liberation movement?' The model answer reworked familiar territory – much of it simply a verbatim extract from the agreed propaganda line of December 1949. The main points, then, were that over 96 per cent of the MCP were 'alien Chinese who consequently care little for Malayan unity or independence', and that their violence was 'of a most morbid type, consisting of intimidation, extortion and murder', while their aims, doctrines and techniques were 'implacably Stalinist'.[147]

The second question – 'In whose interests are we fighting?' – broached more difficult territory, as did questions 4 and 6: 'What is the purpose of continuing the fight in Malaya?' and 'What is the justification for our remaining in Malaya?' In other words, the Colonial Office recognized that MPs were frequently forced to justify why Britain was fighting in Malaya. However, the government had neglected the 'why we fight' theme in Malaya, as it raised the awkward issue of how far to acknowledge that the battle against Communism had strong *economic* motivations. Undoubtedly one reason why Attlee's government was so concerned about the MCP was not simply the fear of South East Asia turning Communist, but also, and more importantly, the fact that Malaya annually earned Britain more dollars than did all Britain's own exports.[148] In a very real sense the campaign against the MCP was a battle to retain the dollars earned by Malaya's rubber and tin industries. But to admit this fact openly risked playing straight into Communist hands, providing them with a tacit admission that Labour really were the old-fashioned, exploitative imperialists denounced by the *Daily Worker* and *Pravda* alike. Attlee's government therefore tended to hedge. It thereby avoided letting Communist propagandists score an easy point, but simultaneously incurred the scorn of certain influential Conservatives, such as Rab Butler, who felt that Labour ought to be more forthright in acknowledging the hard financial reasons that underlay Britain's defence of Malaya.[149] This reluctance to be entirely forthcoming about what Britain was fighting for is clearly revealed in the model answers: Britain was fighting 'in the interests of all law-abiding citizens of Malaya', 'against the predatory ambitions of international communism', and with the aim of 'guid[ing] the Federation of Malaya to responsible self-government within the Commonwealth'.[150] No reference was made, in any of the eleven answers, to less altruistic reasons for the sacrifice of British lives in Malaya. The coyness of the answers on these difficult questions suggests that the prepared responses were unlikely to convince determined anti-imperialist and Communist hecklers.

These questions and answers thus offer a telling indication of the sorest points for Attlee's government on Malaya in mid-1950. Concern about the state of public opinion in Britain is also evidenced by the extent of the briefing paper's distribution: 100 copies were dispatched to Denis Healey at Transport House, 620 to Labour Party constituency headquarters and 50 to Conservative Central Office.[151] At the same time, apprehension was growing over American ignorance about the Emergency. The immediate effect of the outbreak of war in Korea was to reduce dramatically American press coverage of the Malayan campaign. Whitehall feared that Americans might criticize Britain for not pulling her weight in Korea, and in October 1950 Shinwell warned the Malaya Committee that the American public was 'inclined to be critical' of Britain's effort in Malaya.[152] The only remedy was to ensure that Malaya did not slip from American consciousness – provided, of course, that American commentators did not dwell on 'British exploitation of the colonies', as they were sometimes wont to do.[153] In practice this meant offering inducements (such as free flights to Malaya courtesy of the RAF) to American correspondents to lure them to the colony, and greater efforts to place articles in the American press.[154]

For a variety of reasons, then, considerable importance was attached by Attlee's government to opinion in the United Kingdom and elsewhere on Malaya. The aim was not only to ensure that 'banditry' or 'terrorism' in Malaya was properly understood, but more broadly to stem Communist propaganda on the Emergency lest dissension on this issue turn into a deluge of trade union hostility to the Labour government's foreign policy. Besides undertaking 'corrective' work, Whitehall information officers also needed to ensure that Malaya simply remained news. The problem with the *Daily Worker* was that it paid too much attention of the wrong sort to Malaya, but the reverse was true of most of the mainstream press. Fleet Street's inattention to Malaya alarmed the Colonial Office at least as much as anti-imperialist attacks – increasingly so as the Emergency lengthened. Ensuring that Malaya was reported continued to be a necessity for Attlee's Conservative successors. We turn now to examine the effort both Labour and Conservative governments put into intervening in the presentation of the Emergency by the mass communications media themselves.

Government Relations with the News Media

The Malayan Emergency coincided with a period in Britain when television started to become a mass medium.[155] Yet as far as one can gather from surviving records, successive governments still attached greater importance to press coverage of the Emergency than to either the radio or television output of the BBC, or to Independent Television. Certainly the BBC's Overseas Service was regarded, as ever, as a useful branch of overseas propaganda, and it was kept fully informed by the Foreign Office of the official government line on propaganda to the Far East in general, and Malaya in particular.[156] However, the relationship between the BBC, on the one hand, and the Malayan authorities and Whitehall, on the other, was not always untroubled during the Emergency.

The BBC's Far Eastern Section broadcasts on the Emergency were criticized by Gurney. As we have seen, he charged that the BBC was 'the worst offender in creating the impression that life in Malaya . . . consists of a series of incidents'.[157] As in each Emergency that this volume examines, one of the foremost aims of those leading the counter-insurgency was that an air of 'normality' should predominate, with terrorism appearing atypical and geographically limited. In Malaya, as elsewhere, this remained a pious wish as the desire for more 'good news' ran entirely counter to conventional news values – a fact Church House knew only too well, as Higham's response to Gurney reveals:

> It is, I am afraid, only too true that not only the BBC but also the UK Press tend to direct nearly all their attention to terrorist activities in Malaya. As you will know from your experience in Palestine, this is simply because exciting incidents in the terrorist campaign are 'news', whereas ordinary peaceful development which is going on all the time is not news.
> We feel that by and large the BBC are doing their utmost to help us, but it is difficult for them to depart from their principle of producing their news broadcasts in the same way as a newspaper produces its news columns, i.e. solely on the basis of news-value.[158]

Nevertheless, Higham promised that the Colonial Office would tackle the BBC on Gurney's behalf and attempt to persuade Jacob to station a permanent correspondent in South East Asia, as both Gurney and the Regional Information Officer were advocating.[159] An approach to Ian Jacob was duly made, which he countered with a criticism of his own: the conventional complaint of broadcasters against the military in wartime, namely, that the authorities in Malaya were not releasing enough news.[160] (Already aware of this deficiency, Gurney was actually taking steps to remedy it – with the appointment of Josey to superintend the release of news on police operations, and by establishing the Joint Information and Propaganda Committee.) Although relations remained cool between local BBC staff and Radio Malaya (a government-controlled station), who regarded one another as rivals rather than partners, criticism of the BBC tailed off as the Emergency progressed. And the BBC's coverage of the Emergency in Britain itself does not appear to have come under fire in the way that British press reportage did.[161]

  Why, then, both in Westminster and Kuala Lumpur, was the press scrutinized so closely? Both the civilian and the military leaders of the campaign held a strong belief that the press, particularly local papers, played a critical role in determining the shape of the Emergency. Press reportage had an operational effect on both 'bandit' activities and civilian morale. If the press could be encouraged not to carry details of certain types of MRLA activities, such as the slashing of rubber trees, it was felt that this would reduce the likelihood of a copy-cat effect in other parts of the colony. Thus it was important, at certain times, to urge the press *not* to report terrorism.[162] At other times, the problem was perceived as not whether but *how* the press reported terrorism. It is a commonplace that the military in wartime regard the press as inimical to the smooth conduct of a campaign, and certainly the commanders of the forces in Malaya viewed the press as predisposed towards hostility, and likely to have a deleterious effect on morale, unless carefully briefed and managed by the military themselves. Successive High Commissioners and military commanders thus laboured to mould a pliant press: one which would willingly withhold information about bandit activities at certain times, but also strike the desired balance between reporting terrorism in such a way that the true nature of the 'bandits' was revealed and presenting optimistic reports of security force operations. Both the vernacular press and the world press correspondents in Malaya were expected to fulfil the duties accorded them by the military.[163]

  The history of the military's relations with the press in Malaya was not a particularly happy one. The relationship was frequently, and mutually, antagonistic. On the military's part (and that of the Malayan government as a whole), dissatisfaction was regularly voiced over press reportage of the Emergency – either that there was not enough of it, or that it gave a misleading impression. But as Alec Peterson realized in 1952, press suspicion of the authorities was partly the product of a defective propaganda set-up. It had been a tactical error to 'place the responsibility for Press releases about the Emergency in the hands of a department which was known to be engaged in operational propaganda'.[164]

Despite the steps taken early in the Emergency to lure journalists to Malaya, and to ensure 'responsible' reportage, in June 1950 Gurney still felt that the British press was 'not doing enough to present to the people at home a true picture of the work being done in Malaya by the Government and security forces'.[165] In the authorities' eyes, the problem was not so much that the UK press represented terrorism in too favourable a light, as that it was apt to be critical of the counter-insurgency campaign, and pessimistic in its estimations of how soon the Emergency would end. Journalistic pessimism threw the unerring optimism of the military in Malaya into sharp relief. As the Emergency lengthened, the upbeat tenor of military press briefings in Malaya made the commanders of the security forces look either deluded, if they genuinely thought the bandits would soon be eliminated, or deceitful, if they did not.[166] Matters were worsened by the lack of aptitude of a string of military commanders for public relations work. Boucher, the first General Officer Commanding in Malaya, was debarred by Gurney from attending press conferences in early 1949, after a string of gaffes.[167] As we have already seen, Briggs also ran into trouble for his remarks at press briefings, which went further than Boucher's in insisting Malaya was on a 'war footing' and that Communist 'banditry' in Malaya was the local manifestation of an international Communist campaign.[168]

In mishandling the press, however, Templer outdid both Boucher and Briggs. As his (by no means hostile) biographer has remarked, in his personal relations with the press Templer was 'singularly unsuccessful'.[169] He conceived of the press as an ancillary weapon in the military campaign, and treated correspondents with the brusqueness – if not outright rudeness – that characterized his dealings with military subordinates:

> He did his best with senior responsible visiting journalists: the Joe Alsops, Vernon Bartletts, or Chester Wilmots. With them he was able to establish a rapport; with the local pressmen he was always uneasy, often hostile. Essentially he did not like or trust journalists, and in Malaya, despite his good intentions (such as the proposed monthly background briefing for editors and foreign correspondents), he found it difficult to keep his temper with them. He would not permit any press censorship in Malaya, but if a newspaper printed something he didn't like he would send for the editor and tell him so, in no uncertain terms. He took the view that the press ought to be supporting his – and the Government's – objectives and that they should subordinate to these objectives, in the national interest, their irreverence or sensationalism, and even their desire for scoops. When they did not do so, he was furious.[170]

Much of this refers particularly to the local press. However, as has been seen in the case of Templer's relationship with *The Times*'s correspondent, Louis Heren, he was not above insisting – with equal vehemence – that the British press also get on side, and that, to this end, the Colonial Office tackle Fleet Street editors on his behalf. There was actually no need for Templer to insist that the Colonial Office keep the press in check at its end. For some months before Templer's appointment as supremo in Malaya, Blackburne and the Colonial Office Information Services Department had been keeping a watchful eye on British press coverage of the Emergency, and attempting to correct 'any serious errors of fact' that arose.[171] However, the Colonial Office was not prepared to break the longstanding tradition of leaving *opinion* free from governmental regulation, and bridled at Templer's exhortations that it should.

Templer's attitude to the press very much prefigured that of Sir John Harding (Governor of Cyprus between 1955 and 1957). Both were irked by press criticism of their leadership of the campaign against terrorism, and sought drastic powers which would compel the press to report events more favourably. Cloake's assertion that Templer never permitted 'any press censorship' in Malaya thus requires some qualification. Malaya's Emergency Regulations allowed very stringent measures to be taken against editors of the local press who the administration thought were lending comfort to the Communists. Templer, however, was discontented with this provision for remedial action against errant editors. In June 1952 he sought powers to oblige the press to carry government announcements on the counter-insurgency campaign verbatim – a measure which had been tried in Palestine. As the Colonial Office's T.C. Jerrom remarked, such a move was 'just the sort of thing which would be likely to annoy the Press'.[172] His colleagues agreed, and during Templer's visit to London that month, Sir Thomas Lloyd did his best to dissuade the High Commissioner from assuming such powers of compulsion over the press. Templer was only bought off with the agreement of the Colonial Secretary, Oliver Lyttelton, that he could at least extend the existing Emergency Regulations to cover the Singapore press.[173]

Thus the press came under considerable scrutiny, and criticism, during the Emergency. The local press was censured for sensationalism and playing up bandit successes, which was thought to lower morale. On assuming the office of Colonial Secretary in November 1951, Lyttelton quickly reached the opinion that: 'Much of the journalism in Malaya is in the inferential or deductive manner, and there is in my experience no Press which is more difficult to handle, more unpredictable in its comments, or more speculative in its guesses.'[174] Similarly British correspondents were reprimanded for either ignoring the Emergency or reporting it in too pessimistic, or irresponsible, a vein. But how fair was this criticism? Was Templer simply over-reacting because his lack of skill at handling the press had the unfortunate corollary of ensuring that his press conference tantrums were reported in full? Is it possible that the relative lack of coverage of the Emergency resulted in undue anxiety over what scant reportage there was of MCP terrorism and security force operations against it?[175]

In examining the extent of dissent in the British press, the most obvious starting point is to investigate how far the British press reproduced the government's favoured terminology and interpretation of terrorism.

What immediately becomes apparent is the heterodoxy of language. British newspaper correspondents certainly wrote of 'bandits' in Malaya, but gave them many other names besides. In the first month of the Emergency alone, the *Daily Herald* had variously described the armed members of the MCP as 'gangsters', a 'terror gang', 'Chinese gangsters', 'terrorist killer squads' and 'guerrillas'.[176] And although the press frequently did use the officially preferred designation of 'bandit', journalists were not universally in favour of its application, particularly as the Emergency wore on. Some felt (as the Foreign Office came to) that calling the MCP 'bandits' betokened a lack of seriousness about the Emergency. In the first of a series of widely read articles on the Emergency in the *Daily Telegraph*, Malcolm Muggeridge (then its deputy editor) railed against the ludicrous

> efforts of the authorities to write down this conspiracy by calling it an 'Emergency' and its adherents 'bandits'.
> The first term suggests a temporary disturbance rather than a revolt in rapid process of turning into a civil war. The other, with its Robin Hood connotation, was chosen to get over the difficulty of calling the terrorists Chinese Communists (which they are) when their opposite numbers in China had been recognised by Britain . . .[177]

The *Daily Mail* was similarly critical of the refusal to link the Malayan 'bandits' with Mao's Chinese Communists. Journalists who disparaged the official terminology, and the reluctance to proclaim an international Communist conspiracy which underlay it, did so because they felt that those in authority underestimated the enemy.[178] Thus, despite their criticisms, they were certainly not going to berate the government for heavy-handed counter-insurgency tactics, nor did they ever contest the essence of the government's interpretation of the MCP: that it was a sectional rather than a national movement. Whatever certain newspapers said against the term 'bandit', they certainly regarded it as preferable to the language employed by the *Daily Worker* – a publication which the *Daily Mail* called 'the only Russian newspaper printed in English': 'In the perverted language of that Red Sheet the bandits who are murdering British settlers and soldiers in Malaya are "fighters for freedom", whereas the 17 men shot down in a recent ambush are called "quislings".'[179]

All sections of the press tended to place greater stress on the Communism of the insurgents than did the official propaganda line – at least as it was formulated in the earlier phase of the Emergency. But again, some qualification is required. Although the propaganda guidelines initially prescribed an underemphasis on the Communism of the enemy, the reasons (it will be recalled) were largely domestic: the Malayan government did not want Communism to appear a powerful, and thus attractive, bandwagon. However, Westminster and Kuala Lumpur did not deny that the bandits were Communists, even if they baulked at suggesting CCP involvement in the MCP insurrection. There was never any attempt to insist that the 'bandits' were apolitical (even if that appelation suggested as much). Indeed, much of the early Colonial Office propaganda for the trade unions on the Emergency *relied* on instilling an understanding that the enemy in Malaya were Communist.

Where certain correspondents did exceed the official line was in repeatedly asserting that external aid (namely from China) was being received by MCP. Here again, Louis Heren was especially vexatious, periodically reporting that the MCP was receiving Chinese reinforcements. In September 1951, he asserted that 'the closeness of the liaison between Communists in Malaya and the Chinese Government will probably never be known, but the stories of surrendered men prove that some kind of organisation does exist'.[180] Gurney was so concerned by the 'mischievous and dangerous' article that he sent a note to all local press editors asking them to refrain from reproducing Heren's report, which if repeated would have 'an encouraging effect on bandit morale'.[181] When, the following June, Heren relayed Peking Radio's claim that China was giving 'sympathy and aid' to the people of Malaya, his report was subjected to rigorous investigation, and was used by the Foreign Office to bolster its view that the government ought now to publicize China's links with the MCP.[182]

There were, then, points of dissent. Although many British newspapers referred to events in Malaya as a 'war', they did not regard themselves as thereby obligated to support government policy. When Labour was in power, sections of the right-wing press found ample room for criticism of Attlee's handling of the Emergency. The decision to recognize the PRC attracted particular condemnation. Echoing the sentiments of planters and tin miners in Malaya, the *Daily Mail*, for example, was scathing about the injurious effect on morale in Malaya of the recognition of Communist China, and accused (as Muggeridge later would) Attlee's administration of having to deny any connection between the PRC and banditry in Malaya in order to avoid offending the newly recognized state.[183]

For their part, the more liberal and left-wing press also found much to criticize. When Churchill won the General Election in October 1951, the *Herald* and *Manchester Guardian* feared that political progress in Malaya, set in motion by Briggs and Gurney, would be relegated to the back burner by Churchill's personal appointee to the vacant post of High Commissioner, General Templer. The new Colonial Secretary, Lyttelton, seemed to confirm such fears on his visit to Malaya in November 1951, when he began his tour with the remark that the military campaign against the bandits had first priority.[184] Templer's methods were not universally praised in the British press. His imposition of collective fines on villages in 'black areas' which refused to pass information on 'bandit' activities to the authorities was regarded with distaste by the Labour Party, and newspapers including the *Daily Herald*, the *Observer* and, while Heren was stationed in Singapore, *The Times*.[185] Similarly, the burning down of villages which Templer felt were harbouring or aiding MRLA terrorists, and whose inhabitants refused to co-operate with the security forces, was greeted with protest.[186]

Broader aspects of the counter-insurgency campaign, and not merely collective punishment measures, were also attacked by the more left-wing press. Both the *Manchester Guardian* and the *New Statesman and Nation* published letters and articles by Victor Purcell (before and after the publication in 1954 of his scathing indictment of Templer, *Malaya: Communist or Free?*) suggesting that, under Templer, the campaign against the MCP had become something of an anti-Chinese pogrom. Purcell argued that the 'hearts and minds' measures directed at Chinese 'squatters' had fuelled racial antagonism. Moves such as the wholesale resettlement and mass detentions of rural Chinese had fuelled the mistrust with which expatriates and the Malayan authorities viewed *all* Malayan Chinese: a 'fashionable barbarism' had set in.[187] The *Manchester Guardian* was correspondingly critical of the inhumanity of aspects of the security forces' behaviour towards captured, or suspected, terrorists; for example, alarm was voiced when (what appeared to be) a practice of displaying dead terrorists' bodies outside rural police posts came to light in August 1952.[188] In the same year the *Daily Mirror* campaigned against the practice among the Army in Malaya of drawing up 'league tables' of bandit 'kills'.[189]

However, if there was dissent over the conduct of the counter-insurgency campaign, it is important to realize its limits. Press divergence from Whitehall's official propaganda line was actually remarkably limited when one considers the nature of the battle against the MCP, and the far greater visibility of the security forces as compared to their opponents. Despite Templer's maladroitness with the press, he gradually won many admirers. With hindsight Templer himself recognized what his critics during the Emergency had known all along: that the press was uncommonly generous towards him. We have already encountered Templer's *ex post facto* opinion that all but the 'extreme left wing papers' reported the Emergency well. In fact, as Victor Purcell pointed out in 1954, it was *The Times*, not the radical press, which was the biggest thorn in Templer's side, and, Heren apart, there was 'a widespread agreement to represent Templer's regime in Malaya as an outstanding success and the war against the Communist Terrorists as as good as won'.[190]

On almost all Whitehall's main points of concern, Fleet Street showed little sign of a serious revolt against the government, or in favour of an immediate abandonment of Malaya. For example, the information departments of the Foreign and Colonial Offices worried that the length of the campaign would encourage disaffection among the British public, and possibly even lead them to believe that, as the *Daily Worker* urged, operations against mere bandits could not conceivably be so protracted.[191] Thus they were concerned to stress that the impenetrable nature of the jungle, rather than an enemy with widespread popular support, prolonged the 'mopping up' of the MCP; Malaya's jungle interior had to be made real to those outside the territory. This 'seeing is believing' theme was one which visual media (such as films and newsreels) were particularly suited to conveying. British press correspondents in Kuala Lumpur and Singapore also echoed the theme, warning readers that, had they only seen the jungle for themselves, they would know better than to question the duration of the Emergency. In this respect, Major Arthur Campbell's widely read, semi-fictional account of the Suffolk Regiment's Malayan tour, *Jungle Green* – which came complete with a dust-jacket endorsement of its authenticity from Templer himself – must have gratified Whitehall public relations officers with its visceral evocation of conditions in the jungle.[192]

Similarly, Whitehall's fears that the uneven nature of the encounter between the heavily armed security forces and the minimally armed Malayan terrorists might result in press hostility were unfounded. For example, some behind-the-scenes agonizing occurred before the introduction of heavy bombers to the Malayan campaign. These would be used (among other purposes) to drop 1,000 lb – and, later, 4,000 lb – bombs on suspected terrorist hide-outs.[193] Whatever their functional value, though, as Colonial Under-Secretary of State J.J. Paskin remarked at a Chiefs of Staff meeting in February 1950:

> The political objection to heavy bombers being sent was that not only would Russian propaganda make out that the employment of heavy bombers was inhuman but also public opinion in this country might consider that the sending of these bombers implied that the situation had seriously deteriorated.[194]

Moreover, the arrival of Lincoln bombers might suggest that unjustifiably severe methods were being employed against mere 'bandits'. As the IRD's assistant head, Watson, minuted, 'bombing villages, as opposed to troops, and especially merely suspect villages, produces terrible reactions among liberals etc. everywhere'.[195] And in Foreign Office eyes, the presentational problem posed by the use of the heavy bombers provided a further incentive for openly acknowledging the 'bandits' as Communists – harsh treatment of openly avowed Communists being presumably less likely to stir liberal consciences.[196] Thus, prior to the amendment of the propaganda line (in July 1950), Gurney decided to give *no* publicity in Britain to the bombers' presence in Malaya. For its part, the Foreign Office hoped to play down any leaks, and by a new sleight of hand, to describe the planes as 'medium' (rather than heavy) bombers. The lack of protest in the British press, throughout the Emergency, over the use of Lincolns might suggest that the down-playing strategy worked. Alternatively, one might hypothesize that few newspapers felt any qualms about the dropping of 1,000 lb (or 4,000 lb) bombs on 'bandits' whom they had never scrupled to call 'Communist', even if Whitehall had.

Dissent in the British press was actually remarkably muted for an Emergency which lasted so long, and which was undoubtedly not always a 'clean fight' – on either side. The clearest illustration of how far consensus prevailed, and how few friends the *Daily Worker* had in Fleet Street, relates to a series of shocking photographs that paper published in April and May 1952. These photographs were unquestionably the most horrifying visual images thrown up by the Emergency. The first depicted a smiling British marine holding up the severed head of a Chinese insurgent.[197] Panic ensued in Whitehall at the prospect of a liberal outcry, and the 'propaganda handle to our opponents' which such material provided.[198] The initial assumption, however, was that these must be fakes, designed to serve the needs of Communist propaganda.[199] However, investigations by the Admiralty revealed that such photographs had indeed been taken, and furthermore that the practice of cutting off CTs' heads was fully sanctioned by the military.[200] Indeed, General Templer, in the heat of this controversy, argued that decapitation was an essential last resort in identifying enemy personnel killed in combat, whatever propaganda coups this might hand to Britain's opponents, internal or external.[201] But for all the Cabinet's and Colonial Office's discussions on how best to minimize the damage, no other British newspaper replicated the photographs, or even commented adversely on the practice of severing heads.[202] (Some papers indeed had argued earlier in the campaign that *more* use ought to be made of head-hunting Dyak trackers.) Thus the expected storm of public protest never arose.

What makes the press's neglect of the *Daily Worker*'s photographs all the more significant is that striking images of the conflict in Malaya were so rare. The fact that the most arresting image of the Emergency depicts *British* methods, and not terrorist atrocities, serves to suggest that the MCP either lacked the ability to generate shocking images of their struggle in Malaya, or was denied publicity for its more terrifying activities. Shortly after the appearance of the *Daily Worker*'s photographs an article in the *Daily Telegraph* stated that there had been a ban on publicizing terrorist atrocities in official reports. In the wake of the decision to outlaw decapitation, this practice was now being reconsidered: 'there have been shocking cases in which British soldiers killed in action have been needlessly and hideously disfigured by the terrorists. Men, women and children have been slashed to death, and almost every day an emergency communiqué gives the bare outline of these murders.'[203] Some commentators, such as Purcell, concluded that 'by the standards of the guerrillas of the Peninsular and Boer Wars and the Maquis in France, the Malayan bandits were very mild fellows indeed'.[204] But it does seem that the MCP did indeed mutilate some of their victims – Blackburne's private diary of his trip to Malaya testifies to this – and that, unlike similar mutilations carried out by Mau Mau, such acts were not used to vilify the MCP. Presumably the reason was governmental reluctance to trade in such images – a reticence which, as we shall see, initially affected government propaganda on Mau Mau. Despite the absence of horrific images of MCP misdeeds, however, the 'bandits' remained castigated as terrorists. On the whole, the British press never wavered in its belief (shared by, or perhaps derived from, the government) that the MCP was no nationalist movement, and that any measures were justified against such an enemy.

The Role of Film and Newsreel

As we have seen, film was regarded as a key tool of the counter-insurgency campaign within Malaya. But the role of film in the Emergency was not restricted to the Tarzanesque film-strip hero who encouraged 'anti-bandit' sentiment among rural Malayan audiences. Film also performed important functions beyond Malaya, particularly with regard to British and American audiences. Most crucially, film made an invisible campaign perceptible. Operations which were hidden by their very nature, and frequently under-reported in the British press, were given a more palpable form through the medium of film. During the Emergency British cinema-goers were provided with one feature film set in Malaya (*The Planter's Wife*), one long documentary (*Operation Malaya*), several Malayan Film Unit (MFU) shorts, and sporadic newsreel stories on the jungle war. None of these, other than the MFU shorts, were *direct* celluloid offerings of the British or Malayan government. However, all the filmic treatments of the Emergency were touched by the colonial authorities in Britain, Malaya (or both) in some way.

The lengthiest filmic treatment of the Emergency was Ken Annakin's feature, *The Planter's Wife*, released in September 1952. Purporting to be an authentic (albeit fictionalized) account of the planters' life in Malaya, the locations were in fact shot in Ceylon, while the actors never left Pinewood Studios.[205] The film certainly made no attempt to conceal whose side it was on: the opening frames provide a dedication to the planters of Malaya, 'where only the jungle is neutral and where the planters are daily defending their rubber trees with their lives'. The plot contained two parallel sources of dramatic tension: the efforts of the planter, Jim Fraser, to protect his beloved rubber trees from destruction at the bandits' hands, and his wife's attempts to save their marriage from an imminent collapse, precipitated by Jim's insistence that she return to the safety of

England with their young son. Annakin went to some lengths to show conditions in Malaya: the bandits slashing rubber trees on the heavily fortified estates, and extorting food and protection from the terrorized workforce; and the planters living in a state of permanent fear and vigilance (though still managing to enjoy a few stengahs in the club). The ending, however, was resolutely optimistic, the bandits having been defeated during a shoot-out at the Frasers' plantation, and the marriage salvaged.

The peculiarity of this morale-raising tribute to Malaya's planters was that it never really explained what the conflict was about, to the extent of ignoring the bandits' political orientation altogether. The avoidance of any mention that the 'bandits' were Communists was all the more surprising given that the film had one eye firmly fixed on the American market, as evidenced by the choice of an American star, Claudette Colbert, for the eponymous role.[206] This piece of strategic casting, together with producer John Stafford's remarks (in a Rank publicity release[207]) that he hoped the picture would 'help make the American people as a whole more aware of the part Britain is playing against Communism in the Far East', suggests a striking coincidence of aim between the film-makers and government propaganda strategists. At the time *The Planter's Wife* was under production, the latter were making concerted attempts to encourage more American reporters to visit Malaya, and were also commissioning articles on the Emergency for the US press.

Press reports from 1951 suggest that there was substantial governmental involvement in the film. The *Daily Worker* reported that the National Film Finance Corporation (the state film bank) had put up considerable backing for the film.[208] The *Daily Mirror* related, in May 1951, that both Jim Griffiths and Malcolm MacDonald were giving a new film about the 'forgotten women who run homes in conditions of constant terror' their 'fullest co-operation': this because 'too many people at home and abroad tend to forget the war we are fighting in Malaya'.[209] One sure sign that the film met with the approbation of Churchill's administration is that in June 1952, while Templer was in London, he agreed that a copy of the film should be sent to Malaya for him to view and then record a prologue to it.[210]

However, with its somewhat unfortunate implication that the Malayan Emergency was essentially a battle to safeguard a vital raw material – rubber – for the West, *The Planter's Wife* ran the risk of antagonizing anti-colonial *American* audiences.[211] And in Britain, the omission of political context met a puzzled, and generally hostile, response. As the *Daily Express*'s Leonard Mosely put it: '*The Planter's Wife* is the sort of film you make after the producer has instructed the director: "Give me an exciting picture about the war in Malaya but keep politics out of it" . . . rather like telling the story of Adam and Eve without the serpent'.[212]

In fact, with the exception of the *Daily Herald*'s reviewer (who felt the film was 'a fine and merited tribute to the courageous spirit most of us like to think is typically British'[213]), no British press film critic gave the film unqualified praise. The *Daily Worker* gloated that *The Planter's Wife* was 'the most viciously dishonest war propaganda film ever made in Britain', though, at the same time, the film offered triumphant evidence that imperialist apologists could 'offer no more high-minded justification of their determination to stay [in Malaya] than the plea that plundering Malaya's natural resources is "earning dollars"'.[214]

The pattern of official encouragement of filmic treatment of the Emergency (albeit stopping short of financial assistance) was repeated with David Macdonald's documentary film *Operation Malaya*. In 1952, Macdonald approached the Colonial Office in search of funds for his latest venture: a film which would do for the Malayan Emergency what his *Desert Victory* had done for the Desert Rats' war against Rommel in North Africa. While Templer welcomed the proposal, he refused to finance it on the grounds that he understood it to be a commercial venture.[215] Macdonald was, however, given every assistance by the Malayan authorities in producing the film, which was released in 1953, and the credits acknowledge grateful assistance to the Police and Armed Forces of Malaya. Templer himself featured in the film, which served as a panegyric to his achievements.

It is easy to appreciate the propaganda value of the film to Templer and the British government. Documentary was an ideal medium for showing the nature of the terrain in Malaya, and thus for illuminating why operations in the colony were so protracted. In *Operation Malaya* the jungle, more than once, was described as an 'impenetrable canopy'. But additionally, several other aspects of the Emergency were illuminated, in a far from impartial fashion. The New Villages, for example, were featured as safe havens where Chinese peasants could not 'be contaminated by the ideologies the terrorists represent'. Most importantly, *Operation Malaya* gave faces to those whom the narrator called the 'unseen enemy who [are] not prepared to stand and fight, only to murder and run'. The audience was thus able to view the Communist terrorists at work: terrorizing villagers, shooting suspected informers, laying ambushes for British troops and opening fire on the unsuspecting patrol. Yet these scenes of terrorism in action were also the film's greatest weakness, in that they detracted from the sense of documentary realism – as contemporary critics hastened to point out.[216] *Operation Malaya* took Grierson's dictum that documentary was 'the creative treatment of actuality' a little too far. It did not require a particularly canny viewer to realize that terrorism could not be filmed as it took place, in the way *Operation Malaya* purported to show. What had been billed in the promotional publicity as exciting shots of jungle warfare were in fact reconstructions.

In many respects, the newsreel treatment of the Emergency bore considerable resemblance to *Operation Malaya*. As with newspaper editors, newsreel companies faced criticism that they were not doing enough to bring the conflict in Malaya to British audiences. In October 1950, Air Commodore Harvey (a Conservative backbencher) asked the Minister of Defence, Emanuel Shinwell, whether he realized that 'many pictures and newsreels are to be seen showing the Americans fighting gallantly in Korea and very little of the British Forces fighting a long and gallant battle in Malaya'.[217] Such criticisms were fairly routine from disgruntled Conservatives, but there was real substance to Harvey's complaint. In 1948, only two of the newsreel companies released *any* story relating to the Emergency.[218] Matters improved slightly in 1949, with all four companies (British Gaumont, Universal, British Movietone and Pathé) issuing at least one item on Malaya. Bearing in mind, however, how short newsreel stories often were, this still does not amount to any appreciable coverage of a conflict in which thousands of members of the British forces were now involved.

In 1949 there was, though, a significant development in terms of newsreel coverage of the Emergency: the MFU began to supply footage, shot by its own cameramen, to the newsreel companies. Thereafter, throughout the Emergency, virtually all the newsreel stories about Malaya viewed by British cinema audiences actually originated from the same source: the MFU.[219] As the MFU's output grew (having received substantial inputs of both finance and enthusiasm under Hugh Greene's leadership), so did the volume of stories on the Emergency carried by the newsreel companies. Thus the MFU's distribution of raw footage ensured that images of the Malayan Emergency reached British screens. Had it not done so, it is difficult to envisage that Malaya would have received very much attention at all from the newsreel companies. The expense of stationing a camera crew in Malaya over such a long period would have been prohibitive. And given the frequent reluctance of the Emergency's military commanders to allow journalists near the scene of operations, it is surely questionable whether they would have co-operated with commercial cameramen in the way that they clearly did with the MFU.

The role of the MFU was such, then, that one cannot regard the newsreels as being entirely independent purveyors of images and news stories about the Emergency. The newsreel companies really functioned as a covert branch of official propaganda, in that audiences were unaware of the original source of the film material they viewed. The companies were naturally free to edit the MFU footage they received and to dub a soundtrack in their own house-style. Accordingly, the companies did not release identical stories on the Emergency, but the stories necessarily bore a heavy resemblance to one another, and tended to be issued around the same dates. A comparison of the MFU 'dope sheets' (the MFU's own written commentary on the footage it sent out, some of them still preserved in the Pathé archive) with the stories assembled by the commercial companies reveals a high degree of correlation. The dope sheets also indicate why film was regarded as such a crucial propaganda medium, with one commentary explaining:

> No words ... can describe the nightmare conditions but the pictures you are about to see, taken by a MFU cameraman, who accompanied the patrol, dramatically portray the hazardous task which faced these men, showing their fortitude in an attempt to contact a terrorist gang and in their fight against almost impenetrable jungle ...
>
> This will perhaps serve as a photographic monument to the courage and fortitude of the men whose task it is to bring the terrorists into the hands of law and order for Malaya and for the world.[220]

As the foregoing example might imply, the majority of newsreel stories featured British forces on operations in the jungle. The newsreels thus reinforced the government's 'seeing is believing' theme. Filmic images revealed the nature of the jungle: the waist-high swamps and swathes of dense foliage which made progress so slow. The soundtrack further reinforced the visual message. As one Movietone commentary ran, this was 'largely a battle of hide and seek in the forest, for throughout the Peninsula the jungle affords ideal concealment for the murderous gangs now at work in Malaya'; thus the Gurkhas faced an 'extraordinarily difficult task of rounding up the Reds'.[221] The concluding statement – 'It seems certain that the battle of Malaya is bound to be a long-drawn-out affair' – was exactly the conclusion which the British government hoped those familiar with Malaya's terrain would draw.[222]

Despite the inadequacy of words to describe the Malayan conditions, in longer stories the commentaries often became unusually evocative. For example, a Pathé story from June 1950 told viewers that 'the very jungle is on the bandits' side ... the thick undergrowth, the lallang grass that cuts like a knife, damp oppressive heat that saps a man's strength and an enemy who can go a hundred miles without breaking cover'.[223] In this conflict neither the jungle nor the newsreels were neutral, as the commentators' parting shots frequently made clear: 'It's a tough job our boys tackle',[224] 'Gallant men of Malaya – we salute you!'[225] or 'the new generation of jungle warriors earns the admiration of a nation'.[226]

Stories also often highlighted the importance of new military technology, particularly aircraft, including the Lincoln bomber, whose introduction to Malaya had initially caused colonial officials such anxiety.[227] Newsreel audiences saw planters learning how to use the latest American carbines, their targets consisting of human-shaped cardboard cut-outs kitted out in MCP's distinctive green beret with red star insignia![228] In contrast, the newsreels also depicted the 'native trackers': the Dyak head-hunters whose head-severing prowess was so starkly revealed by the *Daily Worker*. The newsreels, however, glossed over the head-hunting skills of the 'natives' in favour of their skill at tracking terrorists.[229] Furthermore, newsreel stories also managed, intermittently, to reveal the terrorists themselves to British audiences, although the problems David Macdonald experienced in filming terrorism were also experienced by the MFU cameramen. Not surprisingly, then, the viewer never encountered Malayan terrorists in action, but occasionally saw CTs who had either surrendered or been wounded (if not killed) in the course of operations.

To sum up, the newsreels provided an unerringly optimistic, patriotic account of the Emergency. A complex political situation was reduced to the level of British troops stamping out 'Reds' and bringing lawlessness under control. Each company insisted, along with Movietone, that 'the supreme value of Malaya as a dollar earning country makes it essential that effective steps against the terrorists should be taken';[230] nor was the wisdom of Templer's methods ever doubted.[231] Receiving both raw footage and guidance as to its presentation from the MFU, the newsreel companies proved a remarkably pliant weapon in the official propaganda campaign on the Emergency.

Conclusion

As we have seen, from as early as 1956 the contribution of propaganda to the success of the counter-insurgency in Malaya was acknowledged. Less well documented has been the importance attached by the governments in London and Kuala Lumpur to propaganda *beyond* the Federation. Governmental efforts to ensure that the Emergency was properly understood by the British (and to a lesser extent, American) public were more extensive than one might have expected, and some of this work was of a rather covert nature, such as the IRD's involvement in passing anti-Communist material to the TUC. What the case study reveals is not only the importance attached to language and terminology, but also the extent to which a wide variety of factors, some only tangentially related to the terrorist campaign itself, affect how terrorism is presented. As has been demonstrated, conditions in China (and the British government's recognition of China), the hope of creating tensions between Soviet and Asian Communist parties, and the Attlee administration's problems with Communists at home all shaped the manner in which terrorism was presented, and the extent to which it appeared to British governments necessary to mediate the perception of Communist terrorism. With hindsight, successive British governments appear rather over-sensitive to criticism of the counter-insurgency. However, it is surely the complexity of the aims which underlay the determination to get the presentation of terrorism right, rather than the extent of dissent on Malaya in Britain, that explains such sensitivity.

Notes

1   G. Greene, *Ways of Escape* (Penguin Books, London, 1980), p. 110. Greene, who spent three months reporting the Emergency for *Life* in 1951, highlighted the lack of dramatic tension in Malaya, writing that 'the war (to call it by the right name) showed no sign of ever reaching a climax. While the whole world became excited over whether war was on or off in Korea, the forgotten war in Malaya dragged on.'

2   T. Royle, *War Report* (Grafton Books, London, 1987), p. 254.

3   On the press coverage of the Korean War, see P. Knightley, *The First Casualty. From the Crimea to the Falklands: The War Correspondent as Hero, Propagandist, and Myth Maker* (Pan Books, London, 1989), ch. 14, and Royle, *War Report*, ch. 7.

4   Greene, *Ways of Escape*, p. 110.

5   L. Heren, *Growing Up on 'The Times'* (Hamish Hamilton, London, 1978), p. 144.

6   For further background see Darwin, *Britain and Decolonisation*, ch. 3.

7   Overseas Planning Committee, 'Malaya in Home and Overseas Publicity: Aims and Objectives', paper no. 556, 6/12/44; CO 875/20/2.

8   Stubbs, *Hearts and Minds*, p. 12.

9   The term 'squatters' referred to those Chinese Malayans who, during the Japanese occupation, had left the towns and sought refuge in the fringes of the jungle, where they existed by subsistence farming; N. Barber, *The War of the Running Dogs: How Malaya Defeated the Communist Guerrillas 1948–60* (Fontana, London, 1971), p. 16.

10   Anthony Short, *The Communist Insurrection in Malaya 1948–1960* (Frederick Muller, London, 1975), pp. 49–50.

11   'Internal Security in Malaya', by J. Dalley, 14/6/48; CO 537/6006.

12   The English-language press in Malaya was active in demanding a tougher line against the MCP. In the early part of June 1948, the *Malay Mail* produced a stream of criticism of the government's weakness, and following the murder of three planters in Sungei Siput on 16 June the *Straits Times* printed a 'Govern or Get Out' editorial, urging that the local State of Emergency in that state be extended throughout Malaya; Stubbs, *Hearts and Minds*, p. 67.

13   Rejecting the orthodox interpretation that the Emergency was declared too late, Frank Furedi has recently argued that in fact the declaration was a preventive manoeuvre by the Malayan government, 'motivated by the long-term consideration of pre-empting the growth of opposition'. To this end the government fostered ethnic cleavages in Malaya which would prevent the emergence of a homogeneous nationalist movement; 'Britain's Colonial Wars: Playing the Ethnic Card', *Journal of Commonwealth and Comparative Politics*, 28 (March 1990), 70–89, p. 71. See also Furedi's 'Britain's Colonial Emergencies and the Invisible Nationalists', *Journal of Historical Sociology*, 2, iii (1989), 240–64 and, for a lengthier exposition of his thesis, *Colonial Wars and the Politics of Third World Nationalism* (I. B. Tauris, London, 1994).

14   'The Colonial Empire Today: Summary of Our Main Problems and Policies', CO International Relations Department paper, annex, May 1950; CO 537/5698.

15   This version of events was adopted in a secret report entitled 'Director of Operations Malaya, Review of the Emergency in Malaya from June 1948 to August 1957' (Kuala Lumpur, 1957), p. 3; WO 106/5990. It is also the line taken in, among many other accounts, a 28-page pamphlet by J.H. Brimmell, *A Short History of the Malayan Communist Party* (Donald Moore, Singapore, 1956). Brimmell is described on the cover as

a 'student of international communism for 10 years', who had worked for the British Embassy in Moscow (1946–48), with the Foreign Office in London (1948–51) and in the Commissioner-General's Office in Singapore (1951–3). The latter, it should be noted, was also the headquarters for the IRD's regional operation in South East Asia.

16 Furedi, 'Britain's Colonial Wars', *Journal of Commonwealth and Comparative Politics*, p. 72; see also his footnote 4, pp. 87–8.

17 'Communist Influence in Malaya', May 1948; CO 537/3755.

18 Stubbs, *Hearts and Minds*, p. 69.

19 Joint Intelligence Committee, JIC/7/49, minute by Roberts dated 17/1/49; CO 537/4762.

20 On 10 May 1950, during a session of Parliamentary Questions on Operations, Malaya, Colonel Gomme Duncan asked whether the Minister did not 'agree that the use of the term "bandits" is rather reminiscent of a comic opera show and is not applicable to an enemy organised on this scale?'; H.C. Debs, vol. 475, 10/5/50, col. 369, extract in CO 537/5977. Criticism of the term 'bandits' began to emerge very soon after the start of the Emergency: for example, a critical article in *The Economist* entitled 'What Is Wrong with Malaya?', urged that the Communists 'should be called insurgents, for they are more than a collection of bandits', and that the 'chief mistake' would be to underrate them; *The Economist*, vol. CLV, 18 (17/7/48), p. 104.

21 Brief for the Malaya Committee Meeting on 18 May 1950, FZ1017/11G; FO 371/84478. This has also been the view taken by many later commentators on the Emergency, including Noel Barber, *War of the Running Dogs*, p. 10.

22 Minute from J.D. Higham to Blackburne, November 1948; CO 537/4762.

23 Telegram from Arthur Creech Jones (Secretary of State for the Colonies) to Malcolm MacDonald (Commissioner-General for South East Asia), 19/8/48, no. 162; CO 537/5123.

24 Minute by J.B. Williams, 19/8/48; CO 537/3746.

25 W.S. Morgan (Head of Information Services Branch, CO) wrote to the COI's Mary Burke, drawing her attention to 'the question of terminology': 'We have now been advised by the Malayan Government that we should always use the term "bandits" to describe the Communist terrorists, and that we should avoid the use of any expression which will give the idea that they represent a nationalist or representative movement in rebellion against the established Government'; letter dated 18/12/48; CO 537/5123.

26 Summary of a statement by Malcolm MacDonald in the COI's fortnightly *Commonwealth Survey*, 30 Oct. 1948, no. 10; CO 537/5123.

27 On the contrary, officials in Malaya were adamant that support for the MCP was coerced. As Sir Henry Gurney (Gent's replacement as High Commissioner) wrote: 'it is universally agreed here that the support which they get here is almost wholly through intimidation and cannot by any stretch of the imagination be described as "popular". It is impossible to overstress the extent to which intimidation and extortion is practised'; Gurney to Sir T. Lloyd, 8/10/48; CO 537/3758.

28 See J.B. Williams's minute to Seel, 19/8/48; CO 537/3746, and a telegram from Gurney to Creech Jones, 7/2/50, FZ1016/8; FO 371/84477.

29 J.B. Williams to Seel, 19/8/48; CO 537/3746.

30 Gurney to T. Lloyd, 8/10/48; CO 537/3758.

31 Telegram from MacDonald to Creech Jones, 20/4/49, no. 117; CO 537/4751.

32 Telegram from Gurney to Creech Jones, 6/10/49, no. 1132, FZ15684/10140/61; FO 371/76021.

33 This was an aim which the IRD was working towards; see a minute by Ralph Murray (Head of IRD), 27/10/49, FZ15684/10140/61; FO 371/76021.

34 Letter by Paskin to M.E. Dening (Superintending Under-Secretary, FO), 17/10/49, FZ15684/10140/61; FO 371/76021.

35 Secret letter by Dening to Paskin, 28/10/49, FZ15684/10140/61; FO 371/76021. Guy Burgess's views can be found in in the same file; see his minute to Hibbert, dated 20/10/49.

36 Dening to Paskin, op. cit., FO 371/76021.

37 Minute by P.D. Coates, 22/10/49, F15684/10140/61; FO 371/76021.

38 Telegram from MacDonald to Creech Jones, 21/10/49, no. 288, F16669/1017/61; FO 371/76005.

39 Ibid.

40 Top Secret letter by J.H. Watson to O.H. Morris, 1/12/49, F17639/1071/61; FO 371/76005.

41 Secret, 'Note by the Colonial and Foreign Office. Malaya. Attitude towards Communism in Malaya and China', para. 4, F17630/1017/61; FO 371/76005.

42 Ibid., para. 6.

43 Ibid., para. 8.

44 Telegram from Creech Jones to MacDonald, 16/12/49, no. 686, transmitting the final line as agreed by the FO and CO, F17630/1017/61; FO 371/76005.

45 Ibid.

46 Letter from Gurney to Creech Jones, 12/1/50, FZ1016/6; FO 371/84477.

47 Statistics cited by Barber, *War of the Running Dogs*, p. 87.

48 Quoted in Short, *Communist Insurrection*, p. 217.

49 Barber, *War of the Running Dogs*, pp. 88–91.

50 'Publicity in Malaya', memo by R.H. Scott, 18/4/50, brief for the 1st meeting of the Malaya Committee, to be held on 19 April 1950, FZ1017/4G; FO 371/84478.

51 Ibid. Briggs's linkage of the PRC with the Malayan bandits was also discussed in the Cabinet Malaya Committee; MAL C (50), Minutes of the 1st Meeting, 19/4/50; CAB 134/497.

52 The proposal to create a Cabinet Malaya Committee was first mooted by the Minister of Defence, Emmanuel Shinwell. In a minute dated 27 March 1950 by N.D. Watson to Sir Thomas Lloyd, Shinwell's initiative is mentioned. The rationale behind the proposed committee is given as 'the public interest which [Malaya] is at present arousing'; Watson to Lloyd, CO 537/5997. Minutes of the committee are to be found in CAB 134/497. The 1st meeting of the COI's Far Eastern Publicity Committee was held on 13 March 1950; agendas, minutes and papers of the committee are in INF 12/303.

53 Brief for the 2nd meeting of the Cabinet Malaya Committee, 22/4/50, FZ1017/2G; FO 371/84478.

54 MAL. C. (50), 4th Meeting, Minutes, 8/5/50; CAB 134/497.

55 James Griffiths, *Pages from Memory* (J.M. Dent, London, 1969), pp. 97–8.

56 'Supplementary brief for the Minister of State, for the Cabinet Malaya Committee meeting on Monday 19 June', by R.H. Scott, 16/6/50, FZ1017/15G; FO 371/84478.

57 Extract from a letter from Higham to Gurney, 19/5/50; CO 537/5984.

58 Both can be found in FZ10110/30G; FO 371/84482.

59 'Secret. Note by Colonial Office and Foreign Office. MALAYA. Attitude to be adopted in publicity towards Communism in Malaya and China', op. cit., p. 1; FO 371/84482.

60 Extracts from minutes of the Joint Information and Propaganda Committee; CO 1022/482/48.

61 'The Situation in the Federation of Malaya from the Point of View of the Director of Operations', May 1951; CO 537/7263.

62 Short, *Communist Insurrection*, p. 305.

63 Memo from the Secretary for Defence, 'Official Designation of Communist Forces', no. 15/17/52, 20 May 1952; CO 1022/48.

64 Barber, *War of the Running Dogs*, p. 10.

65 L.W. Pye, *Guerrilla Communism in Malaya: Its Social and Political Meaning* (Princeton University Press, Princeton, N.J., 1956), p. 88.

66 Short, *Communist Insurrection*, ch. 12, pp. 309–21.

67 Cloake, *Templer*, p. 256.

68 Telegram from Vincent del Tufo (Officer Administering the Government) to Oliver Lyttelton (Secretary of State for the Colonies), 17/12/51, no. 105, FZ1018/1; FO 371/101223.

69 Monthly Political Intelligence Report, no. 75, 15 January–15 February, FZ1018/20; FO 371/101223.

70 *The Times*, 'Malayan Emergency II: Discontents in a Plural Society' (12/8/52), p. 5.

71 See Heren, *Growing Up on 'The Times'*, p. 150 and Julian Paget, *Counter-insurgency Campaigning* (Faber and Faber, London, 1967), p. 62. Purcell, Barber and Templer's biographer, John Cloake (himself an FO official at the time of the Emergency), all give late 1952 as the date of discovery; see Cloake, *Templer*, pp. 254–5.

72 Cloake states that the Malayan government delayed publication so that the Communists would not be able to work out how Special Branch had got hold of the document; *Templer*, p. 292.

73 See *Daily Telegraph* (28/10/52), 'Terrorists Limit Malaya Targets', by Denis Warner. Warner quoted briefly from the captured document: '"We are not losing the war nor abandoning our object of a People's Republic of Malaya, but we must limit our activities"'; no act of terrorism was to be committed unless it had a military objective. General Sir Robert Lockhart was also reported at a press conference to have commented on the 'marked decline in terrorist activity'.

74 Templer apparently became so incensed with Heren that in February 1953, at the High Commissioner's behest, Lyttelton made an 'indirect and unofficial approach' to *The Times* which left Sir William Haley (the recently appointed editor) 'a bit shaken', in Lyttelton's words; Cloake, *Templer*, p. 293.

75 Letter from Major D.L. Lloyd Owen, Military Assistant to Templer, to W.P. Oliver, HQ Eastern Command, 6/1/53; Templer Papers, National Army Museum, 8301-6. Heren himself makes this point in *Growing Up on 'The Times'*, p. 152.

76 In 1956 it was calculated that it took an average of 1,800 hours of 'jungle-bashing' for every 'contact' with the insurgents; Paget, *Counter-insurgency Campaigning*, p. 68.

77 Cloake, *Templer*, p. 261.

78 Cloake states that the earliest recorded usage of this phrase by Templer was in a speech to the Malayan Chamber of Commerce on 26 April 1952, although many felt he had coined the expression before that date; *Templer*, footnote 1, p. 477. Others, including Stubbs, suggest that Gurney had used the phrase before Templer; *Hearts and Minds*, p. 2; and see Short, *Communist Insurrection*, p. 416.

79 The lengthiest monograph devoted to this subject is Stubbs's *Hearts and Minds*; but see also Short, *Communist Insurrection*, ch. 16, 'Battle for the Mind', and Robert Thompson's *Defeating Communist Insurgency: Experiences from Malaya and Vietnam* (Chatto and Windus, London, 1966), ch. 8, 'Information Services'. The latter was employed during the Emergency initially as Chinese Affairs Officer in Ipoh, rising to become Malaya's Defence Secretary before the end of the Emergency. He was then invited to help the American government in defeating Communism in Vietnam.

80 Paget, *Counter-insurgency Campaigning*, pp. 76–7. Robert Thompson also denies that Communist propaganda was very effective: 'Communist propaganda is less effective than it is given credit for, and in many cases would be lost on the people altogether if it were not backed up by terrorism'; *Defeating Communist Insurgency*, p. 97.

81 See CC(53)20, 17 March 1953; CAB 128/26. In the Cabinet discussion on whether or not to hand Lee Meng over, Lyttelton expressed strong opposition (shared by Templer) to the exchange, as it 'would make an unfortunate impression on public opinion in Malaya and would be construed by the terrorists as proof of the power and prestige of the Soviet bloc'. Eventually, after Lee Meng's death sentence had been commuted

by the Sultan of Perak, it was decided not to exchange her for Saunders, despite the public pleading of Saunders's wife; Barber, *War of the Running Dogs*, pp. 156–61.

82 Transcript of Sir John Sterndale-Bennett's address, P10113; FO 371/1397.

83 Minutes of a Meeting of [Malaya's] Joint Information and Policy Committee, 18/8/50; Trends of Bandit Propaganda; CO 537/6579.

84 J.N. McHugh, *Anatomy of Communist Propaganda July 1948–December 1949* (Malayan Government Printer, Kuala Lumpur, 1950); copy in CO 875/72/1.

85 Pye, *Guerrilla Communism*, pp. 182–7.

86 Ibid., pp. 226–30. The Malayan authorities found that many SEPs they interviewed had an extremely limited understanding of Communism.

87 Federation of Malaya Police Operational Intelligence Summary, no. 86, 8/3/50; CO 537/5986.

88 Pye, *Guerrilla Communism*, p. 102; see also George Thomson (Public Relations Secretary, Singapore), 'Propaganda in the Current Emergency', 29/11/50; CO 875/72/1.

89 Letter from Gurney to Higham, 25/4/50; CO 537/6579. Three years earlier Gurney had made precisely the same criticism of the BBC with respect to publicity it had given to the threats of Zionist terrorists in Palestine. Blackburne passed on the criticism to the BBC's Grenfell Williams, informing him of Gurney's view that 'such publicity is exactly what the terrorists themselves want'; letter dated 12/6/47, BBC WAC R28/42/4.

90 Record of a discussion between *The Times*'s H.L. Brigstocke and A.J.W. Hockenhull (CO) for Oliver Woods, dated 6/1/52, in *The Times* Archive, Malaysia file.

91 Part of the 'hearts and minds' strategy was, thus, to show Malayans that Britain was committed to setting the colony on the path to independence at an early date, and to encourage a Malayan 'national identity' among the diverse ethnic constituencies.

92 On resettlement see Stubbs, *Hearts and Minds*, pp. 101–7. By the end of 1954, 547,000 people had been resettled.

93 This was one of the main criticisms of Templer made by Victor Purcell, a Chinese-speaking former member of the Malayan Civil Service, in his *Malaya: Communist or Free?* (Victor Gollancz, London, 1954). In January 1953, the *Observer* reported the opinion of a senior resettlement officer in Johore State, who thought that 75 per cent of the New Villagers were 'choking with animosity against us'; 'The Vanishing Enemy in Malaya' (4/1/53), p. 7. The disaffection of the resettled Chinese peasants was also the theme of Han Suyin's novel, *And the Rain My Drink* (Jonathan Cape, London, 1956), based on her first-hand experience as a doctor in one such community.

94 Purcell, *Malaya: Communist or Free?*, p. 6.

95 Briggs's remark was discussed by the Cabinet Malaya Committee, 18/5/50, MAL. C. (50) 5th Meeting; CAB 134/497.

96 Short, for example, writes that 'In general, at least until 1951, MPC propaganda was reckoned to be far superior to that of government'; *Communist Insurrection*, p. 417. This perception was also apparently shared by SEPs. The Weekly Report on Malaya for the period 10–18 Feb. 1950, no. 55, quoted a recently surrendered terrorist as saying: 'There appears to be no government propaganda whereas Communist propaganda is good and is constantly put out to the people'; FZ1015/9; FO 371/84475.

97 MAL. C. (50), 5th Meeting, op. cit., CAB 134/497.

98 At a meeting on 7 June 1950, Briggs admitted his statement on propaganda should have been corrected; Minutes of the 15th Commissioner General's Conference held at Bukit Serene; CO 537/6011.

99 For example, in November 1950, Air Commodore Harvey MP reported to the House, after a visit to the Federation, that 'our propaganda out there was practically nil' – there was 'none worth talking about'; H.C. Debs, vol. 480, 3/11/50, cols 484–5.

100 Telegram from Gurney to Creech Jones, 14/2/49, no. 216; CO 537/4750.

101 Minute by T.C. Jerrom, 1/1/53; CO 1022/46.

102 Short, *Communist Insurrection*, p. 417, footnote 2.
103 A large collection of early propaganda leaflets can be found in CO 875/71/6.
104 Memo on the Commission-General, Singapore, by R.H. Scott, 22/2/51, FZ1016/ 28; FO 371/93007. For a lengthier exposition of Regional Information Office work in Asia, see 'The Work of the Regional Information Office at Singapore', P1016/31/G; FO 953/1637.
105 Minutes of the first meeting of the Joint Information and Propaganda Committee, held in the Department of Public Relations, Kuala Lumpur, 10 Feb. 1950. Minutes are contained in CO 537/6579.
106 Josey, however, was not an unadulterated success in the post; M. Tracey, *A Variety of Lives: A Biography of Sir Hugh Greene* (The Bodley Head, London, 1983), p. 128.
107 CC 37(50), 19 June 1950; CAB 128/17.
108 Tracey, *A Variety of Lives*, p. 117.
109 Ibid., p. 122.
110 Walk, 'Coming In from the Cold', p. 52; and Lucas and Morris, 'A Very British Crusade', p. 104.
111 Greene, Secret 'Report on Emergency Information Services, September 1950– September 1951', p. 1; CO 537/7255. For an account of Greene's time in Malaya, see Tracey, *A Variety of Lives*, ch. 8, pp. 126–37.
112 Greene, Report, op. cit., p. 3.
113 The most famous ex-bandit of this kind was Lam Swee, whose denunciations of the MCP's terror strategy (such as *My Accusation* (Malayan Government Printer, Kuala Lumpur, 1951)) were regarded as excellent anti-Communist propaganda.
114 Greene, Report, op. cit., p. 5.
115 Telegram from MacDonald to Creech Jones, 24/8/49, no. 237; CO 537/6571.
116 Report by Stanley Hawes to MacDonald, 3/4/50; CO 537/6571.
117 Hawes to MacDonald, 1/4/50; CO 537/6571.
118 Greene, Report, p. 7.
119 Ibid., pp. 9–11.
120 Tracey, *A Variety of Lives*, p. 134.
121 Force 136 was the wartime Special Operations Executive unit sent to conduct undercover sabotage activities in occupied Malaya, alongside the Malayan Communist resistance.
122 Cloake, *Templer*, pp. 236–7.
123 Secret covering letter from Peterson to Templer, dated 20/8/52, accompanying his 'Report and Recommendations on the Organisation of Information Services in the Federation of Malaya'; CO 967/181.
124 Paget, *Counter-insurgency Campaigning*, p. 69.
125 Secret, Director of Operations Review of the Emergency in Malaya, op. cit., 12/9/57; WO 106/5990.
126 Army Operational Research Group, Report no. 5/56, 'Psychological Warfare Research: Its Role in the Cold War' (March 1956), prepared by F.H. Lakin; WO 291/1509. As a result of research carried out with SEPs, the report stated that psychological warfare efforts had played an important part in the surrender of about half of 432 ex-terrorists interviewed.
127 Letter from Templer to Lewis Hankins, Delaware, USA, 3/12/68; Lloyd Owen Papers, NAM, 8011-132-1.
128 See the results of Ministry of Information surveys in CO 875/52/6.
129 On the CO survey see *Manchester Guardian* (23/12/48) and *Daily Mail* (21/12/48).
130 Barber, *War of the Running Dogs*, p. 87.
131 See, for example, *Daily Worker*, 'An Iron Hand in Malaya', by a Special Correspondent (17/6/48), p. 2.
132 *Daily Worker* (18/6/48), editorial, p. 1.

133 *Daily Worker* (9/7/48), editorial, p. 1. The *Daily Worker* also lost no time in pointing out that the designation 'terrorist' had been applied to the Malayan Communist resistance by the Japanese during their occupation; 'Malaya: The Real Terror' by Jack Woddis (26/9/48), p. 2.

134 Naturally the *Daily Worker* recorded many such protests, no matter how small. For example, it reported on 4 Sept. 1948 that the London area committee of the Electrical Trades Union (ETU), representing 57,000 workers, had demanded the immediate withdrawal of British troops; p. 1. On 7 Sept. it chronicled the delivery of a message to the War Office from a deputation of girls at a north London furniture factory, who wanted their 'boyfriends here, not Malaya'; p. 6.

135 Creech Jones to MacDonald, 19/8/48; CO 527/5123.

136 Minute by Higham to Blackburne, 19/10/48; CO 537/5123.

137 Minute by N.D. Watson to J.D. Higham, 26/10/48; CO 537/5123.

138 Higham to Blackburne, 19/10/48. Blackburne agreed on the general principle but thought that (in the short term) it was sufficient that these representatives attend a press conference shortly to be given by Malcolm MacDonald. Blackburne to Watson and Higham, 21/10/48; CO 537/5123.

139 Minute by Watson to Higham, 26/10/48; CO 537/5123.

140 Ibid.

141 'Labour and Trade Union Organisation in the Federation of Malaya and Singapore', report by Awbery and Dalley; CO 875/22/2.

142 Minute by Haler to Brigadier Johnson, 24/9/48; CO 875/22/2.

143 Letter from Ralph Murray to Blackburne, 24/1/49; CO 875/22/2.

144 *Daily Herald* (28/10/48), editorial, p. 2. The occasion for this editorial was the TUC's 800-word declaration exposing the Communist strategy of sabotage and disruption, and the General Council's proposal that the Communist World Federation of Trade Unions (WFTU) suspend its activities.

145 See, for example, an article by the *Malayan Monitor's* Lim Hong Bee in the *Daily Worker* (28/4/49), 'They Are Silent Now about Malaya'. He noted a shift in terminology: the bandits were being 'hastily promoted to "Communists"' and 'even comparatively "respectable" labels like "rebels" and "insurgents" [had begun] to creep into British official statements'.

146 Minute by Blackburne to Jeffries, 23/3/50; CO 875/72/1.

147 'The Emergency in Malaya. Notes (prepared in July 1950) on certain questions which are frequently asked as regards the nature of the challenge, the necessity for meeting it and the long term objectives of our policy in Malaya'; CO 875/72/1.

148 In 1948, Malaya brought in over $170m, rising to $350m in 1952, as a result of the boom in rubber and tin prices triggered by the Korean War; see A.J. Stockwell, 'British Imperial Policy and Decolonization in Malaya, 1942–52', *Journal of Imperial and Commonwealth History*, 13, i (1984), 68-87, p. 78. On the necessity of holding Malaya see a memorandum by Creech Jones dated 1/7/48, CP(48) 171; CAB 129/25.

149 In a debate on 'The Far East and South East Asia', Rab Butler insisted, with reference to Malaya: 'We must face up to the fact that the standard of living of the average British worker depends as much on exploiting, developing and saving the resources of South East Asia as it does in developing and saving our coal here'; H.C. Debs, vol. 475, 24/5/50, col. 2188.

150 Answers to questions 2, 4 and 6 respectively; CO 875/72/1.

151 Distribution list in CO 875/72/1.

152 MAL. C. (50), 10th Meeting, minutes for the meeting on 17/10/50; CAB 134/497.

153 Ibid.

154 See minute by P.L. Carter (FO IPD), 24/10/50, PG14545/6; FO 953/1031; and telegram from Crichton (RIO, Singapore) to Carter, 27/10/50, P1063/31; FO 953/750.

155 In 1948, 344,000 black-and-white television licences were sold in Britain, whereas by 1961 the figure had risen to 11,268,000; Seymour-Ure, *The British Press and Broadcasting since 1945*, pp. 76–7.

156 See correspondence in BBC WAC E2/325/1.

157 Letter from Gurney to Higham, 25/4/50; CO 537/6579.

158 Letter from Higham to Gurney, 7/5/50; CO 537/6579.

159 Ibid.

160 Letter from Sir C. Jeffries to Jacob dated 18/5/50, in which he refers to criticisms made by Jacob; CO 537/6579.

161 One noteworthy feature of the BBC's Home Service talks output in the 1950s is that terrorism had now, and for the first time, become a subject for discussion in its own right. With simultaneous Emergencies in Malaya, Kenya and Cyprus in the mid-1950s, terrorism had become a phenomenon open to discussion in more general, and conceptual, terms. See, for example, Home Service talks broadcast on 14 Jan. 1954 ('The Anatomy of Terrorism') and 13 Oct. 1955 ('The Form and Tactics of Post-war Terrorism').

162 For example, in Nov. 1948 Gurney wrote to Creech Jones telling him that he had asked the local press to refrain from publishing news of rubber-slashings in Perak State, 'so as to avoid putting similar ideas into the heads of bandits in other areas'. He also asked Creech Jones to advise the British press not to carry information on the rubber sabotage; telegram from Gurney to Creech Jones, 26/11/48, no. 1515; CO 537/3758.

163 Thompson, *Defeating Communist Insurgency*, p. 101.

164 Peterson, 'Report and Recommendations on the Organisation of Information Services in the Federation of Malaya', p. 4; CO 967/181.

165 Minutes of the 15th Commissioner-General's Conference at Bukit Serene, 7/6/50; CO 537/6011.

166 See, for example, the *Observer*'s report of 18/11/51, 'Malaya Has Blackest Week'.

167 Telegram from Gurney to Creech Jones, 6/2/49, no. 180A; CO 537/4750.

168 Telegram from Gurney to Creech Jones, 19/4/50, no. 341. Agreeing that Briggs had contravened the agreed line, Higham optimistically minuted to Watson that he was 'sure Briggs won't wish to make press conferences an everyday occurrence', 22/4/50; CO 537/5997.

169 Cloake, *Templer*, p. 292.

170 Ibid., p. 292.

171 See letter from Blackburne to M.C. Sheppard, 7/5/50; CO 875/53/1.

172 Minute by Jerrom to Higham, 16/6/52; CO 1022/339.

173 Telegram from Templer to Lyttelton, 7/8/52, no. 1587; CO 1022/339.

174 Lord Chandos, *Memoirs of Lord Chandos* (Readers Union, London, 1964), p. 364.

175 This hypothesis would seem to be borne out by the comments of the Colonial Office's B.O.B. Gidden. Writing to Watherston in Kuala Lumpur on the subject of an *Observer* report which had been highly critical of the counter-insurgency campaign (Michael Davidson's 'Increase of Terrorism in Malaya' piece in the *Observer* of 11/2/51), Gidden remarked, 'On the whole the correspondents of the London newspapers do not report the emergency with much understanding. . . . It is all the more disappointing when our main difficulty has been to get correspondents to report from Kuala Lumpur at all, to meet examples of irresponsibility like the present one'; letter from Gidden to Watherston, 21/2/51; CO 537/7262.

176 See, respectively, the *Daily Herald*'s reports for 16, 17, 19, 22 and 28 June 1948. The Colonial Secretary, Creech Jones, himself used the term 'gangsters' to describe the insurgents in the early stages of the Emergency; on 9 July 1948 the *Daily Herald* quoted him as stating, 'This is not a movement of the people of Malaya. It is the conduct of gangsters who are out to destroy the very foundations of human society and orderly life.'

177 *Daily Telegraph* (19/2/52), 'The Last Chance in Malaya', by Malcolm Muggeridge.
178 As the *Times* correspondent, Heren, wrote in the first of a series of articles entitled 'The Enemy in Malaya' (19/2/52), 'to label the Communist armed bands as bandits is more misleading than the grandiloquent Communist term, Malayan Races National Liberation Army. Indeed, it would be unwise to underestimate the strength of the Communist organisation and its ability to take advantage of any deterioration.'
179 *Daily Mail* (28/3/50), editorial, p. 1.
180 *The Times* (25/9/51), 'Terrorist Strength in Malaya'.
181 Telegram from Gurney to Griffiths, for Higham, 2/10/51, no. 932, FZ1016/82; FO 371/93011.
182 *The Times* (23/6/52), 'Aid for Malaya Terrorists'. See minutes by Mary Fisher to Anthony Gann (24/6/52) and by Gann to Jerrom and Higham (26/6/52) on a possible revision of the propaganda line; CO 537/7777.
183 *Daily Mail* (20/3/50), 'Peril Grows in Malaya, Says Man on the Spot', by Lachie McDonald.
184 For Lyttelton's account of press 'misrepresentation' of his initial statement, see *Memoirs of Lord Chandos*, p. 363.
185 Privately, it also appears that Jim Griffiths regretted the introduction of collective punishment measures to Malaya by Templer's predecessor Gurney. In a minute to Sir Thomas Lloyd, he remarked: 'I am very doubtful of either the wisdom or the effectiveness of this kind of punishment'; Griffiths to Lloyd, 18/7/50; CO 537/6007.
186 In this respect, Templer was continuing a practice initiated by Gurney, who had authorized the destruction of Jenderam village in February 1951.
187 *New Statesman and Nation* vol. XLV, no. 1141 (17/1/53), 'Strong Arm in Malaya', Victor Purcell, p. 59. These claims were made at much greater length in his book the following year.
188 *Manchester Guardian* (20/8/52). This issue also re-emerged the following year, with *The Times* printing two letters on the display of dead bodies (31/12/53 and 4/1/54).
189 J.B. Oldfield provides a sympathetic explanation of this practice in *The Green Howards in Malaya* (Gale and Polden, Aldershot, 1953), p. xxii.
190 Purcell, in a letter headlined 'Pot-Shot at a Proconsul', *Spectator*, vol. 192, no. 6555 (12/2/54), p. 176.
191 In March 1951, Robert Scott claimed to have detected such signs. In his brief for the Malaya Committee Meeting to be held on 12/3/51, he wrote, 'Parliamentary and public opinion is restive about the way the Malayan campaign drags on'; brief dated 10/3/51, FZ1016/33G; FO 371/93007.
192 A. Campbell, *Jungle Green* (George Allen and Unwin, London, 1953).
193 To give some indication of the extent of RAF involvement in the campaign, in 1952 the RAF attacked nearly 700 targets, flew 4,000 offensive sorties and dropped over 4,000 tons of bombs; Short, *Communist Insurrection*, p. 371.
194 Extract from COS (50) 23rd meeting, 2/2/50, minute 4; CO 537/5974.
195 Minute by J.H. Watson, 18/2/50, P1063/2G; FO 953/750.
196 As D. MacFarlane, the IPD's regional adviser for the Far East, minuted, 'If we openly acknowledged the situation in Malaya as a Communist revolt instead of bandit trouble to be put down primarily by police methods our publicity could be on different lines.' Minute dated 2/3/50, P1063/3; FO 953/750.
197 *Daily Worker* (28/4/52). Further photographs of the same ilk appeared on 30 April and on 3, 8 and 10 May. The Editor sent the originals to Churchill, stating that 'these shocking disclosures will arouse all decent citizens to demand an immediate end to this dirty war'. Letter from J.R. Campbell to Churchill, 8/5/52; CO 1022/45. On the practice of head severance and an earlier scandal over its employment in Burma, see Mockaitis, *British Counterinsurgency*, pp. 37–8 and pp. 52–3.

198 Draft telegram to Templer, conveying the unanimous opinion of the Cabinet on the *Daily Worker*'s photographs, 6/5/52; CO 1022/45.
199 Some provincial papers also jumped to this conclusion, including the *Yorkshire Evening Post* and *Lancashire Evening Post* (29/4/52).
200 This was confirmed in a letter from the Private Secretary to the First Lord of the Admiralty to the Prime Minister, 1/5/52; he included a statement by the Admiralty verifying that the photographs had been taken on an operation in April 1951, in which it had been impossible for the jungle patrol to bring back the entire body of the dead terrorist for identification. As identification was always required, the severing of heads was permitted if no other method of identifying the body (such as a photograph or fingerprint) was possible; CO 1022/45.
201 As Templer put it, 'War in the jungle is not a nice thing but we cannot forgo the necessity for exact identification of Communist dead'; telegram from Templer to Lyttelton, no. 559, 6/5/52; CO 1022/45.
202 For the Cabinet discussions on this affair see the minutes in CC(52)47, dated 29/4/52 and CC(52)49, dated 6/5/52; CAB 128/24. In the latter meeting, the Cabinet decided to override Templer, finding that the political odium involved in the severance of heads outweighed any military advantage gained.
203 *Daily Telegraph* (23/5/52), '500 Sea Dyaks for Malaya', Denis Warner.
204 Purcell, *Malaya: Communist or Free?*, p. 232. See also Short, *Communist Insurrection*, p. 505.
205 Jack Hawkins, the male lead, provides an anecdotal account of the filming in his memoir *Anything for a Quiet Life: The Autobiography of Jack Hawkins* (Elm Tree Books, London, 1973), pp. 100–1. The crude demarcation between studio and location footage was picked up by the *News Chronicle*'s film critic in a review of the film on 20 Sept. 1952. A lengthier treatment of the role of film in the Malayan and Mau Mau Emergencies is contained in the author's 'Two Faces of 1950s Terrorism: The Film Presentation of Mau Mau and the Malayan Emergency' in *Small Wars and Emergencies*, 6, i. (Spring 1995), pp. 17–44.
206 In the United States the film was released under the title *Outpost in Malaya*.
207 Publicity material available at the National Film Archive in the library of the British Film Institute [hereafter NFA].
208 *Daily Worker* (21/5/51), 'Rank View of War in Malaya', Rose Grant. I have not been able to find documentary confirmation of this in official records.
209 *Daily Mirror* (21/5/51).
210 Note of a meeting on Information Services, June 1952; CO 1022/492.
211 In its lack of context or explanation of the Emergency, the film also departed significantly from the novel on which it was based, S.C. George's *Planter's Wife* (Jarrolds, London, 1951). Considerable background detail on the Emergency and the MCP is provided on pp. 66–8 and pp. 99–104.
212 *Daily Express* (19/9/52). Similarly, Milton Shulman, writing in the *Evening Standard* (18/9/52), complained that 'By avoiding the use of the word Communist throughout the film, *The Planter's Wife* has escaped the political implications of its theme with the obviousness of a short-sighted ostrich with its head in the sand'.
213 *Daily Herald* (19/9/52).
214 *Daily Worker* (17/9/52).
215 Note of a Meeting on Information Services; CO 1022/492.
216 See for example C.A. Lejeune in the *Observer* (29/8/53) and *The Times*'s film critic on 27/8/53.
217 H.C. Debs, vol. 478, 18/10/50; Parliamentary Question on 'Malayan Operations (Publicity)'; extract in FO 953/762.
218 Universal News released two stories about troops setting off for Malaya in the autumn of 1948 (in the issues of 26/8/48 and 9/9/48), and British Movietone News released one of a similar character on 9 Sept. 1948. The other two newsreel

companies, Pathé and Gaumont British, carried no items about the Emergency until 1949.

219 Only occasionally did the newsreel companies send out cameramen; see Ronnie Noble's account of his trip to Malaya to film an interview with Templer, *Shoot First!*, pp. 241–52.

220 MFU dope sheet accompanying Pathé issue no. 52-25, 'Jungle Raid in Malaya' (23/4/52).

221 A later Movietone item of 24 March 1952, which focused on the role of the helicopter in the Malayan campaign – again using MFU footage – ended with an almost identical phrase, the commentator stressing the 'incredibly difficult job of rounding up the Reds'. Issue no. 56908, 'Malayan Operation', 24/3/52.

222 Movietone, issue no. 51299, 'Malaya Round Up', 13/1/49. See also Movietone's issue no. 53884 (15/6/50), containing a story entitled 'British Ministers See Malaya in Close-Up'.

223 Pathé, issue no. 50-48, 'Bandits Face New Tactics' (15/6/50).

224 Ibid.

225 Gaumont British, issue no. 1901, 'Cameronians on 32 Day Jungle Patrol' (24/3/52).

226 Pathé, issue no. 50-12, 'Guards Harass Malayan Guerrillas' (9/2/50).

227 Gaumont British's issue no. 2151, 'Lincolns in Operation Termite' (16/8/54), consisted largely of aerial footage showing the Lincolns dropping their 75 tons of bombs on 'jungle hideouts'.

228 Pathé, issue no. 52-103, 'US carbines for Malaya' (22/12/52); as the commentary explained, 'These people have often suffered sudden murderous attacks from the terrorists and they welcome the carbines as a further protection to their families and homes.'

229 See, for example, Gaumont British, issue no. 1888, 'Sarawak Governor Presents George Cross to Native Tracker' (7/2/52).

230 Movietone, issue no. 53614, 'Malaya's New Director of Operations' (27/4/50).

231 A choice example is Pathé's issue no. 52-28, 'Templer gets tough' (3/4/52), in which the commentator remarks that 'If villagers cut off food supplies to the bandits, the trouble would quickly end. This is the lesson he [Templer] taught a village when he cut rations because they supplied food to a murder gang.'

3 'Worse Than Communists':[1] Propaganda and the Mau Mau Insurgency in Kenya, 1952–60

Introduction

In some respects the Mau Mau Emergency in Kenya was another 'invisible war', rather akin to that in Malaya. Graham Greene, who travelled from Malaya to Kenya in 1953, wrote:

> In Indo-China, even in Malaya, there was something approaching a front line. . . . Here the war was secret: it would happen the day after I left or the day before I arrived. It was a private African war which could be hidden so easily from white eyes, just as seventeen bodies lay for weeks unnoticed in a squatters' village on the outskirts of Nairobi, a mile from the highway and the houses of officials.[2]

The campaign was fought largely in the forests of Kenya's central highlands, which made the conflict between Mau Mau and the security forces as difficult to capture on film as were operations in Malaya's jungles. Furthermore, the excesses of the counter-insurgency campaign, and the ferociousness with which Mau Mau was suppressed, were only partially revealed during the Emergency itself.

Yet to suggest that the Mau Mau Emergency was invisible is patently absurd at another level. Unlike the concurrent campaign in Malaya, Mau Mau was frequently front-page news in Britain. Mau Mau – with its depraved oaths and the apparently primeval savagery of its 'terrorism' – was the very stuff of tabloid sensationalism. As the Colonial Office's H.G. Hall ruefully pointed out, two months prior to the declaration of a State of Emergency in Kenya:

> We must resign ourselves to the fact that there is little or nothing we can do to prevent a situation such as the one which exists in Kenya from being depicted in the UK press in a sensational man-ner. . . . To the Sunday newspaper reader, Mau Mau presents all the lurid aspects of melodrama – a secret society with a blood-curdling initiation oath, the terror which stalks by night, the lone European settler waiting for 'the war horn to blow' and so on.[3]

A string of 'experts', including the prominent psychiatrist Dr J.C. Carothers, anthropologists Max Gluckman and Louis Leakey, and the former Governor of Kenya Sir Philip Mitchell, produced a stream of explanations of the phenomenon of Mau Mau, which were supplemented by a number of White Papers.[4] By the end of the Emergency, Mau Mau had been the subject of three feature films (of varying degrees of seriousness),[5] numerous novels,[6] eye-witness accounts and second-hand instant histories.[7] For government propagandists, then, keeping Mau Mau in the public eye was certainly never a problem.

In the years since 1960, Mau Mau has continued to exert a powerful fascination over historians, sociologists and political theorists, film-makers and novelists, and the popular imagination alike. Since the late 1960s, and particularly after the publication of Rosberg and Nottingham's *The Myth of 'Mau Mau': Nationalism in Kenya*,[8] much of the academic outpouring on Mau Mau has had a distinctly revisionist flavour, seeking to elucidate the myths of Mau Mau spun while the insurgency was in progress. Whereas the literature on the Malayan Emergency has overlooked the extent to which British government propaganda was undertaken outside Malaya, several works on Mau Mau have stressed the primacy of British and Kenyan government propaganda in the mystificatory process. A number of academics, along with certain former Mau Mau leaders, have proposed that the colonial authorities were supremely, and enduringly, effective in propagating their own defamatory version of Mau Mau. In 1967, writing a preface to Donald Barnet and Karari Njama's *Mau Mau from Within*, four former Mau Mau leaders (Kaggia, Kubai, Murumbi and Oheko) wrote that:

> British propaganda – and not only British – has been remarkably successful in equating the revolt of a large section of the people of Kenya with barbarism and savagery, so much so that even many Africans in Kenya are today reluctant to discuss this vitally important episode in our history with candour.[9]

Similarly, Robert Buijenthuis (writing in 1973) claimed that the Kenya government and settlers 'enjoyed an almost complete control over the means of communication and of publicity' and were thus able to 'impose their myth of the Mau Mau, a myth which is still extremely powerful in Europe and elsewhere and which still makes it quite difficult to comprehend fully the whole phenomenon'.[10] Most recently, Frank Furedi has asserted that 'the colonial government went to great lengths to portray Mau Mau as an irrational force of evil, dominated by bestial impulses and influenced by world communism'.[11] As testimony to the effectiveness of this propaganda effort, Furedi insists that even 'the European left, generally inclined to support anti-imperialist movements, looked upon Mau Mau as an unfortunate and distorted product of colonialism'.[12]

However, these statements offer certain assertions that this chapter will contest, such as the validity of regarding the Kenya settlers *and* government as a homogeneous bloc which controlled the presentation of Mau Mau, and whether official propaganda really attempted to insinuate that the hand of Communism lay behind Mau Mau. More broadly, how far should the narrow range of interpretations of Mau Mau, and the recurrence of certain key motifs in the contemporaneous literature on Mau Mau, be read as a triumph of government propaganda? For all the pronouncements that have been made about the dominance and durability of government propaganda on Mau Mau, a full-length study of this aspect of the counter-insurgency campaign is lacking.[13] This chapter will assess the way in which colonial officials and the governments of Churchill, Eden and Macmillan interpreted the upsurge of violence in Kenya, what they understood by Mau Mau terrorism, and how propaganda was used to influence the perception of Mau Mau in Britain, Kenya and further afield.

The Background to Mau Mau

In the early 1950s, Kenya had an indigenous population of approximately 5 million, together with about 30,000 settlers – the cumulation of five decades of colonization by Europeans. Throughout the inter-war years, the colony had been far more in the British public eye than had Malaya. As the settler novelist and anthropologist Elspeth Huxley wrote to Margery Perham, 'For many years this colony has been a minor storm-centre of controversy and discussion. The very name seems to send people's temperatures up.'[14] This may have been partly due to the 'exotic reputation of the settlers'[15] – who surpassed even Somerset Maugham's gin-swilling planters in their reputation for indulgence in alcohol and extra-marital liaisons. Huxley felt that Britain's chattering classes, swayed by their distaste for Kenya's settlers, disapproved of the colony's government, believing it to have 'treated the native population with injustice, bigotry, and unrestrained racial greed'.[16] The institution of apartheid in South Africa provided an ominous warning of where 'unrestrained racial greed' might lead, and, as Perham suggested, many Britons feared that the Kenyan settlers might attempt to reproduce Pretoria's experiment in East Africa.[17] The settlers had already effectively created their own colony-within-the-colony: the 'White Highlands', 7.5 million acres (30,000 km²) of Kenya's best agricultural land on which a controlled number of Africans were permitted to 'squat' (that is, cultivate a smallholding on a European farm, in exchange for a certain amount of labour on the settler's estate). The majority of Kenya's African population, however, lived in 'native reserves', which by the start of the 1950s were hugely overcrowded, leading to an influx of migrants into and around Nairobi. Given that during the 1940s the settlers had begun to push the 'squatters' off their farms (the long-term aim being to transform the old labour-tenancy system into a wage-labourer economy[18]), and bearing in mind the operation of a colour bar in Kenya, it is small wonder that British liberals feared the settlers were increasingly tempted by the South African model.

For their part, Kenya's African population gained in militancy as they were squeezed from the most fertile agricultural land, and as the reserves became increasingly crowded. This was particularly true of the Kikuyu – the ethnic group which in the 1950s was almost exclusively identified with Mau Mau. In the 1920s the Kikuyu Central Association (KCA) was founded to articulate economic and political grievances. Of all Kenya's tribes, the Kikuyu became the most rapidly politicized. As the Kenya government and settlers saw it, the KCA's clever propaganda – instilled into young minds at the Independent schools – had duped a generation of Africans into believing that their land had been stolen by the whites. The 'White Highlands' was an area which the Kikuyu had inhabited before the colonization of Kenya, and continued to do so as 'squatters' thereafter. Thus government propaganda struggled to disprove the KCA (and later Mau Mau) claim that this land had been illicitly wrested from the Kikuyu. Living cheek by jowl with the European settlers, on their farms or in congested Nairobi, it was the Kikuyu who bore the brunt of the dislocation caused by the colonization of Kenya. In the 1940s, the Kikuyu inhabitants of the Central Province were swiftly drawn into a capitalist market system, undergoing a major social transformation.[19] While some were co-opted into the new system, many remained dissatisfied, and these formed the backbone of Mau Mau.

The KCA was one indication that many Kikuyu were far from content with their conditions either as 'squatters' or in the reserves. Another indication that they were rebelling against the impact of colonialism was the rise of a number of messianic religious cults. Of these religious sects, Sir Philip Mitchell (Governor of Kenya, 1944–52) wrote in his memoirs:

> They were – and are – all much the same; a doctrine derived from misreading the Old Testament and mixing in some magic, a varying amount of sexual licence and a reversion to tribal spirit worship; practices of a generally orgiastic nature, often revoltingly obscene and including an element of terror; and as frequent collections of cash for the prophet as the faithful who have been gathered in will stand.[20]

Mitchell attributed Kikuyu membership of these cults to both an innate tribal tendency towards atavism and to the terrorism through which the sects controlled their members. It was from these *dini* cults, as they were known, at least as much as from the KCA or Kenya African Union (KAU, a more conservative organization), that colonial officials in the early 1950s regarded Mau Mau as springing.[21] In other words, the Kikuyu were not seen as simply becoming politicized; rather, their membership of these strange cults betokened what W.H. Ingrams (the Colonial Office's expert on African affairs) termed 'a mystical reaction to frustration'.[22] Frustration felt by the Kikuyu produced 'pagan revivals', and these were manipulated by Kikuyu leaders with a political programme, Ingrams wrote in April 1952:

> The nationalist movement among the Kikuyus is building itself up on the pagan core . . . and there has been an artificial revival of paganism. The movement, known as Mao-Mao [*sic*], at first abjured co-operation with the whites, independent schools sprang up overnight, and after things had settled down, it developed a left and a right. There followed the Kikuyu oath, which originally related only to land but is now focused on a pledge to get rid of the white conqueror by all means, murder included.[23]

At the time Ingrams wrote his report few in Britain had heard of Mau Mau. It remains virtually impossible to say when the Kenya government first became aware of Mau Mau's existence, not least because the colonial administration in some senses called Mau Mau into being. In other words, Mau Mau was not a name which the Kikuyu organizers of a secret, oath-bound movement, dedicated to gaining land and freedom, used to denote their own organization. Memoirs of former Mau Mau leaders concur that 'Mau Mau' was a name imposed on them, and there are numerous different versions of how the movement came by this particular appelation.[24] The term 'Mau Mau' came into currency in 1950 at the trial of nineteen Africans accused of having administered an illegal oath binding its takers to a certain secret Mau Mau association. Thereafter, in August 1950, Mau Mau was proscribed, and 'through its repeated and constant use by Government, press and radio, the appelation "Mau Mau" was irrevocably linked with the underground movement and the revolt which followed some three years later'.[25]

What became known as 'Mau Mau' was an offshoot of both the KCA and the KAU: the KCA had been administering an oath to squatters in the Highlands since 1946. Similarly, the young militants in the KAU, unbeknown to their more conservative seniors, were involved in administering an oath, which (according to Bildad Kaggia) committed its takers to unity, a readiness to do anything for the movement, a pledge never to sell their land, and to the brotherhood of all members.[26] The activity which turned into 'Mau Mau' was thus fairly diffuse: neither geographically confined, nor restricted to any one category of Kikuyu. As D.W. Throup has written, Mau Mau was an amalgam of urban, unemployed and destitute Kikuyu in Nairobi, the dispossessed squatters of the White Highlands, and the poor peasants, tenants and members of the junior lineages in the Kikuyu reserves.[27] Several confusions arose within the colonial administration, as it struggled to grasp the transformations occurring within the Kikuyu. While, in the early 1950s, the Kenya government became (erroneously) convinced that Mau Mau could be equated with the KAU, district officials often reported news of oathing ceremonies in the forests as evidence of the *dini* cults, when in fact it was Mau Mau activity.[28]

When the Colonial Office realized in the summer of 1952 that something was seriously amiss with the Kikuyu, the top echelon of the Kenya government was accused of having been oblivious.[29] The situation appeared all too reminiscent of Malaya in the months before the Emergency, where the High Commissioner (Gent) had seemingly failed to realize the scale of the MCP threat. Like Gent, Mitchell was replaced as Governor by a man whose character was seen as better fitted to management of a crisis situation – although Sir Evelyn Baring turned out to be a less happy choice than Gurney had been in Malaya. With hindsight, the Colonial Office believed that Mitchell had gravely underestimated the seriousness of Mau Mau. Shortly after the State of Emergency was declared (in October 1952), Gorrell Barnes mused that:

> there must have been something very wrong in the organisation of the Government in Kenya and/or in the relations between the Kenya Government and the Colonial Office. It is really very difficult to explain how it is that we heard virtually nothing until the second half of August about a threat to law and order, which burst into full flower during September and October and is now known to have been developing for several months, if not years.[30]

In August and September 1952, the British press began to carry reports of an 'anti-white underground organisation called Mau Mau'.[31] Although the anti-European nature of Mau Mau was frequently mentioned, events in Kenya were also reported as a 'wave of crime' with 'spivs ... being rounded up at the rate of 100 a day'.[32] With the exception of sensationalist accounts such as that which the *Sunday Dispatch* carried on 24 August – announcing Mau Mau's planned 'night of the long knives', when all the Europeans were to be massacred – most press reports suggested that events in Kenya were still easily under the government's control. Thus there was some Parliamentary and press criticism when the Kenya government announced stringent Emergency regulations 'designed to protect law-abiding Africans from intimidation by lawless elements, particularly the Secret Society known as the Mau Mau'.[33] The Labour MP and fervent anti-imperialist Fenner Brockway wrote to Oliver Lyttelton (the Colonial Secretary) to complain that the new powers 'read more like the regime of a totalitarian state, the other side of the iron curtain, than a society moving towards democratic freedom'. Mau Mau terrorism, feared Brockway, had been overstated by the settlers.[34]

Revisionist accounts of the Emergency's origins have agreed that the Kenya government over-reacted to Mau Mau in the early autumn of 1952. While the administration may well have been largely ignorant of Mau Mau and complacent about it before the autumn of 1952, in September and October there was a complete volte-face. Now Mau Mau was seen as an imminent, revolutionary challenge to the colonial authorities, and repressive measures were regarded as essential to quell it. According to this analysis, the Emergency regulations, the declaration of a State of Emergency and the concomitant 'Operation Jock Scott' (a swoop on the leaders of the KAU, who were subsequently imprisoned), together with the settlers' precipitate moves to eject Kikuyu 'squatters' from their farms, instigated a Kikuyu revolt. Thrown from their land, thousands of young Kikuyu men had little to lose in joining the Mau Mau gangs forming in the forests. Thus Mau Mau became a revolutionary challenge to the government only when the latter made it one.[35]

Certainly it seems unlikely that Mau Mau was in a position to launch an all-out attack on the settlers or the colonial administration, even if it had wished to. That would have required a degree of planning, co-ordination and military preparedness which the movement did not possess. Mau Mau was never a tightly disciplined organization like the MCP. However, in the interregnum before Baring's arrival, the Kenya government allowed itself to be tempted (or bullied) by the settlers into believing that a revolutionary conspiracy was about to engulf the colony.[36] Huxley's fictional treatment of Mau Mau, *A Thing to Love*, depicts 'the conspiracy' (i.e., Mau Mau) as plotting to massacre Kenya's white population on Christmas Day.[37] And doubtless many of her fellow settlers imagined Mau Mau to be concocting such schemes in the 'pathological atmosphere' of summer and autumn 1952.[38] Nor were Kenya's settlers ever reticent in making their views known to Government House. After the declaration of the State of Emergency, it became clear that, whatever Mau Mau had been previously, it was now in open revolt against the colonial state. Determining the nature of that revolt – what its aims were and the strategy which underlay its violent tactics – was no easy matter.

Interpretations of Mau Mau

By the end of September 1952, Mau Mau was believed to have killed thirty-seven Africans.[39] There had also been a spate of cattle-maiming and killing on European farms, and oath-taking was widespread. On 3 October, Mau Mau claimed its first settler victim. Following the murder of 'loyal' chief Waruhiu on 7 October, Baring sent Lyttelton an alarmist, and somewhat contradictory, estimate of the threat posed by Mau Mau. The movement had considerable support, he wrote, from various quarters:

> It has been said that about 5 per cent of the members of the Mau Mau movement are fanatical African nationalists, about 20 per cent are thugs and the remaining 75 per cent have joined from fear and would to a greater or lesser degree be glad to be rid of the whole thing.[40]

Baring was rather hazy on what Mau Mau's actual intentions were: it was 'determined to destroy all sources of authority other than Mau Mau' and was 'anti-Christian'. And though he spoke of it in one breath as a 'criminal action', in the next he referred to Mau Mau as 'a planned revolutionary movement', which if not stopped would lead to 'a great deal of bloodshed and something approaching civil war'. Baring was also clearly alarmed at the ease with which Mau Mau could apply its violent tactics to Kenya's white population:

> The murder of chief Waruhiu was on the best Chicago model with the use of a high-powered car and a gunman who did not know his victim by sight. The trail seems to point towards his hereditary enemies the Koinange family. Planned murder of this type can be used as well to strike down a European as an African victim.[41]

The 'planned' aspect of Mau Mau violence caused Baring particular concern. It suggested that the recent killings were not sporadic, spontaneous outbursts but part of a broader Mau Mau conspiracy: 'a plan, a rather ragged and a rather African one, but none the less formidable for that'.[42]

Baring's report set the tone for governmental pronouncements on Mau Mau. Lyttelton's statement to the House of Commons in October 1952, which explained the Kenya government's Emergency measures, borrowed wholesale from Baring's correspondence: 'Mau Mau terrorism is carefully planned, centrally directed and its object is to destroy all authority other than Mau Mau. Its leaders are establishing their own courts in an attempt to usurp the functions of Government.'[43] What Baring's report lacked – as did most analyses of Mau Mau emanating from

135

the Nairobi Secretariat and Whitehall alike – was any real attention to the aims of the movement, and how its tactics were directed to the realization of those political objectives. There was remarkably little discussion about what Mau Mau sought to achieve, and how it intended to accomplish those aims: whether Mau Mau was a nationalist movement, and what the function of its terrorism was; whether Mau Mau (like the Jewish terrorist groups in Palestine, or the Malayan Communists) was seeking publicity as much as any physical objective.

Several explanations can be advanced. In the initial months following the declaration of a State of Emergency, Mau Mau activity was far less than anticipated. By the end of 1952, three more settlers had been killed, which seemed to confirm the much-vaunted 'anti-European' aspect of Mau Mau, and several more Kikuyu had also died. Certain signs presaged an intensification of the conflict. In November, Baring informed the Colonial Office that Mau Mau adherents had been making raids on lonely farms and stealing weapons. Baring forecast armed resistance in the forests, and attacks by armed gangs on farms 'with the intention of killing the Europeans in them'; 'we are in the process of moving in some areas from a police operation to a small scale guerrilla war'.[44] Similarly, the Kenya Commissioner of Police predicted on 10 December 1952 that 'gangster crime against poorly defended and isolated persons and places' would continue, and that Mau Mau's intention was to extend and exhaust the forces of law and order.[45] Despite these predictions, Mau Mau initially appeared a rather pusillanimous enemy: during attacks on European farms in December 'the gangs deliberately avoided taking European life',[46] and appeared generally to have adopted a 'passive attitude'.[47]

Matters changed in 1953. Within the first three months of the year, Mau Mau activity begged (and beggared) explanation. However, the interpretations offered were more concerned with the psychology of Mau Mau than with its political agenda. The nature of Mau Mau 'terrorism' in early 1953 perhaps serves as another explanation for why there was little discussion of Mau Mau strategy. After the events of early 1953, few in the Kenya administration were inclined to discuss Mau Mau as a rational movement. Two highly charged Mau Mau acts of violence deserve special mention. The murder of an entire settler family and the massacre of 'loyalists' at Lari changed the psychological climate within Kenya, limiting the parameters of debate on Mau Mau. In January 1953, the murder of Mr and Mrs Ruck and their three-year-old son sent a shock wave through the settler community. Several features of this Mau Mau attack particularly horrified Kenya's white population: the purportedly horrific mutilation of the bodies[48]; the fact that a mother and young child had been killed; and the symbolic weight which the Ruck family bore in the settlers' collective imagination. As a later account put it,

It was as if Kenya subconsciously saw in them a symbol of the settler ideal at its best, and in their passing, the doom of that ideal . . . neither rich nor poor; simple, decent, sound; in the best sense, good: this was the Ruck family, a microcosm of settler Kenya at its best.[49]

Furthermore, the revelation that one of the Rucks' most trusted servants had been involved in the attack intensified the settlers' rage against the Kikuyu in general.

The murders had several consequences, the most direct of which was a march of several hundred settlers on Government House, to demand that they themselves should have a greater say in the prosecution of the 'war' against Mau Mau.[50] The Ruck murders hardened the settlers' incomprehension of Mau Mau into a blinding fury at their betrayal by previously trusted Kikuyu servants and workers.[51] Many now regarded *any* counter-measures against Mau Mau as acceptable. Graham Greene suggests that Mau Mau was initially met with considerable bewilderment by the settlers – that those Kikuyu whom they imagined they had so successfully rescued from savagery, and tamed into model servants, could repay them in such a fashion:

> The Kikuyu were not savage, they made good clerks and stewards. It was as though Jeeves had taken to the jungle. Even worse, Jeeves had been seen crawling through an arch to drink on his knees from a banana-trough of blood; Jeeves had transfixed a sheep's eye with a seven kie-apple thorn; Jeeves had had sexual connection with a goat; Jeeves had sworn, however unwillingly, to kill Bertie Wooster 'or this oath will kill me and all my seed will die'.[52]

After the Ruck murders, many Kenyan Woosters sent their Kikuyu Jeeveses packing: 60,000 Kikuyu drifted back to the native reserves from the Rift Valley, one-third of them under compulsion.

Those who sought explanations for Mau Mau behaviour, rather than simple vengeance, most commonly posed psychological questions: what had happened to the Kikuyu tribe to make it possible for a man to, for example, carry his master's son home on one day and murder the child on the next? As we will see, a number of influential analyses of Mau Mau adopted the view that the phenomenon was best seen as a form of collective madness – a schizophrenia, enabling its adherents to switch effortlessly between two personae: faithful servant at one moment, blood-lusting savage the next. This obsession with plumbing the psyche of Mau Mau concentrated attention on its oath ceremonies. Their significance was debated in the press and by academic experts, who endeavoured to establish whether the oaths represented a reversion to, or a perversion of, old Kikuyu tribal custom, and what effect they had on their takers.[53] Fascination with Mau Mau's irrational aspects was heightened after the Lari massacre in March 1953.

The killing of 97 Kikuyu on the Lari ridge on 26 March 1953 was, according to Fred Majdalany, 'the definitive horror by which every other act of Mau Mau would be measured'.[54] Immediately after the event, the Kenya government and the Colonial Office insisted that the Lari massacre was the result of a cold-blooded plan by Mau Mau to murder the loyal inhabitants of Lari. An attack on Naivasha police post some miles away had been a cunning diversionary tactic, with Mau Mau gangs from miles around using its cover to descend on Lari.[55] Retrospective accounts have challenged this version of events. Some accounts assert that loyalists and the security forces were responsible for the killings.[56] Others point out that Mau Mau resentment against the inhabitants of Lari was based on a genuine grievance over land ownership.[57] At the time, however, sensational reportage blurred any such dispassionate analysis: the *Manchester Guardian* related 'terrible stories' told by survivors: 'One woman was forced to watch a terrorist hold her child while he slowly removed its head by repeated blows. Another woman, held by terrorists, saw her son's throat cut and the murderers drink the blood.'[58] After Lari, the belief that Mau Mau represented a 'rapid return to the savage'[59] became commonplace and arguably made discussion of its political objectives appear irrelevant, if not nonsensical.[60] In Maughan-Brown's words, Lari served to 'short-circuit any attempt at a political reading of "Mau Mau", and to invalidate in advance any future criticism of settler or "security force" actions'.[61]

One feature of many contemporaneous interpretations of Mau Mau is their fundamental irrationalism: as though Mau Mau was itself so far removed from the realms of rational politics that commentators could discuss it only in quite extraordinary, and entirely apolitical, terms. Thus Lyttelton in his memoirs wrote that:

> I can recall no instance when I have felt the forces of evil to be so near and so strong. As I wrote memoranda or instructions, I would suddenly see a shadow fall across the page – the horned shadow of the Devil himself.[62]

He described Mau Mau's aims as 'nakedly – power, and the expulsion of the white man'.[63] To accomplish this, the 'daemonic figure' of Jomo Kenyatta had employed 'the methods of African witchcraft' – the Mau Mau oath being 'the most bestial, filthy and nauseating incantation which perverted minds can ever have brewed'.[64] Many accounts similarly concentrated on the atavistic aspects of Mau Mau. Sir Philip Mitchell's memoirs, published during the Emergency itself, suggested that some dislocation was inevitable when the Kikuyu were being pushed 'head over heels like a schoolboy being thrown into the swimming-bath, into the twentieth century and all its works, and thrown too from somewhere far back beyond the first century'.[65] Mau Mau was thus a revelation of the primitive heart of darkness lurking in the African psyche, scarcely concealed beneath a thin veneer of civilization: the death throes of 'the black and blood-stained forces of sorcery and magic, stirring in the vicious hearts and minds of wicked men'.[66]

Mitchell's thesis that Mau Mau's psychotic behaviour sprang essentially from the inability of certain Kikuyu to adapt themselves to Western civilization was far from original, and indeed typified interpretations of Mau Mau advanced during the Emergency. The most prominent proponents of versions of this theory were Dr Louis Leakey and Dr Colin Carothers. In *The Psychology of Mau Mau*, a pamphlet commissioned by the Kenya government, Carothers concluded that Mau Mau arose from the Kikuyu's contact with an 'alien culture'. They had consequently lost the 'supportive and constraining influences' of their own culture but not its 'magic modes of thinking', which left them vulnerable to exploitation by 'relatively sophisticated egotists'.[67] In like fashion, Leakey in the first of his two volumes on the organization, *Mau Mau and the Kikuyu*, argued that:

> It is probably because the speed of progress has been too rapid that it has made a part of the population unbalanced in their outlook and thus paved the way for movements like Mau Mau, in the hands of an unscrupulous few.[68]

In his second book, *Defeating Mau Mau*, Leakey proposed that Mau Mau was best understood as a religion, in which the oath ceremonies featured as a 'sort of ritual "Confirmation Service"'.[69] Rather than simply being a perversion of old Kikuyu rituals, Mau Mau's ceremonies were a parody of Christianity: Mau Mau had its own hymns, while its oaths served as an apostolic creed. Thus the oath ceremonies had come to replace initiation rites as the turning-point in a young Kikuyu's life. Having been 'initiated', followers were easily persuaded to kill 'for God and in a righteous cause', and this quasi-religious zeal served to explain why 'so many normally peace-loving Kikuyu' had become 'fanatical, murdering maniacs'.[70]

Leakey's explanation of Mau Mau as religion introduced a fresh metaphor into the limited vocabulary with which the phenomenon was discussed. The commonest images clustered around the linked themes of illness, madness and adolescence. As we have seen, the confrontation between tribal society and modernity was believed to produce a kind of schizophrenia.[71] Analogous with the theory that the Kikuyu were in two minds was the notion, articulated here by Sir Michael Blundell, that they were 'poised between two worlds, the old one of the witch doctor and strict tribal and communal customs, and the new one all around them which seemed to them to have few rigid disciplines and to offer vast prospects of personal advancement if only they could enter it'.[72] In another recurring image, Mau Mau adherents were likened to adolescents – drawing again on the motif

139

of the Kikuyu as 'poised between', though here between the states of childhood and manhood, rather than savagery and civilization. In Leakey's words, Mau Mau members existed in a 'dangerous state of intellectual adolescence'.[73]

Such explanations of Mau Mau differed little from contemporary thinking on African psychology as a whole. The 'two worlds' theme had been fully treated in Thorold Dickinson's 1946 feature film *Men of Two Worlds*, based on an idea by the Colonial Office's Noel Sabine.[74] Similarly, the ease with which de-tribalized Africans, removed from their rural environment and exposed to an alien urban setting, could lose their traditional morals and adopt criminal ways was the subject of Harry Watt's film *West of Zanzibar*, which examined how credulous 'natives' were lured into the illicit ivory trade by cunning Indians.[75] In short, psychological interpretations of Mau Mau lacked specificity. True, Leakey paid some attention to Kikuyu grievances – 'real and imaginary', as they were often prefixed – but many other commentators did not.[76] Some, including Lyttelton himself, entirely denied that Mau Mau might have arisen from land hunger or poverty.[77]

Arguably, as the Emergency progressed those whose task it was to inflict a military defeat on Mau Mau thought more coherently about Mau Mau's motives and *modi operandi* – perhaps because by 1955 the intensity of feeling aroused by Mau Mau's earlier actions was starting to abate. Indeed, after March 1953, no Mau Mau action ever conjured up the passions stirred by Lari. Military commanders had to grapple with several at least superficially puzzling aspects of the campaign. By the end of the Emergency, according to government statistics, Mau Mau had killed thirty-two white civilians, as against 1,821 of their fellow Kikuyu.[78] Even before the State of Emergency was declared, the movement had consistently been characterized as 'anti-white'. Why then did its members make so comparatively few attacks on settlers? Why, if their aim was to drive the white man out of Kenya, or Africa as a whole (as some commentators had it[79]), did Mau Mau kill so many more Kikuyu than Europeans? And why, when Mau Mau had formed itself into large gangs in the forest – a development Baring reported in June 1953[80] – did they appear so faint-hearted? After the melodrama and passion of the early months of the Emergency, the counter-insurgency was, in some respects, rather an anticlimax. The enemy were frustratingly difficult to locate; as a disgruntled Lancashire fusilier put it to a *Manchester Guardian* correspondent, 'You don't want fusiliers for this job. What you want is a thousand ruddy rat traps.'[81] When security force patrols did run into Mau Mau gangs, the fighting was over very quickly, partly (as Baring tacitly admitted) because the security forces shot anything that moved.[82]

General Sir George (Bobbie) Erskine, who arrived in Kenya in June 1953 as the Director of Operations – at both the settlers' and Baring's request[83] – adopted a more no-nonsense approach to the interpretation of Mau Mau than many of his civilian colleagues. He sought logical explanations for the aspects of Mau Mau which to others appeared to defy rationality. As John Lonsdale has observed: 'He recognized that Mau Mau had grievances and an aim, to eject the Europeans. The connexion between strategic end and nauseating means was crisply rational.'[84] Of Mau Mau oaths, Erskine wrote:

> Secrecy was necessary, hence the oaths were administered. Money was necessary, hence the oath had to be paid for. The whole tribe must act as one, hence oaths were administered forcibly. Discipline was necessary, hence judges and stranglers became part of the organization. It was perfectly clear that violence was intended. Oaths became more and more bestial and binding.[85]

And while others pondered why the 'night of the long knives' massacre of Europeans had failed to occur, Erskine found the absence of attacks on settlers no more mystifying than the oaths. Mau Mau's initial aim had been to unify the Kikuyu, Embu and Meru tribes 'behind the theory that political aims could only be achieved by armed force', but the terrorist leaders 'never succeeded in convincing the majority of the affected tribes that this action could succeed'.[86] Ultimately, Erskine suggests, Mau Mau failed to convince, either through persuasion or terror, and the murders of Europeans which had occurred 'were inflicted not as part of an overall plan but as a method of obtaining arms and supplies, raising morale or for reasons of personal prestige'.[87]

Erskine's dispassionate approach to Mau Mau, and his insistence (from as early as October 1953) that bullets alone would not suffice to solve Kenya's problems, earned him the disapproval of many of Kenya's settlers.[88] Settler hostility became more pronounced when he attempted to put his philosophy – that Mau Mau had political causes and needed a political, as well as military, solution – into practice by offering Mau Mau adherents a series of surrender offers. However, Erskine's approach was continued by his successor, Lieutenant-General Sir Gerald Lathbury. He too believed that Mau Mau had clearly identifiable aims, which he defined more closely than Erskine had: to defeat the government, or to force it into negotiations which would provide the Kikuyu with land and a measure of self-government; to frighten Europeans into leaving the colony; and to win the support of other tribes.[89] And at a time when the Mau Mau gangs' reluctance to fight suggested to some, including Blundell, that Mau Mau no longer had any aim other than survival, Lathbury insisted that there was still purpose to Mau Mau's activities, and that the terrorists believed that, by prolonging their campaign, 'a financially exhausted and economically crippled Kenya Government would call off operations and grant concessions'.[90]

This stage, of course, was never reached. When Lathbury wrote his valedictory report in November 1956, not only he, but *all* the British forces in Kenya were preparing to depart. The defeat of Mau Mau now appeared not just inevitable but imminent. Whether Mau Mau was ultimately a failure has been as much debated in the retrospective literature as the vexed matter of whether Mau Mau was a nationalist movement. On the latter point, there remains no consensus, and even radical academics have tended to qualify their use of the adjective 'nationalist' when applied to Mau Mau. Furedi – one of the few to insist that Mau Mau was nationalist – still cautions that it was 'not a conventional nationalist movement'.[91] Maughan-Brown, on the other hand, argues that only the educated, literate wings of Mau Mau could be described as consciously nationalist. Those on the other side of the literate/non-literate divide conceptualized their reasons for fighting in pre-political terms such as a piece of land, higher wages or better education.[92] Not surprisingly, former Mau Mau members' memoirs tend to claim that the movement was both a great success and a 'true liberation movement' – in Kaggia's view, 'the first of its kind of the continent'.[93] Itote ('General China') also asserts that Mau Mau was victorious, though for rather different reasons: 'It was not even a territorial battle to gain certain areas: it was a matter of keeping our struggle in the forefront of world opinion. . . . Mere survival was victory.'[94] Itote thus affirms that Mau Mau was engaged in a battle for publicity. But whereas colonial officials regarded publicity as being an essential aim of the Irgun and Lehi, the Malayan Communists and, later, of EOKA, the same was not true of their understanding of Mau Mau. Becoming obsessed with Mau Mau's psychological origins and with the depravity of its actions, many colonial officials (and authorities on Mau Mau) appear to have overlooked Mau Mau's ends, or insisted that the movement had none other than perversion itself. Believing that Mau Mau members themselves made a fetish of their means, many fell victim to their own myth of Mau Mau.

Propaganda and the Campaign against Mau Mau

During the Emergency little attention was paid to Mau Mau propaganda, or to whether Mau Mau's intention was to gain publicity. Whereas the Communists in Malaya were believed, like Communists the world over, to be extremely adept at propaganda organization the same was not held generally true of the 'ragged, rather African plan' that was Mau Mau. Those Mau Mau (or KAU) leaders who were believed to be astute propagandists were quickly removed from the scene in October 1952 during Operation Jock Scott. Mau Mau was thus left without public spokesmen. In fact, public speeches in support of Mau Mau had been illegal since its proscription in 1950. Thereafter the Kenya government nevertheless believed that effective KAU orators such as Kenyatta – whom they tried to enlist to make anti-Mau Mau speeches – were able to transmit subversive messages to their audiences by means of subtle gestures and nuanced language indecipherable to European listeners.[95] In August 1952, the Kenya government decided to ban KAU public meetings despite 'the admitted evil of preventing legitimate expression of political opinion'.[96] Consequently, after the round-up of October 1952, Mau Mau lacked both leaders and orators.

The government's determination to remove the KAU leadership was motivated by a belief that it contained men of considerable organizational ability without whom Mau Mau would collapse. Among the leadership's achievements, the Kenya government numbered a successful propaganda campaign which had persuaded the Kikuyu that the 'White Highlands' had been theirs in the past until illegally expropriated by white settlers. The Kenya government and settlers alike disputed the veracity of the charge, and one of the themes of official propaganda was to explode as nonsense Mau Mau's 'myth' of the 'White Highlands' as stolen Kikuyu territory. While colonial officials refused to countenance that men such as Kenyatta felt genuinely aggrieved over land, they regarded the repetition of the 'big lie' about the 'White Highlands' to be an effective application of Goebbels's technique to a Kikuyu audience only too ready to believe the message.[97] Kenyatta and other Mau Mau leaders were thought to be cynically exploiting a credulous peasantry for motives of personal gain, in terms of money and/or power – or even, as a Kenya CID report on Mau Mau in April 1952 proposed, 'the assuaging of sexual desire'.[98] Their adherents, softened up by the insidious influence of the Independent schools, readily swallowed the bait. According to Kenya's CID, demonstrable proof that the 'stolen land' propaganda was taking effect could be seen in the growing Kikuyu anti-European sentiment, evidenced by an arson campaign on settler estates in early 1952.[99] Kikuyu who resisted the lure of the 'big lie' were persuaded by other means: namely, the physical and psychological intimidation which accompanied the oath-taking ceremonies.

The Kenya government's anxiety that Mau Mau, the KAU and their fellow-travellers were successfully subverting the Kikuyu through their propaganda also led to a clampdown on the vernacular press. Like Kenyatta's covertly subversive speeches, the vernacular press was believed to be 'full of anti-European propaganda and encouragement of race hatred' but 'so cleverly conducted that it was virtually impossible to get convictions for sedition'.[100] Restrictions on the press formed one prong of the repressive measures taken in September 1952. Thus, by the time the State of Emergency was declared in October, the administration had ensured that Mau Mau had few opportunities to produce propaganda other than of the deed. The nature of the ensuing conflict – Mau Mau's flight to the forest in the months after the Emergency declaration, and its leaders' avoidance of the limelight in order to prolong a campaign of attrition – ensured that there was no opportunity for chosen journalists to meet with Mau Mau leaders, as a handful had met with the Irgun leaders in Palestine.

Mau Mau's propaganda was therefore limited to hand-produced literature (the 'hymn books' and manifestos) intended mainly for the fighters in the forest, and to its actions. In this respect, the oath ceremonies could be seen as a form of propaganda – expressions of Mau Mau ideology.[101] The killing of 'loyalists' similarly generated a powerful message to opponents of the movement – potent enough to cause the collapse of many trials of Mau Mau adherents through lack of witnesses willing to testify. Likewise, attacks on settlers' estates clearly produced a psychological result, though whether it was the one Mau Mau wished to evoke is quite a different matter.[102] Moreover, as Itote has written, whatever Mau Mau intended by particular activities, the overall effect of the movement's very existence was a challenge to the colonial government.

The Targets of Government Propaganda

However circumscribed Mau Mau's ability to produce propaganda at the conventional level was, by the end of October 1952 the Colonial Office and Kenya government were in no doubt that the challenge it posed required an immediate improvement in the government's own propaganda. Sustained attention needed to be directed towards the presentation of Mau Mau far beyond Kenya itself.

The United Kingdom

The most obvious indicator of governmental concern about domestic opinion on Kenya was the appointment of Granville Roberts – formerly the *East African Standard*'s agricultural correspondent – as Government of Kenya Public Relations Officer in London.[103] His duties included briefing reporters on the Emergency and encouraging a steady flow of good news from Kenya. A staple of Roberts's (and the Colonial Office Information Department's) work was to guard against British press misrepresentation of the Kenyan situation. As in previous Emergencies, this was necessary for international, as well as domestic and colonial, reasons. The Director of Information Services, Charles Carstairs, made this clear in December 1952, when he wrote that:

The Government's handling of the emergency in Kenya is not

receiving as good a Press as it should, and could; and it is in the interest alike of H.M.G. and of the Kenya Government itself that action should be taken as soon as possible to remedy this. A bad Press abroad reacts on Kenya itself: witness the alacrity with which West Africans and Indians have sprung to the defence of Jomo Kanyatta [sic] and his associates. Moreover bad publicity helps to increase the flow of P.Q.s and thus adds materially to the burden of unproductive work both here and in Nairobi.[104]

In autumn 1952 the British press had indeed proved awkward. During the lengthy wait for Baring's arrival in Kenya, the Beaverbrook press became extremely critical of Lyttelton, not regarding Baring's unfortunate mishap with an axe (he had nearly severed his hand while chopping wood) as sufficient justification for leaving the troubled colony Governorless for some months.[105] The press was unhelpful in other ways: either by sensationalizing Mau Mau or by going to the opposite extreme, and alleging, as did an article in October's New Statesman, that Mau Mau was a creation of settler propaganda, exaggerated in order to justify settler calls for repression of the KAU.

There were other reasons why British opinion needed attention. Even if, as Carstairs sometimes suggested, the press became more 'responsible' early on in the Emergency, Kenya was very much in the public eye and for that reason alone merited careful Colonial Office scrutiny. Indeed, Lyttelton later made clear that he had been particularly irritated by the attention paid to Kenya by Labour's backbenchers, whom he likened to 'a factious and yelping pack of terriers'.[106] The visit of two of Labour's most dogged anti-imperialists, Fenner Brockway and Leslie Hale, to Kenya (allegedly at the KAU's invitation and expense) in October 1952 doubtless helped to persuade the Colonial Office that British socialist opinion on Kenya would be troublesome.

More marginal than Labour's anti-imperialists, though only a little less vexatious for the government, was the British Communist Party. As Carstairs commented in December 1952:

There is . . . clear evidence that, however little Communism may have had to do with Mau Mau, Communists and their friends are making systematic propaganda use of the situation, and are allying themselves with African and other non-European nationalist sentiment.[107]

This was as true of the CPGB as its comrades overseas. The Daily Worker quickly began to report the Emergency along much the same lines as it had reported, and continued to report, the Malayan Emergency. As in Malaya, the colonial authorities were depicted by the Daily Worker as trying to destroy trade unions and legitimate nationalist aspirations of the Kenyan people by scapegoating a so-called terrorist organization, and using that as grounds for oppressing the entire Kikuyu population.[108] As the counter-insurgency campaign progressed, and allegations of security force atrocities became rife, the Colonial Office no doubt paid more attention to the *Daily Worker* as its charges found echoes in more respectable quarters.

Kenya

It goes without saying that propaganda was urgently required in Kenya itself as a result of the Mau Mau disturbances. As we have already seen, the Kenya government took the precaution of limiting the channels of publicity open to its opponents at an early stage. Censorship was heavily applied in other ways too: whereas the Malayan authorities had found it impossible to prevent the import of the *Daily Worker* into the Federation of Malaya, their Kenyan counterparts felt no compunction at banning not only the *Daily Worker* but a lengthy list of subversive publications.[109]

Clearly, though, positive propaganda was needed as the counter-weight to censorship. Three main constituencies had to be reached, each demanding very different treatment. First, Mau Mau members had to be induced to surrender, through propaganda as well as military defeat. One recent article has suggested that the propaganda campaign was 'at least as intense as the military one'.[110] Second, 'loyal' and wavering Africans required persuasion that, to use an early Kenya information office slogan, 'Mau Mau is an evil thing'. They also had to be reminded that a form of constitutional democracy, such as Kenya was tentatively progressing towards, was far more devoutly to be wished for than the return to savagery presaged by Mau Mau. Third, Kenya's white settlers also required propaganda extolling democracy's virtues: as Carstairs ruefully minuted in July 1953, 'Africans are not the only people in Kenya in need of guidance and indoctrination.'[111]

Indeed, far from the settlers and the colonial authorities sharing a complete identification of outlook, there was considerable friction between the two groups. The settlers regarded career colonial civil servants and their Whitehall masters as lacking a proper understanding of the 'natives' – the sole preserve of Kenya's permanent settlers.[112] Angered by what they perceived as Colonial Office softness towards Mau Mau, the settlers protested, and were rewarded with the inclusion of settler representatives on the 'War Council'.[113] The embittered expatriates were no more fond of journalists than of colonial officials, and felt that they were unfairly criticized in the international press for demanding stringent measures which, in their eyes, were the only remedy for Mau Mau.[114] To rectify this 'misrepresentation' Blundell launched a campaign designed to secure better coverage for Kenyan affairs in January 1953 under the banner 'The Truth about Kenya'. The initial aim was to collect sufficient funds to enable the settlers to send their own public relations officer to London. His brief, as Blundell told Leslie Hore-Belisha, was to 'put over what white settlement has done in Africa and counter many of the slanders which are made against us'.[115]

For their part, the colonial authorities reciprocated the settlers' animosity, although were more discreet in venting it. The two groups had an essential difference of outlook on how Kenya should be governed. From a Colonial Office perspective the settlers either did not understand, or did not accept, Westminster's post-war commitment to seeing the colonies progress towards self-government, albeit at a differential pace determined by particular local circumstances.[116] The settlers' hankering after times past, and their ruthlessness in dealing with Mau Mau (many of the detainees' allegations of brutality and torture concerned the Kenya Regiment, which was drawn from the ranks of the settlers[117]). caused very real problems for government propagandists whose job was *inter alia* to publicize Britain's achievements in Kenya. They feared that observers outside the colony would tar the Colonial Office with the same brush as the more extreme settlers. The latter were, unfortunately, not easily muzzled; as Bill Gorrell Barnes remarked to Sir Thomas Lloyd in February 1953, 'if only the silly element of the settlers could be kept quiet, it could be imagined that there are some splendid fellows among them who are thinking constructively even in these times'.[118]

Likewise the military leadership – whom one might have imagined more sympathetic to the settlers' frustration – shared Colonial Office irritation. Erskine, in particular, quickly developed an antipathy towards the settlers: they were all 'common middle class sluts', he wrote to his wife.[119] They also had a regrettable tendency to extrapolate from their limited local knowledge the overall state of military operations:

> The settler is not a good judge of the situation. He looks at things entirely from the situation in his own locality – if he loses a few cows he thinks we are doing badly. He does not know the Reserve or the Forest and he can't understand why we don't brush up all the gangs and march home! The settlers are difficult as you know and far too many of them have the South African outlook to the African problems.[120]

The military leadership also resented the settlers' resort to illegal methods and the excesses of the Kenya Regiment which cast a slur on the British troops' own good name. Through propaganda, though, the Colonial Office hoped to dilute the 'South African outlook' of Kenya's white population.

The Empire-Commonwealth

Propaganda was also directed at audiences beyond Britain and Kenya. The Colonial Office was particularly concerned that various members of the Empire-Commonwealth might take exception to the British response to Mau Mau. As A.H. Joyce of the Commonwealth Relations Office (CRO) pointed out to Charles Carstairs in January 1953:

> It matters a great deal in terms of Commonwealth relationship and understanding that we should do our utmost to show to the world that our policy in Kenya derives from no selfish Imperialistic motives (which is still suspected), but is designed wholly in the interests of the inhabitants of this territory.[121]

In short, the repression of Mau Mau had to be projected as part of Britain's effort to prepare Kenya for ultimate self-government, rather than as a prolongation of direct rule. To ascertain the state of colonial and dominion opinion on Mau Mau, the Colonial Office sent regular letters of enquiry to Governors and High Commissioners. As the Colonial Office feared, the indigenous populations of many colonies and dominions were indeed opposed to the government's handling of Mau Mau, although sometimes for entirely contradictory reasons.

India's political leaders and its press were outspokenly critical of Britain's handling of Mau Mau, regarding the latter as a legitimate expression of Kenyan nationalism.[122] Indian hostility was particularly alarming as Kenya contained a substantial Indian population, and the possibility that India entertained imperialist designs upon East Africa was one with which the Colonial Office toyed.[123] The British and Kenya governments were also concerned that Indians might be involved in Mau Mau.[124] As a consequence, India was bombarded with publicity material on British policy in Kenya, though six months after the start of the Emergency the High Commissioner in India still professed himself to be 'disturbed at the bad publicity we are getting over Kenya'.[125] This was underlined when Nehru remarked in various speeches in 1953 (the year that the Central African Federation was created) that the 'course of events in East, South and Central Africa were [sic] all part of a general design to crush the natives and ensure the continuing domination of the white settlers'. He even went so far as to suggest that Mau Mau might not really exist at all.[126]

Nehru's words had a galvanizing effect not only on newly independent states and colonized peoples, but also on settler opinion in South Africa, the Rhodesias and Kenya. South Africa was equally outspoken on the British handling of Mau Mau, but from a diametrically opposed perspective. Malan's Nationalist Party, and most of white South Africa, regarded Mau Mau (like the ANC) as a Communist-controlled conspiracy against minority rule in sub-Saharan Africa.[127] They feared that 'unless a firm policy is followed in the African Colonies, Mau-Mau and worse will spread throughout the continent'.[128] Nehru's rhetoric appeared as proof positive of India's imperialist designs in the continent. Britain found herself caught between the two. Both India and South Africa criticized HMG at once for its policy in Kenya *and* for failing to moderate the perceived extremism of the other's views. Pretoria resented New Delhi's public proclamations on Kenyan affairs, and 'expected that if the United Kingdom Government [were] going to take notice of what any other Government says about policy in African colonies, they [would] pay particular attention to the opinions of the only member of the Commonwealth in Africa'.[129] Propaganda was consequently required on all sides: to persuade Indians that Britain was not over-reacting to Mau Mau, while simultaneously reassuring South Africa of Britain's anti-terrorist mettle and debunking the myth of Communist involvement in Mau Mau.

The United States

Americans, like white South Africans, shared a tendency to perceive Mau Mau as a manifestation of international Communism. Although East Africa had not traditionally been a region of especial concern to America, the globalization of the Cold War transformed American notions of where their national security lay. As John Gunther put it in 1955, Africa was now America's 'Last Frontier':

> Africa lies open like a vaccuum, and is almost perfectly defenceless – the richest prize on earth. What is more it is defenceless in a period of Cold War. Besides it pants for development. If we do not help it to develop, somebody else will.[130]

There could be no mistaking who that 'somebody else' was. While Gunther himself was quite categorical that Mau Mau had nothing to do with Communism, other American journalists were not.[131] Foremost among them was Robert Ruark, *Life* correspondent and popular fiction writer, whose novel *Something of Value* was (Lonsdale suggests) the 'best known account of Mau Mau'.[132] Ruark articulated the fears of what was doubtless a considerable proportion of Americans when he wrote of Mau Mau in *Life*, in February 1953:

> I am convinced that its prime exponent, Jomo Kenyatta, is by no means his own man. He was educated abroad, boasts of spending several years in Moscow, is married to a white woman, and is a highly intelligent fellow. Mau Mau's top leaders are unknown,

but they have cunningly exploited the grievances of many simple, misguided people.[133]

Loose conjecture that Kenyatta's stay in Moscow made him a Communist (or as near as dammit) was common enough. But Ruark claimed to have evidence, albeit of a somewhat tenuous kind: a letter had come into his possession, 'translated into halting English by an Indian clerk', which described Mau Mau as 'the African's Communist Unit'. Ruark at once insinuated that Russian and Indian influence underlay Mau Mau, and he later made even greater play with the international conspiracy behind Mau Mau in *Something of Value*.[134] Ruark's writing was sensationalist and alarmist, with its intimations that Mau Mau might spread to other tribes, 'joining up with racial strife to the south and all the way north'.[135] However, it was also undoubtedly popular, and was precisely the sort of 'very ordinary tripe' (as the CO's Dixon Barton referred to Ruark's article) which British propaganda sought to counter.[136]

Even if Mau Mau had not appeared to hold potential for Communist involvement, its sensational and sexual aspects fascinated American audiences. Furthermore, Americans were perhaps also more inclined to perceive Mau Mau as a racial dispute between blacks and whites, and to suggest that Kenya's colour bar was one factor behind the Kikuyu revolt, and hence to see in the confrontation an echo of their own racial strife.[137] This was not quite the image of Mau Mau which Britain wanted to project, preferring to depict it as an inter-Kikuyu dispute, and so in this respect also British propaganda was a necessary antidote.

Propaganda Organization

With so many audiences to be reached, each needing specialized treatment, the propaganda organization in Kenya required immediate improvements in the autumn of 1952. When the Colonial Office turned its attention to the state of Kenya's information services it found the same state of neglect and disorder as it had already discovered in Malaya, and would shortly in Cyprus.[138] On 23 October, Carstairs warned Lyttelton that an efficient information machine did not exist in Kenya. Information activities were broken up and scattered about various agencies, with 'no one point – short of the Chief Secretary and Governor – at which a view can be taken of information problems as a whole'. The most urgent requirement was thus for a single Director of Information who would actually be privy to the policy-making process.[139] This disorganization should have surprised no one. As early as April 1952, Ingrams's report on the prospects for Communism in East and Central Africa had warned that the region's most urgent need was for improved information services. These were particularly poor in Kenya.[140] Consequently, when the Emergency began the Colonial Office regretted having closed the United Kingdom Information Office to East Africa in 1949.[141]

Mau Mau activities in the months preceding the Emergency focused attention on Nairobi's press-management arrangements. With the appearance of sensationalist press articles on Kenya, the Colonial Office advised Nairobi that such reporting was virtually inevitable, but that certain steps might also be taken. Haler recommended that the Kenya authorities should seize every opportunity of putting over in speeches, official communiqués and radio talks a 'factual review of the situation'; full information about developments should be supplied both to the local press and to the Colonial Office Information Department, which would consider having a 'senior and publicity-minded official' address the Lobby.[142] As in other Emergencies, releasing speedy, accurate reports of terrorist incidents was of the essence:

> You will appreciate the desirability of issuing to the press prompt and adequate information about the situation. We have found it is always better to seize the initiative in matters of this kind by making an official statement *before* the press have had time to publish unofficial (and often highly exaggerated) versions of an event.[143]

Kenya's response was to send Granville Roberts to London to tackle Fleet Street face to face, and provide the Colonial Office Information Department with 'accurate information about the law and order situation'.[144]

Whatever could be done at the London end to influence the press and pre-empt unhelpful reportage, it was imperative that the Kenya government put its own house in order, particularly if it was to produce successful propaganda for internal consumption. Baring was aware of this, but his proposed remedies for the propaganda organization's deficiencies met with sharp Colonial Office disapproval. For many months Whitehall remained dissatisfied with information work in Kenya and Baring's attitude towards it.[145] Tension arose between the Governor and the Colonial Office primarily because of Baring's *idée fixe* that Kenya must be equipped with a psychological warfare officer. Baring's obsession with this notion suggested that his grasp of the rudiments of propaganda work was none too firm. He first made his request for a psychological warfare expert to Gorrell Barnes in November 1952.[146] Although sceptical about the notion of a 'psychological warfare' wizard, the Colonial Office information department agreed that it was vital to fill the hitherto non-existent post of Director of Information, and the vacant position of Kenya Government Press Officer.[147] No one suitable being found in Kenya itself, the Colonial

Office and Baring settled on Brigadier William Gibson for the Directorship and Alastair Matheson as Press Officer. The two men arrived in Kenya in February to set about reorganizing information work.

While the 'myth of Mau Mau' literature gives the impression that British/Kenya government propaganda was so successful that a well-oiled machine must have co-ordinated the defamation of Mau Mau, in reality Kenya's propaganda organization was riven with personal animosities, confusion and mistrust. Visiting Kenya in April 1953, Lyttelton's Parliamentary Private Secretary (PPS), Hugh Fraser, reported that Gibson was 'setting about his job competently'.[148] Baring, however, was not yet content with the shape of his information department. In June, several further alterations were proposed by Nairobi, including the removal of Granville Roberts from London to Nairobi, 'to give news from Kenya the right slant for London papers', and putting the Army in charge of 'sitreps' (situation reports) on operations.[149] In other words, the Army would be responsible for the release of news relating to the counter-insurgency campaign, while Matheson would, in Baring's words, be able to 'devote more time to fossicking out information from the Members [of Legco] and me'.[150]

Colonial Office personnel were divided in their response. There was general agreement that Granville Roberts was better off staying in London.[151] However, the proposal to have the Army issue news was more controversial: the Colonial Office had already had to warn Gibson to give his press releases a 'less "Shikari" flavour'.[152] Indeed, the Colonial Office had been anxiously weeding out sporting and hunting metaphors from Kenya's press releases following complaints (from as far afield as West Africa) that operations against Mau Mau were described in terms more redolent of big-game shoots than a conflict between two sets of human antagonists.[153] The Colonial Office had similarly cautioned the BBC for inappropriate language – only to find that the Corporation was merely replicating the vocabulary of Kenya's official press releases.[154] The Army might be insensitive to the nuances of language, and, as E.B. David recognized, there was a danger in alotting the military a news-disseminating role:

> The presentation of emergency news, even if it is largely of an operational character, very often carries a political slant, and it is easy for this to be overlooked or not realised by an Army press officer. We have had difficulties over this in Malaya . . .[155]

Although the Army did in fact take on this role, Lyttelton warned Baring that he should encourage greater balance in the news. Previously there had been 'far too much purely military and security news', statistics on the killing of Mau Mau adherents and so on, and 'far too little about the good things and large areas of peace and progress, against which

Mau Mau events should be seen'.[156] Lyttelton also complained that Baring had sent insufficient information for the 'frequent skirmishes in the House of Commons'. To rectify matters, he suggested that the new Deputy Governor, Sir Frederick Crawford, be given special responsibility for information policy as a whole.

When Crawford duly became Deputy Governor, he was warned by the Colonial Office that Kenya's propaganda work was inadequate, with too little attention being paid to 'the human approach to a human problem': namely, the winning of hearts and minds.[157] If the Colonial Office hoped that Crawford would remedy the deficiencies, it was sorely disappointed. In Crawford, Baring had found an ally for his request that a psychological warfare expert be sent. When Harold Evans (then Carstairs's deputy in the information department) visited Kenya in August 1953, he found a mood of despondency:

> They are worried on two counts – (a) the "outward projection" problem . . . and (b) the apparent failure to get into the minds of the Kikuyu, either the active Mau Mau or the people on the fence.
>
> Of the two, (a) is the less difficult though it is difficult enough – especially if, as Gibson, Reiss [the African Information Officer] and company suggest, there is very little actual achievement in African development to publicise, or, at any rate, achievement on the kind of scale that will be taken notice of by the Press outside Kenya. Baring and Crawford showed no signs of sharing these doubts, however, and their concern was to expand or adjust the information machinery to make it more effective.[158]

It was clear that a serious rift was developing between Gibson and the information staff on the one hand, and the Governor and Deputy Governor on the other. As Evans tellingly remarked, 'It is an indication of a not very satisfactory state of affairs that Gibson was not even present at these interviews, since it would seem to imply that he does not carry the full confidence of Baring and Crawford.'[159] Recriminations were mutual. The propaganda team were excluded from policy-making, and even felt that policy was lacking. Gibson made this point to Evans, and repeated it to Hugh Fraser MP shortly after, who took a less sympathetic view: absence of government policy 'never worried Dr. Goebbels, nor must it worry the Propaganda office'.[160] For their part, Baring and Crawford blamed the failure to reach the Kikuyu on a shortcoming in propaganda and, more pointedly, on deficiencies with the propaganda personnel. As Evans was well aware, they were paying for their misconception of propaganda work, while Gibson was unpopular precisely because they were paying him a miracle-worker's salary:

It was obviously a crass misunderstanding of the role of information services – as we knew at the time – to think that you had only to pay enough money to get a miracleman who would transform the situation. I have said as often as I can, to as many people as I can, that information services can *not* produce miracles: that they are only an instrument of policy: and that the policy must be right and the facts favourable before they can produce results.[161]

Baring, however, persisted in thinking that even if Gibson was not a miracle-worker one could still be found. He wanted a fresh appointee to take care of external projection, being unsure whether Matheson was up to the job,[162] and to compensate for Gibson's lack of 'a newspaperman's sense of urgency'. Baring and Crawford also had the influential support of General Erskine. Indeed, the renewed request for a psychological warfare expert was pointedly made by Erskine to Harding (the Commander of the Imperial General Staff), *not* to Lyttelton:

> The Governor and myself feel we need a man of high quality who will focus his attention on a psychological approach to the Kikuyu tribe to present the best of our intentions and actions. This requires a man who has knowledge of how to put ideas across and who understands the technique of psychological warfare.[163]

The Colonial Office was concerned that Erskine and Baring did not appear to know what they wanted, or even what psychological warfare was.[164] Carstairs also sagely suggested that even if they acquired 'some sort of "wizard"', he in turn would be relegated. He had in mind not only Gibson's experience, but also the 'Malayan parallel', which was 'not encouraging'. There Templer had chosen his own 'wizard' without UK intervention (a barbed reference to Alec Peterson), 'had sanctioned the building up of a large organisation and was now tearing it down'.[165]

The second weakness with the Governor and Commander-in-Chief's case was that they seemed already to have someone who matched their own vague requirements, namely one who 'knew the African mind in general and the Kikuyu mind in particular'.[166] Dr Louis Leakey professed to know the Kikuyu better than any other white man,[167] and had the added advantage of being 'strongly anti-Mau Mau'.[168] Local knowledge was at a premium given that, as E.B. David put it, 'the vast mass of the Kikuyu tribe' were 'the battleground on which this struggle is being waged'.[169] Psychological warfare in the narrow sense (which David defined as 'exerting pressure on a particular group of people in order to condition their minds in a particular direction, and not to be over-scrupulous about how this is done') *might* be used to induce Mau Mau adherents to surrender, though David cautioned that he thought its potential in Kenya was 'very small'. Such measures, however, were inappropriate to build up the Kikuyu's determination to resist terrorism:

> We frankly cannot see how any outside 'expert' is going to help
> you on this nor do we believe that any new organisation can provide
> a short cut or a substitute for the necessarily arduous and slow
> task of winning the people over, a task in which all Government
> Departments should be made to realise that they have a part to
> play, and in which the Information Services must feature more
> largely than any, being the means by which Government policy
> is made known – Government's 'loudspeaker' in effect. Better
> co-ordination, more effective direction, wider imagination – all
> these may perhaps be needed, but surely they do not require a
> newcomer; and the appreciation and assessment ... [of Africans'
> 'mental capacity, susceptibilities' and so on] must be based on the
> information and views obtained from your Intelligence set-up, your
> Leakeys, Provincial Administration and those with greatest under-
> standing of the Kikuyu mind.[170]

In brief, David advised that better use be made of Gibson – that
he co-ordinate information work and be brought into 'much closer
association with your inner counsels than he is today'.

The upshot of this firm guidance from the Colonial Office was that
Nairobi finally dropped its insistence on importing a psychological warfare
expert, and decided to concentrate instead on creating a 'very much
hotted up information and propaganda service, and to develop themes,
targets and channels'.[171] To this end, in September 1953 Crawford
reported the setting up of a secret 'Propaganda Working Party', which
would include Louis Leakey, Ben Ryan, and 'certain African Kikuyu
experts'.[172] This initiative was directed towards two vital objectives.
The first was to take informed advice on how best to influence the
'African mind'. In this respect it is significant that the first meeting of
the African Information 'Working Party' (on 2 November 1953) decided
to invite Dr J.C. Carothers, a 'world authority on African psychiatry', for
a two-month visit 'to investigate the psychological factors underlying
Mau Mau with a view to strengthening the support of loyalists and
assisting the rehabilitation of others'.[173] Second, the working party
was an attempt to overcome the gulf between the African information
officers (under John Reiss) and the propagandists whose work was for
external consumption. The committee also gave the Deputy Governor,
Crawford – its chairman – an overview of *all* branches of propaganda
work.

By the time the propaganda working party first met, then, the Emergency was in its thirteenth month. Propaganda was regarded by the
Colonial Office as 'one of the main keys to solving the Emergency', but
the setting up of an efficient propaganda machine had proved immensely
time-consuming and troublesome. Baring proved remarkably tenacious in

his wrong-headed determination to find a psychological warfare expert as a panacea for all Kenya's ills.[174] The real problem, of course, was less one of propaganda than of policy. In particular, the colony did still have a long way to go before its land-holding arrangements, the African standard of living and level of political representation could reasonably be expected to win the hearts and minds of interested outsiders, let alone of Kenya's African population.

Propaganda Themes and Channels

One of the earliest concerns of Foreign Office propagandists was that the Emergency in Kenya should not be perceived as a re-run of Malaya: an interminably protracted campaign against an elusive enemy which had at least moral support from like-minded regimes abroad. The Head of the Information Policy Department (IPD), A.C.E. Malcolm, wrote to Carstairs the month after the Emergency was declared, requesting

> material to substantiate the thesis that Kenya is not, repeat not, going to develop into 'another Malaya' and I should dearly like to have a handful of sound arguments to put into circulation. On the face of it there is altogether too much similarity for the propagandist's convenience: bush = jungle; Mau Mau = bandits; non-juring African victims = non-Communist Chinese squatters; civilian apathy = civilian apathy; planters = planters. I am sure this is all very superficial but I am trying to put myself in the position of the friendly but ignorant foreigner who needs some comforting facts that he can repeat to his friends.[175]

What Malcolm essentially hoped was that Mau Mau should be presented (as Cleary suggests it was) as 'a small, unpopular, easily controllable, savage tribal uprising'.[176] Carstairs reassured the IPD that propaganda on Mau Mau would emphasize the inter-Kikuyu nature of the conflict: 'facts illustrating African opposition to Mau Mau' would be communicated to the press daily.[177] Indeed, throughout the Emergency Baring was requested to supply material to illustrate both that Mau Mau's casualties were primarily African, and that fellow Kikuyu formed the front line of defence against Mau Mau terrorism.[178] The irony in this was – as Malcolm himself soon realized – that the basic themes of propaganda on Mau Mau were identical to those on Malaya: that the victims of terrorism were of the same ethnicity as the terrorists; that the terrorists did not enjoy external support, nor were they a legitimate nationalist movement; and that Britain was doing much to promote the social and political advancement of the colonial inhabitants.[179] Labelling Mau Mau 'terrorists' was, once again, central to the delegitimizing process, and again the British and Kenya governments employed labels self-consciously: Gibson himself stated that the 'normal words for Mau Mau supporters are "terrorists" or "gangsters"', with the term 'thug' inadvertently slipping into official communiqués on occasion.[180]

The portrayal of the Mau Mau uprising as a civil war was, from Britain's point of view, a comforting fact in its own right – not that it was a complete distortion. The Emergency was projected as a confrontation less between dissatisfied colonial subjects and their rulers – a black versus white conflict – than between progressive and regressive factions of the same tribe. The Kenya government and settlers were absolved from any real responsibility for the Emergency, while explanations of what had caused this internecine Kikuyu conflict drew on other similarly self-serving (though probably genuinely held) beliefs. The origins of the 'civil war' were thus explained in terms of Kikuyu psychology, as an Information Paper written by Gorrell Barnes for West African ministers demonstrates:

The exact nature, organisation and origins of Mau Mau are in some respects obscure. It is almost entirely a Kikuyu movement, and it appears to derive from certain peculiarities of Kikuyu tradition and tribal organisation. It is shot through with witchcraft, which has always played a very big part in Kikuyu tribal customs, particularly in relation to the use of land. It has indeed been suggested that Mau Mau represents, in part, a last effort of the witchdoctors to retain their influence in the face of the advance of education and civilisation.[181]

In other words, the Colonial Office projected a view of Mau Mau – common enough in settlers' and others' analyses of the movement – as an atavistic reversion to primitive savagery. Mau Mau's barbarism resulted from a peculiarity within the Kikuyu which rendered many of them incapable of responding to the challenge of civilization. The effect of this line of reasoning was further to deflect blame from Kenya's colonizers, as even in the mid-1950s few in Britain felt qualms about the very notion of a 'civilizing mission'. One Kenya missionary's contemporaneous account of Mau Mau made this absolution more explicit, when (defending missionary behaviour) he remarked that 'the shaking of a whole society to its very depths was *not exactly anybody's special fault*' (emphasis added).[182] Moreover, the positive result of this dislocation was progress, and a steady stream of works by Kenyan settlers, as well as government propaganda, drew attention to the advantages which colonization had brought Kenya.[183]

Stress on Mau Mau primitivism was also calculated to make the movement appear unlike a nationalist one. Propaganda laboured to delineate laudable ('progressive' and moderate) nationalism and unacceptable (unrepresentative and violent) nationalism, to Mau Mau's detriment. The indisputable fact that Mau Mau was largely confined to one tribe, the Kikuyu (and its 'cousins', the Embu and Meru), reinforced the message that Mau Mau was not a manifestation of 'orthodox' nationalism. As Gorrell Barnes's paper explained, Kenya's other tribes believed that Mau Mau leaders aimed 'not at African but at Kikuyu dominance in Kenya':

> There is in fact in Mau Mau a strong element of exclusive nationalism, based not on racial and national pride, but on envy and hate. This basis is demonstrated, as in other cases (cf. Hitler's nationalism) in extreme ruthlessness towards the Kikuyu itself, who have so far been the most numerous victims of the Mau Mau.[184]

If Mau Mau was 'nationalist', it belonged to the illegitimate strain.

The other main themes of propaganda on Mau Mau all supported the central thesis that it was a retrogressive Kikuyu affair. In particular, details (or alleged details) of Mau Mau's oath ceremonies were regarded by the Colonial Office and Kenya information services as especially suited to the task of rectifying any 'misconceptions' about Mau Mau. Indeed, when Lyttelton announced the declaration of a State of Emergency in Kenya, he emphasized that Mau Mau pursued its aims 'by forcing secret oaths upon men, women and children by intimidating witnesses and law-abiding citizens'. Africans who refused to take the oath were strung up from rafters until they became unconscious, while those who did participate were committed to the murder of Europeans.[185] The oath ceremonies and Mau Mau terrorism were thus inseparable.

The Colonial Office Information Department and Foreign Office Information Services Department both commissioned articles about the oath ceremony and acquired rights to reproduce press articles which were thought to carry the desired message.[186] Several points about the oath ceremonies were stressed. Initially, the oaths were represented as an attempt by Mau Mau's leaders to attract followers by promising a return to old Kikuyu customs. The oaths were thus more or less traditional to Kikuyu society.[187] The ceremonies were also a means of accumulating profit for Mau Mau leaders, as Lyttelton told the House of Commons in November 1952.[188] However, as Mau Mau oaths, and activities, became more extreme, the primitivism and cannibalism of the oath ceremonies were employed as explanations of how men could be made to perform acts such as those reported to have taken place at Lari – including the drinking of decapitated babies' blood.[189] The oaths were now depicted as a wilful perversion of Kikuyu custom, so degrading that all who took part were instantly cast out of 'normal' Kikuyu society, and bound to Mau Mau as the only alternative society which would accept them.[190]

Material on Mau Mau oaths was thus supplied as an antidote to the criticism that Mau Mau arose from real political and economic grievances, and that Britain's repression of 'terrorism' was an inadequate response. For example, the Colonial Office seized upon the idea of providing India with lurid details of the oaths as the most suitable means of countering that country's 'misperceptions', H.T. Bourdillon writing:

> I think this is a suitable opportunity to counter the Indian sug-
> gestion that Mau Mau is a popular and ultimately progressive
> liberation movement to which the complete solution is concessions
> by Her Majesty's Government, and in this connection to draw the
> Indian Government's attention to the notorious Mau Mau oaths
> and ceremonies, details of which will already have been or might
> simultaneously be given to them by the UK High Commissioner.[191]

However, there was a disadvantage in using salacious details about the oaths in this way. As the Emergency progressed, the oath ceremonies became (or were purported to become) so perverted that the British government baulked at openly publicizing details of Mau Mau's sexual depravity. No matter how much the government wanted Mau Mau to be correctly understood – and the security forces' activities against such an inhuman enemy to be free from criticism – it was also committed to upholding public standards of decency. Consequently, when a European Member of Legco, Group Captain Briggs, requested in 1953 that Kenya's Publicity Officer in London fully inform MPs of the latest form of the Mau Mau oath, the Governor delicately responded that he did not propose to use Granville Roberts as 'a source of information on bestiality and unnatural practices'.[192] This predicament arose more sharply in 1954, when a Parliamentary delegation of both Conservative and Labour MPs visiting Kenya was given information on Mau Mau's later oaths, which were so perverted that

> the only possible deduction to be drawn from them is that we are
> now faced in Kenya with a terrorist organisation composed not of
> ordinary humans fighting for a cause, but of primitive beasts who
> have forsaken all moral codes in order to achieve the subjugation
> of the Kikuyu tribe and the ultimate massacre of the European
> population of the Colony.[193]

However, the MPs were not permitted to publish details of Mau Mau perversions – which included intercourse with dead sheep and the drinking of prostitutes' menstrual blood – in the main body of their report. The report was published as a White Paper, but the Cabinet decided, on Lyttelton's recommendation, that the report's appendix

159

(detailing Mau Mau oaths) was of such obscenity that it could not be included in a government publication.[194] MPs, however, were allowed to read the obscene details in the privacy of the House of Commons Library.

In fact, the government had always been less coy in private about publicizing salacious material. Ways were found to make the more obscene oaths known to those whose acquaintance with them would do the government's cause the most good. The *Daily Express* railed against the government's censorship of the 'banned' appendix – 'Unprintable they no doubt are, but, while they remain unprinted, how can the public form a true picture of this crisis?', the editor opined[195] – but in fact the paper had only itself to blame for its exclusion from the circle of editors circulated with a copy of the appendix.[196] Access to secret material was used as a reward for editorial good behaviour, and for some time before the publication of the White Paper selected editors had been privy to confidential material on Mau Mau oaths.[197] Editors who were shown such documents were obviously not intended to publish them but, having been privy to government confidences, they were perhaps rather less inclined to demand publication, and all the more ready to praise the manner in which Mau Mau was being handled. Thus *The Times* welcomed the government's restraint in withholding obscene material, and claimed that the paper itself had felt obliged to forgo publication of some details sent back from its Kenya correspondent.[198]

A double standard thus underlay government propaganda: public prudishness and private prurience. Had the government been genuinely committed to preserving the public from the more obscene details, it would surely have baulked at the publication of Robert Ruark's *Something of Value* in Britain. Leakey was proved wrong in his opinion, voiced in *Defeating Mau Mau*, that to give 'full details of the horrible, filthy and degrading acts . . . would be to ensure that [the] book was never published, or if it was, that it would be banned'.[199] Ruark not only managed it, but when his novel was turned into a feature film in 1957 (admittedly without some of the novel's excesses), Churchill himself recorded a prologue. Details of the oath ceremonies were also provided to British troops arriving in Kenya in a background pamphlet issued by GHQ East Africa. The paragraphs outlining Mau Mau ceremonies were fairly tame, but the booklet also came with a detachable, 'confidential' appendix, 'issued by GHQ East Africa to certain recipients of the pamphlet'.[200] This contained material identical to that in the White Paper appendix.[201] In short, Blundell's false modesty in describing the oaths could be read as an unintentional parody of the governmental dual standard:

I do not intend to give full details of the increasing horror of the Mau Mau oaths. . . . Suffice it to say that masturbation in public, the drinking of menstrual blood, unnatural acts with animals, and even the penis of dead men all played a part in this terrible destruction of the Kikuyu mind.[202]

If it is easy to comprehend the centrality of Mau Mau oaths to government propaganda, it is less obvious why those responsible for propaganda eschewed linking Mau Mau and international Communism. Indeed, the utility of implying a linkage appears such that some writers have assumed that official propaganda did precisely this: thus Furedi's remark that the colonial government attempted to portray Mau Mau as 'influenced by world communism'.[203] The examples Furedi cites – Carothers's pamphlet, Leakey's work and the Corfield Report – do not substantiate his claim. Only Corfield paid any real attention to the question of Mau Mau's relationship with Communism, and he concluded that the movement had 'virtually no connection with Communism, but was developed by Kenyatta as an atavistic tribal rising aimed against Western civilisation and technology and in particular against the Government and the Europeans as symbols of progress'.[204] His view in fact exemplifies that of the Colonial Office.

From this statement, it would be a mistake to extrapolate that the government was unconcerned about the prospect of Communist infiltration in Africa, or that it did not worry that the Kremlin might be aiding Mau Mau. The Colonial Office's 'expert' on Communism in the colonies, Harold Ingrams, reported in 1952 that although Communism in West Africa was more advanced, a latent threat existed in East Africa:

> since Communist tactics require the keeping open of sores caused by the friction between imperialist rulers and subject peoples awakening to nationalism, until such time as they can be profitably brought to a head, it has to be remembered the potential dangers in East and Central Africa are greater than in West Africa for there are far more possible causes of friction, largely due to the multi-racial problem.[205]

The Colonial Office consequently took seriously the possibility that the Soviet Union might be (or become) involved in Mau Mau but, unless evidence existed, was reluctant to portray the movement as a Kremlin puppet.

Such scruples exercised the Foreign Office Information Research Department rather less. The latter had been involved in anti-Communist propaganda work in Africa since its inception.[206] The IRD's very *raison d'être* – namely publicizing the Communist threat and promoting the democratic way of life – predisposed it towards regarding Communism as more pervasive than did other departments. Moreover, the nature of its work, and the unattributable character of much of its output, doubtless inclined the IRD to be more creative with the facts than colleagues in the

Colonial Office. Consequently friction arose between members of the CO Information Department and the IRD over how to handle the question of Communism and Mau Mau.

From the onset of the Emergency, articles periodically appeared in the British and American press suggesting that the Soviet Union was behind Mau Mau. These the Foreign Office carefully noted. An article in the *Kansas City Star* of 24 October 1952, for example, stated that: 'It seems a fairly safe guess that if Communists are not yet connected with this terroristic movement, they soon will be', and criticized the British government's imperialistic policies which had resulted in the Mau Mau movement.[207] Articles such as this prompted the Foreign Office Information Policy Department, in consultation with the Colonial Office, to issue a press release through the BIS which asserted – among other 'Facts about the Mau Mau' – that 'there is no evidence that either Mau Mau or its policy is in any way inspired or directed by Communists'.[208] But, ever keen to promote its own business, the IRD wanted to gain rather more mileage from a possible Communist connection with Mau Mau than this outright rejection, and it began to press the Colonial Office to put together an 'Intel' (an attributable background briefing note) on the subject. One senses from the IRD's insistence to Harold Ingrams that the Intel should 'discuss possibilities and presumptions' that factual accuracy was not an absolute requirement.[209] Unfortunately for the IRD, certain members of the Colonial Office were less willing than Ingrams to play on 'presumptions' about a possible Communist intrigue. Dixon Barton, in particular, was adamant that the Colonial Office should not play the IRD game. He therefore toned down Ingrams's draft Intel considerably, to reflect his own belief that 'there are not, as yet, any features of the Mau Mau disturbances which suggest Communist influence'. Similarly, Jomo Kenyatta's period spent studying in Moscow was insufficient basis for any presumptions, Barton insisting that 'there is no evidence that he has been influenced by Communist techniques in any share he has had in planning the present disturbances'.[210]

Despite Ingrams's and the IRD's promptings that Britain might appear complacent if it absolutely rejected any link between Communism and Mau Mau (given that Communists would, at the very least, hope to capitalize on the discomfort Mau Mau caused Britain[211]), the line adopted appears to have been closer to Barton's. The issue, however, remained something of an open sore between the IRD and Barton for some months. Barton maintained a continuous watch against rearguard IRD activities. For example, he moved to scotch rumours in the British press in December 1952 to the effect that the Soviet Embassy in Addis Ababa was supplying aid to Mau Mau.[212] On this occasion the Foreign Office issued a telegram stating that it 'would be difficult to choose a more inconvenient spot [than Addis Ababa] for subversive activities. . . . Ethiopia itself is too backward to provide fertile ground for communist activities.'[213] Barton was then dismayed to find, in June 1953, that the IRD regarded Ruark's article in *Life* as 'second hand evidence of Communism behind Mau Mau', and was using its publication to call for a fresh 'Intel' on the subject.[214] Barton's response is testimony to the reluctance of the Colonial Office to create propaganda on a basis of a known untruth:

> I am afraid I cannot force myself into proving what I do not believe . . . and I thought all this had been thrashed out with the FO's IRD some time ago. As I have said, that FO Department gets the summary of Intelligence every month; they can be reminded of that and be, yet again, told that when we have anything approaching 'evidence' of Communism being behind Mau Mau we will make a point of telling them.[215]

Truthfulness was, of course, the traditional basis for attributable government propaganda. This was perhaps the main reason why British propaganda on Mau Mau on the whole avoided playing the Communist card. Denials of Communist involvement in Mau Mau were not always as unambiguous as Barton's. Official propaganda never disavowed that Communists sought to profit from Britain's misfortune in Kenya, and not everyone was as scrupulous about evidence. Some allowed ideological conviction to outweigh the lack of demonstrable proof that Communism was behind Mau Mau. Lyttelton himself was reluctant to follow Barton's line too assiduously, and could not resist suggesting that Mau Mau had at least borrowed its organizational structure from the Communists.[216] Even in his memoirs, published after the Emergency was over, he repeated his conviction that Communists had aided and abetted the insurgency.[217] (Others regarded Mau Mau's organization as borrowing as much from Nazism as Marxism-Leninism, in the same way that EOKA in Cyprus was variously likened to both strains of totalitarianism.[218]) Cleary argues that British propaganda during the Emergency deliberately implied 'low-level communist involvement, and nefarious Indian activities'.[219] But that is perhaps to overstate what play Britain made of the Communist connection. However, his conjecture that Britain did not play upon American fears of Communism because to do so would have been 'contradictory to general United Kingdom policy which . . . was to persuade the United States to see the world less in stark black and white terms, and to treat subversion as an internal problem' is persuasive. It would have interfered with the presentation of Mau Mau as isolated and containable to suggest that international Communism was fuelling the insurgency, and might have attracted unwelcome US State Department attention to British policy in Kenya.

If Mau Mau was neither properly nationalist nor Communist according to British propaganda, for what, then, was it fighting? While propaganda certainly sought to explain what had caused Mau Mau (thus the employment of Carothers *et al.*), it paid little attention to the rather different question of what cause Mau Mau adherents fought for, other than to state what the movement was against. Repeated attempts were, however, made to deny the veracity of Mau Mau's own version of what it fought for, namely, land stolen by white settlers.[220] Gorrell Barnes's information paper for West African ministers was insistent on this point: the 'White Highlands' was not the only, or the best, agricultural land in Kenya; furthermore, this area had belonged to the Masai, to whom the settlers had paid adequate compensation.[221] In short, the land was neither stolen nor the Kikuyu's traditional preserve. On this point, Leakey's testimony was invaluable. His books and articles were adamant that Mau Mau propaganda on the White Highlands was spurious. The Kikuyu *had* lost a certain amount of land to white settlement, but

> the just and genuine land grievances of the Kikuyu were quite insufficient to stir up the degree of anger against the white man that Mau Mau wished to engender. It therefore became necessary to falsify history for the benefit of the growing generations and to tell the youth of the tribe that other land – which had never been in Kikuyu possession and which was now in European ownership – was also land that had once been Kikuyu property and had been 'stolen' from them.[222]

Others took Leakey's argument even further, to the point of suggesting that Mau Mau had no legitimate grievances at all. Indeed, much of the counter-insurgency literature subscribes to the belief that leaders of insurgencies consciously manufacture grievances through which to mobilize insurrection.[223] Similarly, Lyttelton utterly denied that Kikuyu discontent might arise from economic conditions, to the point that even some like-minded observers felt he had protested too much.[224] As far as Mau Mau was ascribed aims, these were couched in negative terms. Mau Mau was 'anti-European, anti-Asian and anti-Christian'.[225] Anti-white sentiment was attributed to Kikuyu 'xenophobia' – a groundless hatred, rather than to the Kikuyu experience of discrimination.[226] Thus the explanation of Mau Mau's 'aims' reiterated the irrationality of the movement: when the settlers and British administration had done so much to develop Kenya, to want rid of them was simply illogical.

As the Emergency progressed, propaganda increasingly played on the internecine aspect of the rebellion, particularly after the Lari massacre, and once it had become clear that there would be no 'night of the long knives' against Europeans. However, it is far-fetched to argue, as does Waruhiu Itote, that the government did not 'advertise' the deaths of white settlers.[227] Even if government propagandists had wished to, they would certainly not have persuaded the mainstream British and American press to share their news values. The balance of the journalistic scales consistently tipped towards the murder of whites, in however small numbers, rather than of Africans in much larger numbers. If, in the Western popular imagination, Mau Mau is remembered (or was perceived at the time) as a movement which killed scores of – rather than thirty-odd – white civilians, the fault is not primarily the British government's. The press, novelists and film-makers all played their part in pandering to their audiences' perceived preference of having whites cast in the role of Mau Mau's principal victim.[228]

Positive Propaganda

The foregoing has attempted to unravel the main themes of negative propaganda on Mau Mau. However, the corollary to this branch of the information services' work, within and beyond Kenya, was the positive projection of past British achievements in the colony, and the promotion of policies for Kenya's future. To this end Lyttelton requested in December 1952 a steady flow of 'information regarding creditable events or developments in Kenya generally and particularly places not affected by Mau Mau'.[229] The intention was partly to demonstrate that only one area of Kenya was infected with Mau Mau: beyond it there were 'large areas of peace and progress' – just as in Malaya there were both 'black' and 'white' areas.[230] While this theme had the advantage of underlining the message that Mau Mau was a Kikuyu affair, it carried the danger that the Kenya government might seem too complacent, simply glossing over Kenya's dire situation, while feeding journalists endless copy about African welfare and development which they had no wish to file.[231]

The merits of the Kenya government's work and the iniquities of Mau Mau were, nevertheless, simultaneously driven home to Kenyan and international audiences. With respect to the Kikuyu, Embu and Meru tribes, the Kenya Information Working Party codified its themes thus:

A. Mau Mau is an evil thing. It is the invention of wicked and unscrupulous men. It is bringing misery and hardships to thousands.
B. The task of destroying Mau Mau lies principally with the Africans themselves. Europeans and Asians will help them.
C. Europeans, Asians and Africans can then march forward to progress and prosperity.
D. Concurrently with these, publicity for the progress and developing prosperity of law-abiding Africans.[232]

Although these points were couched in more sophisticated language

165

for non-African audiences, the list serves to illustrate the interaction of positive and negative themes. In publicizing the Kenya government's progressive measures, the Kenya information services had to steer a delicate line: neither suggesting that terrorism had paid (by forcing the government to introduce constitutional reform quicker than it would have done without the impetus of an Emergency), nor implying that the government was deliberately slowing the pace of reform in order to punish Kenya's entire indigenous population for the misbehaviour of Mau Mau. In other words, they hoped to show Africans that progress was being achieved despite rather than because of Mau Mau. In the face of the Colonial Office's regular requests for more positive material, Crawford, the Deputy Governor, was insistent that despite the difficulties of getting 'betterment and welfare material published in the UK, when it seems to have so little news value to English editors compared with Mau Mau news', efforts were being made to provide inspiring stories, and to uplift African lives through typically British pastimes:

> We do most heartily agree in the need to offset the inevitable effects of the Security Force operations, and to bring some laughter and joy back into the lives of the people. Cycling clubs, more football, an extension of African broadcasting, cheaper radio sets, rediffusion and bands, the Scout movement, an African civil servants' club, open-air cinemas (Schlesinger Jnr. has been here and has bitten) – quite a lot of new stuff is going on; and we *are* doing what we can to see it gets publicity.[233]

The Importance of Images

While Africans in Kenya were being persuaded that 'British administration is in the best interests of the inhabitants' and that 'white settlement is essential to the economy of the country',[234] in London Granville Roberts was doing his best to place material for positive background articles on Kenya in the British and international press. Although Roberts's work primarily involved liaison with the press, reflecting the overall bias of the British and Kenya governments' propaganda effort on the Emergency,[235] positive themes lent themselves rather better to newsreel than press treatment. Newsreels were better suited to 'soft' stories which did not require the explanation of complex political background than to hard news. In addition, the Kenya government consciously encouraged the newsreels to carry upbeat stories on Kenya to rectify the initial bad impression of the colony which Westminster felt had been created by early newsreel treatment of the Emergency.

As in Malaya, the government directed the flow of newsreel coverage of events to follow its own agenda, regarding newsreels and photojournalism as vital means of showing audiences far from the 'battlefield' the nature of the terrain, and, in Kenya's case, to 'combat the idea that Mau Mau is the only thing going on in Kenya'.[236] This interventionism was all the more necessary in Kenya's case because of the unfavourable images emanating from the colony in the early months of the Emergency. Given the type of warfare being waged between Mau Mau and the security forces it was unavoidable that, as in Malaya, images of the enemy in action would not be forthcoming whereas security force operations would be all too visible. Because Kenya achieved greater prominence in the British press than had (or did) Malaya, more space was correspondingly devoted to photographic images of the Mau Mau Emergency. These pictures frequently showed Kikuyu peasants being rounded up during 'sweeps' of Mau Mau-'infected' areas, detained behind barbed wire fences (in what the *Daily Worker* called 'concentration camps'), or being driven in wire cages on the back of Army trucks. With the exception of the *Daily Worker*, most British papers which carried such photographs did so without intent to harm the government or arraign the security forces' *modus operandi*.[237] Some even suggested that the Kikuyu Home Guards were remarkably accurate at distinguishing Mau Mau adherents from the mass of Kikuyu suspects, thus masking the fact that vast numbers of Kikuyu who lived in badly affected areas were detained simply on suspicion of Mau Mau activity.

Newsreels screened in Britain also devoted some attention to the large-scale 'sweeps' in Kenya. Here too the images were not left to speak for themselves, but were anchored by commentaries which urged the viewer to accord the security forces their complete support, and stressed the latter's efficiency in weeding out the guilty from the innocent. The first Pathé issue to treat the 'Mau Mau crisis', on 6 November 1952, showed the Army rounding up suspects, taking care to screen them ('as it is all too easy for the innocent to suffer'), while insisting that 'All who carry the mark of Mau Mau must be hunted out so that peace may come to this troubled colony.'[238] Indeed, the fiction that Mau Mau adherents could be physically distinguished from other Kikuyu was one to which the newsreels – and feature-film makers – remained wedded throughout the Emergency.[239]

However, the pro-security force bias of newsreel commentaries failed to convince all interested viewers in Britain that the companies backed the government's cause. In particular, MI5 expressed concern (in an area not normally within its sphere of interest) that the 'general impression' left by the press and newsreels was 'of Africans being manhandled and oppressed by white imperialists'.[240] MI5's 'very severe criticism . . . about the inadequacy of information giving the Government side of the picture about Kenya' was passed on to the Colonial Office. In turn, the latter's Mary Fisher felt that 'the newsreel point is worth pressing home. There is no Govt. [*sic*] film unit supplying stuff about e.g. burnt European farms to counterbalance commercial stuff about – I gather – manacled Kikuyu.'[241] Carstairs thus wrote to Baring (who, even before MI5 made its criticisms, had already been requested by Lyttelton to supply positive photographic and newsreel material[242]) asking him to influence 'those responsible for the newsreel material' so that they would 'treat matters more objectively and comprehensively, and perhaps even be given facilities to do so'.[243]

Whereas the Malayan Film Unit was able to provide commercial newsreel companies with footage, Kenya's information services were woefully inadequate in terms of film output and facilities. It was a deficiency which was well recognized, though not one which was rectified with the utmost dispatch. During his 1953 visit, Harold Evans reported to Carstairs that Kenya needed to get a 'good cameraman and ensure a steady flow of footage of positive developments'.[244] Clearly matters changed over the course of the next few months, perhaps under the impetus of a reorganization of Kenya's information services, whereby the African information services merged with the external propaganda services. The first annual report of the Department of Information (for 1954) enthused about the department's good relations with the BBC and cinema newsreels, which 'regularly sought and accepted' its advice.[245] By the end of 1955, the department was able to boast that 13,000 feet of 13 mm film had been shot for newsreel and television companies – making a total of twenty-eight stories, fifteen of which were used by one or more company.[246]

The Department of Information also set about the task of supplying international audiences with a mass of photographic material. Some of these photographs projected positive images of development in Kenya.[247] There was also something of a 'black market' in Mau Mau atrocity photographs. Just as the Colonial Office instigated the surreptitious distribution of details about bestial Mau Mau oaths, so too did it encourage Baring to provide photographs showing Mau Mau's atrocities against humans and animals. Like the oaths, these photographs were felt to be too repugnant and shocking for open circulation. When an early set of human atrocity photographs arrived in Whitehall in December 1952, Carstairs warned the Foreign Office that:

> These the Secretary of State is most anxious not to have broadcast or put in the papers, as some of them are particularly horrible, but we suggest that some sets be sent abroad to be shown at agreed discussions to suitable persons and we propose to keep a set in this Department for similar use.[248]

By the first week of January 1953, Carstairs was able to report that 'sets of photographs (selected) of human atrocities in Kenya have been shown at great discretion to persons who it is thought would benefit by seeing them'.[249] In Westminster, MPs of all shades had already seen the photographic evidence of Mau Mau's abominations essential to a proper understanding of the movement. Lyttelton explained his decision to let MPs see the material thus:

> If these were plain murders or mutilation of cattle it would be bad enough. But the savagery with which these crimes are committed beggars description, and it is for that reason only that I have, with the greatest reluctance, placed certain photographs in the Library.[250]

Photographs confirmed the message of written propaganda. As Lonsdale graphically coveys:

> The iconography of the war was horrible, with pictures of ham-strung cattle grotesquely knelt upon the grass and burned black babies lying decapitated in the ashes of their homes. It looked very like a war between savagery and civilisation. On the side of order blond youths in slouch hats, backed by honest spearmen in blankets, represented the finest examples of their race, each in their proper place. African troops were also shown with guns, starched into civilisation by the creases in their khaki. On the side of chaos crouched wild-eyed men in rags and ringlets, just out of the trees.[251]

The British government was not alone in believing images – whether filmic or photographic – to be among the most salutary correctives to wrong-headedness on Mau Mau. Pathé's treatment of the trial of those accused of the Lari massacre exemplifies this 'seeing is believing' approach. Perhaps as a result of pressure from Baring to adopt a more 'objective' approach, the newsreel company produced its most emotively pro-Kenya government piece yet. Containing shots of the aftermath of the massacre (charred huts, the burnt remains of bodies, mangled bicycles, followed by lingering shots of hospitalized African children, virtually mummified in bandages), the newsreel item of 11 May 1953 was prefaced with an unprecedented warning to viewers: 'This story contains harrowing scenes. But Pathé News believe that only by showing them can the situation be brought into its true perspective.'[252] The item also showed some of the very shots which had upset MI5 so greatly – Africans manacled in detention camps with identification numbers round their necks – but the commentary made a great point of juxtaposing camera-man Bill McConville's initial feeling of slight sympathy, with his bitter conclusions: 'I felt some pity for them even if they were guilty. . . . Later when I had seen the victims of the Lari massacre for myself there was no pity in my heart'. Indeed, the overall thrust of the piece was to reinforce the settlers' demands for immediate (and none too painstaking) justice:

> No, there was no pity in my heart. If these were the murderers, then I, like all in Kenya, would expect swift justice. Too long has

this proud and faithful land suffered from the Mau Mau's crusade of evil. Justice *must*, and will, be done.[253]

In short, the piece was remarkably favourable to the Kenya government at a time when even Winston Churchill was having grave doubts as to the wisdom of trying 200 people for the same crime; as Baring was informed, the Prime Minister had reacted 'very strongly' against the possibility of a mass execution.[254]

Similarly, though without actually reproducing images of Mau Mau atrocities, several contemporaneous writers on Mau Mau asked their readers to believe that such photographs would remove any misconceptions that it was a nationalist movement. Stoneham, for example, wrote that their 'hideous corpses cry out, not for "conciliatory measures", but for vengeance on their slayers'.[255] His proposition that such images 'could never be produced for general publication . . . [though] it would be salutary to send copies of these nauseating pictures to those who suggest a compromise with this infamous gang of savages' was, unknowingly, close to official policy. However, there were occasions on which the British and Kenya governments did make atrocity photographs more widely available. For example, in 1954 an anonymous pamphlet entitled *The Mau Mau in Kenya* was published, which was almost entirely devoted to horrific images of Mau Mau terrorism, and was clearly a government production, given its preface by Granville Roberts. And if the photographs were indeed so shocking that they evoked a desire for revenge, one has to question the prudence of the Kenya government in issuing African troops in Kenya a fully illustrated booklet containing an ample selection of the most gruesome human and animal atrocity photographs.[256] Given that the allegations of brutality and torture which plagued the counter-insurgency campaign were predominantly against locally raised forces, and that the Kenya government's defence of the 'loyalists' rested on the claim that some of Mau Mau's savagery was bound to rub off on those who came into contact with it, it seems of dubious wisdom deliberately to fuel antagonism with such provocative images.[257]

Defensive Propaganda

It was the excesses of the security forces which undoubtedly formed the biggest sticking point for British and Kenya government propaganda. As had been already discovered in Palestine and Malaya, countering allegations of security force atrocities was no easy business. In Kenya the allegations were unquestionably not all malicious, or fabrications of mendacious Mau Mau propaganda – an assertion which British propaganda made about EOKA's similar atrocity claims in Cyprus only months later. No matter how savage and barbaric Mau Mau's killings appeared, opinion both in Britain and elsewhere in the mid-1950s was not prepared to overlook security force 'misbehaviour' on the scale and of the seriousness of that apparently occurring in Kenya. The cases which did come to light in courts martial revealed a disrespect for the Queensberry rules which, even in the circumstances, appeared excessive: eardrums burnt by cigarettes,[258] a seventy-year-old man virtually roasted alive in his hut,[259] suspects kicked into a cauldron of boiling water 'for fun',[260] and so on.

The first allegations of torture by the security forces surfaced in December 1952, when Nairobi reported to the Colonial Office that forty-five prisoners had been assaulted – including torture by bastinado – and that European police officers were among those involved.[261] Initially the Colonial Office attempted to gloss over such allegations. Early in the Emergency, Lyttelton briefed Granville Roberts and his own press officers that there was no evidence against any of the accused and, consequently, no action would be taken on any of the charges brought against the security forces, but that Baring had made his condemnation of 'inhuman methods' clear.[262] But it became ever clearer that mud was sticking with a certain amount of reason, and Church House prescribed preventive measures to ensure that malpractices did not occur, in preference to large doses of whitewash after the event. As E.B. David pointed out to the Deputy Governor, if the Kikuyu were to be persuaded that 'members of the Security Forces are genuinely their friends', such measures were a vital prerequisite.[263]

As it was, there were all too many disturbing and problematic features of the counter-insurgency campaign for the Colonial Office's liking. Certain civil and military methods of containing Mau Mau aroused unease. For example, Baring's commitment to collective punishment measures rang alarm bells among those who had been responsible for publicity on the Palestine and Malaya campaigns. The very practice had now gone out of favour, with Templer himself, who had so vehemently defended its implementation in Malaya, now apparently urging that collective punishment was somewhat counter-productive. Thus in December 1953, Lyttelton informed Baring:

> I do not demur to sparing exceptional use of communal punishment, but you should know that experience in Malaya, which I have just discussed with General Templer, strongly supports my view that its effectiveness is limited and that the bitterness it induces in innocent people who have suffered from it often defeats what should be our primary purpose of persuading waverers to come out on our side and above all to volunteer information.[264]

The behaviour of the security forces generated yet more concern among

171

those charged with propagating a progressive image for Kenya. One of the earliest features of military operations to trouble the Colonial Office was the number of people being shot 'while attempting to escape'. This recurrent phrase in the 'sitreps' transmitted by the Kenya authorities conjured up even more distasteful Nazi connotations than did the imposition of collective punishments. By February 1953 the number of Kikuyu killed in these circumstances was, in the words of the East Africa Department's Rogers, 'not inconsiderable and it is very noticeable'.[265] The total, by April 1953, stood at 430 Mau Mau 'terrorists or suspects' shot 'while attempting to escape or resisting arrest' over a six-month period.[266] With typical Colonial Office understatement, Rogers wrote to Potter (Kenya's Member for Law and Order): 'I confess that those of us who are fully aware that the situation cannot be handled with kid gloves are still a little concerned about the number of these shootings.'[267] In publicity and humanitarian terms, it was preferable that the security forces should take more prisoners rather than killing so many Africans in questionable circumstances.

The security forces were also increasingly accused of beating and torturing Africans in (or on the way to) detention camps, and, in some cases, of actually killing them. By the time of Erskine's arrival in June 1953, these allegations were so serious that one of his first actions was to make a strenuous denunciation of brutality and public commitment to ending it: 'Every officer in the Police and the Army should stamp at once on any conduct which he would be ashamed to see used against his own people.'[268] Although Erskine referred to the practice of 'beating up' Africans, he privately admitted that much worse had been going on, telling his wife that 'there had been a lot of indiscriminate shooting' before his arrival.[269] While Erskine hoped to end this too (and claimed, rather implausibly, that he had), he defended many aspects of the counter-insurgency which attracted considerable criticism in the United Kingdom. His overall attitude was reflected in his injunction to Harding to resist the woolly liberal cry, 'Don't be too beastly to the Mau Mau.'[270] On the one hand he claimed that Mau Mau adherents could be 'easily identified as they have long hair, long beards, and are filthy dirty' and that 'locals [were] entirely satisfied when we kill this type' – thus justifying a more discriminating 'shoot-to-kill' policy in the prohibited areas.[271] On the other hand, he also rationalized pattern bombing of the prohibited areas – despite the indiscriminate death this would bring – on the grounds that if these areas were renamed as a 'bombing range nobody would attempt to waste their time and sympathy with people who deliberately chose to live in a bombing range'.[272] Others, however, doubted the efficacy of pattern bombing. Many Labour MPs expressed moral scruples at the use of Lincoln bombers, and even the *Daily Telegraph* questioned the practice on utilitarian grounds, with one of its hostile reports on pattern bombing being used as ammunition by

Churchill in a meeting with the Chief of the Imperial General Staff, Harding.[273] Although bombing continued, more serious efforts had to be taken by Erskine at his press conferences to justify the strategy and cite statistical proof of its success.[274]

During the course of 1953 accusations against the security forces mounted, as did evidence substantiating certain alleged cases of torture. Baring's earlier protestations to the Colonial Office that neither he nor senior officers had been able to obtain 'reliable confirmation of allegations of the use of inhuman methods amounting to something like torture' were no longer adequate to staunch the tide of public alarm in Britain and elsewhere.[275] With some reluctance on Baring's part, proceedings began to try authenticated cases of mistreatment of prisoners or suspects. Although one might have expected that these trials and courts martial would at least have allayed suspicions that the Kenya government was involved in a wholesale cover-up, they did not produce this palliative result, instead having several unfortunate side-effects. First, they publicized, and verified, the appalling inhumanity practised by certain members of the security forces. Second, the relative infrequency of trials as against the number of allegations made suggested (to those with a will to believe it) that those cases coming to court were only the tip of a sizeable iceberg, whose hidden bulk the Kenya government had every interest in keeping submerged.[276] Third, the good faith of the Kenya authorities in stamping out brutality was called into question because many of the accused were let off so lightly – either being found not guilty, or given the softest of sentences.

It is worth examining in some detail two of the most serious cases to illustrate the extent of the problems they caused for government propagandists. In November 1953, Brian Hayward, a nineteen-year-old Kenyan settler, was tried in Tanganyika for brutality during screening operations in its Northern Province (where Kenyan Security Forces had authority to chase Mau Mau gangs). He pleaded guilty to twenty charges of assault, including whipping prisoners on the soles of their feet, burning their eardrums with lighted cigarettes, and tying leather thongs round their necks. As punishment, he was sentenced to three months' imprisonment without hard labour and fined 2,000 shillings.[277] This leniency had been counselled by the magistrate:

> It is easy to work oneself into a state of pious horror over these offences but they must be considered against their background. All the accused were engaged in seeking inhuman monsters and savages of the lowest order – some might even have lost relatives.[278]

Such remarks, quite apart from Hayward's misdeeds themselves, engendered 'public alarm' – to use Lyttelton's phrase[279] – in Britain. The decision of the Kenya authorities in December 1953 to reprieve Hayward and reinstate him in his former position seemed to confirm that the Kenya government, and not just the judiciary, was insensitive to African sentiment within the colony and humanitarian sentiment the world over. On 5 December, Lyttelton saw fit to telegraph Crawford (whose position ought to have given him a certain sensitivity to public opinion) to warn him about the message being transmitted:

> You must know that public opinion here has become extremely concerned with the behaviour of the Kenya Security Forces as disclosed by the published facts in this case and that of Griffiths. Reinstatement of Hayward after conviction for this type of offence will inevitably be interpreted as confirming alleged lax attitude of Kenya authorities towards behaviour of this kind.[280]

The case of Griffiths – mentioned by Lyttelton – came to court a month after Hayward's reprieve, and was even more damaging for the Kenya government and security forces. During it, details emerged about various security force malpractices. Army units had kept 'scoreboards' detailing Mau Mau 'kills' – this competitive spirit having been fostered by certain officers giving monetary rewards for 'kills'. The trial thus publicized abuses which had been privately known of for some months: Erskine, for one, had known that 'scoreboards' were widespread. He had therefore altered the presentation of Emergency statistics in such a way that Mau Mau casualties were no longer attributable to particular units, on the grounds that the old system tended 'to make the matter a cup tie and introduce[d] an element of competition useful in some ways but dangerous in others'.[281]

The Griffiths court martial also uncovered other unsavoury procedures (reminiscent of those in Malaya), such as the severing of hands from Mau Mau adherents' corpses to aid later identification of the bodies. Severed hands had also, on occasion, served as the gruesome props of Army 'practical jokes'. The Griffiths case also coincided with a flurry of press reports, inspired by Fenner Brockway, who had unearthed different evidence of an inappropriately 'sporting' atmosphere among British troops in Kenya. In an open letter to the Secretary of State for War, Anthony Head, Brockway stated that the November issue of the Devonshires' regimental journal depicted the campaign in Kenya '"as though it were a hunt for game"', and that it provided more proof of monetary rewards having been offered for kills.[282] Brockway's evidence, in short, suggested that the sporting language of Kenya's press releases (which the Colonial Office had tried to eliminate) accurately represented the spirit in which the counter-insurgency was being prosecuted. Much of the British press sided with Brockway, including papers which were not his natural allies. The Times, for example, affirmed that although many of the Mau Mau had 'done savage and murderous deeds, nevertheless they remain human beings. . . . All the sternness in the world is admirable, but not the atmosphere, which such incidents rightly conjure up, of an afternoon's shoot or a pig-sticking match'.[283]

The Kenya government's suggestions for dispelling popular and press agitation following these revelations were not particularly helpful. Crawford lamely proposed more negative propaganda on Mau Mau:

> Any idea in Britain that Mau Mau are misguided savages, fighting for their land, and no worse than Communists, should be exploded. They are utterly merciless, cunning, and by their system of oathing and secrecy, are present everywhere.[284]

The Colonial Office, however, along with the Labour Opposition, pressed for an inquiry into security force behaviour as the only method of clearing the air and dispelling the impression that neither Westminster nor Nairobi took the issue of brutality seriously enough.[285] The subsequent Commission confirmed that all the malpractices had indeed occurred, and while its report exonerated British troops serving in Kenya, it concluded that the Home Guard – beyond the scope of its inquiry – was indeed a problem.[286] This report went some way to pacifying British newspapers, at least temporarily, which were only too glad to relate to their readerships that British boys were innocent.[287]

However, the Griffiths court martial reveals that for the British government the presentation of security force activities in Kenya was at least as difficult as mediating the presentation of their opponents' 'terrorism', and almost certainly a good deal more so for much of the campaign. As Erskine revealingly remarked in a letter to his wife in March 1954, 'This man Griffiths has given me more trouble than the Mau Mau.'[288] The same appears just as true, as far as official propagandists were concerned, of the misdeeds of the security forces in general as of Griffiths in particular.

Quite aside from the misdeeds of individual members of the security forces, the government also regarded as political liabilities other officially sanctioned aspects of the counter-insurgency campaign. In particular, the high number of Mau Mau members executed gave cause for concern in Westminster and Whitehall, as did the fact that some Kenya district officers favoured public executions.[289] The macabre spectacle of public hangings from 'portable gallows' prompted the Colonial Office to intervene, once again, in Baring's handling of the Emergency. As early as December 1952, Lyttelton urged Baring to take precautions against 'herding [detainees] in front of the gallows' – in view of 'previous publicity'.[290] But like the issue of security forces' brutality, the number of prisoners executed was to become an open sore for the British and Kenya governments. In this case the inflammation worsened as the crimes punishable by death in Kenya became more tangential to the principal offence of participation in terrorist activity. New Emergency Regulations made 'consorting' with terrorists a hanging offence, and Churchill himself interceded to prevent Baring from adding the possession of incendiary material to the lengthening list, his objection being that this stipulation would make possession of a box of matches a hanging offence.[291]

How far the actual extent of security force ill-treatment of Kikuyu suspects and prisoners was uncovered at the time, either through Kenya's courts or the efforts of tenacious journalists, is a moot point, and one which really falls beyond the scope of this study.[292] One can, however, fairly safely assume that the extent of atrocities was never fully uncovered by the courts: the very culture of Kenya's administration was one of concealment rather than disclosure. As *The Times*'s Colonial Editor, Oliver Woods, wrote in confidence to his Editor, 'where incidents occur, there is naturally a conspiracy of silence'.[293] Five years after Woods made his assertion, the Hola Camp incident provided a vivid, and all too public, illustration of his point. That episode was partly so scandalous because – quite apart from eleven prisoners' deaths – it was revealed that various individuals had initially attempted to blame the deaths on 'infected water', when in fact they were due to guards over-zealously enforcing the policy of using physical force on prisoners who refused to work.[294] It seems reasonable to infer from this incident that other, more successful, 'cover-ups' occurred during the Emergency – though the nature of successful 'cover-ups' is such that they are extremely hard to divine after the event.

However, if one accepts that some atrocities were deliberately concealed, the question arises of whether others colluded with the Kenya administration and military. D.H. Rawcliffe, writing in 1954, claimed that there was a 'tacit conspiracy involving the Kenya Government, the police and the Press not to reveal or even hint at anything which the outside world would term acts of brutality or callous behaviour towards the Kikuyu'.[295] Such an assertion does not appear warranted. During a campaign in which the main theatres of military operations were designated 'prohibited areas', press correspondents doubtless found their access to them constrained, if not prohibited, by the military. But the British press was certainly not mute over controversial aspects of military operations in Kenya. Some papers, of course, were more vocal than others. The *Daily Mirror*, for example, allowed Labour's anti-imperialists full reign. Barbara Castle wrote a series of articles in December 1955 which examined cases she had uncovered during a recent trip to the colony of beatings and brutality suffered by African prisoners.[296] And in private, *The Times* credited itself with being 'largely responsible for creating a critical opinion' on the question of executions in Kenya.[297]

The obduracy of certain Fleet Street papers over the question of brutality was indeed such that in December 1953 (and on other occasions) Baring saw fit to complain in his habitually oblique fashion to Lyttelton that 'adverse comments [were] beginning to be made about the ir-responsibility of local and certain UK newspapers in commenting on Kenya affairs'.[298] His hostility towards the press was echoed by Louis Leakey, who complained that 'incidents of an unpleasant character' had attracted

> a wholly undue amount of publicity in the popular overseas press, which seldom takes the trouble to point out that for every such unpleasant incident which comes to light there are tens of thousands of cases where persons, similarly placed, have acted with complete correctitude.[299]

Further evidence that many British press correspondents actively sought to uncover the 'truth' about security force behaviour in Kenya, rather than conspiring to keep silent, may be adduced from a confidential memo penned by Oliver Woods while visiting Kenya in January 1954. Arguing that brutality in Kenya was not in fact as widespread as was sometimes alleged, Woods wrote:

> I think one very strong argument in favour of the view that atrocities are not frequent is this. There have been at times as many as 60 highly trained correspondents of English, American and other newspapers in this country. Some of them have been here a long time now, travelled much, and even speak the language. Most of them tend to be anti-settler and they are very keen on ferreting out misbehaviour but the fact is that more cases have appeared in the courts of law than in the newspapers.[300]

His conclusion on the question of brutality was that there was 'a lot of rough stuff but . . . little real sadism'.[301] Even if this muted conclusion is accurate, 'a lot of rough stuff' was still more than enough to make the task of British and Kenya government propagandists an extremely trying one.

How Successful a Campaign?

On the surface it appears that official propaganda on Kenya was uncommonly successful. Mau Mau was portrayed in films, novels as well as the British (and most of the American) press as the expression of retrogressive savagery which Whitehall publicists put such effort into projecting. The range of expressed opinion on Mau Mau itself was thus exceedingly narrow. This, however, is not to say that British/Kenya government propaganda, or it alone, had *caused* people to think of Mau Mau in this light. It is hard enough to gauge popular attitudes, let alone to establish how people acquired any particular opinion, and this makes it extremely difficult to judge the success of any attempt to shape public opinion.

There are grounds, however, for suggesting that official propaganda on Mau Mau was in fact less successful than it superficially appears. From the outset serious weaknesses flawed the propaganda organization in Kenya. Many complaints were made, particularly in the early stages of the campaign, that propaganda was uncoordinated, and that sufficiently powerful messages were not being transmitted. Even as the military operations drew to their close, some still felt that the propaganda effort had never overcome its initial problems. In February 1955, for example, Elspeth Huxley wrote to Blundell on the subject of the negligible publicity the Kenya government's amnesty offer to Mau Mau members had been given: 'What a pity that Kenya has never been able to achieve an efficient and imaginative Public Relations Department', to which Blundell replied, 'In the strictest confidence the truth of the matter is that Sir Evelyn Baring is not the world's highlight for publicity.'[302]

Blundell's assertion is ambiguous. It might mean either that Evelyn Baring was not the sort of character who attracted international attention, or, more probably, that he performed inadequately before press reporters and cameramen – a point which others have made.[303] Huxley's assertion is also corroborated by others. General Hinde felt that Kenya's psychological warfare effort suffered from a lack of humour, remarking that 'in any form of propaganda appeal should be made to the African sense of humour, even if, in the case of the Kikuyu, it is not as strongly developed as in other Tribes'.[304]

Why then was Kenya never able to develop an 'efficient and imaginative Public Relations Department'? One key reason was that propagandists in Kenya were marginalized from decision-making. As we have seen, Gibson complained that he could not create effective publicity for policies over which he had no control. Granville Roberts, more geographically remote, similarly felt hampered by the lack of briefing from Kenya's policy-making élite. As he told Blundell in June 1954:

> My channels [in the UK] are wide open and good enough, I think. The gap is at your end. A long letter from the Acting Governor has been my sole recent fountain of policy explanation of the sort I obviously must have and an Information Department geared for a purpose in Kenya which appears to be insensitive to reaction outside, is not really very much use to me.[305]

These dissatisfactions gave added piquancy to the personal animosities between various key personnel. For example, as well as criticizing the Governor and Deputy Governor, Roberts was also virulently hostile to Gibson (an easy target, given his high salary and the high expectations of him). As his remarks to Blundell appear to confirm, he was responsible for spreading 'poison around both in Nairobi and London' concerning the adequacy of Kenya's information team.[306]

The distance between propagandists and policy-makers in Kenya partially explains why the former were sometimes less than happy with the policies they had to publicize. More broadly, one might question whether, when it came to promoting future British policy for the colony, the propagandists had sufficient positive material to work on. Certainly in 1954 both the Swynnerton plan for land reform and agricultural development and the Lyttelton constitution promised Kenya's Africans certain advances. The former provided that Africans would be permitted to grow (under state regulation) cash crops such as tea and coffee, while the latter allowed limited African political participation in Kenya's administrative structures: Kenya would henceforth have an African Minister for Community Development, and eight African members of Legco, directly elected.[307] But were these measures enough to satisfy African aspirations or merely sufficient to suggest that Mau Mau violence had in some limited way paid off? Given the growth of nationalist African politics when restrictions were lifted on political activity, and the rapid pace at which Kenya proceeded towards independence, it seems hard to argue that the reforms did other than whet the appetite they hoped to sate, and doubtful whether they were the stuff around which imaginative propaganda could have been built.

As for the success of propaganda on Kenya beyond the colony, the results were mixed, and tend to confirm Jacques Ellul's adage that propaganda is far more successful when working with the grain of public opinion than when it attempts to alter strong convictions. Thus one could argue that white European or American audiences did not need a great deal of persuasion that Mau Mau was an atavistic reversion to savagery, as the image of the Mau Mau terrorist was not far removed from the popular stereotype of the untamed African. Propaganda was less successful, however, in India where it faced the task of altering the perception of Mau Mau as a legitimate nationalist challenge to imperial rule. Consequently, despite the attention paid to opinion in India, the Dominions Office and Colonial Office found that their message did not easily penetrate the Indian audience. Even after eighteen months of the Emergency, those Departments were still troubled by the need to 'counter the Indian suggestion that Mau Mau is a popular and ultimately progressive liberation movement to which the complete solution is concessions by Her Majesty's Government'.[308] However, the British and Kenya governments were perhaps surprisingly successful in altering the popular misconception on both sides of the Atlantic that Mau Mau was a Communist movement. As Cleary has pointed out, BIS efforts to scotch American press reports that Mau Mau was Communist-infiltrated were reasonably effective,[309] though of course there remained individual

179

Americans (and others, including many settlers) who remained convinced to the contrary.

In terms of influencing media presentation of Mau Mau, the British and Kenya governments' publicists appear to have been fairly successful, though, as with public opinion, one can never entirely satisfactorily distinguish between various influences shaping the 'output'. We have already seen how the newsreel companies – after initial MI5 worries about the dangerous images they purveyed – became willing purveyors of positive stories about Kenya government progressiveness. As for the press, just as in previous Emergencies, personal contacts were one of the staples of Colonial and Foreign Office publicity work. In this instance the Kenya government was fortunate to be on excellent terms with Oliver Woods, although *The Times* was not always uncritical. Granville Roberts also judged his personal network of contacts and 'clubbability' with opinion formers to have been invaluable, as he informed Blundell:

> Vera and I find that our small dinner parties are far pleasanter and more effective than cocktail 'do's', although more expensive! It helps to maintain the only sort of liaison which is really effective in London circles.[310]

Even the liberal British press, including the *Manchester Guardian* and *New Statesman and Nation*, adopted remarkably consensual positions on Mau Mau. As Maughan-Brown has remarked, both publications revealed 'an initial scepticism about the settler interpretation of "Mau Mau" giving way progressively to an increasing reliance on that interpretation'.[311] The *Manchester Guardian*'s Patrick Monkhouse, for example, was one of the Colonial Office's approved article-writers on Mau Mau.

Yet one must qualify this impression of undiluted approbation on the part of the press for the counter-insurgency in Kenya. It must be borne in mind that the objectives of official propaganda were twofold: to denigrate Mau Mau, and to create support for British policy in Kenya and the counter-insurgency campaign. Despite the hard line taken on Mau Mau by almost all British papers (with the obvious exception of the *Daily Worker*), and the extent of personal contacts between Whitehall and Fleet Street, government publicists were far less successful on the second point. Indeed, those responsible for information work on Kenya found themselves in the uncomfortable position of having to explain (if not outright defend) security force atrocities. Much of the British press was simply unprepared to defend measures against Mau Mau, or the Kikuyu as a whole, which appeared indefensible.

On the second count, then, propaganda was less than successful (although of course Church House never actually defended the worst atrocities). It was easy to make Mau Mau appear retrogressive and savage, but much harder to convince people that certain measures against Mau Mau were necessary. However, the failure does not lie primarily with those responsible for government propaganda. We should be wary of making Baring's mistake of thinking that propagandists could achieve results independent of the actions of the military and policy-making élite. The reason why propaganda failed in at least part of its mission has less to do with the propaganda organization itself (though its deficiencies did not help) than with the impediments placed on it by the actions of others. As Evans pointed out in September 1953:

In a multiracial community undergoing the strains and stresses now being experienced in Kenya, the official information services are bound to run into criticism, the criticism not infrequently being aimed at the information services when government policy is the real objective.[312]

Notes

1 Letter from F. Crawford (Deputy Governor) to E.B. David (CO East Africa Department), 16/12/53, CO 822/489.
2 Greene, *Ways of Escape*, p. 143.
3 Letter from H.G. Hall to C.A. Hartwell, Secretariat (Nairobi), 12/9/52; CO 822/436.
4 'Report to the Secretary of State for the Colonies by the Parliamentary Delegation to Kenya, January 1954' (Cmd 9081, 1954); East African Royal Commission (Dow) Report (Cmd 9475, 1955); and F.D. Corfield, 'Historical Survey of the Origins and Growth of Mau Mau' (Cmnd 1030, 1960).
5 These were *Simba* (Rank, 1955, dir. Brian Desmond Hurst); *Safari* (Columbia, 1956, dir. Terence Young) and *Something of Value* (MGM, 1957, dir. Richard Brooks).
6 Among them were Robert Ruark's *Something of Value* (Doubleday, Garden City, N.Y., London, 1955) on which Brooks's film was based; Elspeth Huxley's *A Thing to Love* (Chatto and Windus, London, 1954); C.T. Stoneham's *Kenya Mystery* (Museum Press, London, 1954); M. Harding's *Mask of Friendship* (Collins, London, 1956); and W.B. Thomas's *The Touch of Pitch* (Allan Wingate, London, 1956).
7 Eye-witness accounts were provided by a number of Kenya settlers, most notably C.T. Stoneham's *Mau Mau* (Museum Press, London, 1953) and *Out of Barbarism* (Museum Press, London, 1955). Kenya missionaries also provided their interpretations of Mau Mau, for example, T.F.C. Bewes's *Kikuyu Conflict: Mau Mau and the Christian Witness* (Highway Press, London, 1953), as did journalists who had been in Kenya for all, or part, of the insurgency, including A. Campbell's *The Heart of Africa* (Longmans, Green, London, 1954) and J. Gunther's popular *Inside Africa* (Hamish Hamilton, London, 1955). There were also several narratives of the hunt for Mau Mau leaders in the forest provided by those involved in the gangs: P. Goodhart and I. Henderson, *The Hunt for Kimathi* (Pan Books, London, 1958); F. Kitson, *Gangs and Counter-Gangs* (Faber

and Faber, London, 1960); and W. Baldwin, *Mau Mau Manhunt: The Adventures of the Only American Who Has Fought the Terrorists in Kenya* (E.P. Dutton, New York, 1957).

8 C.G. Rosberg, Jr and J. Nottingham, *The Myth of 'Mau Mau': Nationalism in Kenya* (Praeger, New York, 1966).

9 Barnet and Njama, *Mau Mau from Within*, p. 9.

10 R. Buijtenhuis, *Mau Mau Twenty Years After: The Myth and the Survivors* (Mouton, The Hague, 1973), p. 43.

11 F. Furedi, *The Mau Mau War in Perspective* (James Currey, London, 1989), p. 4. Likewise, Luise White has recently written that the 'propaganda campaign was at least as intense as the military one'; 'Separating the Men from the Boys: Constructions of Gender, Sexuality, and Terrorism in Central Kenya, 1939–59', *International Journal of African Historical Studies*, 23, i (1990), 1-25, p. 18. See also R.B. Edgerton, *Mau Mau: An African Crucible* (I.B. Tauris, London, 1990), pp. vii–viii.

12 Furedi, *Mau Mau War in Perspective*, p. 4.

13 David Maughan-Brown has produced a full-length monograph on the fictional treatment of Mau Mau which discusses the relationship between 'colonial fiction' (that is, novels written by settlers, or those espousing the settlers' point of view) and the dominant ideological constructions of Mau Mau emanating from non-fictional sources. His scope, however, does not extend to an examination of government propaganda on Mau Mau in any but the broadest terms: D. Maughan-Brown, *Land, Freedom and Fiction: History and Ideology in Kenya* (Zed Books, London, 1985). A recent article by A.S. Cleary, 'The Myth of Mau Mau in Its International Context', *African Affairs*, 89, 355 (April 1990), 227–45, goes some way to rectifying the lack of academic literature on how the 'myth' was manufactured.

14 Letter from Huxley to Perham, 10/3/42, in E. Huxley and M. Perham, *Race and Politics in Kenya* (Faber and Faber, London, 1956), p. 23.

15 A. Clayton, *Counter-insurgency in Kenya, 1952–60: A Study of Military Operations against Mau Mau* (Transafrica, Nairobi, 1976), p. 37.

16 Huxley and Perham, *Race and Politics*, p. 23.

17 Ibid., letter from Perham to Huxley, 15/3/42, p. 25.

18 See D.W. Throup, *Economic and Social Origins of Mau Mau, 1945–53* (James Currey, London, 1987), ch. 5, 'The Kikuyu Squatter Problem'.

19 Furedi, *Mau Mau War in Perspective, passim.*

20 Sir P. Mitchell, *African Afterthoughts* (Hutchinson, London, 1954), p. 248.

21 Ibid., pp. 248–52. For a widely read contemporaneous account of these messianic movements, see N. Farson, *Last Chance in Africa* (Victor Gollancz, London, 1949), ch. 18.

22 This phrase was used by Ingrams in a report he wrote for the Foreign Office IRD entitled 'Communist Prospects in East and Central Africa' in April 1952; CO 537/7780.

23 Ibid., p. 56.

24 For Mau Mau members' accounts, see: Barnet and Njama, *Mau Mau from Within*, pp. 51–4; B. Kaggia, *The Roots of Freedom, 1921–1963: The Autobiography of Bildad Kaggia* (Transafrica, Nairobi, 1975), p. 115; W. Itote, *Mau Mau in Action* (Transafrica, Nairobi, 1979), p. 166; J.M. Kariuki, *'Mau Mau' Detainee: The Account by a Kenya African of His Experiences in Detention Camps 1953–60* (Penguin Books, Harmondsworth, 1964), pp. 50–1.

25 Barnett and Njama, *Mau Mau from Within*, pp. 52–3.

26 Kaggia, *The Roots of Freedom*, p. 107.

27 Throup, *Economic and Social Origins of Mau Mau*, p. 11.

28 Furedi, *Mau Mau War in Perspective*, p. 109.

29 The lengthiest report that the Colonial Office had yet received on Mau Mau was a letter from Henry Potter (Government House, Kenya) to P. Rogers (CO), dated 17/8/52; CO 822/436.

30 Secret memo by W.L. Gorrell Barnes to Sir T. Lloyd, 18/11/52; CO 822/439. See also minute by Gorrell Barnes to Lloyd, 19/2/53; CO 822/440.

31 *News Chronicle* (21/8/52), 'Bayonets warning in Kenya'.

32 Reuters report (21/8/52).

33 Kenya government press release, 'Law and Order in Kenya: Text of 8 Bills Published'; CO 822/437.

34 Letter from Fenner Brockway to Oliver Lyttelton (Secretary of State for the Colonies), 19/9/52; CO 822/437. This view was echoed by an article in the *New Statesman and Nation* shortly afterwards – to which Kenya's settlers took great exception; vol. XLIV, 1126, (4/10/52), p. 366. The article was attacked by Stoneham in *Mau Mau*, p. 47.

35 See Rosberg and Nottingham, *The Myth of 'Mau Mau'*, p. 277; Maughan-Brown, *Land, Freedom and Fiction*, pp. 48–9; Barnet and Njama, *Mau Mau from Within*, p. 149. Furedi takes this view further, arguing that the declaration of an Emergency was a pre-emptive strike against latent nationalism, instigating a 'secret war designed to prevent the emergence of a broad radical anti-colonial movement'; 'Britain's Colonial Emergencies and the Invisible Nationalists', *Journal of Historical Sociology*, 2, ii (Sept. 1989), 240–64, p. 255.

36 Throup, *Economic and Social Origins of Mau Mau*, p. 231.

37 Huxley, *A Thing to Love*, pp. 55–7.

38 This phrase was used by Perham in her introduction to Kariuki's *'Mau Mau' Detainee*, p. 14.

39 D.H. Rawcliffe, *The Struggle for Kenya* (Victor Gollancz, London, 1954), p. 55.

40 Letter from Baring (Governor of Kenya) to Lyttelton, 9/10/52; CO 822/444.

41 Ibid. Mau Mau acts of violence were frequently described in the gangster idiom, by the British press as well as by the Kenyan authorities. Baring's description of Waruhiu's death was replicated by the press, the *Daily Mail* (8/10/52) telling its readers that the chief had been murdered in a 'Chicago-style hold-up'. The British Information Service in the US also encouraged such analogies, describing Mau Mau in a press release of 7 Nov. 1952 as 'the unholy union of dark and ancient superstition with the apparatus of modern gangsterism'; CO 822/448. Some commentators believed that Mau Mau had been influenced by Hollywood gangster movies, with Stoneham writing that the average Mau Mau member 'has been reared on a diet of Hollywood violence and garbled accounts of underground warfare in Europe and the East'; *Mau Mau*, p. 28.

42 Letter from Baring to Lyttelton, 9/10/52; CO 822/444.

43 Telegram from Lyttelton to Baring, 21/10/52, no. 684, containing the text of his statement to the House of Commons on the imposition of a State of Emergency; CO 822/438.

44 Telegram from Baring to Lyttelton, 24/11/52, no. 782; CO 822/439.

45 Kenya Commissioner of Police, Situation Appreciation for the week ending 10 Dec. 1952; CO 822/477.

46 Commissioner of Police, Situation Appreciation for the week ending 31 Dec. 1952; CO 822/477.

47 Letter from the Commander-in-Chief, Middle East Land Forces, to War Office, VCIGS, 5/11/52; WO 216/811.

48 As one account put it, 'The official police photograph of Michael Ruck as Mau Mau left him is something unlikely to be surpassed in grievous nauseating horror'; F. Majdalany, *State of Emergency: The Full Story of Mau Mau* (Longmans, London, 1962), p. 124.

49 Ibid., p. 124.

50 See the first-hand account of Sir Michael Blundell in *So Rough a Wind* (Weidenfeld and Nicolson, London, 1964), pp. 123–9.

51 Commissioner of Police, Situation Appreciation for the week ending 28 Jan. 1953; CO 822/477.

52 Greene, *Ways of Escape*, p. 145. See also John Lonsdale, 'Mau Maus of the Mind: Making Mau Mau and Remaking Kenya', *Journal of African History*, 31 (1990), 393–421, p. 407.

53 The *Manchester Guardian* carried a protracted exchange between Mitchell and Gluckman (Professor of Social Anthropology at Manchester University) on this subject; Gluckman, 'The Mau Mau Rituals: Tribal Religion and Witchcraft' (19/3/54); Mitchell, 'The Mau Mau Rituals: Fancy and Fact' (10/5/54), and response by Gluckman on 26/5/54.

54 Majdalany, *State of Emergency*, p. 147.

55 See, for example, Lyttelton's statement on 31/3/53; H.C. Debs, vol. 513, 31/3/53, 'Kenya (Massacre, Uplands)', cols 1037-40.

56 Maughan-Brown cites two Kenyan accounts which deny that Mau Mau carried out the attack: H.K. Wachanga, *The Swords of Kininyaga*, and K. Muchai, *The Hardcore: Land, Freedom and Fiction*, p. 27.

57 Maughan-Brown, *Land, Freedom and Fiction*, pp. 27–8; Furedi, *Mau Mau War in Perspective*, p. 122; B. Berman, *Control and Crisis in Colonial Kenya: The Dialectic of Domination* (James Currey, London, 1990), p. 349.

58 *Manchester Guardian* (28/3/53), 'Mau Mau Massacre of Loyal Kikuyu', p. 6. Such accounts of the Lari massacre were also current many years after the event; see Mitchell, *African Afterthoughts*, p. 254, and Majdalany, *State of Emergency*, pp. 141–7.

59 Commissioner of Police, Situation Appreciation for the week ending 1 April 1953; CO 822/477.

60 See Perham's conclusion in Huxley and Perham, *Race and Politics*, pp. 271–2.

61 Maughan-Brown, *Land, Freedom and Fiction*, p. 28.

62 Lyttelton, *The Memoirs of Lord Chandos*, pp. 394–5.

63 Ibid., p. 394. Lyttelton was not alone in thinking that a handful of power-hungry men manipulated the Mau Mau movement; see also Stoneham, *Mau Mau*, pp. 132–40.

64 Lyttelton, op. cit., p. 394.

65 Mitchell, *African Afterthoughts*, p. 260.

66 Ibid., pp. 260–1.

67 J.C. Carothers, *The Psychology of Mau Mau* (Government Printer, Nairobi, 1954), p. 15.

68 L.S.B. Leakey, *Mau Mau and the Kikuyu* (Methuen, London, 1952), p. 85.

69 L.S.B. Leakey, *Defeating Mau Mau* (Methuen, London, 1954), p. 42. The whole of Chapter 4 (pp. 41–52) is devoted to Leakey's analysis of the 'Mau Mau religion'.

70 Ibid., pp. 51–2.

71 For example, pondering the question of how it was that, towards the end of the campaign, captured Mau Mau adherents proved so willing to turn on their erstwhile comrades-in-arms, Blundell concluded that 'it was part of the extraordinary schizophrenic psychology of Mau Mau in the Kikuyu mind'; *So Rough a Wind*, p. 195.

72 Ibid., p. 105. See also F. Corfield's 'Historical Survey of the Origins and Growth of Mau Mau', ch. 2.

73 The phrase was used in an article by Leakey commissioned by the Kenya government; copy in CO 1027/7. Carothers (somewhat more inclined to criticism of the settlers than Leakey) likened a dissatisfied Kikuyu to the child of 'inconsistent, indecisive parents . . . ever trying unsuccessfully to discover the length of the chain that binds him'; *Psychology*, p. 13. See also Blundell, *So Rough a Wind*, p. 197.

74 *Men of Two Worlds* (Ealing, 1946, dir. Thorold Dickinson).

75 *West of Zanzibar* (Ealing, 1954, dir. Harry Watt).

76 Leakey, *Defeating Mau Mau*, ch. 2. Carothers, on the other hand, writes more generally of African psychology and the dislocation caused by the encounter with Western culture. This, he suggests, produces an attempt by Africans to turn back the clock to an illusory 'Golden Age' before Europeans arrived; *Psychology*, pp. 10–11.

77 In his memoirs Lyttelton attacked the Labour Opposition's claim that Mau Mau's

causes were essentially economic as 'a convenient but false argument'; *Memoirs of Lord Chandos*, p. 395. This was a point he repeatedly made during the Emergency, as will be seen.

78 Mau Mau also killed sixty-three European and 524 African members of the security forces. As for Mau Mau losses, 1,070 were executed between Oct. 1952 and Feb. 1957, only a third of whom had been found guilty of murder. See 'The History of the Emergency in Kenya'; CO 822/1220. Between 1952 and 1956, 10,399 Mau Mau were killed by the security forces according to official sources; GHQ East Africa, Emergency Statistics; WO 276/92.

79 Gunther, *Inside Africa*, p. 352.

80 Secret letter from Baring to Lyttelton, 9/6/53; CO 822/692.

81 *Manchester Guardian* (8/1/53).

82 Baring made this point, in self-defence, against the charge that the ratio of 'kills' to captures of Mau Mau members by the security forces was suggestive of more than a little trigger-happiness: 'The real trouble is that in very thick forest everything happens in a few seconds and the Mau Mau Kikuyu seen are either shot or escape.' Secret letter from Baring to Lyttelton, 17/7/53; CO 822/692.

83 C. Douglas-Home, *Evelyn Baring: The Last Proconsul* (Collins, London, 1978), pp. 236–7.

84 Lonsdale, 'Mau Maus of the Mind', *Journal of African History*, p. 414.

85 Report by Erskine, 'The Kenya Emergency, 7 June 1952 – 2 May 1955'; WO 236/18, p. 1. Also cited by Lonsdale, op. cit.

86 Erskine's report, op. cit., p. 2.

87 Ibid., p. 5.

88 A statement to this effect was made at a press conference on 21 Oct. 1953, when Erskine warned that Kenya's biggest problem was the political one of finding a way for different races to cohabit amicably; press conference notes for 21/10/53; WO 236/17.

89 Appreciation by the Commander-in-Chief, East Africa, Jan. 1956; CO 822/772.

90 'The Kenya Emergency, May 1955–November 1956', by Lieutenant-General Sir Gerald W. Lathbury, p. 1; WO 236/20. In a speech to the Royal African Society on 25 Nov. 1954, Blundell had suggested that 'We know today that instead of the aim of the elimination of the European and the Asian and the establishment of the Kikuyu-dominated government, the objective is that of survival.' Transcript of Blundell's speech in WO 236/17.

91 Furedi, *Mau Mau War in Perspective*, p. 6.

92 Maughan-Brown, *Land, Freedom and Fiction*, pp. 46-9.

93 Kaggia, *Roots of Freedom*, p. 193.

94 Itote, *Mau Mau in Action*, p. 5. Rosberg and Nottingham also claim that Mau Mau, particularly towards the end of the campaign, kept going in order to gain publicity; *The Myth of 'Mau Mau'*, p. 299.

95 Telegram from Baring to Lyttelton, 10/10/52, no. 616; CO 822/443.

96 Letter from Hartwell to Rogers, 25/8/52; CO 822/435.

97 Huxley, in Huxley and Perham, *Race and Politics*, p. 255.

98 Secret, 'Memorandum on Mau Mau Intimidation', Nairobi CID, c.52/166 (undated, 1952) para. 15, p. 5; CO 822/438.

99 Ibid., p. 5.

100 Note by Gorrell Barnes on discussions with Whyatt (Attorney-General in Kenya's Legislative Council [Legco]) and Davies on the Kenya Law and Order Bills, 12/9/52; CO 822/437.

101 See Maia Green, 'Mau Mau Oathing Rituals and Political Ideology in Kenya: A Re-analysis', *Africa*, 60, i, (1990), 69–86.

102 Certainly the result (heightened settler obduracy) was unintentional if, as Leakey suggests, the aim was to create an exodus of fearful Europeans; *Defeating Mau Mau*, pp. 28–9.

103 A letter from Lyttelton to W. Teeling MP (17/10/52), mentions the dispatch of 'an experienced journalist to London'; CO 822/438.

104 Minute by Carstairs to Gorrell Barnes, 10/12/52; CO 1027/7. In apparent contradiction of his opening sentence, Carstairs had written to A.C.E. Malcolm (Head of the Foreign Office's IPD) only four days earlier, saying that 'On the whole coverage given to Kenya affairs, and the quality of the comment on it, is good'; letter from Carstairs to Malcolm, 6/12/52; CO 1017/7. Perhaps this discrepancy can be explained by an element of bravado on Carstairs's behalf in his letter to Malcolm – an attempt to convince a 'rival' department that the Colonial Office information staff had the Mau Mau situation well in hand.

105 Correspondence on this issue can be found in CO 822/545.

106 Lyttelton, *Memoirs of Lord Chandos*, p. 401.

107 Minute by Carstairs to Gorrell Barnes, 10/12/52; CO 1027/7.

108 See, for example, *Daily Worker* (22 and 31/10/52).

109 For a list of publications banned in Kenya see CO 822/1774.

110 White, 'Separating the Men from the Boys', *International Journal of African Historical Studies*, p. 18.

111 Minute by Carstairs, 1/7/53; CO 1027/40. For an exposition of propaganda themes to be directed to Europeans, see 'Secret. Appreciation of the Situation' by Major-General Hinde, 5/3/53; Hinde MSS, File 10, MSS Afr. s.1580, Rhodes House.

112 Maughan-Brown argues that the settlers assumed that only they 'knew' Africans – a belief rudely shaken by Mau Mau, whose activities proved that they had been ignorant of developments on their own estates; *Land, Freedom and Fiction*, ch. 3.

113 Blundell, *So Rough a Wind*, pp. 154–7.

114 For amusing anecdotal evidence to this effect, see Campbell, *Heart of Africa*, p. 247.

115 Letter from Blundell to Hore-Belisha, 21/1/53; Blundell MSS, Box 3/1, MSS Afr. s.746, Rhodes House. This box also contains Blundell's correspondence with Kendall Ward, who was appointed as the representative of the resulting organization, 'The Voice of Kenya', with offices in London's Old Bond Street.

116 On a trip to Kenya in 1949, Kenneth Blackburne remarked that the settlers 'seem to want to keep the African for ever in a menial position . . . they treat them like dirt'; diary entry for 17/4/49; Blackburne MSS, Box 9/1, MSS Brit. Emp. s.460, Rhodes House.

117 Mockaitis, *British Counterinsurgency*, p. 50; Clayton, *Counter-insurgency*, pp. 37–52.

118 Letter from Gorrell Barnes to Sir Thomas Lloyd, 19/2/53; CO 822/440.

119 Letter from Erskine to Lady Erskine, 17/1/54; IWM 75/134/1.

120 Report on the situation in Kenya, written by Erskine to Harding, 9/11/53; WO 216/860.

121 Letter from A.H. Joyce to C.Y. Carstairs, 1/1/53; CO 1027/7.

122 On the unfavourable attitude of the Indian press, see a telegram from the UK High Commissioner in India to the CRO, no. 1325, 24/10/52; CO 822/448.

123 The UK High Commissioner in India kept a careful watch over India's attitude to East Africa; see P. Rogers to A. Cohen, 6/11/51; CO 822/581.

124 One extreme view of Indians' complicity in Mau Mau was presented in Kenya's Intelligence Digest, no. 189, Aug. 1954: 'Mau Mau is directed and financed by Indian Communists, but the Indian community in general, with the exception of the Moslems, has gone disturbingly close to showing actual sympathy for the terrorists'; DO 35/5342.

125 Telegram from the UK High Commissioner in India to the CRO, no. 482, 24/4/53; CO 822/448.

126 Cleary, 'Myth of Mau Mau', *African Affairs*, p. 237.

127 Ibid., pp. 227–8.

128 Confidential Memorandum, 'South Africa: Attitude of the Union Government to

United Kingdom Policy in Colonial Territories', by the Acting UK High Commissioner in South Africa to Secretary of State for Commonwealth Relations, 15 Jan. 1954; DO 35/5343.

129 Ibid.

130 Gunther, *Inside Africa*, pp. 3–4.

131 Addressing the issue of whether Mau Mau was Communist, Gunther stated: 'Allegations that the Mau Mau conspiracy is Communist-inspired, or that the terrorists are supplied with arms from Soviet Russia, or are led by Russian agents are nonsensical. No responsible British authority on the spot gives them any credence whatever'; *Inside Africa*, p. 368.

132 Lonsdale, 'Mau Maus of the Mind', *Journal of African History*, p. 407. *Something of Value* was first published in London in 1955.

133 *Life* (16/2/53), 'Your Guns Go with You', in CO 822/461.

134 See *Something of Value*, pp. 284–304.

135 *Life* article, op. cit.

136 Minute by Dixon Barton to E.B. David and H. Hall, 16/6/53; CO 822/460.

137 See, for example, Gunther on the colour bar in Kenya, *Inside Africa*, pp. 324–5; see also Farson on the necessity of working out 'an equitable, co-operative partnership of black and white in Africa'; *Last Chance in Africa*, p. 384.

138 This should have come as no surprise. On his trip to Kenya in 1949, Blackburne had found the information staff making no serious attempt to deal with the press, and, in the African information service, no consultation over policy; Blackburne diary, 16/4/49; Blackburne MSS. Box 9/1, Brit. Emp. 460, Rhodes House.

139 Memo on 'Public Relations – Kenya', prepared by C.Y. Carstairs for Lyttelton, 23/10/52; CO 1027/40.

140 'Measures for Countering Communist Propaganda in East and Central Africa', W.H. Ingrams, p. 109; CO 537/7780.

141 Minute by Carstairs to Gorrell Barnes, 10/12/52; CO 1027/7.

142 Minute by Haler, 8/9/52; CO 822/436.

143 Letter from H.G. Hall to Hartwell (Nairobi Secretariat), 12/9/52; CO 822/436.

144 Letter from Hartwell to Hall, 20/9/52; CO 822/436.

145 In December 1952, Carstairs repeated his earlier claim that 'the information organisation in Kenya can hardly be said to exist'; memo to A.C.E. Malcolm, 6/12/52; CO 1027/7.

146 In a letter from E.B. David to Sir Frederick Crawford, 26/8/53, mention is made of Baring's initial proposal being contained in a letter to Gorrell Barnes of 18 Nov. 1952; CO 822/701.

147 Carstairs to Gorrell Barnes, 10/12/52; CO 1027/7.

148 Notes by Hon. H. Fraser MP on the Emergency in Kenya, April 1953; CO 822/479.

149 Before Gibson and Matheson's arrival, the CO had used Baring's telegrams and notes on events as press releases; Gorrell Barnes to Sir Charles Arden-Clarke, 1/1/53; CO 822/467. The idea that the Army should take over seems to have come from Erskine; letter from E.W.M. Magor (Nairobi) to Hall, 19/6/53; CO 822/469.

150 Letter from Baring to Gorrell Barnes, 17/6/53; CO 1027/40.

151 Minute by Carstairs, 1/7/53; CO 1027/40.

152 Ibid.

153 Minute by Barr on Baring's 'sporting terms' creeping back into his telegrams, 23/4/53; CO 822/454.

154 Carstairs wrote to Gibson on 16/6/53 to relay the 'considerable resentment' among West Africans at the choice of language used in the BBC Overseas Service News bulletins to report operations in Kenya. Although Carstairs thought it unlikely that they could do much to influence correspondents' choice of words, he urged Gibson to ensure that 'government and military handouts and statements do not offend in this way'. The BBC, for its part, blamed the military authorities in Kenya

for the offensive phraseology; letter from A.H. Wigan (Head of BBC Foreign News Department) to A.J. Haler, 4/8/53; CO 1027/31.

155 Minute by E.B. David to Carstairs and Gorrell Barnes, 30/6/53; CO 1027/40.

156 Letter from Lyttelton to Baring, 10/7/53; CO 1027/40.

157 Draft letter from E.B. David to Crawford, 27/7/53; CO 1027/40.

158 Letter from S.H. Evans to C.Y. Carstairs, 11/8/53; CO 822/701.

159 Ibid.

160 'Report of Visit to Kenya, 17 Sept.–5 Oct. by Hon. H.C.P.J. Fraser MBE MP'; CO 822/479.

161 Letter from Evans to Carstairs, 11/9/53; CO 1027/40.

162 Letter from Evans to Carstairs, 11/8/53; CO 822/701.

163 Telegram from Erskine to Harding, 12/8/53; WO 216/857.

164 As Evans wrote: 'Crawford said that for his part he did not know what a "psychological warfare expert" was, which gave me the opportunity to say that it puzzled us no less'; letter to Carstairs, 11/8/53; CO 822/701.

165 Minute by C.Y. Carstairs, 18/8/53; CO 822/701.

166 Letter from Evans to Carstairs, 11/8/53; CO 822/701.

167 Leakey, Mau Mau and the Kikuyu, p. viii.

168 Letter from Evans to Carstairs, 11/8/53; CO 822/701. Crawford, however, felt that while they 'might make use of him as an adviser . . . it would be impossible to employ him as an executive because of his difficult temperament'.

169 Top Secret letter from E.B. David to Sir F. Crawford, 26/8/53; CO 822/701.

170 Ibid. David's letter has also been quoted by Charles Townshend, who regards it as 'as clear an expression of British counter-insurgency doctrine as any that could be found'; Britain's Civil Wars, p. 36.

171 Letter from Crawford to David, 17/9/53; CO 822/701.

172 The idea had in fact been floated in more skeletal form by Baring to Lyttelton in a telegram of 21/8/53; CO 822/696.

173 Baring reported this to Lyttelton, requesting that no publicity be given to Carothers's visit, on 6 Nov. 1953; telegram from Baring to Lyttelton, 6/11/53, no. 1173; CO 822/696. Minutes of the meetings of the African Information Working Party can be found in CO 1027/41.

174 The hankering for greater use of psychological warfare techniques did not disappear altogether. In October 1955, this time at General Lathbury's insistence, the War Council established a Psychological Warfare Staff to assist in bringing about Mau Mau surrenders; see F. Furedi, 'Kenya: Decolonization through Counter-insurgency', in Gorst et al., Contemporary British History, pp. 159–61.

175 Letter from A.C.E. Malcolm to Carstairs, 22/11/52; CO 1027/7.

176 Cleary, 'Myth of Mau Mau', African Affairs, p. 228.

177 Letter from Carstairs to Malcolm, 6/12/52; CO 1027/7.

178 See for example a telegram from Lyttelton to Baring, of 7/12/52, no. 895; CO 1027/7.

179 Letter from Malcolm to Carstairs, 24/12/52; CO 1027/7.

180 Letter from Gibson to Carstairs, 30/6/53; CO 1027/31.

181 Outline of Information Paper for West African Ministers on the 'Situation in Kenya', by Gorrell Barnes, 8/12/52; CO 1027/7.

182 Bewes, Kikuyu Conflict, p. 36.

183 This was the type of work which Blundell's Voice of Kenya campaign sponsored. Blundell also claimed, shortly after the declaration of an Emergency, to be 'gingering up the Government here [Kenya] to put a largeish sum of money into the estimates yearly to provide better public relations for the colony'; letter to Gerald Sayers, Conservative Research Dept., London, 30/12/52; Blundell MSS, Box 6, file 1.

184 Outline Information Paper for West African Ministers, 8/12/52; CO 1027/7.

185 Telegram from Lyttelton to Baring, 16/10/52; CO 822/438.

186 See, for example, correspondence between F.J. Bradshaw (FO ISD) and Barnes (COI) on the COI acquiring rights to a bloodthirsty excerpt from C.T. Stoneham's *Mau Mau*; CO 1027/7.

187 See BIS press release no. 4, 7/11/52; CO 822/448.

188 On 7 November 1952, Lyttelton stated that the leaders of Mau Mau charged 'a substantial fee' for the administration of the oath, and that the movement was thus the 'unholy union of dark and ancient superstition with the apparatus of modern gangsterism' – remarks which were carried in a BIS press release; CO 822/448.

189 See the report on Mau Mau oaths given to the Parliamentary delegation visiting Kenya in 1954; CO 822/800.

190 This point was emphasized by Leakey, in *Defeating Mau Mau*, p. 87.

191 Letter from H.T. Bourdillon to P.R. Sedgwick, 9/3/54; DO 35/5343.

192 Undated extract from the proceedings of the Kenya government; CO 822/474.

193 Memorandum, entitled 'Mau Mau', given to the Parliamentary Delegation in Kenya, 13 Jan. 1954; CO 822/800.

194 CC(54) 10, Minutes of 22 Feb. 1954, item 9; CAB 128/27.

195 *Daily Express* (24/2/54).

196 Even as the Cabinet decided not to publish the appendix, Ministers agreed that it should be 'communicated to newspaper proprietors by the most appropriate channel'. CC(54) 10, op. cit.; CAB 128/27.

197 In January 1954 details of the Mau Mau oath – no doubt those given to the Parliamentary Delegation – were supplied to the editors of *The Times*, the *Observer*, the *Daily Telegraph*, the *Manchester Guardian*, the *Spectator* and the *New Statesman and Nation* through Granville Roberts; see Minutes of a Meeting of the African Information 'Working Party' on 18/1/54; CO 822/800.

198 *The Times* (24/2/54), editorial, 'United Views on Mau Mau'; unlike the *Express's* editor, *The Times* felt that publication of the report alone 'should put an end to the propagation of the malicious (or merely woolly-minded) idea that Mau Mau is a "liberation movement"'.

199 Leakey, *Defeating Mau Mau*, p. 84.

200 *The Kenya Picture* (Government Printer, Nairobi, undated, though with a foreword by General Erskine dated 5/1/54); copy in Erskine's papers, Box 75/134/4 (IWM).

201 Clayton states that this appendix had to be returned after it had been read by the recipient of the pamphlet; *Counter-insurgency*, p. 7.

202 Blundell, *So Rough a Wind*, p. 168.

203 Furedi, *Mau Mau War in Perspective*, p. 4.

204 Corfield, 'Historical Survey', ch. 10, 'External and Internal Influences on Mau Mau'.

205 Ingrams, 'Communist Prospects in East and Central Africa', April 1952, p. 1; CO 537/7780.

206 This is evident from a letter from Ralph Murray to Blackburne, 12/12/49; CO 537/6569.

207 Extracts from the *Kansas City Star* of 24/10/52 contained in a letter from J.G. Boyd (IPD) to C.Y. Carstairs, 5/11/52; CO 822/448.

208 BIS press release no. 4, 7/11/52; CO 822/448.

209 Minute by W.H. Ingrams to Rogers, 4/11/52; CO 822/461.

210 Minute by D. Barton to Rogers, 6/11/52. This was reflected in his rewording of the Top Secret Intel, no. 228, 17/10/52, 'Situation in Kenya: Possibility of Communist Connections with Mau Mau'; CO 822/461.

211 Minute by Ingrams to Carstairs, 7/11/52; CO 822/461.

212 Such a story was carried by the *Daily Mail* on 1/12/52; it was also carried by the US magazine *Time* on 8/12/52.

213 Telegram from FO to Asmara, no. 2, 26/1/53, 'Activities of Russian Legation, Addis Ababa'; CO 1027/7. Barton caustically minuted, of this rebuttal of the

rumours, 'What the FO doesn't say is that we have had a lot of difficulty with their IRD over Communism being at the back of Mau Mau'; minute dated 30/1/53.

214 Minute by Barton, 1/6/53; CO 822/461.

215 Ibid.

216 *The Times* of 3/11/52 reported Lyttelton's remarks while in Kenya that 'Certain features of the Mau Mau organisation, such as cells, bore the mark of a pattern which was painfully familiar in many other situations' – though he stressed that it was not helped financially from outside Kenya; nor were there parallels with Malaya.

217 In his memoirs, Lyttelton at once acknowledged the absence of proof, but asserted his belief in a Soviet and Indian intrigue; *Memoirs of Lord Chandos*, p. 399.

218 Stoneham, for example, writes of Mau Mau as influenced by both Communists and Nazis; *Mau Mau*, pp. 27–9.

219 Cleary, 'Myth of Mau Mau', *African Affairs*, p. 241.

220 For example, in November 1952, the FO's IPD took exception to an article by Alexander Campbell in *Time*, which implied that the basis of Mau Mau was the problem of landlessness; letter from J.G. Boyd (IPD) to Carstairs; CO 822/448. A BIS hand-out, which stressed that Mau Mau represented the sort of secret society that was an 'endemic in disease in Africa', was recommended as an antidote.

221 Outline Information Paper for West African Ministers, 8/12/52; CO 1027/7.

222 Leakey, *Defeating Mau Mau*, p. 23.

223 F. Kitson writes in *Low Intensity Operations: Subversion, Insurgency, Peace-Keeping* (Faber and Faber, London, 1991): 'One of the most remarkable instances of a cause being manipulated, if not invented, in order to make a wide appeal is afforded by the Mau Mau movement in Kenya'; p. 31. For a critique of counter-insurgency literature see P. Schlesinger, 'On the Shape and Scope of Counter-insurgency Thought' in *Media, State and Nation*, pp. 66–91.

224 In a broadcast from Nairobi, Lyttelton said that 'Mau Mau is not the child of economic pressure' – a line which he stuck to with a rigidity even Blundell thought misplaced; *So Rough a Wind*, p. 104.

225 Text of a broadcast by Lyttelton in Nairobi on 4/11/52; CO 822/459. As for Mau Mau being anti-Christian, Berman and Lonsdale argue that it was 'non-Christian' rather than anti-Christian; B. Berman and J. Lonsdale, *Unhappy Valley: Conflict in Kenya and Africa. Book 2: Violence and Ethnicity* (James Currey, London, 1992), p. 441.

226 Undated article, 'Kenya and Mau Mau' (probably early 1953) by Ingrams; Ingrams MSS, Box 4, file 5, MSS Brit. Emp. s.428, Rhodes House.

227 Itote, *Mau Mau in Action*, p. 187.

228 Thus in *Simba* and *Something of Value*, although the audience is made aware that Africans are also victimized by Mau Mau, the plots centre on the murder of white settlers.

229 Telegram from Lyttelton to Baring, 7/12/52, no. 895; CO 1027/7.

230 Telegram from Lyttelton to Baring, 10/7/53, undated; CO 1027/40.

231 This was alleged by the *Daily Telegraph* (30/3/53).

232 Memorandum on the work of the Information Services in Kenya, 'Information to the Kikuyu, Embu and Meru in Central Province'; CO 1027/40.

233 Letter from Crawford to E.B. David, 3/9/53; CO 1027/40.

234 Ibid.

235 The volume of press work is shown in the annual reports produced by Kenya's Information Department for the years 1954 and 1955; CO 1027/54.

236 This phrase was used by Carstairs of his request to Nairobi to furnish more positive material on Kenya; minute to Gorrell Barnes, 10/12/52; CO 1027/7.

237 The *Daily Mail* on 14 Nov. 1953, for example, launched a vituperative attack on the *Daily Worker*, which had published three photographs the previous day of

Kikuyu suspects seated behind barbed wire fences in postures of surrender, with the intention of 'shaming our country in the eyes of the world', as the *Mail*'s editor put it.

238 Pathé, issue no. 52-90 (6/11/52), 'Mau Mau Crisis'.

239 The films *Something of Value* and *Simba* both show Mau Mau initiates receiving ceremonial gashes on the arm during oath ceremonies, setting them apart, and ensuring that if caught by settlers there could be no doubt as to whether punishment was deserved. But Leakey points out that although Mau Mau initiates initially received seven ceremonial gashes as part of the oath ceremony, this practice was soon abandoned precisely because it rendered adherents too readily detectable. Thus there was 'no outward sign by which one can tell whether a man is a Mau Mau supporter or not'; *Defeating Mau Mau*, p. 121. See also Kariuki, '*Mau Mau' Detainee*, p. 66.

240 Minute by Mary Fisher to Evans and Carstairs, 2/1/53; CO 1027/7.

241 Ibid.

242 Telegram from Lyttelton to Baring, 7/12/52, no. 895; CO 1027/7.

243 Draft letter from Carstairs to Baring, 8/1/53; CO 1027/7.

244 Letter from Evans to Carstairs, 11/8/53; CO 1027/40.

245 'Annual Report of the Department of Information for 1954', p. 2; copy in CO 1027/54.

246 'Department of Information, Annual Report, 1955', p. 4; CO 1027/54.

247 Again, this was a Colonial Office demand which took Nairobi some time to satisfy; minute by C.J. Bonington, dated 30/4/53; CO 1027/7.

248 Letter from Carstairs to A.C.E. Malcolm, 6/12/52; CO 1027/7.

249 Minute by Carstairs to MackIntosh, 8/1/53; CO 1027/7.

250 H.C. Debs, vol. 509, 16 Dec. 1952, 'Kenya', col. 1237.

251 Lonsdale, 'Mau Maus of the Mind', *Journal of African History*, p. 405.

252 Pathé, issue no. 53-34 (11/5/53), 'The Mark of Mau Mau'.

253 Ibid.

254 Telegram from Lyttelton to Baring, 28/5/53, no. 500; CO 822/702.

255 Stoneham, *Mau Mau*, p. 96. See also Blundell, *So Rough a Wind*, p. 140.

256 The pamphlet was designed to be distributed to battalions of the King's African Rifles on their return to Kenya from Malaya and to members of the East Africa Pioneer Corps on return from the Canal Zone. Its cover set the tone for the contents: against a blood-red background was a photograph of a panga lying next to an African toddler, disembowelled and virtually sliced in half down the middle. A copy can be found in WO 236/17.

257 The OAG (during Baring's convalescent absence from Kenya in the summer of 1953) explained the incidence of torture and inhuman treatment of Mau Mau suspects in this way; telegram no. 993, 10/7/53; CO 822/489.

258 This was one of the accusations in the Hayward case, examined below.

259 *The Times* (22/12/53).

260 *Reynolds News* (13/1/57).

261 Telegram from Deputy Governor to Lyttelton, 16/12/52, no. 917, CO 822/439.

262 Telegram from Lyttelton to Baring, 12/2/53, no. 141; CO 822/471.

263 Letter from E.B. David to Crawford, 29/7/53; CO 1027/40.

264 Telegram from Lyttelton to Baring, 4/12/52, no. 870; CO 822/439.

265 Letter from Rogers to Potter, 12/2/53; CO 822/474.

266 Telegram from Baring to Lyttelton, 20/4/53, no. 459; CO 822/474.

267 Rogers to Potter, 12/2/53; see also Sir T. Lloyd's minute dated 15/4/53; CO 822/474.

268 'Message to Be Distributed to All Officers of the Army, Police and Security Forces' by Erskine, dated 23/6/53; WO 236/17.

269 Letter from Erskine to his wife, 28/11/53; Erskine private papers (IWM).

270 Telegram from Erskine to Harding (CIGS), 14/6/53; CO 822/693.

271 Letter from Erskine to Harding, 7/7/53; CO 822/693.
272 Ibid.
273 COS (53) 144th Meeting of 22/12/53, minute 4; in PREM 11/696.
274 See the brief for Commander-in-Chief on Air Operations, for a press conference on 20/10/54; WO 236/17.
275 Telegram from Baring to Lyttelton, 11/2/53, no. 180; CO 822/471.
276 Oliver Woods wrote in Jan. 1954 that there had been 150,000 arrests made during the Emergency, twenty-four cases of complaints tried and five convictions; he thought that for every case which came to court there were probably ten which did not – which seems rather optimistic; 'Confidential Note on Brutality in Kenya, 28/1/54'; Woods MSS, Confidential Memoranda (1953-70), *The Times* Archive.
277 Telegram from Twining (Governor of Tanganyika) to Lyttelton, 12/11/53; CO 822/503.
278 Reuters report from Dar es Salaam, 12/11/53; CO 822/503.
279 Telegram from Lyttelton to Twining and Baring, 20/11/53, no. 556; CO 822/503.
280 Telegram from Lyttelton to Crawford, 5/12/53, no. 1151; copy in Harold Ingrams's private papers; MSS Brit. Emp. s.428, Box 4, File 5, Rhodes House.
281 Telegram from Erskine to Harding, 29/6/53; CO 822/474.
282 *The Times* (22/12/53), 'Regimental Notes on Mau Mau MP's Letter to Minister'.
283 *The Times* (22/12/53).
284 Letter from Crawford to E.B. David, 16/12/53; CO 822/489.
285 Attlee requested during Question Time on 30 Nov. 1953 that the Prime Minister order an inquiry into the evidence presented during Griffiths's court martial; H.C. Debs, vol. 521, 30/11/53, col. 770.
286 'Summary of Report by the McLean Court of Inquiry into allegations made during the trial of Captain G.S.L. Griffiths DLI, against conduct of British Security Forces in Kenya'; PREM 11/696.
287 See, for example, the *Daily Mirror* (28/1/54).
288 Letter from Erskine to his wife, 7/3/54; Erskine private papers (IWM).
289 Between the start of the Emergency and April 1957, 1,074 Mau Mau prisoners were hanged. Of this total, only 321 were executed for murder, while 54 were hanged for 'oath administration' and 207 for the yet more nebulous offence of 'consorting'; execution statistics can be found in CO 822/1256.
290 Telegram from Lyttelton to Baring, 11/12/52, no. 919; CO 822/439.
291 Note from Churchill to Lyttelton, 5/12/54; PREM 11/1424.
292 On the question of how far the principle of 'minimum force' was adhered to in Kenya, see Mockaitis, *British Counterinsurgency*, pp. 49–50; J. Newsinger, 'Minimum Force, British Counterinsurgency and the Mau Mau Rebellion', *Small Wars and Insurgencies*, 3, i (Spring 1992), 47–57; and Mockaitis's 'Reply', *Small Wars and Insurgencies*, 3, ii (Autumn 1992), 87–9.
293 Confidential memorandum on 'Brutality in Kenya', by Oliver Woods, op. cit.
294 The incident occurred in March 1959, at the remote Hola Camp (where the remaining Mau Mau 'hard core' detainees were imprisoned). The outcry over the prisoners' deaths led to the publication of a White Paper later in 1959: 'Documents Relating to the Death of Eleven Mau Mau Detainees at Hola Camp in Kenya', Cmnd 778. Documents relating to the Hola case can be found in CO 822/1261. A personal account of the events of March 1959, written by an ex-Administrative Officer in the Kenya adminstration, is contained in W.H. Thompson's transcript memoir, 'Only the Foothills' (IWM), and for an account of Baring's role in the affair, see Douglas-Home's *Evelyn Baring*, pp. 289–9.
295 Rawcliffe, *The Struggle for Kenya*, p. 68.
296 *Daily Mirror* (7/12/55) 'A One Woman Probe into Kenya', p. 2; (9/12/55) 'The Truth about the Secret Police', p. 2; (10/12/55) 'Why Was This Report Kept Dark?', p. 2.

297 Memo by George Kinnear, Kenya correspondent; Kinnear MSS (1941-54), *The Times* Archive.
298 Telegram from Baring to Lyttelton, 31/12/53; CO 822/696.
299 Leakey, *Defeating Mau Mau*, p. 117.
300 Confidential memorandum, 'Brutality in Kenya', op. cit.
301 Ibid.
302 Letter from Huxley to Blundell, 22/2/55, and repley from Blundell to Huxley, 9/3/55; Blundell MSS, Box 3/2.
303 Campbell, *The Heart of Africa*, p. 271.
304 Minute (undated) by Hinde, on War Council Minute 1436, 'Psychological Warfare'. Hinde MSS, file 3; MSS. Afr. s.1580, Rhodes House. The settlers' criticisms of Kenya government propaganda were also related by *The Times*'s correspondent, George Kinnear, who thought the allegations had 'some foundation' – but cautioned that few Europeans really knew what was in the Kikuyu mind; Kinnear MSS, confidential letter dated 19/2/55, File 1941-54, *The Times* Archive.
305 Letter from Roberts to Blundell, 14/6/54; Blundell MSS, Box 3/2.
306 Letter from Evans to Carstairs, 11/9/53; CO 1027/40.
307 Berman, *Control and Crisis in Colonial Kenya*, pp. 396–7.
308 H.T. Bourdillon to P.R. Sedgwick, 9/3/54; DO 35/5343.
309 Cleary, 'Myth of Mau Mau', *African Affairs*, pp. 240–1.
310 Letter from Roberts to Blundell, 26/1/56; Blundell MSS Box 4/file 3. See also a letter from a Tory MP praising Roberts's work; letter from 'Cub' Alport to Blundell, 2/3/55, Blundell MSS Box 3/file 2.
311 Maughan-Brown, *Land, Freedom and Fiction*, p. 158.
312 Letter from Evans to Carstairs, 11/9/53; CO 1027/40.

4 'Mischief in the Air':[1] EOKA and the Struggle for Enosis in Cyprus, 1955–59

The Background to the Dispute

From 1950 onwards the British administration in Cyprus was aware that the movement among Greek Cypriots for union with Greece (*Enosis*) was gaining ground. Enosis had been a romantically cherished notion throughout the period of British rule, and arguably since the time of the Greek war of independence. In the past, however, desire for union had taken a more inchoate form – a sentimental attachment, which was infrequently acted upon and only occasionally strained Anglo-Greek relations on the island.[2] But in 1950 the fresh decade heralded a new departure in the movement for Enosis. In January 1950 the Greek Orthodox Church organized a 'plebiscite' which revealed a 96 per cent majority in favour of Enosis. Naturally, as the polling had been carried out through the agency of Orthodox priests, this result did not reveal the antipathy of the Turkish-Cypriot minority who had no wish to see the island being united with Turkey's traditional antagonist. While the British administration did not accept the result, the plebiscite demonstrated the will of the Orthodox Church to mobilize Greek-Cypriot opinion and to force the issue to the forefront of the Governor's attention.

The plebiscite also brought to the administration's attention the radicalism of the Bishop of Kition, who was elected as the new Ethnarch, Archbishop Makarios III, later that year. As Ethnarch he was both the political and spiritual leader of the Greek Cypriots – the figurehead of the Enosis movement, and later dubbed the 'Arch-Terrorist' behind EOKA's campaign of violence.[3] Makarios, and the Orthodox Church in general, were seen by the Cyprus government as catalysing the Greek Cypriots' rapid politicization. Not only did the Church preach a gospel of Enosis but through the Ethnarchy (its ruling body, headed by Makarios) it had lobbied an initially reluctant Greek government into support for the cause of union. By 1953 the Papagos administration had swung behind Makarios. Unbeknown to the British government, it was also providing material aid for the embryonic resistance movement covertly being planned by a small committee including Makarios and General George Grivas.[4]

British colonial officials also believed that the Cypriot Communist

Party (AKEL) was whipping up Enosis agitation. That Cypriot Communists should be advocating Enosis was somewhat surprising, given the antipathy of the Orthodox Church towards godless Communism and the hostility of the royalist Athens political establishment to proponents of an ideology defeated at such cost after World War II. As Communists were treated with considerably less than toleration in Greece itself, the Cyprus government concluded that AKEL's stated support for union was a duplicitous move, dictated by Moscow, designed both to gain electoral support in Cyprus itself (where Enosis was undoubtedly popular among Greek Cypriots) and to foment unrest in a sensitive area of the Mediterranean. Their main goal was thus understood to be the disruption of NATO, by sowing the seeds of discord between the precariously allied Greek and Turkish states.[5]

Cold War considerations permeated Britain's response to the development of the Enosis movement, shaping official perceptions of the island's strategic importance. The strategic necessity of Britain's continued rule over Cyprus was the predominant theme of Westminster's initial response to Enosis agitation, voiced most notoriously by a junior Colonial Office minister, Henry Hopkinson, when he told the House of Commons that 'certain territories in the Commonwealth . . . owing to their particular circumstances can never expect to be fully independent'.[6] Hopkinson's unfortunate 'never' was responsible for his subsequent removal from office, and has also been credited with propelling events in Cyprus from protest to physical violence. Yet for all the Colonial Office's publicly stated certainty that Cyprus was too valuable ever to achieve self-government, the island's strategic value was questionable. As a former senior official of Britain's last colonial administration in Cyprus has written, 'the military case for retaining possession and control of the island in fact rested more on the negative argument of denying it to a hostile power than on the positive argument of its operational value'.[7] And after the disastrous Suez operation, launched from Cyprus, playing up the latter's military value became a redundant propaganda theme. Britain's position in Cyprus was thus not always easy to defend, but as the case for Cypriot self-determination was annually laid before the UN General Assembly by successive Greek governments, the administrations of Churchill, Eden and Macmillan were repeatedly called upon to justify Britain's retention of the island.[8] As during the Palestine Emergency, Britain's behaviour came under fierce international scrutiny. In response, the British government tried to emphasize that Cyprus was not simply a colonial issue but an international problem, whose solution required the agreement of three states: Britain, Greece and Turkey.

In many respects the State of Emergency in Cyprus, declared in November 1955 after the outbreak of terrorism in April, differed from the two other counter-insurgencies concurrently being wound down in Malaya and Kenya. When the fluent Greek-speaking poet and novelist

Lawrence Durrell (appointed in late summer 1954 as Director of Information Services[9]) arrived in Cyprus he noted 'something which marked Cyprus off from the rest of the Mediterranean – an agricultural island being urbanized too quickly, before its inhabitants had really decided what was worth preserving about their habits and surroundings'.[10] This observation brings to mind analyses of Kenya before the eruption of Mau Mau violence: the theory that terrorism resulted from prematurely catapulting the indigenous population into the twentieth century. But despite this apparent parallel, as far as British colonial officials were concerned discontented Greek Cypriots could not be dealt with in quite the same way as Mau Mau or Malayan malcontents. Greek Cypriots were fellow Europeans, and they were agitating not for independence but rather to be ruled by a state for which many of the classically educated British establishment had considerable admiration. Thus the resort to terrorism was less easily attributed to a racially determined propensity towards bloodshed than had been the explosion of Mau Mau violence in Kenya, even if by August 1958 Harold Macmillan had reached the conclusion that 'Murder was quite respectable in Cyprus. We all made the amendments to the Decalogue which suited us. In our case it was adultery, in the case of the Cypriots it was murder.'[11] The campaign for Enosis was certainly seen as more sophisticated than Mau Mau, being waged on several levels simultaneously: while Grivas planned and executed a phased campaign of sabotage and terrorism in Cyprus, the Greek government and Makarios (before his banishment to the Seychelles in 1956) engaged in diplomatic warfare, bringing the grievances of the Greek Cypriots to a wide international audience. The Greek government also provided moral support to the insurgents through the medium of Athens Radio. Thus it did not take the British government long to realize that this campaign was one in which propaganda would be heavily used, on all sides.

British Interpretations of EOKA Violence

When the first bombs exploded in Cyprus on April Fool's Day, 1955, the Cyprus government, while not exactly treating the explosions as a joke, certainly had little idea of the seriousness of the campaign of violence they portended. Government House had received some prior intimations that the Enosis movement might soon explode in violence. Most noticeably the growing belligerency of sermons preached in Greek Orthodox Churches hinted that the Church would not shrink from violence if necessary.[12] In addition, the capture of an explosive-laden ship, the *Ayios Georgios*, on 25 January 1955 had led to the trial for conspiracy of a handful of Grivas's co-conspirators. One of these, Socrates Loizides, helpfully provided the administration with a document testifying the existence of a well-armed and organized secret revolutionary organization which was plotting the overthrow of the Cyprus government.[13] However, rather than alerting the administration to potential danger, the discovery of this plot seems to have induced premature complacence, and a belief that revolt had been nipped in the bud – when in fact it had not yet begun.[14]

Certainly, on 1 April the Cyprus government had no clear idea of who lay behind the bomb-throwing, and discovered the existence of EOKA (Ethniki Organosis Kyrion Agoniston, National Organization of Cypriot Fighters) only when the latter revealed its existence in pamphlets scattered in Nicosia after the bombings. The identity of 'Dighenis', the pseudonym of the leader who signed EOKA's leaflets, remained a mystery for some time. Indeed, Grivas later charged that the Cypriot Communists – piqued at having been out-manoeuvred by EOKA in the struggle for mastery of the Enosis movement – unmasked him as Dighenis.[15] Not until the British Army captured some secret diaries kept by Grivas did they discover the planning behind the terrorist campaign, and something of the role that Makarios played in the decision to opt for violence rather than diplomacy, as will be seen.

Early press reports in Britain of violence in Cyprus reflected the vagueness felt by Colonial officials as to the nature of the terrorist organization. For example, a report in *The Times* of 22 June 1955 related the Cyprus Police Commissioner's remarks that the terrorists had now decided on 'a definite policy of murder' but that he had no clues about the perpetrators or the underground movement EOKA.[16] Similarly, the following month, the *Daily Herald* referred to EOKA as the Cypriot terrorist organization '*suspected* of being behind the latest wave of bombings' [emphasis added].[17] Analysis of the terrorists' objectives was necessarily patchy, with historical analogies being drawn in the absence of firm evidence; the *Sunday Dispatch* told its readers in July 1955 that while the leaders of EOKA were mysterious, their tactics were those of the 'Palestine terrorists' – namely to 'frighten the British out'.[18]

Early estimations of the Cypriot violence, by both Westminster and Fleet Street, did concur on one point, from which there was no deviation throughout the Emergency: that EOKA violence was specifically a campaign of terrorism. The foregoing case studies have revealed the importance attached to terminology – to the correct labelling of acts of political violence – by those responsible for upholding order. Thus what had initially been known as 'banditry' in Malaya became officially 'Communist Terrorism' later in the counter-insurgency campaign. In the case of Cyprus, however, the activities of EOKA were scarcely ever given any appelation other than 'terrorism', even before it had become apparent who was behind the violence and what they intended by it. Field Marshal Sir John Harding, who replaced Sir Robert Armitage as

Governor in September 1955, was educated in the nuances of language by the Colonial Office personnel to whom he reported: on one occasion he was talked out of a piece of legislation which would brandish EOKA fighters who refused his surrender terms as 'outlaws' – a designation which the Colonial Office felt carried dangerously romantic connotations, unlike the term 'terrorist'.[19]

After April 1955 some weeks elapsed before the Cyprus administration began to talk with more confidence about EOKA's strategy. As the months passed a pattern emerged of EOKA attacks on police stations, with Greek-Cypriot constables forming the most frequent victims of EOKA assassination; the intention seemingly was to break police morale and intimidate Greek Cypriots into withdrawing from what was a largely Turkish force. Attacks on police stations throughout the island were a means of dispersing and drawing in ever more British armed forces – of 'militarizing' the struggle – while simultaneously offering 'opportunities to acquire much-needed arms with which to carry the struggle forward'.[20]

By autumn 1955, confidential Intelligence appraisals of EOKA (though they still revealed nothing of Grivas's 'communications with nationalist leaders in Cyprus, with the Ethnarchy or with Greece, or even whether such communications exist'[21]) deemed propaganda and the search for publicity as central to the terrorist violence. An Intelligence report, written as though by 'Dighenis' himself, stated:

> I shall realise this aim (*Enosis*) by the effect which my activities in Cyprus will have on public opinion here, in the UK and in the US. My main object of attack is public opinion, *not* any particular physical target.[22]

The theory that terrorism was essentially a headline-grabbing strategy was not confined to government officials. Where the British press attempted to offer an analysis of EOKA violence the linkage of terrorism and propaganda often reappeared, as it did in instant, journalistic histories of the Emergency. As Dudley Barker put it:

> [EOKA's] first aim was to influence world opinion. Primarily, the battle of Cyprus was a propaganda battle. Neither Grivas, Makarios, the sponsors of EOKA, nor the members of the Greek Government who had consented to the plan, imagined that the British could be driven from the island by force; although there was at one time a fear that Grivas could rouse the whole Greek population of Cyprus into rebellion, such a step was never really contemplated. What it was hoped to do was so to persuade public opinion, internationally, and in Britain itself, that Cyprus was being oppressed, that the British Government would finally be pushed into giving up the colony to Greece.[23]

The idea that EOKA sought international sympathy, while raising the stakes of occupation for the British government to an unacceptable level, was also found in contemporaneous novels with a Cyprus setting.[24]

As the campaign progressed into 1956 and beyond, other aspects of EOKA's terrorism became more prominent. The variety of EOKA's targets and day-to-day tactics suggested that violence had other functions besides simply keeping the cause of the Greek Cypriots (increasingly presented as self-determination rather than Enosis) in the minds of diverse international audiences. In the course of that year EOKA's actions included blowing up British aircraft, placing a bomb under the Governor's bed (which failed to explode), shooting an off-duty eighteen-year-old British soldier while he was bathing, mining troop vehicles, murdering a picnicking British couple, kidnapping a seventy-year-old British man, mining a drinking fountain used by British soldiers after their customary Sunday football match with locals, and disembowelling two soldiers.

There was a growing element of enforcement terror to EOKA's activities with the continued targeting of Greek-Cypriot policemen and other actual or potential 'traitors'. This terrorization of Greek Cypriots was a dimension of EOKA's activity emphasized by British propaganda, for it suggested that a reluctant indigenous population had to be frightened into support for the terrorist organization. As during the Malayan and Mau Mau Emergencies, British propaganda emphasized that the majority of the terrorists' victims were of the same ethnicity as their attackers as a convenient way of demonstrating how far the insurgents were from being a popular national resistance movement. However, the fact that much of EOKA's violence was also indirect – apparently random killings of British civilians unconnected with either the administration or the security forces – encouraged analysts of the campaign to attribute a *provocative* function to EOKA's actions. In other words, the ostensible senselessness of the acts themselves, which surely meant that EOKA could not be intending to win sympathy (certainly not from British public opinion), suggested that EOKA was aiming at two distinct goals. The first was to frighten the British by raising the stakes of staying in Cyprus to an unacceptable level.[25] The second was to provoke repression by the British authorities. Repressive measures, more than the deeds of EOKA themselves, would then mobilize international (and Greek-Cypriot) support and lend authenticity to EOKA's claim that the British were the real terrorists in Cyprus. The Cyprus Intelligence Committee interpreted Grivas's motives thus: the government would be forced to react with harsh, illiberal laws and the use of armed force, which would lead to 'incidents' Grivas could 'use as "atrocity" stories, to show the people abroad that the Cypriots are being oppressed and harshly treated, and so damage Britain's reputation'.[26] British repression would serve EOKA in other ways. As Lawrence Durrell put it, the terrorist hoped 'to bring down upon the community in general a reprisal for his wrongs, in the hope that the fury and resentment roused by punishment meted out to the innocent will gradually swell the ranks of those from whom he will draw further recruits'.[27] Such interpretations of EOKA terrorism formed the basis of Cyprus government press releases, and they were widely carried by the British press, though Harding expected press reports on EOKA's aims to point out simultaneously the ineffectiveness of such methods.[28]

A number of British newspapers refused to ape Harding's public insistence that terrorism was being beaten and that it was perpetrated by a numerically insubstantial 'hard core' in the mountains. Government-friendly papers such as the *Daily Express* certainly toed the Tory line that 'there is no "resistance movement" in Cyprus. . . . There is a small, utterly ruthless and brutal band of terrorists whose . . . methods arouse widespread disgust and fear',[29] but others, including the *Manchester Guardian*, the *Observer* and the *Spectator*, thought differently.[30] As had become common during Emergencies involving terrorism, lessons and precedents were frequently sought from previous counter-insurgency campaigns, and the *Spectator*, in August 1956, found the most apt parallel for Cyprus developments in the Irish 'war of Independence':

> EOKA has demonstrated once again what the IRA proved in the 1917–21 period: well-organised violence not only can pin down large armies of occupation, but can create a world opinion so hostile to the occupier that he is forced to listen to rebel demands.[31]

Several papers, then, were inclined to see EOKA as successful to the extent that it had considerable public backing. During EOKA's campaign no less than in the other Emergencies studied the precise relationship between the 'water and the fish' remained a vexed issue. Not only did elements of the British press disagree with the colonial authorities, but the latter themselves were far from unanimous on the issue of the degree of popular support EOKA enjoyed. Most significantly, Durrell himself became convinced that EOKA was not the 'small body of revolutionaries, unknown to the general public' he had initially taken it for.[32] By late 1956 he believed the Greek Cypriots to be largely behind EOKA. This was not simply a product of EOKA 'terrorization' but of British blunders. Westminster and Nicosia had acted insensitively, refusing to find a formula whereby Enosis was not ruled out in perpetuity. Moreover, in hanging the EOKA terrorist Karaolis, the British had irrevocably embittered the Greek Cypriots. Force was then the only option open to crush EOKA, but the chances of military counter-measures succeeding were lessened as popular support for the terrorists increased.[33] Believing that persuasion could no longer be effective, Durrell resigned his post as the head of the Cyprus Information Office.

Durrell's view on leaving office could scarcely have been further removed from Harding's. The latter was never reticent with his opinion on the terrorists' relative popularity and strength: even after his replacement as Governor by Sir Hugh Foot in December 1957, he continued to produce articles for various British newspapers on the state of EOKA and the counter-insurgency campaign.[34] Harding viewed EOKA much more in terms of conspiracy than of popular discontent. Terrorism was a tool in the personal control of Archbishop Makarios, who would turn it on or off at will, using violence in tandem with political negotiations (whether at Government House, Nicosia or at the UN), as a reminder to the British of the consequences of non-compliance with his political demands. Lulls in terrorist activity served as a demonstration of how easily normalcy could be resumed in Cyprus if only the appropriate political bargain were struck. Harding's term in office was characterized by a reluctance to deal with those with 'blood on their hands' (hence his deportation of Makarios to the Seychelles in March 1956 and unwillingness to release him unless he denounced terrorism) and an apparently unwavering confidence in the efficacy of force in breaking the 'hard core'. EOKA was thus seen as numerically insignificant: it might have coerced some support – or passive acquiescence – from the Greek-Cypriot community at large, but it remained unrepresentative. When Harding announced in July 1956 that constitutional reform would proceed in Cyprus (despite the dangers of reform being misread as a concession to terrorism), he did so on the grounds that 'the great mass of the people' were 'heartily sick of violence and all its consequences'.[35]

The arrival of Sir Hugh Foot as Harding's replacement in December 1957 was widely regarded as signalling a Westminster-inspired retreat from the inflexibility of Harding. Foot's view of terrorism, and of the relationship between EOKA and the mass of Greek-Cypriot people, was more akin to Durrell's than Harding's. The campaign itself had moved on. The months between March 1957 and March 1958 saw a self-declared 'truce' by EOKA (albeit one in which there were frequent bursts of violent activity, as British propaganda hastened to point out). The lull in terrorist activity, however, was not matched by inactivity on the part of the security forces, which kept up the relentless pursuit of Grivas and his mountain gangs. Their cordon-and-search operations, with the resultant detention of increasing numbers of Greek Cypriots in what EOKA termed 'concentration camps', provided Grivas with fertile opportunities to make allegations of brutality against the security forces during the truce. In this period, EOKA honed the 'smear technique', as it became officially dubbed.

In March 1958 there was a recrudescence of terrorism, which Foot saw as 'deliberately planned to hit the headlines of the world Press during the UN debate and to present a picture, not only of Greek-Cypriot determination to achieve its aims and of defiance of our authority, but also of our "repressive measures"'.[36] Unlike Harding, Foot did not draw a sharp distinction between the terrorists and the Greek Cypriots in general. While mindful of the rights and fears of the Turkish minority, he was determined to reach a political solution which would satisfy at least some of the Greek Cypriots' grievances. Foot's wife Sylvia appears to have spoken for both of them when she reflected: 'It seemed to me that EOKA was composed to a greater or lesser extent of every Greek in Cyprus. It seemed to our weary hearts that we were once more up against the disastrous and childish and utterly hopeless theory that Force could overcome Ideas.'[37] It was precisely this theory, associated with Harding, that Foot sought to abandon. The intensification of EOKA terrorism in late 1958 (October seeing the heaviest casualties of the Emergency, including the climactic murder of Mrs Cutliffe, a British soldier's wife), and the constant threat that tension between the Greek- and Turkish-Cypriot communities might imminently explode into fully-fledged civil war, required a continuation of the security forces' counter-terrorist operations. But Foot was determined to persist in exploring negotiated options for a settlement which would accommodate both Greek and Turkish aspirations. He was rewarded with the discovery in early 1959 that the Greek government was no longer willing to tolerate its defence policy being disrupted by Grivas, and that, with pressure, Makarios could be detatched from his insistence on Enosis. The resulting settlement consequently uncoupled self-determination (or Enosis) and self-government, allowing Cypriots the latter but not the former, with Makarios as the head of an independent Cypriot state.

EOKA's Explanation of Its Strategy

Expositions of the Cyprus campaign left by EOKA's leader, George Grivas, reveal that propaganda was indeed a key function of violence.[38] Predictably, in works which aimed chiefly at self-justification after the apparent fruits of his campaign had been plucked by Makarios, Grivas does not refer to his organization as a terrorist one, but rather as a liberation movement employing well-established principles of guerrilla warfare.

In his treatise on guerrilla warfare, Grivas set out EOKA's strategic objectives as follows:

> By deeds of heroism and self-sacrifice to draw the attention of inter-national public opinion, especially among the allies of Greece . . .
> By continually harassing the British in Cyprus, we must show that

we are firmly determined not to yield, whatever the sacrifice, but that on the contrary we are prepared to continue until international diplomacy exercised through the UN, and the British in particular, are compelled to examine the Cyprus problem and reach a speedy settlement in accordance with the aspirations of the Cypriot people and the whole Greek nation.

It should not be supposed that by these means we should expect to impose a total defeat on the British forces in Cyprus. Our purpose is to win a moral victory through a process of attrition, by harassing, confusing and finally exasperating the enemy forces, with the objective of achieving our main aim.[39]

Grivas claimed to have employed a 'sound knowledge of mass psychology' in his campaign. EOKA's activities and the capacity of members to withstand 'danger and privation' served to stimulate the Greek Cypriots' faith in the cause.[40] But not only did deeds have this persuasive effect, the organization had also taken pains with its leaflets and word-of-mouth propaganda. Such propaganda helped bolster domestic and international belief in the justice of the cause, serving to 'draw attention to those acts of our opponent which were more likely to discredit him internationally'.[41] Grivas had responsibility for propaganda within Cyprus, while the Greek government and Makarios were charged with publicizing the Enosis cause abroad.

Grivas's works also confirm the phased nature of the campaign. The first phase would, through dramatic incidents of sabotage, awaken the British and the world to EOKA's existence and aims. This period would also see the conversion of the 'youth of Cyprus into the seedbed of EOKA'.[42] The next objective was to 'terrorize the police and to paralyse the administration, both in the towns and the countryside'. Grivas hoped that this would result in demoralization of the police and the intervention of the Army in protection duties which would overstretch them; attempts would subsequently be made at the United Nations to solve the Cyprus question. His strategy was basically two-pronged: execution groups in the towns would pick off selected individuals (be they Britons or traitorous Greek Cypriots), while mountain 'guerrilla' groups in Cyprus's more impenetrable regions would harry the security forces, keeping them engaged in a protracted search for a well-hidden enemy. In addition, Greek-Cypriot schoolchildren and students would serve as the vanguard of the 'revolution', carrying out valuable leafleting duties and forming a reserve of potential new recruits to EOKA. Their frequent demonstrations in the towns also provided Grivas with further ammunition against the British security forces, which attacked even children with impunity.

If much of EOKA's strategy had been divined by (or become apparent to) the British, in one respect Grivas's explanation of the organization's *modus operandi* differs entirely from British official interpretations of terrorism: namely, Grivas's insistence that EOKA chose only 'direct' targets.

His protestations that EOKA was fighting a war, only a more efficient and selective one, echo the claims of early Russian Anarchists that they had invented a new, clinical form of war:

> The truth is that I was fighting a war in Cyprus against the British, and if they did not recognise the fact from the start they were forced to at the end. The truth is that our form of war, in which a few hundred fell in four years, was far more selective than most . . . We did not strike, like the bomber at random. We shot only British servicemen who would have killed us if they could have fired first, and civilians who were traitors or intelligence agents.[43]

This seems more than a little tendentious when one recollects the most publicized EOKA atrocities, which were precisely those that contradicted Grivas's 'rules of engagement': the killing of a picnicking British couple, the shooting in the back of Mrs Cutliffe, and the killing of soldiers who were scarcely in a position to fire first (the Lefkoniko drinking fountain incident, or the shooting of a young soldier while bathing). The fact that Grivas went to considerable lengths to dissociate EOKA from the murder of Margaret Cutliffe suggests that, if his organization *had* been trying to incense British opinion and provoke repressive measures (and even reprisals) from the security forces – as his opponents thought – then he may also have been unprepared for the scale of the unpopularity that such activities would bring him.[44] So if terrorism was meant to have a provocative function, and affect public opinion in a way which would provoke as much outrage as sympathy (depending on the audience), it would seem that Grivas was not fully prepared to accept the consequences of what he had planned.[45] Grivas's eagerness to justify himself, and to eulogize his own role in the struggle for Enosis – seen in the Diaries, his subsequent memoirs and treatise on guerrilla warfare – indicates a man who craved respect rather than ignominy. He might claim that his young acolytes who formed EOKA's 'close-range execution squads . . . did not care who called them "thug" or "coward"', but such accusations almost certainly stung 'Dighenis' himself.[46]

The British Publicity Organization

When Durrell arrived at the Government Information Office in Nicosia, it required a thorough shaking-up:

> The Information Office had a beguiling air of good-natured shabbiness, and its awkward mirrored rooms gave one the impression of entering an abandoned barber's shop on the Rue Cherif Pacha

in Cairo. I had been led to believe that much needed to be done, but I was unprepared to find so few of the means for doing it. My inheritance seemed in pitiable shape; a cellar full of discarded blocks and photographic equipment so shabby and mouldering as to be a disgrace; an aged film van or two; a moribund house-magazine; and various other odds and ends of little practical use. Absolutely no briefs save the Colonial Report a year out of date; and a mountain of posters showing pictures of the Queen decorating coal-black mammies with long-service medals – the very thing to make Greeks and Turks, with their colour-bar, dance with rage.[47]

As Armitage had recognized, 'with our disorganised information services, our propaganda has been conducted with one arm behind our backs, and our other paralysed from the wrist downwards'.[48] Following Durrell's appointment, and a visit by Harold Evans to Cyprus in 1954, measures were set in hand to establish an Information Office capable of countering pro-Enosis propaganda.

In Britain, government publicity on Cyprus was handled by various agencies in Whitehall. The Colonial Office Information Department (COID) was the principal source and co-ordinator of publicity in Britain on Cyprus, liaising directly with Durrell and his successors in Nicosia. The international dimension of the problem also necessitated the involvement of several Foreign Office departments: the Information Policy Department (IPD), Southern Department and United Nations Department all fed policy and advice to the Colonial Office, while the Information Research Department advised on the Communist aspect of the Cyprus Emergency and the propaganda mileage that could be gained from exploiting it. The Foreign Office IPD was also responsible for co-ordinating the propaganda effort in Britain and Cyprus with that of the British Information Service (BIS) in New York. The attention paid by Makarios and the Greek government to courting American sympathy for the cause of self-determination (as the goal of Enosis was rephrased for international audiences) demanded a continuous counter-publicity effort by the BIS.

The large number of organizations involved in Cyprus publicity work encouraged government critics (including some of Eden's and then Macmillan's own backbenchers) to claim that this overlapping of publicity functions actually prevented the transmission of a clear message. Sir Charles Mott-Radclyffe was one of the most persistent critics, being particularly concerned that the morale of British forces was damaged by the unclear British propaganda line. Tackling both the Colonial Secretary and the BBC in November 1958, Mott-Radclyffe complained that British propaganda was not doing enough to reassure the troops that 'they have the overwhelming support of everyone at home, except a freak minority'.[49] Mott-Radclyffe's criticisms coincided with an influential letter printed in the *Daily Telegraph* (and actually written by one of its own journalists), headed 'Too Many Voices'. Douglas Williams listed ten separate offices in Cyprus alone that dealt with propaganda, and charged that this resulted in a general lack of policy and wastage of both money and staff time. His suggested remedy was the appointment of a senior Press Officer to the Governor's personal staff who would co-ordinate all publicity and propaganda in Cyprus.[50]

In fact at the time of Williams's writing, the Governor of Cyprus was contemplating a reorganization. This was not the first time that considerable thought had been given to the question of rationalizing the complex propaganda set-up both in Cyprus and elsewhere. Harding had proposed several changes in his time as Governor, and particularly favoured the appointment of full-time Cyprus Information Officers in London and New York. This plan was first mooted in early summer 1956 with EOKA terrorism in full flow. The new Director-General of Information in Cyprus, Leslie Glass, wrote to Harold Evans that the Cyprus Information Services were still not geared to 'conduct a world campaign on an international issue'.[51] Evans therefore favoured Harding's scheme of creating new posts. An appointment in London was duly made, with John Fletcher-Cooke becoming the specialist Cyprus Information Officer in July 1956. Fletcher-Cooke's background, as a former Chief Secretary in Cyprus who had previously been seconded to the UK delegation at the United Nations, amply qualified him for the task. However, his appointment caused some alarm in the Foreign Office IPD, which felt that it might be circumvented if material from Cyprus now transferred from Nicosia to BIS in New York via Fletcher-Cooke, by-passing the IPD *en route*.[52] The department specifically opposed the attachment of an equivalent Officer to the BIS in New York. Partly this opposition stemmed from a sense that the wrong problem was being addressed: Harding wanted a new man to create more channels of publicity, whereas the real problem (as the Foreign Office saw it) was that of speed; the news agencies were in a position to transmit news faster than the cumbersome official relay system.[53] Sir Roger Makins, Britain's Ambassador in Washington, had rather different grounds for objection, fearing that 'the very considerable effort now being put into the explanation of our Cyprus policy is reaching near the limit of how far we can go without running into criticism of waging propaganda'.[54]

Fear of being *seen* to be conducting propaganda hampered the government in replying to critics of the publicity effort. For example, when a Parliamentary Question in January 1957 expressed concern as to whether 'the truth about Cyprus' was being given equal prominence with the 'distorted story being circulated by the Cyprus Federation of America',[55] the British Embassy in Washington advised against giving a complete account of the BIS's activities, as they had 'deliberately avoided propaganda warfare with the Greeks' in America. The true extent of British publicity work was that material had been distributed to an average of three to four thousand American editors, commentators and opinion-formers.[56]

The changes initiated by Harding in June 1956 did not satisfy him for long. A year later he reviewed the publicity set-up once again, with several different objectives in mind. First, it was clear that by mid-1957 the Governor was smarting from constant personal criticism of him in sections of the British press, and this moved him to seek tighter supervision over the press in London. Second, following Makarios's release from the Seychelles in March 1957, Harding was planning to initiate a 'spoiling operation *before* Makarios arrives in London and the Ethnarchy/Noel Baker/Benenson/Foley/*Manchester Guardian* clique gets to work' because it was 'more urgent than ever' to dispel misconceptions about the Ethnarchy's objectives.[57] Harding therefore contemplated 'special arrangements . . . outside the normal run of Government publicity', in what he termed a 'highly political assignment'. Third, the question of Cyprus was due for further airing at the UN in the autumn, and Harding wanted to revamp publicity arrangements in America.

The first concern resulted in the appointment of Derek Chudleigh in July 1957 as the Cyprus government's press officer in London.[58] As for Harding's special assignment, various candidates were considered, with much attendant discussion in the Foreign and Colonial Offices as to the merits and demerits of the proposition.[59] Lennox-Boyd discussed with Dr Charles Hill (the Chancellor of the Duchy of Lancaster, in whom was vested oversight of government publicity in Britain and overseas) the need for a special organization. While concluding that one was not necessary, Lennox-Boyd hastened to reassure Harding that he and Hill would 'not hesitate to adopt any measures however unorthodox which may serve our common purpose'.[60] After further agonized debate, the Colonial Office eventually backed down under the weight of Harding's insistence and agreed to appoint the Governor's preferred candidate, Sir Charles Peake (formerly Britain's Ambassador in Athens and one-time head of the Foreign Office News Department prior to World War II), for the special assignment. His role was explained and justified to the Treasury by Sir John Martin as follows:

> to keep a constant watch on what is published and said about Cyprus and its political problems in this country and to let no opportunity slip for refuting malicious and ill-informed comment, and for explaining the facts and our efforts to deal with them. The arrangement is, of course, quite special and arises from the unique situation in Cyprus.[61]

However, the appointment was certainly not popular with the entire publicity team within the Colonial Office. Peake's arrival as 'special adviser on Cyprus publicity and information matters' threw some of the pre-existing propaganda arrangements into uncertainty. How did Peake's role square with that of Derek Chudleigh? And did Peake's arrival herald both a vigorous offensive against Makarios and a general stepping up of publicity?[62]

Evidence of a divergence of opinion between the Colonial Office and Harding became more pronounced when he tried to insist on the appointment of a further special adviser later in the summer of 1957 – this time to handle publicity in America, his third main concern. Harding's determination to plant his own man in New York to explain Cyprus government policy to Americans and the world's press during the UN debate simultaneously annoyed the Colonial Office, the IPD and the head of the BIS in New York, John Peck (a former IRD head). It was particularly unfortunate that Harding had set his heart on appointing the *Daily Telegraph*'s Douglas Williams to the post, as he (Williams) had scorned the choice of Peck as Director-General of the BIS. Harding's proposal itself was enough to make at least one Foreign Office official 'furiously angry':[63] the fact that the Colonial Office seemed to be caving in (again) occasioned the venomous Foreign Office riposte that it was 'behaving in front of the Governor rather like a small bird being hypnotised by a rattlesnake'.[64] However, Foreign Office and BIS disapproval notwithstanding, Williams did go to New York, though in a rather diminished capacity as compared with that envisaged by Harding.[65] Meanwhile, Harold Evans was briefly seconded from the Colonial Office to the UK Delegation at the UN to see whether it could be given 'a fuller and faster service of information and guidance on colonial affairs so that it could move quickly to counter the flow of misrepresentation'.[66]

On arrival in Cyprus Sir Hugh Foot considered rearranging Cyprus publicity work yet again. The office in Nicosia was then under the control of P.J.F. Storrs, entitled Director of Public Relations, who had replaced Leslie Glass, the former Director-General of Information. In the course of the Emergency, then, Cyprus had already had three different (and variously titled) heads of publicity, and in November 1958 Storrs himself was about to depart. Foot pondered appointing T.J. Lennard, Storrs's deputy, to assume general responsibility for publicity, and replacing Storrs with Chudleigh (the London-based Public Relations Officer).[67] After consultation with the Colonial Office, it was decided that Storrs's post would be abolished on his departure in January 1959, and that John Reddaway (the Administrative Secretary) would have overall charge of information services, with Chudleigh as Chief Press Officer. Although to Whitehall this arrangement still looked 'a bit under-powered' and unlikely to 'withstand strong criticism', there was one consolation: Foot personally was far more press-friendly than his predecessor. As O.H. Morris (head of the COID) commented, Foot took 'great personal interest in the press and a powerful intermediary between him and the press [was] not called for' – the implication being that Harding *had* needed such an intermediary.[68] Furthermore, as events turned out, the new provisions for propaganda did not have to be long-lasting. By early 1959 EOKA terrorism no longer had to be countered through propaganda, and Makarios's acceptance of the scheme for independence meant that any future reorganization of information work had to be geared to the needs of an independent Cyprus.

The Themes of British Propaganda

An outline of the propaganda organization highlights a marked lack of continuity in personnel, particularly in the Nicosia information office, but also indicates the importance attached to getting Cyprus publicity right. The twists and turns of the publicity reorganizations frequently paralleled developments in the terrorist campaign or in the diplomatic battle waged between London, Athens and Ankara. As the struggle for Enosis moved from one phase to another, and alternated between violence and diplomacy, there were (of necessity) frequent fluctuations in the tempo of British propaganda and in the themes used both to project British policy and to denigrate EOKA. It is to the broad themes and objectives of British official propaganda that we now turn.

The search for a Communist connection with EOKA

The attractiveness of presenting Enosis agitation as Communist-inspired had already been apparent to some government officials before EOKA revealed its existence with the bombs and pamphlets of 1 April 1955.[69] After that date attention was devoted to the most fruitful means of debunking EOKA in the eyes of likely sympathizers, and, with that objective in mind, some sections of the Foreign Office regarded a Communist terrorist as a doubly attractive proposition. Given that anti-Communism was its very *raison d'être*, the IRD was understandably the most persistent advocate of this linkage between Communism and terrorism. By 1955 that section had become a 'thorn in the flesh' of the Colonial Office with its insistence on presenting EOKA in this rather distorted light – just as its interventions over Mau Mau had become unwelcome.[70]

Initially the idea that Cypriot Communists might be implicated in terrorism did at least have some grounding in reality. In the early 1950s the Cypriot Communist Party (AKEL) had joined those clamouring for Enosis. But as the campaign progressed, it became increasingly obvious how tenuous was the connection between AKEL and EOKA. If the co-operation of the Orthodox Church and AKEL over the 1954 plebiscite had been an unholy alliance, a lasting relationship between AKEL and Grivas was an even less likely proposition. Grivas's wartime resistance movement, after all, had preferred to eliminate Greek Communists rather than the Nazi occupiers. Indeed, despite the IRD's machinations, Grivas owed a greater ideological debt to Hitler than to Marx, as some contemporary analysts of the Cyprus campaign pointed out. According to Byford-Jones:

> it was not generally realised at the beginning of Operation Enosis how much Colonel Grivas was still under the influence of that outmoded dictator Hitler. Like Hitler, he had actually divided Cyprus into twenty Gaus [sic]. Like Hitler, he had put in charge of each an Obergruppen Fuehrer, with like instructions on how to act when the time came.[71]

Working on American anti-Communist preferences, the IRD twisted the same information about EOKA's organizational structure into proof that the terrorists were organized along Communist cellular lines. As EOKA terrorism mounted and began to assume an anti-Communist as well as an anti-British aspect, playing the Communist card relied increasingly on manipulation of dissonant evidence to fit the preferred theme.

In 1955 the government had attempted to tarnish Makarios by alleging a Communist connection. On 29 September 1955 several British newspapers reported the Colonial Office announcement that it had 'definite evidence' of Communist support for Makarios's attempt to overthrow British rule.[72] Although the claim was apparently based on secret intelligence reports, the Colonial Office case rested more obviously on the interview Makarios granted to three Greek-Cypriot Communist mayors, and the fact that he was backing a general strike (organized by the predominantly Communist trade unions) to coincide with Harding's arrival. The *Daily Mirror* perceptively questioned whether the Colonial Office's Communist 'slur' on Makarios was paving the way for his deportation.[73]

However, in their private appraisals of EOKA neither the Colonial Office nor the Cyprus government were entirely certain about the extent to which Communists were involved in the terrorism. When Lord Vansittart placed a Parliamentary Question before the House of Lords in March 1956, enquiring after the extent to which Communism was responsible for the murder of British subjects in Cyprus, Harding advised the Colonial Office to reply that there was 'no *direct* evidence'. He did, however, try to bolster the notion of a Communist dimension to EOKA by reporting allegations that EOKA weapons had been handed over on an opportunistic basis to persons considered to have Communist sympathies, and by positing a theory that anti-British incitement was fomented by Soviet organizations in Beirut and Prague.[74]

Another troublesome feature of the supposed 'Communist threat' in

Cyprus was that AKEL represented a particularly unthreatening breed of Communist, being far more anti-Orthodox Church than they were pro-Moscow. Privately the Colonial Office admitted that – although Harding had detained 133 AKEL members to keep them 'out of circulation' until he had established a constitutional government[75] – the Cypriot Communists were 'not really lost souls but men who could possibly be converted into moderate left-wingers with no communist affiliations'.[76] A lecture given by John Fletcher-Cooke to the Colonial Office Overseas Services Conference in April 1956 made the point that most Communists in Cyprus were 'not really communists at all': they just voted that way because of the dearth of alternatives.[77] If the Communists were not actually behind the terrorist campaign, only supporting it opportunistically, then other means of playing on popular fears of Communism had to be devised. Fletcher-Cooke's lecture provided some useful pointers for future propaganda. His crowning argument was that international Communism stood to gain most from the Cyprus dispute (by destabilizing NATO), and thus represented the reason why Enosis could not be granted in the foreseeable future.[78] Turkey was only forty miles from Cyprus and also had a common frontier with the Soviet Union. If Cyprus were united with Greece, and the latter at some future date turned Communist (as had been a very real possibility in the past), then Turkey would face Communist encirclement. As Fletcher-Cooke dramatically put it, 'Cyprus might become a loaded revolver pointing at her very heart'[79] – a concern which led to the 'inescapable' conclusion that 'British withdrawal from Cyprus in favour of Greece would lead to chaos and bloodshed in Cyprus and the break up of the NATO defence line in the Middle East', from which only the Communists would derive benefit. This reworking of the 'Communist threat' theme became a standard line in British propaganda, with Fletcher-Cooke's lecture forming the basis for a Foreign Office briefing note for Commonwealth MPs, and serving as a source of reference for questions on Communism in Cyprus.[80]

Raising the Communist spectre in Cyprus, then, was somewhat problematic. As Glass remarked in June 1956, Communism in Cyprus was 'not a good subject from our point of view at present. EOKA are violently anti-Communist and the Communists are lying pretty low.'[81] Indeed, as the Foreign Office Southern Department's J.E. Galsworthy minuted, 'although it would greatly help our cause in America if we could show that the Communists were mixed up with terrorism, the fact is that at present EOKA and AKEL are in a state of feud, and the latter have recently come out *against* terrorism'.[82] Some attempts were, nevertheless, made to link EOKA or Makarios with Communism: a BIS pamphlet of August 1957, attempting to discredit Makarios before his impending visit to America, stated that he had 'not scrupled to act in concert with the Soviet authorities' and listed several contacts with

Eastern-bloc diplomats.[83] However, the anti-Communism of the terrorists themselves became increasingly apparent. By 1958 it was clear
that EOKA was routinely targeting Communists and killing them in a
manner which belied Grivas's claim that no 'unnecessary cruelty' was
used in his campaign.[84] While this certainly did not entirely end British
attempts to fuse Communism with terrorism in the popular imagination,
such efforts certainly assumed less prominence in official propaganda,
with other themes and concerns coming to the fore.

Revealingly, British government propagandists had not been alone
in the attempt to work on popular anti-Communism. All sides to the
dispute attempted such a tactic at some stage in the campaign. The
Greek government made discreet attempts to manipulate American
anti-Communism at the élite level. The Colonial Office periodically
learnt of such initiatives when American diplomats sought guidance
on how to interpret the intelligence fed to them by the Greeks. On one
occasion (at the time when a safe conduct for Grivas and key EOKA
members was being considered by Harding) the American Ambassador
in Athens learnt via the Greek diplomatic service that if Grivas were to
'disappear' (i.e. be killed by the British security forces), then EOKA would
fall under Communist control. Athens was clearly hoping to encourage
Washington to put pressure on Britain to cease military operations
during the safe-conduct period.[85] Harding's response on hearing of
the Greek manoeuvre through the Colonial Office reveals how far
the *British* attempts to play on anti-Communism relied on fabrication:
as he remarked of the Greek gambit, it was 'of course purely Greek sales
talk for American consumption. There is not the slightest chance that a
movement like EOKA, born and bred by the Church, would fall under
Communist domination.'[86]

In a rather different manner, Makarios and Grivas both intermittently
played the Communist card. Grivas tried to excite criticism of Britain's
counter-insurgency strategy by showing that it relied on co-opting
Cypriot Communists as an anti-EOKA force. In EOKA propaganda at
the time, and in his subsequent memoirs, he charged that the Cyprus
government had deliberately bungled the arrest of AKEL members,
imprisoning only sufficient to create Communist 'martyrs' to revivify
the Communist movement.[87] Arguably, in the latter stages of the Emergency the British had brought the charge of a 'sell-out' to Communism
on themselves by encouraging the disgruntled Cypriot Left in such
activities as the breaking of an EOKA boycott of British goods. However,
the Cyprus government's strategy actually aimed at remodelling AKEL
and the Communist trade unions into models of soft-left respectability,
effectively de-Communizing them – the antithesis to enlisting Communist support. In a rather different guise, the spectre of Communism in
Cyprus was also periodically raised by Makarios, who was fond of telling
international (especially American) audiences that the British denial of

self-determination to the Cypriots perpetuated a state of oppression in which Communism might flourish.[88]

British government efforts to link Communism and terrorism were eagerly echoed by the right-wing popular press in Britain. The *Daily Express* tried to tarnish certain Communist-dominated trade unions in Britain by revealing support they had given to Communists in Cyprus. Indeed, that paper launched something of a crusade against the Electrical Trades Union in May and June 1956 after its gift of £20 to the Cyprus Emergency Fund became public. Although this rather inconsequential sum had actually been sent to help pay for the legal defence of Communists detained in Harding's round-up, the *Daily Express* represented the money as a 'terror gift' and a 'stab in the back' to the British boys fighting in Cyprus.[89] By a timely coincidence for the *Express*, an electrical apprentice who had just been shot by EOKA while doing his National Service in Cyprus was able to add his own personal feelings of betrayal by his former trade union to those of the paper.[90] This lent credibility to the *Express*'s line that money given to the Cypriot Communists actually fuelled EOKA terrorism. Precisely why this should be so was not explained, suggesting that to convince a (favourably disposed) audience of the correlation between terrorism and Communism one only had to imply – rather than prove – that it existed. To ascertain whether its readership agreed that the 'wicked £20' was 'dirty money' to promote terrorism rather than a honourable gift, the *Express* launched a readers' poll. If the figures of the ballot are to be believed, then the paper had certainly succeeded in persuading an overwhelming majority – no less than 98 per cent – of its respondents that aiding Cypriot Communists was tantamount to promoting terrorism.[91] This fortnight-long campaign by the *Express* had dual functions: to smear a Communist-led British trade union, and to mobilize popular opinion in favour of a harder governmental line on Cyprus. The readers' poll apparently revealed that four out of ten Britons were dissatisfied with government handling of Cyprus because it was insufficiently tough – a statistic which the *Express* clearly hoped the government would heed.

Exposing the complicity of the Greek government

British official propaganda which aimed at discrediting EOKA terrorism sought to expose several more or less hidden hands behind Grivas's violent pro-Enosis activities. The possible aid given by the Eastern-bloc countries to the terrorist movement (and the certain profit they extracted from the whole Cyprus mess) was thus only one international aspect of the Cyprus problem played on by government propaganda. Highlighting the support accorded EOKA by successive Greek administrations was in many respects a much easier task than the complex process of

213

demonstrating how Communists gained from the Cyprus crisis. After all, there was more substance to build on – Greek involvement was scarcely secret – even if it was a less obviously profitable theme. To British propagandists proof of Greek government complicity in terrorism would at least help to undermine its respectability at the UN, where Greece tended to assume the moral high ground by dressing up Enosis as a self-determination issue. The British aim in this case was probably more a matter of tarnishing the diplomatically energetic Greeks by their connection with terrorism than of damaging the terrorists. Conceivably though, evidence of Greek government aid to EOKA might also call into question the extent to which the terrorist organization represented a genuinely popular movement, making Grivas appear simply the pawn of those more powerful than himself.

British denunciations of the Greek government's misdeeds were always presented as defensive actions: answering fire in a propaganda war launched by the Greeks. Indeed, the most tangible Greek backing for EOKA was in the form of propaganda. Thus the Greek government did nothing to prevent Athens Radio from becoming a conduit for EOKA broadcasts, and also supplied for international distribution a mass of propaganda pamphlets (translated into numerous languages) attacking the British position on Cyprus.[92] The pamphlets tended to rely on striking visual images and accompanying text which revealed the ferocity of the British regime in Cyprus and viciousness of the methods used against (in particular) Greek-Cypriot schoolchildren who were campaigning for the right to self-determination.[93] The Greek government's efforts thus formed part of the smear campaign which was simultaneously undertaken by EOKA. Such propaganda therefore had to be countered along the general lines established to counter EOKA allegations against the British as a whole (which will be examined below). Broadly speaking, British counter-propaganda consisted of indicting terrorism where possible, rather than answering in detail the specifics of every accusation of brutality. As the head of the IPD, C.C.B. Stewart, advised:

We do not wish to follow the Greeks along the line of emotional vituperation by spreading counter-atrocity stories; not only are we likely to be much less successful than they are, but in the long run there is probably more to be gained by sticking to a rational presentation of our policy. I do not mean that we should pull our punches about acts of terrorism committed in Cyprus: but our material about these incidents should not be turned into an operation to refute Greek allegations, rather should it be keyed independently to an indictment of terrorism as such.[94]

To this end a pamphlet was produced in the summer of 1956, *Greek Irredentism and Cypriot Terrorism*, which set out the extent of Greek government culpability. A memo on similar lines was also produced the following year, to be sent to British posts overseas when the UN debate on Cyprus began, entitled *Greece and Cyprus: The Policy behind Terrorism*.[95] The British government thus hoped to ensure that Athens was universally associated with EOKA terrorism. In part this end was served by the publication of Greek-Cypriot documents which had fallen into British hands, namely the Grivas diaries and Ethnarchy papers seized after Makarios's deportation. Although, as will be seen, the publication of these documents (after much internal wrangling as to the legal niceties of publishing captured private papers) was principally aimed at discrediting Makarios, they also assisted the effort to establish high-level Greek complicity in terrorism.[96]

However, one sore point emphasized in Greek propaganda remained particularly difficult to counter: dissident opinion in Britain. Such criticism gave Greek propaganda a valuable handle, one of the glossiest Greek government publications being a 160-page book, *British Opinion on Cyprus*, which reproduced various critical articles and cartoons from the British press. As a wry IPD official commented, this was a 'very much abler piece of propaganda than usual largely of course because it is principally written by leading British journalists'.[97] Far from a bipartisan approach being adopted in Parliament over the conduct of the counter-terrorist campaign, Cyprus remained one of the most hotly contested issues between Labour and the Conservative government until the latter part of 1958 – Labour criticism of Tory foreign policy being stoked by the Suez fiasco. Domestic criticism of the government tended to be interpreted in Whitehall as ignorance which could be countered by educational publicity. Regrettably, this 'ignorance' in Britain had a disabling effect on British Information Service propaganda in America, with Peck advising his Foreign Office colleagues that 'our efforts . . . are being largely undermined by what appears from here to be the purely adolescent attitude of HM's Opposition to this question of self-determination'. Consequently, he pleaded for a special effort 'to get some rational and realistic views propagated in England on this specific issue'.[98] With the Foreign Office concurring that 'the attitude of the opposition constitutes the greatest weakness in the presentation of our Cyprus policy in the USA and abroad generally', considerable Colonial and Foreign Office attention was devoted to influencing left-wing opinion at home on Cyprus.[99] To this end, stress was laid on the duplicity of Greek calls for Cypriot self-determination, which masked the Greeks' selfish desire to annex Cyprus, and on the fact that self-determination for Cyprus would inevitably entail a denial of rights to the Turkish minority, who were fundamentally opposed to Enosis.

Perhaps the most vexatious aspect of Greek propaganda was Athens Radio, a source of irritation to the British government from as early as 1954. That a supposedly friendly government would allow, or even urge, a radio station on its soil to broadcast vitriolic incitements to violence against an ally provoked considerable outrage. After its failure to respond to repeated British requests to moderate the tenor of the broadcasts, the Greek government's treachery became a key component of British propaganda against Greece. Through personal contacts with BIS personnel, American opinion-formers were presented with choice extracts from Athens Radio broadcasts. A pamphlet entitled *Mischief in the Air* was also produced, and updated at intervals, presenting transcripts from the most offensive broadcasts.[100] The aim was to demonstrate that Athens Radio had actually *incited* terrorism – an objective made all the more necessary in the light of a decision (taken by the Cabinet in January 1956) to allow Harding to jam Athens Radio broadcasts if he saw fit.

This was a rare step. Indeed, many hostile commentators represented it as unprecedented (forgetting that the Mandatory Authorities in Palestine had been given similar powers to counter the Zionist insurgents' radio propaganda) stressing that Nazi broadcasts during World War II had not been jammed.[101] Given the unorthodox nature of the move, the jamming of Athens Radio needed the accompaniment of more than usually persuasive propaganda. Lennox-Boyd had sold the measure to his Cabinet colleagues on the grounds that the government had the right to 'take any counter-measures necessary to preserve British and Cypriot lives from outrages directly provoked by these broadcasts'.[102] Likewise, in public he stressed that Athens Radio broadcasts had gone beyond propaganda and constituted incitements to murder – almost tantamount to operational instructions to the terrorist organization.[103]

In the United States, where there had been considerable worry that the measure would be badly received, Peck worked on the theme that the broadcasts were equivalent to obscene publications ('horror comics' as he put it) that would be banned in the United States, drawing attention to the limitations placed on freedom of speech even in libertarian America. This strategy was apparently successful.[104] However, at home there was considerable dissent over the jamming of Athens Radio. Although the *Daily Express* welcomed it as a sign that the kid gloves were coming off to deal with what René MacColl termed the 'Communist-tainted, anti-British crew in charge of Radio Athens',[105] two influential weeklies, the *Spectator* and the *New Statesman and Nation*, were highly sceptical of the efficacy and the moral validity of the policy. In a front-page leader the latter regretted that Eden's government had 'abandoned the fundamental rule that criticism, even when abusive, is better answered than suppressed'. This would surely damage Britain's case in Cyprus:

> To try to stop the Greeks from presenting their case must suggest to the outside world that our own is hopelessly weak. The Greeks can rightly retort that they do not jam our broadcasts. They can also point out that despite the animosities of recent months Athens radio continues to relay a daily news bulletin broadcast by the BBC.

By making a British monopoly of the Cyprus air we are suggesting that the Greeks have a monopoly of the arguments.[106]

This particular attempt to deal with Greek propaganda was therefore doubly unsuccessful: the broadcasts continued, despite attempts at jamming, and indeed played their own part in the campaign to discredit the British in Cyprus through atrocity allegations. A series of broadcasts in the summer of 1957 entitled 'Vandals and Sacrilegers' (whose title was its sole source of amusement to the Cyprus government) detailed places where atrocities had allegedly taken place and names of 'participants'.[107] Moreover, the decision to jam Athens Radio helped to harden opinion (in some quarters) against the government's prosecution of the counter-terrorist campaign. The louder this dissent, the harder the task of British propagandists became.

The presentation of Makarios: archbishop as arch-terrorist

'Funny life, isn't it? Wonder what they'd say at home if the Vicar buzzed a brick at the village policeman after Sunday service.'[108]

The first months of the Emergency saw a remarkable transformation of the way in which the Ethnarch of Cyprus was presented to the British public. In October 1954, the *Observer* had drawn a sympathetic portrait of the politicized ecclesiastic:

He is a character as warming as he is striking. His dark dignity and garb make him seem much taller than he is. His beard is flecked with grey, his features are most handsome, his eyes gentle, slightly hooded but good-humoured. Though in conversation he shows a thorough grasp of politics, it is with the underlying spiritual matters that he seems concerned.[109]

By the time that Makarios was deported to the Seychelles in March 1956, however, most of the British press presented a very different picture. Under the headline 'I have hated this man for a long time', the *Daily Express*'s William Hickey wrote:

Beneath the smile, the soft voice, the black robes, the chain round his neck is arrogance. . . . Under the priest's robes is a deceitful, Machiavellian man who has not scrupled to tell lies. . . . He is an enemy of all men.[110]

Makarios's apparently benign features had in fact been a 'fawning mask', as one contemporary commentator put it, and from early 1956 until well after his release, Makarios was cast as the Rasputin of the Cyprus melodrama.[111] His easily caricatured features – indeed, his very visibility in contrast to the invisibility of the terrorists he was said to command – ensured that he became the principal butt of British wrath against the Cypriot terrorists.

The transformation of Makarios from archbishop to arch-terrorist was consciously encouraged by government propagandists. Indeed, mediating Makarios's public image was one of the main concerns of the British publicity organizations in Nicosia, London and New York. Why should this have been so? Clearly the belief that Makarios had played a central role in instigating terrorist violence in Cyprus underlay the determination to vilify him. He needed to be shown in his true colours. However, determining the extent, as opposed to the simple fact, of Makarios's involvement in the origination and direction of EOKA was more exacting. Despite the difficulties with evidence, plausibly demonstrating Makarios's complicity with terrorism became a necessity. The justification for the Archbishop's deportation in March 1956 – that he had acted in bad faith, persistently thwarting Harding's attempts at a negotiated settlement of the self-determination issue during their five months of talks – was not widely seen as sufficient grounds for exiling him. Eden's government had to produce more compelling reasons for its action: thus the concern to present Makarios as the terrorist-in-chief.

In the opening months of the EOKA campaign little was certain about Makarios's involvement with the terrorists. Even after six months of violence on the island, Cyprus intelligence reports reveal a woeful lack of information as to the Archbishop's role. It was known that Makarios had given financial support to Grivas, but unclear whether he had personally solicited Grivas's intervention in the Enosis movement.[112] He was certainly under suspicion. As Ethnarch, he was automatically the political leader of the Greek Cypriots and thus the main champion of Enosis – the cause for which the terrorists were fighting. Furthermore, his ambivalent pronouncements on EOKA violence heightened rumours of his personal involvement with terrorism. Makarios's refusal to denounce terrorism, both in 1955 and repeatedly thereafter, became one of the main sticks with which to beat him.[113] In fact Makarios had been instrumental in inviting Grivas to survey the opportunities Cyprus offered for waging a more militant (though not necessarily terrorist) pro-Enosis campaign.[114] In 1951 Makarios had founded a youth movement, PEON, aimed at inculcating pride in Greek identity and sharpening the desire for Enosis. Grivas had been invited, quite openly, to Cyprus on two occasions before April 1955 to offer Makarios advice on PEON's organization, and in due course this youth movement would become the 'seed-bed' for Grivas's terrorist set-up. But whether Makarios had actually ordered the switch from agitation to terrorism was a different matter. Grivas subsequently claimed not.[115]

At the time of Makarios's deportation in March 1956, intelligence on EOKA, and the Archbishop's role therein, was still poor. The Cyprus government, however, had a tradition of deporting troublesome clerics, having dealt with the 1931 disturbances in this fashion.[116] Moreover, Harding had been bitterly frustrated by the breakdown of his talks, in which he had sought a settlement allowing for self-determination sometime, rather than never (albeit after a period of self-government), in return for a denunciation of terrorism by Makarios. The latter was a non-negotiable prerequisite to constitutional progress as far as Harding was concerned.[117] But the Archbishop had his price. Harding would have to offer a complete amnesty for EOKA fighters and agree to transfer control of the police into Cypriot hands before independence. These shiftings of the goalposts, and the Archbishop's refusal to condemn terrorism, convinced Harding of Makarios's insincerity and led him to believe that, as his biographer Lord Carver later wrote, 'so long as [Makarios] was in Cyprus, whether free or restricted in some way, terrorism could not be effectively dealt with nor any real progress be made'.[118] Although Carver also wrote of the 'gradual accumulation of evidence of his complicity with, support of and even possibly direction of the EOKA terrorist campaign',[119] no tangible confirmation of Makarios's *leading* role seemed to exist at the time. 'Proof' consisted largely of the Archbishop's refusal to indict EOKA, the funeral oration he had given for his cousin (an EOKA member killed by the British security forces during an ambush) and some details of Makarios's aid given to the arms-running during the *Ayios Georgios* affair. The circumstantial nature of this evidence was a problem for British propaganda.

The ground was prepared for Makarios's deportation with the publication of a White Paper reproducing the correspondence between the Governor and the Archbishop during the period of their talks, as a means of highlighting the latter's inflexibility.[120] A statement along the same lines was made by Lennox-Boyd in the House of Commons on 5 March. As the *Daily Herald* astutely remarked the following day: 'The definition of "terrorist" is going to be extended. It is significant that Mr. Lennox-Boyd said in the House yesterday that Archbishop Makarios is now "using the weapon of violence in order to secure agreement on his own lines"'.[121] This was taken as a sign of Makarios's impending deportation, and sure enough he was flown to the Seychelles on 9 March.

After the event, Eden repeated the claims that the government had mounting proof of Makarios's complicity in EOKA terrorism, and that he had used EOKA's acts to strengthen his own bargaining position.[122] But no evidence was actually published until late August 1956. Indeed, the incriminatory extracts from Grivas's diary were not even captured until two security force operations in June and August. For the government this was a dangerously long time-lag, as it was far from unanimously accepted (even in Britain) that its action in exiling Makarios had been justified. Dissent within certain sections of the press – evident when the decision to allow Harding to jam Athens Radio was taken – was now more pronounced. (Significantly, new censorship measures within Cyprus came into effect simultaneously with the deportation of Makarios, which did nothing to endear the Cyprus government to the more hostile elements of the press.) The *Spectator*, for one, thought it unimportant, and unsurprising, that Makarios should have connections of some sort with EOKA: 'what nationalist leader does not have ties with the terrorist elements of his own party?'[123] If deportation was meant to clear the way for more moderate leaders to make their presence known, argued the *Spectator*, then this was nonsensical, given that the only possible contenders were the Turks and the Communists, and that Britain's moral position in Cyprus rested on 'the defence of our oil reserves from Communists'. In short, Makarios's deportation 'gave him all the advantages of martyrdom without the salient disadvantage of being dead'.[124]

For British propagandists it was doubtless a salient disadvantage that Makarios was alive, as they had to find ways of proving his terrorist connection, thus justifying the punitive action. One promising source of material with which to nail Makarios was the documentation seized from the archiepiscopal palace after the deportation. The Head of the IPD counselled that 'if any really compromising material was found there or elsewhere, I would recommend exploitation of it'.[125] But this proved easier said than done. Triangular discussions between the Colonial Office, Foreign Office and the Cyprus government were protracted and inconclusive, revealing wide disagreement over the legality of publishing such documents, and over their suitability for the objective in mind. Harding's desire to publish – and have Makarios damned – was thwarted by his more cautious advisers, who rejected his proposals for a Command Paper containing the documents.[126]

Harding was particularly excited by one captured letter (from the Ethnarchy Secretary to the Greek Prime Minister) which, he claimed, 'establishes beyond dispute the attitude of the Archbishop and Ethnarchy in general towards the terrorist organisation, EOKA' – largely, it seems, because EOKA was referred to as 'the national resistance movement in the island'.[127] But to others this, and other, seized material did not constitute irrefutable proof. Charles Carstairs was an influential sceptic in the Colonial Office, arguing that the allusions to terrorism did not support the inferences drawn from them: consequently, 'nothing much can be built on the oblique references to terrorism'. Furthermore,

> The more serious students of the documents as a whole, such as the *Economist* and the *Spectator*, while perhaps noting the unspiritual tone of so largely ecclesiastical a body, might well take the line that while the [Ethnarchy] Council would not get high marks for candour, there is nothing very horrifying in their pursuing a course

which they hold dear, in the face of the might of Britain, and by whatever diplomatic and negotiating means lay to their hands.[128]

Carstairs's advice that the Ethnarchy documents should not be published was reinforced by legal guidance that publication would breach copyright law, as the material had been taken without the authors' consent. However, in June 1956 new material fell into British hands which altered thinking on how best to debunk Makarios: the Grivas diaries. Substantial portions of the EOKA leader's private diary were discovered by British troops after a narrow brush with Dighenis. Then on 20 August further documents were captured during counter-terrorist operations in Famagusta.[129] These diaries were subsequently seen as the best means of incriminating Makarios – the Ethnarchy documents being held in reserve for possible future use.[130]

The Grivas diaries became one of the mainstays of British propaganda on Cyprus. Grivas's references to 'Genikos', 'The General' or 'G' revealed that Makarios (to whom these pseudonyms referred) had been forewarned about several terrorist attacks, which was construed as testimony to Makarios's leading role in EOKA. Here was the proof of Makarios's complicity that had been lacking in March. But publication of extracts from the Grivas diaries also served broader purposes, including the defamation of Grivas himself. Galsworthy of the Southern Department sketched in the Foreign Office's preferred picture of the terrorist leader which could be drawn from the diaries: 'a most unpleasant individual with a marked tendency towards megalomania and a strong streak of sadism mixed up with twisted religious sentiments. This is the portrait which we wish to project.'[131] To this end, the diaries required a certain amount of editing lest Grivas come across like 'a heroic maquisard from the last war'. As Galsworthy remarked, it was essential 'to publish nothing which might contribute to the myth which Greek propaganda is assiduously trying to build up that Grivas is a heroic and single-minded leader of a noble resistance movement'.[132]

Less than a week after the August capture of the diaries, a Colonial Office statement on them (together with highly selective extracts) was published, producing a flurry of banner headlines in the following day's papers. Of these the most striking was the *Daily Express*'s 'ARCH-TERRORIST MAKARIOS/Hate Diary Brands Him'.[133] The right-wing popular press accepted uncritically Lennox-Boyd's enjoinder that the diary 'proved beyond doubt that Archbishop Makarios was the leader of the terrorist campaign', and that he was 'actually involved in the choice of victims for murder'. At a press conference Lennox-Boyd stated that there could no longer be grounds to criticize the deportation of Makarios:

'Much of the criticism to which I and my colleagues have been subjected about our treatment and deportation of the archbishop was based on the argument that he was a moderate and we were losing a chance of getting moderate support.

That argument has been blown absolutely sky-high by these papers which show him to be the personal director of the whole tragic business.'[134]

If he seriously expected criticism to dry up after the publication of the diary extracts then he must have been sorely disappointed by the persistent hostility of those elements of the press already sceptical over government policy. The most intransigent opponents of the government went so far as to suggest that the diaries were in fact forgeries – nothing but a propaganda ploy along the lines of the notorious Casement diaries. This was certainly the line adopted by the Greek government, and it found favour among the Conservatives' implacable enemies such as the *Daily Worker*. In anticipation of such scepticism, the government took pains to refute the forgery accusation, even issuing photographs of the notebooks in which Grivas had written his diary. After the publication of a major propaganda booklet based on the diaries and entitled *Terrorism in Cyprus*, in September 1956, Kenneth Neale (of the Colonial Office's Mediterranean Department) appeared on the BBC's *Panorama* with further visual confirmation of the diaries' authenticity. David Dimbleby was shown Grivas's beret and cardigan, Sam Browne belt and glasses, which had been found with the diaries.[135] Neale also explained to Dimbleby that the handwriting of the diaries was identical to that on a visa application form filled in by Grivas some years earlier: a fact that had been attested by the Director of the Home Office Forensic Science laboratory.

The charge that the diaries were forged was easier to meet than other criticisms of the government's propaganda strategy. Several influential British dailies and weeklies, while accepting the validity of the diaries, nevertheless questioned the policy underlying their bowdlerized release to the public. The critics' mood of frustration with Eden's government was summed up in the *Manchester Guardian*'s memorable 'Blimp in Cyprus' cartoon, in which Low's hero exclaimed, 'Gad sir, we can't negotiate with that fellow Makarios. . . . He's on the other side!'[136] Sharing the *Guardian*'s scepticism, the *Observer* found the Conservatives' new moralism – particularly the 'sudden squeamishness about negotiating with people with blood on their hands' – 'thoroughly unconvincing'. The editor of the *Observer* also made the point that the extracts did *not* show that Makarios had retained, if indeed he ever possessed, complete control over EOKA, in which case a verbal denunciation of terrorism by the Archbishop would have very little practical effect.[137] Not everyone, then, was convinced either that Makarios was the terrorist-in-chief or that it was productive for the government to set its face so unequivocally against dealing with terrorists: history suggested that this was only to court the humiliation of a subsequent climb-down. Indeed, the *New Statesman* reminded readers of 'the lesson we ought to have learnt from Michael Collins 40 years ago', warning that '"Makarios the terrorist" may prove an even more effective plenipotentiary than "Makarios the ecclesiastical politician"'.[138]

Nevertheless, the booklet which brought lengthy extracts from the Grivas diary to a wide domestic and international audience, *Terrorism in Cyprus*, was the official publication which the Colonial Office and Cyprus government thought most likely to disenchant public opinion with Makarios and Grivas. Great attention was paid to its design and production as this booklet was to be put on sale in Britain at a price that would attract a wide readership: it was 'to look interesting without suggesting that it is a glossy piece of propaganda', with a cover which was 'striking without being garish'.[139] Again, discretion was the watchword of government propaganda.

Entirely related to the goal of exposing Archbishop Makarios's role in terrorism was a further concern of official propaganda: to highlight the involvement of the Greek Orthodox Church in EOKA activity. This would further discredit Makarios and the Ethnarchy Council by showing that the Archbishop had not only instigated terrorism but had also corrupted his Church and its congregation in so doing. Stress on the Church's connivance at terrorism would also help to legitimize the security forces' searches of Church property, detention of priests, and exile of Makarios and two other bishops to the Seychelles – all of which EOKA and Greek propaganda presented as acts of sacrilegious barbarity. The other side to the coin had to be shown, and American audiences, according to Peck, were particularly hungry for stories of 'spiritual intimidation' in Cyprus.[140] In Nicosia there was considerable eagerness to retaliate against an organization which was perceived as having done so much to embitter Greek Cypriots against the British administration in Cyprus. Furthermore, the Orthodox Church's part in the terrorist campaign was one which many Cyprus government officials thought could virtually be relied upon to summon up the righteous indignation of white Anglo-Saxon Protestants, convinced of their own cultural superiority.

It is impossible to tell how far the widespread denunciations in Britain of the Orthodox Church's role in terrorism were due to the government's efforts. This theme had captured the British imagination some time before the Cyprus government brought out its widely distributed pamphlet *The Church and Terrorism in Cyprus*. A Greek Orthodox priest had even been deported from London in June 1956, charged with collecting money for the terrorist organization – an act which outraged the Bevanite Left, but gratified the Tory popular press.[141] However, not only did the tabloid press hark generally on the instigatory role of the Church – the fiery sermons, the slogans daubed on church walls, the corruption of youth

223

– but so too did the clutch of novels based on, and contemporaneous with, the Cyprus Emergency. For example, we find a didactic speech in Appleby's *The Bad Summer* denouncing the role of the Church in tones redolent of Cyprus government propaganda:

'In some ways Cyprus is seven hundred years behind Europe. In the Middle Ages it was perfectly all right for a Christian Bishop to take a leading part in politics, to go into battle wearing armour and swinging a mace. That was part of his job. In the west we've now moved beyond that kind of thinking – but not here. Every priest is an active patriot – or what he calls a patriot – and he will do everything he can for the national cause or what he calls the national cause. In England, when people read about monasteries being searched they think we are being barbarous and sacrilegious. But they should take notice of the bombs and guns we find. Some of them are even hidden in graves.'[142]

The Cyprus government's desire to vindicate its actions against the Orthodox Church was evident from the tone and substance of its pamphlet *The Church and Terrorism in Cyprus*, which appeared in February 1957. Again heavy use was made of the Grivas diaries to demonstrate the Ethnarchy's knowledge of and assistance to EOKA. Further 'proof' also consisted of extracts from Makarios's sermons and references to the captured (and still unpublished) Ethnarchy documents. The pamphlet contended that the Ethnarchy Council minutes revealed 'a tacit recognition of the part which terrorism played in strengthening the Archbishop's negotiating position'. In other words, Harding's interpretation of the documents, which had been questioned by colleagues, was presented as fact.[143] Peck's request for material on 'spiritual intimidation' was amply met in a section dramatically entitled 'The Prostitution of Religion':

The church leaders sought to dragoon their flocks into unquestioning accord with their political adventure by a second process, more subtle than intimidation, more insidious, and with effects more difficult to eradicate. . . . By devoting sermons to politics rather than true religion a confusion is purposely brought about in the pious mind, a confusion between Christianity and Hellenism.[144]

The zealousness of the pamphlet's tone caused some alarm in Whitehall. Cox, of the Foreign Office IPD, thought that 'attacks on Churches, however corrupt, seldom pay publicity dividends', and that it might have been preferable to concentrate on attacking Makarios personally rather than the Church *per se*.[145] The validity of Cox's assertion perhaps depends on the audience in mind. While there did seem to be considerable outrage about the role of the Church among British observers and public opinion, knowledge of the Orthodox Church's involvement in politics was hardly likely to incense Greeks or Greek Cypriots. The latter were, after all, accustomed to the concept of a politicized church, and might have resented British propaganda which impugned a different tradition in the conduct of religious affairs. Yet, as far as Harding was concerned, it was precisely this audience to whom the message should be addressed.[146] More broadly, however, the pamphlet illustrated the Nicosia information team's over-eager approach to propaganda. This was manifest in the jacket chosen for the pamphlet – with a picture of Makarios beside a photograph of a corpse on the front and the text of the Ten Commandments on the back – causing Cox to remark ruefully that 'Nicosia have, before now, displayed a more marked predilection for pictures of corpses than is good for successful propaganda.'[147]

While Nicosia's information office was enthusiastically exposing the Orthodox Church, policy-makers in London and Cyprus debated their next moves. Terrorism had intensified in the spring and summer following the deportations, but by early 1957 pressure was mounting on the government to reassess its attitude towards Makarios. The new Radcliffe constitutional proposals (entailing greater Cypriot involvement in its government) were sent to Makarios in December 1956.[148] By January, the security situation was improving, and the Cabinet was pondering the offer of NATO mediation made by its Secretary-General, Lord Ismay. Clearly, Makarios could not remain in the Seychelles permanently, and the widespread criticism of his deportation had scarcely lessened with the subsequent failure of any new 'moderate' leaders to emerge in Cyprus. Influential voices beyond the Opposition called for his release. The Archbishop of Canterbury repeatedly advocated such a move, even though Makarios had still not indicted terrorism; there was nothing to be gained by anybody 'trying to extort from Makarios the renunciation of violence when whatever the lips say (to quote Euripides) there is no kind of guarantee that the heart has consented thereto'.[149] With EOKA's offer of a truce on 14 March 1957 – on the condition that Makarios was released and included in negotiations – Macmillan's government decided to send a note to Makarios asking him to denounce terrorism in return for his freedom. Even though the Archbishop's response was a less than wholehearted rejection of violence, the Cabinet (amid rumoured acrimony between Harding and Lennox-Boyd) decided that the Archbishop must be freed.[150]

The decision was far from unanimous. Lord Salisbury resigned from the Cabinet in disgust at the freeing of Makarios, even though the latter was still debarred from entering Cyprus. Predictably, the release also brought howls of protest from those sections of the British press which had greeted his deportation with such relish. Under the headline, 'Terror Goes Free', the *Daily Express* editorial tried to whip up popular dissatisfaction with the government's move:

With the blood of 112 Britons and 131 Cypriots on his hands, Archbishop Makarios goes free. A word from him could have saved all those lives. But even now he cannot bring himself to make an unconditional disavowal of violence. . . . It is difficult to see what Mr. Lennox-Boyd hopes to achieve by releasing this mischief-maker.[151]

Apparently this mood found favour with the public. A Gallup poll in April 1957 revealed that while 33 per cent of those polled agreed with the decision to release Makarios, 34 per cent disapproved.[152]

This perhaps suggests that the government needed to start remodelling its projected image of Makarios. However, amid an atmosphere of popular fervour – *against* Makarios in Britain and *for* him in Cyprus – Harding started planning his special propaganda operations against Makarios.[153] Only days after Makarios's release, the Governor wrote to the Colonial Secretary asking that, in anticipation of 'a very ticklish and a very trying period in the next few months', he consider a 'spoiling operation *before* Makarios arrives in London'.[154] The aim was to bring home 'to Parliament and public opinion the insincerity of his whole approach last year to the offer of self-government'.[155] Harding hoped to accomplish this by appointing an influential 'agent' with high-level contacts in both the press and political circles, and through more widespread publication in Britain of *The Church and Terrorism in Cyprus*, while also making covert use of the much-discussed Ethnarchy documents.[156]

However, there was considerable doubt in the Colonial Office Information Department as to the viability of Harding's proposal. Certainly the latter saw a need to take some of the party political heat away from the Cyprus issue, so that government publicity and statements on the Emergency would be listened to objectively and not 'attacked as a matter of normal Party warfare'.[157] But whether this could be achieved through the good offices of a special appointee was doubtful. There was more favour for invoking the *laissez-faire* spirit of Voltaire's prayer, 'Oh Lord, let my enemies make themselves ridiculous.' Pondering Makarios's fevered appearances since his release, Carstairs was moved to suggest that

The general public do not know a great deal about Cyprus, but they recognise Makarios as an obviously slippery customer. It would almost pay us to put him on TV – black beard, shifty glances, prevaricating replies and all. Nevertheless the public are, I think, to some extent still confused by a feeling of uncertainty about what it really is that HMG is trying to do.[158]

And here was the nub of the problem: what was Harding's policy? While crushing terrorism was still his first priority, a political settlement would clearly be necessary at some stage. Harding's refusal to countenance negotiating with Makarios (unless he denounced terrorism, which seemed unlikely given the failure of all previous efforts to prod him in this direction) found ever fewer supporters in the Colonial Office. Why had Makarios been released if not to re-incorporate him into the political process? Carstairs, and others in Whitehall, recognized this, and consequently saw the dangers in continuing to emphasize the slipperiness of Makarios in the absence of any real policy. In the short term, Harding won at least part of the battle, managing to secure the appointment of Sir Charles Peake as his special high-level press contact in London – though even Peake recognized that 'if we do have to do business with Makarios, we shall not have improved our prospects by an organised campaign to blacken his face'.[159]

Thus throughout 1957 and into 1958, official policy was still to present Makarios in a hostile light. The Colonial and Foreign Offices kept a close watch on his appearances on television abroad (particularly in America), looking for signs that Makarios was indeed making himself ridiculous.[160] The panic-stricken response to a rumoured visit to Britain by Makarios in 1958 is perhaps the clearest illustration of popular and governmental touchiness over the Archbishop, the stir being sparked by the Archbishop of Canterbury's invitation to Makarios to attend the Lambeth Conference in summer 1958. The projected visit of Makarios highlights, in particular, the extent to which the government was prepared to intervene at the highest level of the BBC to ensure that Makarios was not presented in too favourable a fashion. As soon as it learnt of Makarios's possible attendance at the Lambeth Conference, the Colonial Office (along with other concerned Departments) immediately began to ponder whether the BBC should be approached and politely requested not to interview Makarios, or, if it insisted on giving him air-time, ensuring that he was subjected to hostile questioning. Any request not to interview Makarios would have to be suitably discreet as the BBC was 'somewhat uppish if so approached', in the words of the Colonial Office's D.M. Smith – a sensitivity which was more than understandable in the light of Eden's heavy-handed treatment of the Corporation during the Suez crisis. Smith, for one, consequently favoured allowing the BBC to put Makarios on air, so long as 'we do what we can to ensure that he is not addressed by the interviewer as "Your Beatitude" (as happened last time) which inhibits the interviewer from asking questions which present Makarios in a poor light'.[161]

As the reference to an unsatisfactory 'last time' suggests, June 1958 was not the first occasion on which the BBC had incurred governmental opposition over interviews with Makarios. Towards the end of Churchill's premiership an interview with Makarios had been broadcast despite a personal approach by the Prime Minister to Sir Ian Jacob, the Director-General of the BBC. Jacob had refused to accede to the demand, apparently feeling that the interview of the Archbishop by Woodrow Wyatt was 'a fair and interesting exposure of a shifty rascal'.[162] Again, in September 1955, the Cabinet had discussed how to respond to a *Panorama* programme which contained an interview with Makarios at 'a most inopportune moment for a broadcast of the kind proposed', and whether or not the Postmaster-General should direct the BBC not to transmit the programme.[163] Once again, however, the broadcast went ahead – with Wyatt using the opportunity to quiz Makarios on his refusal to denounce terrorism.[164]

The pattern of reluctance actually to ban a BBC interview with Makarios outright, despite clear reservations about such broadcasts, was repeated in June 1958. Approaches were certainly made to the BBC in anticipation of his likely visit to London: Dr Charles Hill, during one of his 'informal chats' with Harman Grisewood of the BBC, made some 'forthright, if personal, observations' and believed that the BBC would make any future interview with Makarios 'the occasion for severe hostile questioning of the gentleman'. Similarly Selwyn Lloyd weighed in with a personal note to Ian Jacob, asking him not to interview Makarios for fear of outraging Turkish sensibilities.[165] But no direct attempt was made to prevent any broadcast, more probably through government reluctance to take such drastic action when more informal means would suffice than through ignorance that it had the legal power to ban representatives of terrorist organizations.[166]

While the government pondered how best to deny Makarios favourable publicity, two outraged British citizens were individually taking steps to have the Archbishop arrested on arrival in Britain. A Mr Ivor Worth of Bristol hoped to have Makarios arrested for complicity in the murder of a British soldier in Cyprus, telling the *Daily Herald* that it was 'about time someone came out strongly on the side of our soldiers in Cyprus'.[167] But he lost the first stage of his campaign when a Bristol magistrate told him that Makarios could not be charged without prior evidence and that the government's White Paper on terrorism in Cyprus was unacceptable for this purpose. The government took General Sir Edward Spears's attempt rather more seriously, not least as he apparently had the support of Lord Harding. Finding that the pamphlet *Terrorism in Cyprus* was not going to stand up in court as evidence against Makarios, Spears contacted Harding to ask whether he would swear an affidavit in support of his remarks (indicting Makarios) in Appendix 5 of the pamphlet. Harding's consent caused some consternation in the Colonial Office, as in September 1956 a decision had been taken, with Harding's full assent, that it was not in the public interest to bring Makarios to trial.[168] The Colonial Office consequently warned Harding off swearing an affidavit with the intimation that a libel suit (brought by Makarios presumably) might follow if he did. Having done so much to inflame public opinion against Makarios, the government certainly had no wish in mid-1958 to see Makarios tried for murder, although it was somewhat embarrassing to find that the evidence with which the Archbishop had been denigrated

– principally the Grivas diaries – constituted 'only hearsay' in legal terms.[169]

Although this particular storm blew over when the Archbishop of Canterbury delicately withdrew his invitation to Makarios, the Spears affair – and the popular support that it had attracted – showed how difficult a change of policy over Makarios would be for Westminster's policy-makers and propagandists alike.[170] Would British public opinion accept that Governor Foot was going to negotiate with Makarios and that the latter would therefore have to return to Cyprus, possibly before terrorism had been totally defeated? In the latter part of 1958 the Cabinet feared that it would not.

Ever since his appointment Foot had been anxious to talk to Makarios, regarding him as 'a key figure, if not the key figure, in the whole puzzle', and indeed he had met the Archbishop surreptitiously in Athens in February 1958.[171] However, the alarm engendered in the Turkish-Cypriot community (and in Ankara) when such undercover meetings became public prompted Foot to elevate negotiations to a more formal level, with the inclusion of the Turks. The partnership principle was enshrined in the Macmillan plan of June 1958, which sought to bring together the British, Turkish and Greek governments in talks on Cyprus's future. In the weeks following the announcement of this new diplomatic initiative, Makarios underwent a 'Pauline conversion',[172] gradually coming round to acceptance (in September 1958) of independence, as opposed to self-determination, for Cyprus.[173] The path was gradually being cleared for his reinstatement in Cyprus as the legitimate representative of the Greek Cypriots. But public opinion in Britain represented a severe stumbling block. When Foot's intention to announce the return of Makarios to Cyprus within the next six weeks was debated at a Cabinet meeting in August 1958, the discussion turned on whether British public opinion would permit such a move.[174] In a further Cabinet meeting (less than a fortnight later) it was again felt that public opinion was not yet prepared for 'such a change in our attitude towards the Archbishop'.[175]

If the government now hoped to replace the image of Makarios as arch-terrorist with a portrait of the sort of man with whom one could do business, it was confounded by the renewed ferocity of EOKA terrorism in late 1958. In the British public imagination (or certainly in substantial sections of it), Makarios was still guilty by association. Harding's journalistic efforts did little to help foster public support for any reorientation in government policy. Even as the Cabinet debated the merits of permitting Makarios to return to Cyprus, Harding was cautioning readers of the *Daily Express* that 'there is one thing to remember about the terrible situation in Cyprus . . . Makarios is at the bottom of everything'. Makarios, warned Harding darkly, was an 'implacable foe' who would 'no more give up that aim [of Enosis] than Khrushchev will give up Communism, or Nasser his dreams of an Arab empire'.[176] Even those newspapers which had encouraged the government to allow Makarios to re-enter Cyprus – despite the continued absence of any denunciation of terrorism – found their liberalism hard to maintain in the face of the atrocities of October 1958.

The murder of Mrs Margaret Cutliffe in Famagusta while out shopping for her daughter's trousseau caused an outcry in Britain almost on a par with the rage which had greeted the murder of Sergeants Martin and Paice in Palestine eleven years earlier.[177] Echoes of the troubled final days of the Mandate were also heard in the call of certain Tory backbenchers that Britain must govern in Cyprus or get out.[178] Even the Labour Party rallied round the cry that Makarios *must* now make his opposition to terrorism clear. The security forces' virtual rampage through Famagusta on the night of the murder, and the arrest of almost every adult male resident, received little prominence and much whitewash in most of the British press. Outrage focused on the deeds of EOKA, not on the 'counter terror', as the *New Statesman* dubbed the troops' actions.[179] The *Daily Herald*'s Dennis Pitts was scarcely exaggerating when he wrote that 'the name of Makarios is a filthy word EVERYWHERE in Britain now'. If the Greek Cypriots had previously had a case, then that case was 'tarnished for ever by this monstrous killing'.[180] Makarios's name had never ceased being filthy to those on the political right, and Harding used news of the killing to underline his demand that he must not be unconditionally returned to Cyprus: 'We must refuse to be misled by the would-be appeasers, the philhellenes, and the doctrinaire advocates of outworn political theories . . . and the pious hopes of those who think that leopards do change their spots.'[181]

Undeterred by the appeasement slur, Macmillan's government pressed ahead with its trilateral negotiations, doubtless encouraged by the fact that the Labour Party also preferred diplomacy to an all-out military operation to rid Cyprus of terrorists – the other option being urged on the government in the sombre autumn of 1958. This new element of bipartisanship enabled Macmillan's government to persist on its chosen path, despite the unpopularity that talking to Makarios drew from certain quarters, in the highly charged atmosphere which now surrounded the Cyprus issue. In November 1958 Cyprus was considered to be *the* major problem facing the government, according to a Gallup poll, for the first time since the Emergency began.[182] A significant segment of public opinion was also convinced that toughness rather than negotiation was the key to solving the Cyprus problem, and both those for and against a military expunction of the terrorists were becoming more vocal. There was even a protest against the use of Cypriot sultanas in Winston Churchill's eighty-fourth birthday cake![183]

From the point of view of the government's publicity agencies the need to alter the public perception of Makarios became increasingly evident as the talks of late 1958 and early 1959 moved towards an agreement.[184] Gone was the old spoiling operation against Makarios. Now a special effort was necessary to ameliorate the more unfavourable aspects of his public image in Britain. In other words, the propaganda campaign had to undo much of its work of the previous three years. There is more than a little irony in the fact that, by late 1958, those same Whitehall mandarins who had spent so long debunking Makarios were now scouring the forthcoming histories of the Emergency for 'inappropriate' references to the future President of Cyprus. The volte-face on Makarios resulted in considerable sensitivity over how the history of the Cyprus Emergency would be recorded. Arthur Campbell (author of the popular Malayan adventure yarn, *Jungle Green*) had been commissioned by Harding to write a semi-official history of terrorism in Cyprus. But perhaps unsurprisingly – with a title like *The Flaming Cassock* – Campbell's treatment of the Emergency was not exactly what the Cyprus government had been expecting, and was rejected for publication.[185] The efforts of non-commissioned authors who had produced instant histories were also subjected to pre-publication scrutiny by the Colonial, Foreign and War Offices. And at least two authors were criticized for remarks likely to inflame Greek sensitivities in the delicate early stages of Anglo-Greek *rapprochement*.[186]

However, just as the Whitehall propagandists had sought to camouflage their propaganda activities in the previous months, so in late 1958 they had no desire to *appear* to be whitewashing Makarios. There was even greater fear that the government might seem to be softening its attitude to Grivas. An article in the *Daily Mail*, suggesting that semantic revisionism was under way, was precisely the sort of piece Macmillan's government objected to:

> all the pejorative words like 'thug' and 'terrorist' are being replaced by comforting words like 'guerrilla' and 'patriot'. . . . Roget would have drastically to revise his thesaurus if he were to include all the antonyms which have, overnight, become synonyms. Seldom has evil been transformed more quickly into good, the sinner washed so clean in the springs of unthinking sentiment.[187]

Similar articles should be countered, the Colonial Office recommended, by propagating 'the failure of terrorism and the debunking of Grivas'.[188] In reality, while EOKA had failed to achieve Enosis, the security forces had not defeated terrorism militarily; rather, Grivas had been out-manoeuvred by the politicians, and forced, reluctantly, to abandon his campaign.

The Presentation of EOKA's Activities

Thus far we have concentrated on Britain's efforts to demonstrate the 'hidden hands' behind EOKA terrorism: that is, the complicity of Makarios and the Greek government. Successive Conservative administrations were, in addition, concerned to propagate a negative image of the deeds of EOKA's rank and file. This theme was to some extent interwoven with those already examined. Thus exposure of the part played by Makarios and the Orthodox Church in terrorism served to give EOKA a public face (making Makarios the visible symbol of an otherwise less easily identifiable foe) and to show that supporters of EOKA had joined the movement through spiritual blackmail by the Church, not necessarily of their own spontaneous volition. Likewise, the argument that international Communism would gain most from Cypriot terrorism legitimized the British government's counter-actions, and made EOKA's resort to violence even less defensible.

Both EOKA and the British authorities were engaged in a battle for legitimacy. EOKA sought to demonstrate to the world the bankruptcy of British rule in Cyprus by stressing Britain's over-reliance on force (which EOKA itself had done so much to bring about). With an eye to international opinion, EOKA also re-fashioned its objective as self-determination rather than Enosis. As in previous colonial insurgencies, the British authorities responded to any violent challenge to their rule only partially by attacking their opponents' tactics (i.e. terrorism); the other central theme was the positive projection of British achievements. Hence, as in Malaya and Kenya, much of the propaganda effort went into demonstrating the legitimacy of the colonial presence: the fact that Britain had done much for the colonial inhabitants and that, to some extent, for many of the latter, life went on fairly much as usual.

Britain's case did not rest on any single factor alone, as Leslie Glass spelt out in a note on publicity about Cyprus in June 1956. He pinpointed nine different pillars on which the British argument rested, which may be summarized as follows: (i) Britain's legal sovereignty over Cyprus and responsibility for the island; (ii) Britain's good record in administration and the absence of 'colonial exploitation'; (iii) the scope and genuineness of British offers of self-government; (iv) strategic requirements; (v) the existence of a genuine conflict of interests as between Western defence requirements and the Cypriot demand for self-determination; (vi) the logic of British views on self-determination; (vii) the artificiality of Enosis agitation and the responsibility for inflaming it of the Greek government, Orthodox Church and Greek financial interests; (viii) the 'wickedness of the methods used by the supporters of Enosis', including the 'vileness of terrorism' and 'corruption of youth', and (ix) the 'probable bad results of Enosis', which included the strengthening of Communism.[189] We have seen many of these arguments deployed already, but the list highlights that stressing the 'vileness of terrorism' was by no means the only argument by which the Cyprus government hoped to assert its own legitimacy.

One prominent aspect of British propaganda which did not appear directly on Glass's list was the use of history to bolster the authority of the Cyprus government. Repetition of the historical fact that Cyprus had never been part of Greece was a staple of British official pamphlets and government-inspired articles on the Emergency.[190] Government publicity material (and Tory MPs) constantly reiterated the point that Cyprus had never been Greek; while the majority of inhabitants might speak Greek and share a common Hellenic culture, their aspiration for Enosis was one which had no historical legitimacy, as it did not aim to restore the *status quo ante*. Obviously this was a point which might be expected to cut more ice with British or American audiences than with the Greek Cypriots themselves, to whom it was clearly an irrelevance that they had never actually been ruled by Greece. Indeed, most of Britain's propaganda during the Emergency could be said to have been aimed far more at the international audience than at the inhabitants themselves. The Cyprus government soon became convinced that the task of trying to persuade Greek Cypriots to abandon Enosis was a Sisyphean task that was really beyond its capabilities (though it never quite gave up trying, for all that). As one government official remarked, when the question of political re-education of detainees in Cyprus was under discussion, 'The Communist and Greek Orthodox faiths cannot, I think, be influenced effectively by any kind of propaganda whatsover which any Anglo-Saxons are able to design.'[191] It became commonplace to regard the Greek Cypriots as living in a topsy-turvy 'Alice-through-the-looking-glass' world, gripped by a collective psychosis which rendered them absolutely impervious to British appeals to reason and rationality.

Britain's pack of legitimizing tactics also included the Turkish card – again one which was hardly going to ameliorate anti-British sentiment within the Greek-Cypriot populace. However, in stressing that Enosis was an unviable proposition, it followed that British propaganda would emphasize the existence of a substantial Turkish-Cypriot minority in the island whose rights had to be protected. Thus it would be inappropriate for the British simply to surrender to the Greek Cypriots' demands that Cyprus be allowed self-determination. The Turkish angle was played up quite deliberately, then, as can be seen in the discussion of propaganda policy, particularly between the Foreign Office Information Policy Department and the British Information Service in New York.[192] Arguably, by plugging the Turkish grievances so hard the British government encouraged the Turkish government to adopt a more interventionist role in the Cyprus crisis – perhaps raising Turkish hopes that partition (a policy which HMG considered and then rejected) might be the basis for a settlement, and, in the long term, rendering the Turks dissatisfied with any solution short of this.

Turkey's interest in Cyprus dovetailed neatly with another of Glass's nine pillars of the British case, namely the strategic importance of the island, not simply to Britain but to NATO as a whole, and especially to Turkey, as the most vulnerable member of that alliance. Although the Greek government (also a NATO member) made a point of stressing that a future Cyprus united with the motherland would continue to provide Britain with base facilities, in recognition of her special interests and responsibilities in the Middle East, British propaganda countered that this arrangement would be entirely unsatisfactory. Britain had defence obligations under the Baghdad Pact which the Greeks might not share or 'even approve', and Cyprus was 'so small that it would be extremely difficult to have a military island within an island'.[193] However, arguments in support of Britain retaining Cyprus as a means of defending her multifarious interests in the Middle East became harder to sustain after the Suez crisis of November 1956. Although in January 1957 Harding was still urging the Colonial Office to find means of feeding the British press authoritative articles — 'showing the true value and importance of the Cyprus base to NATO and the Baghdad Pact'[194] — doubts had already been voiced in London and New York over the wisdom of such a course. Only days after the Anglo-French attack on Nasser, Peck had warned that most UN members would henceforth regard Cyprus as the 'imperialist outpost which made aggression possible' (as the air strikes against Egypt had been launched from Cyprus); they would be even more determined to rid Cyprus of the British, and self-determination would 'acquire an aura of even greater magic in the eyes of small nations'.[195] In the later stages of the campaign, then, Cyprus's strategic value had became rather more of a liability than an asset. Indeed, one of the chief reasons why Macmillan's government was so keen to press ahead with a solution based on self-government was that Sandys's post-Suez audit of British defence requirements highlighted the redundancy of the island as a major base.[196] That decision having been reached (and made public), it is hard to see how the government could have motivated the forces to fight for Britain's right to govern a strategically unimportant island for any prolonged period: a speedy settlement was imperative.

Before the decision to give Cyprus independence had been reached, however, the positive grounds on which Britain denied Cyprus the right to self-determination were balanced by the negative reason that the despicable nature of EOKA terrorism itself invalidated the claims of the Greek Cypriots. EOKA's legitimacy was undermined precisely by the methods it had chosen to employ. While it might be imagined government propagandists could have left the presentation of terrorism to look after itself — at least with respect to British journalists, who (however they treated government policy on Cyprus) were unlikely to report EOKA atrocities against British civilians and troops in anything other than outraged tones – an interventionist approach was adopted.

Several aspects of EOKA terrorism were singled out for special emphasis. In official publications and press releases on terrorism, the cowardice of EOKA killers was repeatedly highlighted. EOKA's victims were frequently shot in the back at close quarters in crowded urban areas. During the whole campaign of 1955–59, the British security forces were involved in very few actual 'engagements' with the enemy: EOKA occasionally ambushed security force patrols, but there was scarcely anything resembling a battle or even a prolonged exchange of fire between the sides.[197] The nature of the campaign certainly made for frustration among the troops, and a certain lack of sensational 'news' from the battlefield, as it were, for the press. But the indirectness of EOKA's tactics aided British attempts to portray the terrorists as cowardly murderers, in contradiction to the quasi-legitimate army EOKA purported to be. The fact that the headline-grabbing news from Cyprus consisted largely of urban assassinations meant that the victims (especially if British) could be 'personalized' by the press, making the lives that EOKA terrorism claimed more immediate and more shocking to British readers. Of course, this sense of outrage at the taking of *particular* lives may have been exactly the effect intended by EOKA, but British propaganda was able to exploit this aspect of EOKA's violent strategy to de-legitimize the organization and puncture the self-righteousness of Dighenis's justificatory rhetoric.

EOKA's tactics thus helped ensure that violence in Cyprus was often reported in Britain as a series of tragic human-interest stories. At times British information officers saw this as a trend worthy of encouragement, as can be seen, for example, in the case of Drosoulla Demetriades, whose Turkish-Cypriot fiancé had been the victim of an EOKA street shooting. She came to the attention of the British public as the girl in the striped dress who sat forlornly on a Nicosia pavement, staring at the dead body of her fiancé – in a photograph subsequently regarded as the most enduring image of the Cyprus Emergency.[198] The photograph received wide publicity not immediately after the murder on 25 July 1956, but on 7 August, after Demetriades had been flown to London and given a press conference at the Colonial Office. Her story, and the radio broadcast she had made to fellow Cypriots in which she denounced Grivas, briefly made her the subject of front-page news in the British press. She was 'the beautiful girl who's forgotten how to smile', with a 'mind that hates, coldly and mercilessly, the EOKA terrorists of her native Cyprus'.[199] Harding was pleased with the propaganda use which Nicosia had been able to make of Demetriades, particularly her 'dramatic broadcast attacking EOKA', and a follow-up story was released of how EOKA had beaten up her old mother.[200] EOKA gave the story further mileage by killing her uncle on 15 August in Archbishop Makarios

Street – a location relished by sections of the British press. Although some Whitehall mandarins were, as ever, more scrupulous than others in their desire that British propaganda should be as discreet as possible, consequently feeling that the use of Demetriades for propaganda purposes had been rather too overt,[201] many agreed with Harding on the value of such personalized propaganda. The IPD's Hebblethwaite urged Glass (via Harold Evans) to 'leave no stone unturned in his efforts to provide human stories', as Demetriades' case had done 'more to shake public opinion in, for example, Italy and South America than any other information exercise of ours'.[202]

When terrorism to some extent went into abeyance in 1957 during EOKA's truce – which Nicosia took pains to point out was only sporadically observed by EOKA, thus justifying the fact of its not being observed at all by the security forces – the Cyprus and British governments attempted to keep EOKA terrorism alive in the memory of British public opinion. Towards the end of 1957 discussions occurred between the Foreign Office, Colonial Office and Harding on the question of launching a 'discreet publicity campaign' in the United Kingdom, and a decision was reached that it was 'desirable on general grounds that we should continue to keep in the public mind the nature of terrorism and the terrorists in Cyprus, and particularly at this stage in view of the danger of the situation deteriorating and our having to take sterner measures'.[203] At least the Cyprus Emergency did not suffer the chronic lack of interest that the campaign in Malaya had, and one influential Colonial Office official felt that, even without any special encouragement, 'The press here are already giving pretty good coverage to Cyprus events – sufficient to ensure that the ever-present threat of terrorism and a renewal of violence on a large scale are not forgotten.'[204]

A further reason why rather stale news of EOKA terrorism needed to be kept fresh was that the mass of Greek and Greek Cypriot propaganda alleging brutality on the part of the security forces required an answer and a counter-weight. Answers were not particularly forthcoming. Prolonged behind-the-scenes debates as to whether or not the government should hold a public inquiry into allegations of brutality, or provide evidence for an international inquiry which Greece had urged the UN to undertake, yielded only refusals to air Britain's (undoubtedly not spotless) laundry in public. Maintaining the emphasis on EOKA terrorism, even in periods when there was little of it, was thus one way to counter the propaganda which EOKA was able to produce in such profusion precisely because of its relative inactivity on other fronts.

EOKA and the Smear Technique

As had been the case in Palestine and Kenya, and to a lesser degree in Malaya, the British government was forced on to the defensive during the counter-insurgency campaign, having to concentrate, however reluctantly, on rebutting unsavoury allegations at the expense of positive propaganda. The line that the Greek Cypriots (and their supporters in Greece itself) were deliberately manufacturing groundless anti-British atrocity stories as part of the terrorist strategy formed the basis of the British government's response to the barrage of incriminatory propaganda. In other words, the British hoped to to extricate themselves from having to answer the charges fully by convincing the international and domestic audience that atrocity allegations formed an integral part of *any* terrorist campaign – the implication being that this was as discreditable a tactic in the terrorist arsenal as any other. The reliance of terrorists upon propaganda was to be emphasized.

This was the approach favoured by Harding. He began to be troubled by EOKA's slurs on the security forces early in 1956. In April 1956 the Permanent Representative of Greece to the UN forwarded to the Secretary-General a note giving 'a factual account of atrocities committed by the British forces and authorities against the civil population of Cyprus'.[205] The following month the Greek government applied to the European Commission on Human Rights to ask it to consider whether British methods in Cyprus contravened the obligations set out in the European Convention on Human Rights. In response, the Governor requested Colonial Office permission to introduce legislation against 'malicious and vexatious prosecutions' of members of the security forces by Cypriots, unless they had the prior approval of the Attorney-General to press charges. Unsurprisingly, the Colonial Office discouraged the resort to any such legally dubious manoeuvres.[206] Harding was warned off for the time being. But with both the atrocity propaganda and actual charges of ill-treatment against the troops refusing to disappear, the Colonial Office was far from unconcerned by EOKA's denigratory campaign, which persisted into 1957. The release of Makarios from the Seychelles in March 1957 prompted an invigorated examination of the question of atrocity allegations, as it was feared that the Archbishop would bring them further prominence and credibility when he toured the United States in advance of the 1957 UN debate on Cyprus. The allegations (and Makarios's ability to fuel them) were a major reason why Harding sought at this time to step up the publicity arrangements in London and New York.

The Colonial Office perceived a real danger that the allegations would gain credence in Britain, 'largely from a feeling that there is no smoke without a fire'.[207] Elements of the press viewed as likely to create a stir over EOKA's atrocity campaign included the *Manchester Guardian*, the

New Statesman, *The Economist* and the *Spectator*. Thus concern did not centre solely on papers which routinely accused the British government or armed forces of brutality, such as the *Daily Worker*. Moreover, not only were sections of the press likely to stir matters for the government, but they were almost certainly justified by events; in other words, the smoke did indicate some fire, even if the flames were often artificially fanned. This consideration, too, was tentatively admitted by the Colonial Office in its private deliberations.[208] The fear that a degree of security force brutality (including the use of torture) might be revealed in a public inquiry was one factor which influenced the debate on whether or not the government should meet EOKA's campaign head-on. While some cherished a faint hope that an enquiry might scotch the rumours, instead 'exposing Makarios and EOKA to be a pack of hysterical liars', Harding – like Baring in Kenya – was firmly opposed to any public investigation.[209] He preferred that the CID should investigate privately specific accusations of torture which had some substantiating evidence.[210]

In the spring of 1957 government propaganda, initiated by the Nicosia Public Relations Office, began to present the atrocity allegations as a routine part of the terrorist campaign. One of Harding's major counter-attacks was contained in an eleven-page statement, *Allegations of Brutality by British Forces in Cyprus Refuted*, issued in June 1957. His foreword explained that:

> Wherever terrorism has been employed in the pursuit of political ends, part of the technique has been to try to discredit the forces of law and order by accusing them of scandalously abusing their powers and of indulging in terrorism on their own account. I do not think that any unbiased person who has lived through the past two years in Cyprus could be in any doubt that the Security Forces here have been subjected to a carefully organised campaign of denigration designed to foster hatred among the Greek Cypriot community, and to sow doubt and misgiving outside the Island. Indeed, that this was from the beginning part of his plan has been acknowledged by the terrorist leader *Dighenis*.[211]

The statement also proposed that it would be unrealistic in a campaign such as that being fought in Cyprus to exclude entirely 'the possibility of rough handling of terrorists in the heat of the moment', but argued that, on the very scantiest of evidence, Grivas and Makarios had constructed a 'fantastic illusion of Cyprus in the grip of British terrorism'. The aims behind EOKA's slander campaign were several: not only to throw sufficient mud that some would stick, but also, by encouraging malicious rumours about police 'torture', to find out which of its members had disclosed valuable information.[212] It was suggested that the bulk of accusations could be attributed to EOKA members who had betrayed the organization's secrets during interrogation, and who had subsequently sought to protect themselves against the well-known EOKA punishment for such behaviour. Thus the denial of atrocity allegations provided an opportunity to highlight the internal terrorism operated by EOKA against its own members, and indeed the populace at large. Storrs (the Cyprus Publicity Director) privately told British journalists that the Cyprus government 'was quite prepared to have an inquiry about atrocities if it were effective', but that 'it was no use having a public inquiry as nobody would give evidence'.[213]

The main aim of British counter-propaganda was thus to develop a critique of the smear technique which deflected criticism from the troops and police and focused instead on the terrorists. The accusations of brutality were projected as evidence of EOKA's bankruptcy, signifying that it was a spent force which feared its members cracking under interrogation. Those 'often well-meaning people' who passed on or gave publicity to 'unsubstantiated rumours or allegations' were also criticized.[214] This was a clear dig at a group of Labour MPs (particularly Peter Benenson, Fenner Brockway, Jennie Lee, Lena Jeger and Barbara Castle) who were diligent collators and investigators of Greek-Cypriot allegations against the security forces. Their efforts were untiring: they travelled to Cyprus to examine the accusations, presented their findings at public meetings and in the British press, asked constant Parliamentary Questions, and became the object of widespread detestation within Whitehall. Here again the attitude of the Opposition was one of the most difficult factors to counter in government propaganda abroad, as it was impossible to prevent statements by Opposition MPs being reproduced in the United States or elsewhere.

News Management as a Response to the Smear Campaign

The persistence of the accusations demanded that closer attention be paid to the presentation of security force operations and behaviour in Cyprus, as the spotlight inevitably shifted (despite Harding's best efforts) on to them rather than the terrorists during 1957. This was a consequence not only of the smear campaign, but of the counter-insurgency operations themselves, which were carried on throughout the months in which EOKA was relatively tranquil. Thus the whole process of news management, especially at the Cyprus end, came under close scrutiny. As in earlier Emergencies, the press was perceived as playing a central role.

Unfortunately, Harding proved to be an inept manager of the press. His lack of experience and talent in the realm of press relations was increasingly evident. British press stories of ill-treatment of suspects and even of a counter-terror in Cyprus were often coupled with personal criticism of the Governor, which he took very badly. Furthermore, he developed a tendency to read all press criticism of the handling of the Emergency as a personal slight, even where none had been explicitly intended. Harding's response to hostile press coverage was twofold: to seek greater censorship powers within Cyprus, and to urge the Colonial Office to intervene at the highest editorial level in Fleet Street to correct 'misunderstandings' of the situation. The latter concern was another reason (along with the special 'spoiling operation' against Makarios) why Harding was so keen to appoint Sir Charles Peake as his personal go-between with Fleet Street in 1957.

The Cyprus government had a history of adopting stringent censorship measures before Harding's governorship. As has already been mentioned, the British press reacted unfavourably to censorship regulations introduced when the Enosis campaign was re-animated in 1954. Harding's predecessor, Armitage, was reputed to be 'painfully shy of the press'.[215] Harding, however, was not so much shy of the press as over-confident of his ability to make editors and reporters toe the line, whether through censorship or authoritative briefings. In March 1956 he announced that Durrell had now been appointed as Press Censor, with the task of preventing the importation into Cyprus of newspapers and periodicals from Athens.[216] He stressed that no further measures, such as censorship of outgoing press cables, were envisaged. But the following November Harding assumed much greater powers of press regulation, including the right to ban any publication which he considered prejudicial to the anti-terrorist campaign or to be inciting Cypriots to violence. EOKA's smear campaign was cited as the justification for such measures.[217]

The censorship legislation in Cyprus was widely condemned in Britain, with the *New Statesman* branding it 'the most punitive press law ever enacted in a British territory'.[218] The prosecution of Charles Foley, editor of the *Times of Cyprus* (the *bête noire* of the Cyprus administration[219]), on charges of publishing statements 'likely to cause despondency' and 'likely to be prejudicial to the maintenance of public order', became a minor *cause célèbre* in those sections of the British press which had already made clear their dissatisfaction with Harding's heavy-handedness. Critics felt that Harding was attempting to enforce such conformity within the press that even the smallest measure of partisanship would be eliminated; this would be achieved if Foley's case set the intended precedent – that editors could not write of Greek-Cypriot grievances without simultaneously referring to the Turkish case and the difficulties of the security forces. This precedent seemed not only to be taking the concept of journalistic balance too far but also to be counter-productive. As the *Spectator* wrote:

To attempt to give every side, in fact, is apt to distort the final picture – as the BBC has so often found, to the bored listeners' cost. The freedom of the press has been built up not on a foundation of newspapers all striving to preserve absolute impartiality, but of newspapers representing all the divergent viewpoints.[220]

Through these press regulations and the jamming of Athens Radio, Harding was abandoning the very principles of press and broadcasting freedom and plurality which traditionally informed government media policy. To his critics, the fight against terrorism was insufficient justification.

Those who believed Harding's approach to the communications media to be fundamentally misguided were not restricted to its practitioners. In the Colonial Office there was considerable anxiety over Harding's press management measures. The censorship legislation caused less consternation than his unerring faith in the power of high-level briefings of editors and the lobby to ensure favourable reporting of Cyprus events. Tension between Harding and the Colonial Office occasionally bubbled over into conflict. For example, after a particularly strongly worded condemnation of the 'British terror' in Cyprus by the *Sunday Dispatch* on 25 May 1957, Harding expressed his disbelief that such 'biased comments' should continue to be published despite his telegrams to the Colonial Office containing 'material to enable briefing of the press to be undertaken to counter these allegations'.[221] This drew from Charles Carstairs the rueful remark that he feared nothing would make the Cyprus government 'understand that there is no *sure* way of corking up the Press in this country or of preventing them from drawing their own conclusions and making their own comments on what are reported as *facts*'; the only thing that would really reassure Harding 'would be the total absence of criticism in the UK'.[222] Carstairs's information team in Church House agreed that, as in Malaya and Kenya, 'an extreme sensitivity to press criticism' had developed.[223] The best remedy was to get the news presentation right in Cyprus, thus avoiding reliance on corrective briefings after news stories had already broken.[224]

This was a principle which Harding never quite grasped. To the Colonial Office's chagrin, his plans to 'spoil' Makarios's propaganda tour of America in 1957 similarly rested largely on the principle of rebutting Makarios's allegations *after* the event. A note of frustration crept into internal discussion of Harding's proposals:

The Governor referred to the desirability of giving the press authoritative guidance at the highest level immediately on publication of the various statements likely to come from Makarios in the next few weeks. A short and perhaps unhelpful comment on this is that HMG ought better to regain and maintain the initiative and come out first with a positive move, which would help to make Makarios's obiter dicta irrelevant. It is also perhaps a rather over-simplified view of press relations to think in terms of guidance 'at the highest level' every time Makarios opens his mouth.[225]

Whitehall's irritation at Harding's 'sad lack of knowledge of how the free press in this country works'[226] was aggravated by the Governor's occasional attempts to refute 'biased' press reports by writing in person to the offending editor. This broke another unwritten rule in the Whitehall propagandists' handbook and drew unwelcome attention to Harding's personal sensitivity.[227]

Lack of a clear policy for Cyprus's future was not the only complicating factor for British propaganda on the Emergency. Propaganda cannot easily reverse or palliate awkward 'facts', of which the uncertainty of government policy was but one in 1957. The behaviour and sagging morale of the British security forces in Cyprus presented another problem. Clearly, given the accusations against them, the spotlight shone very harshly on the forces' not always immaculate behaviour. It is hard, even with hindsight and access to official records, to gauge the extent of indiscipline within the forces. No one denied, even at the time, that there were occasions on which the troops' zealousness in carrying out their search-and-arrest operations (or interrogations) absolutely exceeded their brief, becoming little more than a collective venting of anti-Greek fury. Whatever the legitimacy of the rival claims and counter-claims about British reprisals, there were certainly recurring signs of poor discipline and morale among the forces in Cyprus. Some instances reached the British press. As early as July 1955 three privates of the Green Howards were jailed for selling guns – presumably to expatriates looking to defend themselves rather than to EOKA.[228] The following March a group of British soldiers were court-martialled for throwing bombs at their own officers' mess. Their defence represented this action as a drunken attempt to instil a bit of excitement into the monotonous routine of Cyprus service. But in propaganda terms it was an own goal of the first order. More serious, however, were the manifestations of anti-Greek feeling among the British. After the murder of Mrs Cutliffe a set of leaflets was distributed under the aegis of the 'Insurgent Corrective Organisation', which transpired to be the *nom de plume* of a junior NCO in the Signals Unit. The tone was virulent: 'It seems that the only thing the Greek people understand is force. They all live in fear of EOKA. . . . The only course then is to make this race fear the Security Forces. This can only be done by using violence and this organisation will use violence.'[229] Although the serviceman in question was subsequently punished, the incident could scarcely be passed off as the 'joke' that his defence suggested.[230]

Privately the Colonial Office vented concern that Army morale was cracking and feared it was 'in some danger of having our flank turned by our own people'.[231] Although the robust style of General Ken Darling

– who was frequently credited by the press with such sayings as 'The only terrorists I'm interested in are dead ones' – might have been just the tonic which the troops' flagging spirits required, Whitehall reacted with understandable squeamishness.[232] Darling's remarks might damage Britain's case in Cyprus more than they uplifted morale. Indeed, at worst, his remarks might provide a fillip to anti-Greek sentiment within the forces. Admitting that it was 'of course true that there is a morale problem among the Forces in the island' the IPD's P.H.G. Wright wrote frankly to Ralph Murray that:

> There is a certain note of relish which the British popular press find only too easy to attribute to General Darling and the Security Forces; this conflicts with the need to persuade world opinion that we still want reason to prevail and that the policy of repression which is forced upon us by the activities of EOKA is deeply repugnant to the British people as a whole.[233]

Furthermore, the generally poor state of military–media relations in Cyprus, where the press frequently bridled against being refused access to the scene of counter-terrorist operations, threatened to nullify the improvement in dealings between Government House and the press which occurred under Foot.[234]

Undoubtedly there was a sea-change at Government House with the arrival of Foot, who was far more genial with journalists than his predecessor. Sylvia Foot later wrote she was 'glad of the journalists – they were so nice to talk to and so understanding. We liked them and asked them to come and have meals with us – on the record – off the record, what does it matter?': a sentiment which it is hard to envisage Lady Harding ever having entertained![235] The Colonial Office welcomed this thawing in relations. Foot was accessible to the press, yet lacked the interfering tendencies of Harding.[236] But however personable the new Governor was with reporters, the worsening security situation in Cyprus – and the threat of imminent civil war between the Greek and Turkish populations – cast a shadow over their *rapprochement*.

The 'age-old tug-of-war between "News" and "Security"' seemed to pull more in the direction of the latter, even though the military were aware of the value attached to keeping the press on-side.[237] The Director of Operations' Instruction no. 3, of October 1958, specifically told Commanders to afford the press every reasonable facility and treat them with common sense and courtesy, as they could 'do lasting harm to our reputation both in Cyprus and overseas'.[238] But, inevitably perhaps, security considerations sometimes prevailed. Furthermore, the Emergency was nearing its end before Nicosia reported to Whitehall that the mechanisms were fully in place for dealing with atrocity allegations,[239] and it was not until November 1958 that Foot and his public relations team began to give serious consideration to the potential application of psychological warfare methods to Cyprus'.[240]

Visual Propaganda: The Importance of Images

During the Emergency both sides well understood that the visual image was one of the most potent forms of propaganda. In this sphere too, British propaganda was often reactive. Greek propaganda frequently illustrated accusations of security force brutality with photographs depicting young Greek Cypriots with bandaged heads and suspects languishing behind barbed wire in camps. Such images were widespread. British newspapers (editorially hostile to Enosis) also carried photographs of detained or injured Cypriots but tried to use these images to vilify EOKA – whose actions had necessitated the round-up operations during which Greek Cypriots sustained injuries – and to present readers with a palpable depiction of the elusive enemy in Cyprus.[241] The proliferation of 'negative' images (from the British government's point of view) should not, then, be read as entirely the doing of EOKA's propagandists. But clearly the insurgents stood to gain more from such depictions of the security forces' heavy-handedness than the government, and certainly in January 1957 Horace White (Cyprus publicity officer in the CO) felt that 'pictorial publicity' was the government's 'greatest weakness'.[242]

As in previous Emergencies, the chief problem was the invisibility of the enemy and, by contrast, the all too apparent nature of the security forces' activities. However, on the basis of experience from the Malayan and Mau Mau Emergencies, photographs of the *aftermath* of terrorist violence were looked on as an effective weapon in the battle to de-legitimize the enemy – a disincentive to rational discussion of Greek Cypriot grievances.[243] Even photographs of the conditions within the detention camps *could* prove favourable to the government's case if they provided visual confirmation that the camps were far from being the 'British Bergen-Belsen' of EOKA propaganda. This was brought home to the Foreign Office after *Picture Post* ran a four-page photo-story, 'The Truth about the British Belsen', which utterly refuted EOKA's claims.[244] The Rome Embassy then proposed that such material would be useful in countering Greek allegations, and Cox agreed that photographs showing that the detainees were kept in 'reasonable conditions' should be sent to information officers – 'handy for use when necessary'.[245]

Photographs were also increasingly used as illustration for the various Cyprus and British government pamphlets on the Emergency. Such material fell into two broad categories. Depictions of EOKA violence and the victims of their attacks were favoured by the Nicosia Information Office, with its fondness for corpses. These images it regarded as an

integral part of effective anti-EOKA publicity material. Any squeamishness over the 'gruesome' nature of such images was overcome on the
grounds that it was necessary to 'bring home the brutality of terrorism'
to readers of such pamphlets.[246] The second category consisted of
photographs which would 'secure favourable publicity for the British
cause'.[247] The difficulty, as Fletcher-Cooke (Harding's publicity man
in London) appreciated, lay in 'finding photographic subjects which
are likely to increase appreciation of the British policy in Cyprus at
present'.[248] Although the Cyprus government was quite pleased with
the edifying subjects chosen for photography – such as Harding visiting
mixed villages after Greek–Turkish strife, bumper harvests of crops, and
Lady Harding's 'Cypriot welfare activities' – a more jaundiced eye might
wonder whether such images were powerful enough to achieve the
intended effects.[249]

Film, in the shape of both newsreel and television coverage, was
also regarded as a suitable propaganda medium.[250] But here too the
intrinsic difficulties of filming terrorism (which had arisen in the Malayan
and Kenyan Emergencies) re-emerged. Although it was recognized by
mid-1956 that film crews must be given assistance in recording visual
images of the Emergency, the end-product was likely to be one-sided.
As an official of the Commonwealth Relations Office remarked:

> The incidents are almost always shooting or bomb-throwing in the
> dark, or from behind walls, isolated individuals are set upon, and
> the only activities of the security authorities which can be properly
> photographed are the counter-measures. Since these generally
> consist of the arrests, search and interrogation of such suspects,
> in cordoning off districts, or in house-to-house searches, they are
> calculated to emphasize the repressive activities which the actions of
> the terrorists necessitate, and are therefore unlikely to be successful
> as counter-propaganda in North America.[251]

If camera crews wanted action footage, the action they had an opportunity to film could only be that of the security forces. Nevertheless, some
encouragement was given to film-makers and newsreel photographers.
In January 1957 the government agreed to a request from Alfred
Wagg, an American film-maker, to make a television film on the
Cyprus Emergency. The co-operation of the Cyprus government was
pledged on the condition that a British Information Service official
would have the chance to view and comment on the film in the
United States before distribution.[252] And although, as we have seen,
Eden's and Macmillan's administrations were extremely sensitive about
the appearance of Makarios on British television, they did come to
appreciate that television coverage of the Cyprus Emergency *need* not be
unfavourable. Indeed, towards the end of 1958 the Secretary of State for
War recommended to Charles Hill that ITV broadcast a programme on

Christmas Day, entitled 'Christmas in Cyprus', which would 'show the British soldier at play and on duty'. The idea was 'to portray in fact the real behaviour of the British soldier in Cyprus and not as some sections of the Press and some politicians would have it'.[253] And despite the cold feet which later developed – lest the Cyprus negotiations be impeded by transmission of such a film on Christmas Day – the Foreign Secretary approved its transmission on the appointed day.[254]

Although by the time of the Cyprus Emergency television was eroding the popularity of the cinema, newsreels remained a potent (if not the main) source of visual images of the insurgency for British audiences. Subject to less overt government pressure than the television companies, the newsreel companies nevertheless presented the campaign against EOKA in a way that closely approximated to the government's own publicity agenda. In other words, although the images of conflict necessarily focused on the security forces' operations and not on terrorist activities, the commentary prompted viewers towards a sympathetic appraisal of the troops' difficult task.[255] The security forces were invariably presented in a favourable light: young British troops were shown relaxing in certain newsreel stories (calculated, one imagines, to gladden the hearts of anxious mothers of youthful national servicemen serving in Cyprus), as well as on operations.[256] And the unsuccessful nature of the search for Grivas was down-played in bulletins which stressed the perseverance and fortitude of the troops, and the advantages gained from the use of new technology (such as helicopters) in the tracking down of terrorists.[257] In addition, the search for EOKA terrorists in remote corners of the island was projected as a 'civilizing mission' in which British soldiers brought modern medicine to inaccessible mountain villages, doing their best to win the affections of the villagers. As the Movietone commentator remarked: 'It's not easy sweeping terrorists out of holes in corners and at the same time holding the trust of simple people whose only desire is to be left in peace.'[258] And at the time when allegations were rife about British brutality in Cyprus, newsreels repeatedly showed the British Tommy maintaining 'his traditional friendliness' towards the guileless island folk.[259]

Newsreel viewers in Britain were also given a more vivid sense of life in the island than they received from newspaper accounts: the prevalence of EOKA slogans on walls, the Mediterranean climate (although, as a Movietone commentary pointed out with respect to Nicosia, 'there's a sinister quality to this city in the sunshine', and the beaches at Famagusta were 'more useful for filling sandbags'[260]), the narrow streets where many EOKA killings occurred, and dense forest covering Cyprus's mountainous interior. Although most of the newsreel items on Cyprus focused on the Emergency itself, the newsreel companies were mindful, as ever, of showing the lighter side to life: a Christmas party at the Governor's house, the latest fashions at the Nicosia races, and Easter eggs on sale at the NAAFI. Thus governmental concern that 'positive' images of Cyprus should balance the negative was echoed in the major newsreel companies' presentation of the Emergency.

Conclusion

In its propaganda on Cyprus the British government had much 'unofficial' assistance from novelists, film-makers and journalists, who had the same view of terrorism as Westminster. But despite the great effort and attention which went into the production of so many pamphlets and leaflets, and the hours consumed by personal briefings of the press and news management, a question mark hangs over the success of the publicity campaign.

It was a campaign in which propaganda and policy were often completely unsynchronized: at times policy was entirely lacking (or disputed between Westminster and Nicosia), and plans for Cyprus's future changed so rapidly that propaganda could not possibly keep fully abreast. In other words, policy-makers had no clear vision of what propagandists were to sell to Greek Cypriots (or indeed to the domestic population). Although in Britain there was general distaste for EOKA and its activities – reaching its apogee in the attempts by ordinary citizens to have Makarios arrested – it is much more questionable whether Britons were committed to hanging on to Cyprus. Did arguments conveying the strategic desirability of a British-owned island base in the Eastern Mediterranean actually convince people that this justified the sacrifice of young British lives? This, after all, was a much harder task for government propaganda than mobilizing anti-terrorist sentiment. True, there was no great popular pressure on the government to make a precipitate retreat from Cyprus (as there had been in Palestine); only the odd demonstration or protest, and more widespread dissatisfaction over the sending of teenage soldiers to the island. Yet it seems doubtful whether public opinion would have been prepared to endure a protracted military campaign (such as Harding, for one, advocated) to hold Cyprus after the climactic violence of October 1958, had a political solution not been found so soon after (despite the revulsion at dealing with Makarios). Stanley Mayes wrote in 1960 that there was a 'widespread feeling of guilt – a feeling that somehow Britain had not lived up to her principles over Cyprus and that the problem was largely of her own making'.[261] And the high number of courts martial in the security forces, which was revealed after the shooting war was over, suggests that perhaps the troops were less than fully aware of why they were in Cyprus, and increasingly frustrated by a campaign in which the enemy proved so elusive, and so uncooperative after capture.[262]

This highlights one of the central problems for those vested with responsibility for HMG's publicity: many of Britain's projected objectives at the outset were clearly redundant by the end of the campaign. By the settlement of February 1959, Britain did not keep the whole island – only two bases; she had prevented Enosis, but at the price of seeing the Arch-Terrorist become the new President of an independent Cyprus; her security forces had ostensibly defeated terrorism – but had never found Grivas, and indeed suffered the indignity of watching him be received in Athens with full military honours by the Greek government; and if it was imagined at the time that British security forces had prevented EOKA's campaign sparking civil war in the island, inter-communal tension did not abate for long. Attempts to propagate the positive legacy of progress bequeathed by the imperial power ultimately ended in failure too.

Thus if British propaganda was successful in the short term and with specific goals in mind (most notably the denigration of Makarios), any achievements could only be short-lived, as Britain's long-term policy on Cyprus underwent a complete transformation during the course of the campaign. Nothing encapsulates the revolution in British thinking on Cyprus so well as a 1961 photograph of the newly remodelled Makarios shaking hands with the Queen – both 'wearing smiles so warm as to suggest that this is a moment for which both have long waited'.[263]

Notes

1 This was the title of a British propaganda pamphlet which contained extracts from Radio Athens broadcasts. A copy can be found in FO 953/1694.

2 The most notable exception was the 1931 burning of Government House during a demonstration by Greek Cypriots against the payments they had to make to Turkey via the Cyprus government; see N. Crawshaw, *The Cyprus Revolt: An Account of the Struggle for Union with Greece* (George Allen and Unwin, London, 1978).

3 This title was bestowed on Makarios by the *Daily Express* (27/8/56).

4 Grivas had achieved some notoriety during the war and in the subsequent Greek civil war as leader of an extreme right-wing resistance movement, Khi, which had dedicated its efforts rather more to eliminating Communists than the Nazi occupiers of Greece.

5 The Colonial Office line on this point was laid out in a lecture given by John Fletcher-Cooke to the Colonial Office Overseas Service Conference at Rhodes House, Oxford, on 13 April 1956; text in CO 926/450.

6 Cited by Crawshaw, *Cyprus Revolt*, p. 76.

7 J. Reddaway, *Burdened with Cyprus: The British Connection* (Weidenfeld and Nicolson, London, 1986), p. 11.

8 The Greek government sent its first appeal to the UN on 20 Aug. 1954; Crawshaw, *Cyprus Revolt*, pp. 82–9.

9 Durrell was an imaginative appointment, as his pro-Greek proclivities risked antagonizing Cyprus's Turkish minority. But the Colonial Office were more concerned to counter what they saw as extremely pervasive pro-Enosis propaganda; S.H. Evans, 'Information Problems, Themes and Organisation in Cyprus: Some Notes on a Four Day Visit, 22–25 September 1954'; CO 926/179.

10 L. Durrell, *Bitter Lemons* (Faber and Faber, London, 1957), pp. 34–5.

11 Record of a private meeting between Oliver Woods and Macmillan; memo from Woods to Haley, 15/8/58, Cyprus file, 1957, *The Times* Archive.

12 Telegram from Sir Robert Armitage (Governor of Cyprus) to Alan Lennox-Boyd (Secretary of State for the Colonies), 9/12/54, no. 485; CO 926/174.

13 Durrell, *Bitter Lemons*, p. 177.

14 Crawshaw, *Cyprus Revolt*, p. 112.

15 C. Foley (ed.), *The Memoirs of General Grivas* (Longmans, London, 1964), p. 35.

16 *The Times* (22/6/55).

17 *Daily Herald* (1/7/55).

18 *Sunday Dispatch* (10/7/55).

19 See correspondence in CO 926/563.

20 D.M. Anderson, 'Policing and Communal Conflict: The Cyprus Emergency, 1954–60', *Journal of Imperial and Commonwealth History*, 21, iii (1993), 177-207, p. 184. See also Cyprus 'sabotage and incident' reports; CO 926/415 and CO 926/416.

21 CIC(55)27 (Final), 'The Nature of EOKA, Its Political Background and Sources of Direction', 18/10/55; CO 926/455.

22 Cyprus Intelligence Committee, 'Appreciation by Dighenis on 18/11/55', CIC(55)28 (Final), 19/11/55; CO 926/454.

23 D. Barker, *Grivas: Portrait of a Terrorist* (The Cresset Press, London, 1959), p. 76. Another work on Grivas and EOKA dating from 1959 pointed out the pains which Grivas took with news management; W. Byford-Jones, *Grivas and the Story of EOKA* (Robert Hale, London, 1959), p. 58.

24 See, for example, a novel written by a former News Editor of the Cyprus Broadcasting Service, J. Appleby, *The Bad Summer* (Hodder and Stoughton, London, 1958), p. 48.

25 A further CIC report of July 1956, again written from Dighenis's perspective, stated that his chief weapons were 'fear and propaganda'. There was a need to 'provide material on which my propaganda campaign can be based. Armed attacks on the police, the armed forces, and British Government officials will emphasize my line that Cyprus is of no value as a base and costs too much to hold'; CIC (56)18, 'Appreciation of the Situation by Dighenis on 5 July 1956', 6/7/56; CO 926/454.

26 Ibid.

27 Durrell, *Bitter Lemons*, pp. 215–16.

28 This is evident from Harding's reaction to an article in *The Times* on 4 Feb. 1957, 'Crucial Week for Cyprus', which – although almost a verbatim copy of a Cyprus government press release – he attacked for implying that 'EOKA have the power to do as they please', and as another example of the paper's 'poor and unhelpful reporting'; see telegrams from Field Marshal Sir John Harding (Governor of Cyprus) to Lennox-Boyd, nos. 202 (of 3/2/57) and 234 (of 7/2/57); CO 1027/154.

29 *Daily Express* (11/5/56), editorial, p. 2.

30 For example, the *Observer*'s Michael Faber wrote on 4 March 1956: 'Although the core of the organisation is undoubtedly small, it commands widespread support. This support stems partly from fear and partly from the Greek Cypriots' deep emotional involvement with the professed aim of EOKA, itself encouraged by the Orthodox Church and teaching in the schools'; 'Door Shut on Negotiations – Makarios', p. 1.

31 *Spectator* (24/8/56) vol. 197, no. 6687, 'First light', p. 252. The paper was generally critical of the government's handling of the Cyprus dispute over the following two years, and, drawing from the lessons of Irish terrorism, the editor advocated negotiating with Makarios at an early stage.

32 Durrell, *Bitter Lemons*, p. 183.

33 Ibid., p. 242.

34 For example, he wrote a series of three lengthy articles entitled 'Terrorism in

Cyprus' for the *Daily Telegraph*, on 7, 8 and 9 Jan. 1958. He also contributed frequently to the *Daily Express*.

35 Text of a broadcast by Harding announcing the decision to invite Lord Radcliffe to Cyprus as the constitutional commissioner; telegram from Harding to Lennox-Boyd, 11/7/56, no. 1358; CO 926/552.

36 Telegram from Sir Hugh Foot (Governor of Cyprus) to Lennox-Boyd, 10/12/57, no. 1874: CO 926/895.

37 S. Foot, *Emergency Exit* (Chatto and Windus, London, 1960), p. 107. See also the memoir of Penelope Tremayne, who served as a Red Cross nurse in Cyprus during the Emergency, *Below the Tide* (Hutchinson, London, 1958): 'The main significance of EOKA at present is not as an effective instrument but as an idea'; p. 175.

38 General G. Grivas-Dighenis, *Guerrilla Warfare and EOKA's Struggle: A Politico-Military Struggle* (Longmans, Green, London, 1964); C. Foley (ed.), *Memoirs*.

39 Grivas, *Guerrilla Warfare*, p. 5.

40 Foley (ed.), *Memoirs*, p. 12.

41 Ibid., p. 19.

42 Ibid., p. 34.

43 Ibid., p. 43.

44 An EOKA leaflet which appeared shortly after the murder did not exactly deny that EOKA had killed Mrs Cutliffe, but hinted that the murder had been a British plot to bring EOKA into further disrepute; telegram from Foot to Lennox-Boyd, no. 1706, 8/10/58, CO 926/897. The Greek government, however, in denying EOKA involvement, suggested that Mrs Cutliffe had been shot by a jilted lover – an insinuation which caused outrage in Britain (as well as among the forces in Cyprus; see CO 926/908). Grivas persisted in claiming ignorance in his *Memoirs*, echoing the Greek government claim that Mrs Cutliffe 'might have been the victim of some crime of spite or passion'; p. 169.

45 David Rapoport argues that Grivas was also unable to comprehend that he could arouse international (particularly Turkish) opinion in a way that would be ultimately disastrous to his cause; 'The International World as Some Terrorists Have Seen It: A Look at a Century of Memoirs', *Journal of Strategic Studies*, 10 (1987), 901–22.

46 Foley (ed.), *Memoirs*, p. 43.

47 Durrell, *Bitter Lemons*, p. 152.

48 Letter from Armitage to Lennox-Boyd, 30/8/54; CO 926/500.

49 A record of Mott-Radclyffe's meeting with the Secretary of State is contained in a memo from Lennox-Boyd to Sir John Martin, 7/11/58, CO 1027/135. He put a similar case to the BBC, suggesting a reassessment of its programmes for the forces in a letter to Sir Beresford Clarke, 5/11/58, BBC WAC E1/1, 810/1.

50 *Daily Telegraph* (6/11/58).

51 Memo from Glass to Evans, 'World Publicity on Cyprus', 12/6/56, PG11926/18; FO 953/1694.

52 Letter from C.C.B. Stewart (Head of IPD) to J.S.H. Shattock (Political Office with the Middle East Forces), 20/8/56, PG11926/10; FO 953/1693.

53 Memo by C.C.B. Stewart, 'Publicity on Cyprus', 8/6/56, PG11926/10; FO 953/1693.

54 Telegram from Sir R. Makins to FO, 15/6/53, no. 1373, PG11926/11; FO 953/1693.

55 Parliamentary Question for 2/1/57, Cyprus (Information Services) asked by Mr Vane, in PG11926/31; FO 953/1820.

56 Minute by C.C.B. Stewart, 23/1/57, PG11926/31; FO 953/1820.

57 Telegram from Harding to Lennox-Boyd, 6/4/57, no. 640; CO 1027/155.

58 His arrival is documented in FO 953/1825.

59 See the discussion in CO 1027/155.

60 Telegram from Lennox-Boyd to Harding, 13/4/57, no. 599; CO 1027/155.

61 Sir J.M. Martin to Sir Thomas Padmore, Treasury, 19/6/57, RG1682/6; FO 371/130159.
62 Minute by P.R. Noakes, Principal Information Officer in the CO Press Section, to Carstairs on 18/6/57; CO 1027/155.
63 Letter from Joy Wright to John Peck, 23/8/57, PG11926/115, FO 953/1828.
64 Minute by C.C.B. Stewart, 20/9/57, PG11926/115; FO 953/1828.
65 Harding still insisted on paying Williams's fare, feeling that a spoken contract had already been entered into; minute by N. Bicknell, 1/1/58, PG11926/116; FO 953/1828.
66 H. Evans, *Downing Street Diary* (London, 1981), p. 16.
67 Minute from J.D. Higham to Carstairs, 13/11/58; CO 1027/135.
68 Minute by Morris dated 28/11/58; CO 1027/135.
69 As one British diplomat wrote in 1954: 'It would be particularly useful if we could insinuate that the issue of *Enosis* has been gradually exploited and blown up by the Communists, both in Cyprus and Greece, as a Cold War gambit'; telegram from UK Delegation to the UN to FO, no. 163, 14/8/54; CO 926/180.
70 Minute by Barton to Smith, undated; CO 926/180. On a similarly disgruntled note, J.S. Bennett had minuted on 18 Aug. 1954, 'The fact that the American public likes to see Communists behind every trouble in the world does not mean that we must gratify their taste at the expense of truth or wise policy. The *Enosis* problem existed before Communism and would continue without it'; CO 926/180.
71 Byford-Jones, *Grivas and the Story of EOKA*, p. 82.
72 See, for example, *Daily Mirror* and *Daily Herald* (29/9/55). Embroidering the CO statement, the *Daily Express* wrote of a new Russian campaign to infiltrate the Middle East through arms deals with Egypt, which made Cyprus all the more valuable in strategic terms; 'Makarios Asks the Reds for Help', p. 1.
73 *Daily Mirror* (29/9/55).
74 Harding to Lennox-Boyd, 24/3/56, no. 643; CO 926/417.
75 Harding to Lennox-Boyd, 18/1/56, no. 148; CO 926/394.
76 Minute by W.A. Morris to Sir J. Martin, 4/1/56; CO 926/394.
77 Lecture entitled 'Communism and Nationalism in Cyprus', 13/4/56, pp. 5–7; CO 926/450.
78 In a similar fashion, the theory mooted by Claire Sterling *et al.* during the 1980s that the Kremlin was ultimately behind most international terrorism rested on a similar substitution of the question *'cui bono?'* (who benefits?) in place of actual evidence. This point is well made by M. Stohl, 'States, Terrorism and State Terrorism: The Role of the Superpowers', in R.O. Slater and M. Stohl (eds), *Current Perspectives on International Terrorism* (Macmillan, Basingstoke, 1988), p. 183.
79 'Communism and Nationalism in Cyprus', op. cit., p. 11.
80 The briefing paper can be found in FO 953/1698. The same points were reiterated in an official pamphlet, largely for the forces' consumption, *Why We Are in Cyprus*; copy in FO 953/1701.
81 Memo from Glass to Evans, 'World Publicity on Cyprus', 12/6/56; FO 953/1694. However, in July, Fletcher-Cooke urged Glass to knock into shape a pre-existing pamphlet, *Communism in Cyprus*, which the FO had assured Fletcher-Cooke was 'most desirable for information officers' for reference purposes; letter from Fletcher-Cooke to Glass, 16/7/56, PG11926/44; FO 953/1695.
82 Minute by Galsworthy, 2/7/56, PG11926/18; FO 953/1694.
83 These claims were made in a FO pamphlet prepared for BIS, *Propaganda Campaign by Makarios*. Makarios had apparently met M. Sergeev, the Soviet Ambassador in Athens, at the end of July 1957, and the Soviets had pledged support for his campaign. Similar assurances, the pamphlet reported, had been obtained from Czechoslovakia and Poland in August 1957; copy in PG11926/107, FO 953/1827.
84 Foley (ed.), *Memoirs*, p. 43.

85 Telegram from Lennox-Boyd to Harding, 4/4/57, no. 559; CO 926/911.
86 Telegram from Harding to Lennox-Boyd, 5/4/57, no. 629; CO 926/911.
87 Foley (ed.), *Memoirs*, pp. 61–2.
88 See, for example, the transcript of an ABC television programme featuring Makarios in America, 'College News Conference', dated 1/12/57; CO 926/925.
89 *Daily Express* (30/5/56), 'Stab in the Back', Keith Morfett, p. 1. On the following day the paper ran a further front-page story which quoted the Communist-led union as stating that the gift had been for defence of trade union leaders jailed in Cyprus. Then on 5/6/56 the story continued with an exposé of 'Red infiltration' of the ETU leadership; 'Red Infiltration at Top Worries ETU Men'; p. 1.
90 *Daily Express* (6/6/56), 'Be Proud of This Briton', Roy Garrett, p. 1.
91 The poll was launched on 9 June 1956; three days later the *Express* of 12/6/56 reported that 12,000 readers had replied in favour of the editorial line that the £20 was 'dirty money'.
92 Harding reported in Feb. 1957 that an organization called the Pan-Hellenic Committee for Self-Determination for Cyprus (PEAK) had just published a report on its publicity activities from May to Dec. 1956. If the report is credible, then 3.5 million copies of thirty-six different publications in seven different languages had been produced; telegram from Harding to Lennox-Boyd, 16/2/57, no. 313, PG11926/45; FO 953/1820.
93 See in particular the Greek government's major propaganda production in advance of the 1957 UN session, *Some Facts about Cyprus*; copy contained in PG11926/35; FO 953/1820.
94 Letter from Stewart to Peck, 30/6/56, PG11926/22; FO 953/1694.
95 See PG11926/39, FO 953/1820; the principal forms of Greek assistance to the terrorists were given as: initial inspiration; provision of arms and ammunition; provision of funds; training of terrorists; and incitement to violence.
96 By August 1956, Harold Evans was planning the production of an 'attractively designed booklet' (primarily for sale in the UK), entitled *Terrorism in Cyprus*, which would include extracts from the 'captured documents which reveal so dramatically the roles of Makarios and of the Greek Government in the terrorist movement in Cyprus'; letter from Evans to T. Fife Clark (COI), 29/8/56, PG11926/129; FO 953/1701.
97 Minute by Goodall, 13/2/57, PG11926/48; FO 953/1821.
98 Letter from Peck to P.F. Grey (IPD), 13/7/56, PG11926/37; FO 953/1695.
99 Minute by N.E. Cox (FO Southern Department), 17/7/56, PG11926/37; FO 953/1695.
100 Copy in FO 953/1694.
101 The *Daily Herald* on 6/3/56, for example, stated that jamming was to be carried out 'for the first time ever'; p. 1.
102 Lennox-Boyd in a Cabinet meeting of 31/1/56, after the initial decision to jam Athens Radio had been leaked; CM(56) 8, Minutes of the meeting on 31/1/56; CAB 128/30.
103 Lennox-Boyd quoted in the *Daily Express* (28/1/56), 'Jam the Murder Radio', Valentine Hall, p. 2.
104 Letter from Peck to Stewart, 28/5/56; PG11926/8; FO 953/1693.
105 *Daily Express* (7/3/56), 'Now I Can Say It!', René MacColl, p. 6.
106 *New Statesman and Nation* (4/2/56), vol. 51, no. 1300, editorial, p. 113, 'Britain Lowers the Radio Curtain'.
107 On the series 'Vandals and Sacrilegers' see a letter with enclosures from A.D.S. Goodall (FO) to A.S. Aldridge (CO), 16/8/57; CO 926/881.
108 D. Buttenshaw, *Violence in Paradise* (Hodder and Stoughton, London, 1957), p. 83.
109 *Observer* (17/10/54) quoted by S. Mayes, *Cyprus and Makarios* (Putnam, London, 1960), p. 33.

110   *Daily Express* (10/3/56), p. 4.

111   Byford-Jones, *Grivas*, p. 145.

112   Cyprus Intelligence Committee Report (55) 25, 19/11/55; CO 926/454.

113   Much attention was devoted to Makarios's refusal to denounce terrorism when asked to do so by the Archbishop of Canterbury in June 1955. His response that to condemn EOKA 'would involve the risk of exposing me rather unprofitably' seemed to amount to a confession of complicity; Mayes, *Cyprus and Makarios*, pp. 36–7.

114   For more detail on the background to EOKA's campaign and Makarios's role, see Crawshaw, *The Cyprus Revolt, passim*, and Stanley Mayes, *Makarios: A Biography* (Macmillan, Basingstoke, 1981), ch. 5.

115   Grivas reports that Makarios was initially reluctant to go beyond sabotage, a tactic which he certainly *did* endorse; Foley (ed.), *Memoirs*, p. 20.

116   R. Holland, 'Never, Never Land: British Colonial Policy and the Roots of Violence in Cyprus', *Journal of Imperial and Commonwealth History*, 21, iii, (1993), 148-76, p. 149.

117   Harding's cardinal principle during negotiations was that the British and Cyprus governments should 'steadfastly refuse' to discuss constitutional development with any individual or group who refused to declare themselves publicly against violence and disorder; telegram from Harding to Lennox-Boyd, 31/1/56, no. 231; CO 926/548.

118   M. Carver, *Harding of Petherton* (Weidenfeld and Nicolson, London, 1978), p. 216.

119   Ibid., p. 215. See also Sir Anthony Eden, *Full Circle* (Cassell, London, 1960), p. 412.

120   Cmd 9708, *Correspondence between the Governor and Archbishop Makarios* (HMSO, London, 1956). For a brief Cabinet discussion on this White Paper, see CM(56) 18, Minutes for the meeting of 5/3/56; CAB 128/30.

121   *Daily Herald* (6/3/56), 'He might be deported', p. 1.

122   These charges were carried in press reports of the deportation; see for example *Daily Herald* (10/3/56), 'Makarios Goes Out – by RAF', p. 1. However, Mayes rejects the argument that Makarios timed the intensity of terrorism according to how well the negotiations were going, stating that Grivas, rather than Makarios, was calling the shots in the terrorist campaign. Thus it was Grivas who decided to explode nineteen bombs an hour before Lennox-Boyd joined the Harding–Makarios talks on 29 Feb. 1956; *Makarios: A Biography*, pp. 80–3.

123   The *Spectator*, vol. 196, no. 6664 (16/3/56), 'Soft-Centred', p. 332. This line was echoed by the *New Statesman and Nation*, vol. 51 (24/3/56); J.P.W. Mallalieu questioned, 'what on earth would be the point of trying to restore peace by negotiating with someone who was not in touch with the disturbers of the peace?'; p. 263.

124   The *Spectator*, vol. 196, no. 6669, (20/4/56), 'The Plan for Cyprus', p. 516.

125   Minute by C.C.B. Stewart, 12/3/56, PG11926/1; FO 953/1693.

126   Telegram from Harding to Lennox-Boyd, 31/5/56, no. 923; CO 926/450.

127   Ibid.

128   Minute by Carstairs to Harold Evans, 9/6/56; CO 926/450.

129   News of the capture was passed on in a telegram from FO to BIS (NY), no. 200, 26/8/56; CO 926/450.

130   A decision was taken in July 1956 to print the documents for confidential use at FO posts but not to turn them into an official publication, as had originally been envisaged by Harding; Ward (FO) to Bowker, Ankara, 5/7/56; CO 926/450.

131   Minute by J.E. Galsworthy, 11/9/56, PG11926/182; FO 953/1704.

132   Ibid.

133   *Daily Express* (27/8/56), p. 1. Whitehall obviously regarded early publication of these documents as crucial; Harold Evans wrote to T. Fife Clark of the COI that this publication of extracts was necessary 'for immediate policy reasons'; letter dated 29/8/56, PG11926/130; FO 953/1701.

134   *Daily Express* (27/8/56).

135 BBC WAC, *Panorama* script, 1/10/56.
136 *Manchester Guardian* (28/8/56).
137 *Observer* (2/9/56), editorial, p. 6.
138 *New Statesman and Nation* vol. 52, no. 1329 (1/9/56), editorial, 'Must We Deal with Makarios?', p. 229.
139 Harold Evans to T. Fife Clark, 29/8/56, PG11926/130; FO 953/1701.
140 See a minute by the IPD's J. Thomson, in which he refers to a telegram from BIS (NY) asking for such material; minute dated 16/3/56, PG11926/1; FO 953/1693.
141 For two contrasting viewpoints, see the *Daily Herald* (14/6/56), p. 4, and the *Daily Express*, which, in the grip of its campaign against the ETU, ran a front-page headline, 'Priest Collected "Dirty" £900' (14/6/56).
142 Appleby, *The Bad Summer*, p. 73. An earlier Emergency novel, written by another journalist, made even greater play on the role of the Church in terrorism, one of the leading characters being an anti-British bishop. See D. Nash, *Not Yours the Island* (Jonathan Cape, London, 1956); the description of Bishop Athenagoras, p. 10, brings to mind a character strikingly similar to Makarios.
143 *The Church and Terrorism in Cyprus*, p. 23; copy in FO 953/1820.
144 Ibid., pp. 33–4.
145 Minute by N.E. Cox, 18/2/57, PG11926/43; FO 953/1820.
146 Harding urged that *The Church and Terrorism in Cyprus* should be distributed primarily among Greek-Cypriot communities abroad; telegram from Harding to Lennox-Boyd, no. 723, 10/4/57, PG11926/43; FO 953/1820.
147 Minute by Cox, 18/2/57, PG11926/43; FO 953/1820.
148 Crawshaw, *The Cyprus Revolt*, pp. 205–9.
149 Letter from Dr Fisher, Archbishop of Canterbury, to Lennox-Boyd, 22/3/57; CO 926/632.
150 On 20/3/57, the *Daily Express* carried a front-page story of a rupture between Harding and Lennox-Boyd over whether to reopen negotiations with Makarios without first securing his denunciation of terrorism. If there was a dispute, the Cabinet minutes do not reveal it. However, it is apparent from the minutes of meetings before Makarios's release that there were substantial differences; for example, on 18/3/57, Selwyn Lloyd (the Foreign Minister) had advocated that it would be a 'sign of weakness' to embark on discussions with Greek-Cypriot leaders or to release Makarios until terrorism were finally suppressed; CC(57) 21, Conclusions of the meeting on 18/3/57; CAB 128/31.
151 *Daily Express* (29/3/57), p. 6.
152 Gallup, *The Gallup International Opinion Polls*, p. 410.
153 Although Harding's biographer and others have suggested that Harding positively encouraged Macmillan to release Makarios, one has to question, if this is so, what role Harding envisaged for the Archbishop, in the light of his extraordinary propaganda initiative. See Carver, *Harding of Petherton*, pp. 222–4, and B. Lapping, *End of Empire* (Granada, London, 1985), p. 336.
154 Harding to Lennox-Boyd, 6/4/57, no. 640, CO 1027/155.
155 Telegram from Harding to Lennox-Boyd, 14/4/57, no. 669; CO 926/931.
156 Ibid. See also telegram from Lennard (Nicosia Information Office) to White, 4/4/57, no. 623; CO 1027/157.
157 Minute by W.A. Morris to Carstairs and Melville, 8/4/57; CO 1027/155.
158 'Note on Cyprus Publicity in the UK', 12/4/57, C.Y. Carstairs; CO 1027/155.
159 Minute by Peake, 25/6/57; CO 1027/157.
160 British officials were generally pleased with Makarios's public performances; see, for example, a letter from Peck, BIS NY, to P.H.G. Wright (IPD), 12/12/58, PG11910/29; FO 953/1865.
161 Minute by D. Smith to White and Morris, 1/8/58; CO 926/638.
162 The anecdote is related in Harman Grisewood's *One Thing at a Time: An Autobiography*

(Hutchinson, London, 1968), p. 191.

163 See the discussion in CM(55)31, Minutes of the meeting on 15 Sept. 1955; CAB 128/29.

164 Script of *Panorama*, 26/9/55, BBC WAC.

165 See a note from Hill, Chancellor of the Duchy of Lancaster, to the Prime Minister, 16/6/58, and a letter from Selwyn Lloyd to Ian Jacob dated 13/6/58; PREM 11/2226.

166 This suggestion was made by the *Irish Times* (2-3/1/89), when the official papers were first released, which saw in the events of 1958 a foreshadowing of the 'Sinn Fein ban' of 1988. However, British governments have not generally underestimated their powers to compel the BBC to toe the government line, if necessary. As William Clark (Eden's press secretary) noted during the Suez crisis: 'I was struck by the extent to which the BBC was regarded as completely under government control'; *From Three Worlds* (Sidgwick and Jackson, London, 1986), p. 175.

167 *Daily Herald* (28/5/58), 'Informer Wants Makarios Arrested', p. 7

168 Minute by D. Smith to J.D. Higham, 28/5/58, CO 926/639.

169 Macmillan had seemed rather concerned that there should be no valid evidence against Makarios after all, and wrote to the Attorney-General to ask what was wrong with the White Paper accusing Makarios of complicity. This was the reply given by the Attorney-General to Macmillan in a note dated 5/6/58; CO 926/639.

170 Support for Spears can be seen not only in sections of the popular press, which were fiercely opposed to Makarios, but also in letters from MPs and others to the government, suggesting widespread anger over Makarios's possible visit. See letters contained in CO 926/639.

171 H. Foot, *A Start in Freedom* (Hodder and Stoughton, London, 1964), p. 166.

172 Darwin, *Britain and Decolonisation*, p. 281.

173 For the background to this reversal, see Mayes, *Makarios*, pp. 115–20.

174 See the discussion on Cyprus in CC(58)68, conclusions of a meeting on 27/8/58; CAB 128/32.

175 CC(58)69, Conclusions of a meeting on 8/9/58; CAB 128/32.

176 *Daily Express* (6/8/58), 'Beware This Grivas Trick!', Harding, p. 4. The *Daily Herald*, on the other hand, urged the government to challenge Makarios to return to Cyprus and to exert his authority over the terrorists, whose activities were 'killing sympathy for the Greek case and making negotiation impossible'; editorial, 'Try This Key', 5/8/58.

177 This murder also provoked parallels between EOKA and Mau Mau. Charles Foley, former editor of the *Times of Cyprus* and *bête noire* of the Cyprus government, later wrote in his account of the Emergency that the Cutliffe murder 'was more than enough, in the overcharged atmosphere, to convince any doubters that Greek Cypriots were as brutal and bloodthirsty as the Mau Mau'; *Legacy of Strife: Cyprus from Rebellion to Civil War* (Penguin Books, Harmondsworth, 1964), p. 139.

178 The *Daily Herald* (6/10/58), p. 7, carried a report that a backbench Tory revolt was in progress, led by Rupert Speir, MP for Hexham and PPS to the Foreign Minister, who was quoted as saying, 'If the Government doesn't do something drastic, then I'll get my friends together and make it do so. Either we must govern in Cyprus or get out. It could well be a case of getting out.'

179 The *New Statesman and Nation* and the *Observer* paid more attention to the 're-prisals' than the rest of the British press. See the *New Statesman*, vol. 56, no. 1439 (11/10/58), p. 477 and Rawle Knox in the *Observer* (5/10/58), 'Troops and Dogs in Cyprus Murder Hunt', p. 1.

180 *Daily Herald* (7/10/58), 'FIVE BULLETS – a woman falls dead . . . and a cause is wrecked', Dennis Pitts, p. 4.

181 *Daily Express* (6/10/58), 'How to Beat These Murders', Harding, p. 8.

182 Cyprus was still regarded as the most pressing problem in a further poll of December 1958, though by January 1959 it had dropped to fifth on the list; Gallup, *The Gallup International Opinion Polls*, pp. 480, 486 and 491.

183 Foley, *Legacy of Strife*, p. 144.

184 For Foot's account of the process which led to a settlement, see *A Start in Freedom*, pp. 175–81. The ability to reach agreement with the Turkish and Greek governments owed much to the degree of inter-communal strife between the two communities in Cyprus, and the imminent danger in late 1958 that such violence would erupt into civil war – a possibility neither side would lightly countenance.

185 Letter from Piper (CO) to Lieutenant-Colonel Steele (WO), 16/2/59; CO 926/1108.

186 See criticism in CO 926/1110 of Byford-Jones's *Grivas and the Story of EOKA* and in CO 926/1108 on Captain H. Stacpoole's 'Against Two Colonels', which was refused publication rights.

187 *Daily Mail* (19/3/59), 'Here we go again ... deceiving ourselves over Grivas!', Henry Fairlie, p. 8.

188 Specific reference was made to Fairlie's article; see 'Secret. Minutes of the Information Policy Committee Meeting held Friday 20 March 1959'; CO 1027/155.

189 'Note prepared by Mr. Glass, Nicosia, on publicity material about Cyprus, for BIS etc. overseas', 1/6/56, PG11926/22; FO 953/1694.

190 See, for example, the pamphlet *Why We Are in Cyprus*; FO 953/1701.

191 Minute by R. Terrell to J. Thompson, 23/1/56; CO 926/394. As has already been seen, though, not all his colleagues agreed with respect to the 'reformability' of AKEL detainees.

192 See, for example, correspondence in FO 953/1695; a minute by D.E.T. Luard of the IPD suggested that a paper on the Turkish attitude, 'describing the strength of Turkish feelings' on Cyprus, for the use of British information officers might be helpful; minute dated 21/7/56, PG11926/42.

193 *Why We Are in Cyprus*, op. cit., p. 4.

194 Telegram from Harding to Lennox-Boyd, 7/1/57, no. 34; in CO 1027/159.

195 Letter from Peck to Stewart, 9/11/56, PG11926/206; FO 953/1706. Significantly, Peck's suggested remedy, with respect to hostile American audiences, was 'to play the Turkish card very hard'.

196 Furthermore, Britain had no wish to see the NATO alliance in the Eastern Mediterranean crumble, not least as the government was highly alarmed by the overthrow of the friendly regime of Nuri es-Said in Iraq; Darwin, *Britain and Decolonisation*, pp. 280–1.

197 C. Allen, *The Savage Wars of Peace: Soldiers' Voices 1945–1989* (Futura, London, 1990) p. 139. As Harding wrote, in tones redolent of the Malayan Emergency, 'In areas like the Kyrenia Range and the Troodos Mountains or even in the back streets and alleyways of the main towns, this was more like looking for a needle in a bundle of hay than anything I had encountered before'; *Daily Telegraph* (8/1/58), p. 13.

198 D. Barker refers to the photograph of Demetriades as 'one of the most pathetic of the Cyprus emergency'; *Grivas*, p. 132. It subsequently emerged that this photograph had been taken by Nicos Sampson (an EOKA gunman and photographer), who had actually shot Demetriades' fiance before shooting him on film.

199 *Daily Herald* (7/8/56 and 8/8/56). The *Daily Express* (7/8/56) featured the 'striped dress' photograph as a 'flashback to July 25', although this had not been carried at the time of the murder.

200 Telegram from Harding to Lennox-Boyd, 6/8/56, no. 1587, PG11926/78; FO 953/1697.

201 See the criticisms made by the Head of the COID, O.H. Morris, to Harold Evans in a note dated 5/11/57, RGC1682/13/G; FO 371/130159.

202 Letter from S.H. Hebblethwaite to S.H. Evans, 10/9/56, PG11926/132; FO 953/1701.

203 Letter from H.B. Shepherd (IPD) to Peck (BIS NY), 25/10/57, PG11926/116; FO 953/1828.
204 J.D. Higham (CO) to G.E. Sinclair (FO Southern Dept.), 8/11/57, RGC1682/12/G; FO 371/130159.
205 See a note contained in FO 953/1698, 'Reply to Greek Allegations of British Atrocities in Cyprus' (undated, but c. June 1956).
206 See the correspondence in CO 926/564.
207 Minute by Kirkness to Morris, 19/6/57, CO 926/880.
208 Kirkness noted, 'it seems increasingly probable that an investigation would unearth certain instances of brutality, probably by the Special Branch or by interrogators, which cannot be contained in the category of violence in the course of arrest of desperate men'; ibid.
209 Minute by W.A. Morris to Melville, 20/6/57; CO 926/880.
210 A small number of men were tried and found guilty of offences in this way: *The Smear Technique: The Propaganda Use of Mendacious Allegations of Torture*; CO 1027/156.
211 *Allegations of Brutality by British Forces in Cyprus Refuted*, p. 1, 11/6/57, PG11926/85; FO 953/1825.
212 Ibid., pp. 9–10. See also *The Smear Technique*, CO 1027/156.
213 Oliver Woods to Haley, 1/7/57; Oliver Woods MSS, Confidential Memoranda (1953–70), *The Times* Archive.
214 'General Note on Alleged Mal-Treatment of Persons Held in Custody by the Security Forces', enclosed in a letter from P. Storrs to Horace White, 1/3/57, CO 1027/156.
215 Foley, *Legacy of Strife*, p. 32.
216 Telegram from Harding to Lennox-Boyd, 21/3/56; CO 926/507.
217 Reuters report from Nicosia of a statement by Glass, dated 15/12/56; CO 926/507.
218 *New Statesman and Nation*, vol. 52, no. 1343 (8/12/56), unsigned article, 'A Tangled Web . . .', p. 733.
219 As the *Spectator* aptly remarked, the *Times of Cyprus* 'causes more apoplexy in Government circles than any other subject except the inadequacy of living allowances. It is regarded in Government circles with the same loathing as the *Daily Worker* must be in the Carlton Club'; vol. 199, no. 6743, (20/9/57), 'Cypriot and Turk', p. 357.
220 *Spectator*, vol. 198, no. 6707 (11/1/57), 'A Spectator's Notebook', p. 40.
221 *Sunday Dispatch* (25/5/57), 'This British Terror Must Be Stopped', Iris Russell. For Harding's response, see his telegram to Lennox-Boyd, 27/5/57, no. 846; CO 926/880.
222 Minute by Carstairs to Sir John Martin, 28/5/57; CO 926/880.
223 Minute by P.R. Noakes, 3/6/57; CO 926/880.
224 Telegram from Lennox-Boyd to Harding, 30/5/57, no. 789; CO 926/880.
225 Minute by Noakes, 19/5/57; CO 1027/155.
226 Minute by Melville, 29/5/57; CO 1027/154.
227 Shortly after his June 1957 statement on EOKA's atrocity allegations, Harding took umbrage at an article (entitled 'What Have You to Hide, Sir John?') by the veteran foreign correspondent James Cameron, in the *News Chronicle* on 14 June 1957. Two days later Harding forwarded to Lennox-Boyd a letter to the *News Chronicle*'s editor (which Church House urged him to forget); CO 1027/154.
228 *Daily Express* (1/7/55) 'Troops Stole Guns – jailed', p. 1.
229 Text of leaflet distributed in Nicosia on 4/10/58; CO 926/897.
230 *Evening Standard* (5/11/58), '"Vengeance" Briton Jailed in Cyprus', Mark Wilson.
231 Minute by P.H.G. Wright, 10/11/58, PG11910/19; FO 953/1864.
232 *Daily Herald* (23/10/58), 'Bring Me Dead Terrorists', p. 5.
233 Confidential minute by P.H.G. Wright to F.R.H. Murray, 20/11/58, PG11910/23; FO 953/1864.

234 During the July 1958 offensive against EOKA, Foot, according to the *Daily Herald*'s Dennis Pitts, slapped on the 'most rigorous curfew in the island's history . . . imposing total censorship on the press and radio'. Reporters were prevented from moving, even between villages, and telephone communications were cut off for a total of twenty-two hours; (23/7/58), 'Biggest Ever Clamp Now Grips Cyprus', p. 1. See also the *Observer* (10/8/58), p. 4, on the press being barred from observing military round-up operations in central Cyprus. Such complaints were a longstanding feature of the campaign; on 31 Aug. 1957 the *Manchester Guardian* reported that British and American correspondents, together with newsreel and photographic agency representatives, had walked out of a meeting with government and security forces public relations officers, when the latter insisted on its being off the record. The meeting had been called by the journalists who wished to register their complaints of 'suppression, mishandling and delays' in operational and other news.

235 S. Foot, *Emergency Exit*, p. 36.

236 See a minute by O.H. Morris, 28/11/58, CO 1027/135.

237 This phrase was used by Storrs in a letter to O.H. Morris, 27/12/57; CO 1027/162.

238 Director of Operations, Instruction no. 3, 28/10/58, SECRET, RGC1018/53; FO 371/136285. Commanders were also instructed to bring home to all ranks that there was 'a world of difference between quick and effective action against the terrorists, and a "bullying" attitude towards the person halted for checking or screening'.

239 Telegram from Acting Governor to Lennox-Boyd, 11/5/58, no. 628; CO 926/882.

240 In December 1958, Sir John Martin told Lennox-Boyd of the prospective visit of Ralph Murray (now Under-Secretary of State in the Foreign Office) to Cyprus to look into the question of psychological warfare. Minute dated 5/12/58; CO 1027/135.

241 Heavily loaded captions beneath such photographs often prompted the reader into an 'appropriate' response; see for example the *Daily Herald* (7/10/58), where in the wake of the Cutliffe murder a photograph appeared on p. 4, captioned 'A face of cruel dedication . . . a face of stop-at-nothing determination . . . the face of a captured terrorist'.

242 White to Storrs, 8/1/57, PG11926/9; FO 953/1818.

243 Foley describes the discreet distribution of atrocity photographs to journalists at Government House; *Legacy of Strife*, p. 97.

244 *Picture Post* (22/9/56). The story focused on conditions in the most notorious centre, Camp K (Kokkinotrimithia), and utterly refuted any Hitlerian analogy. The photographic illustrations showed prisoners bringing their own beds, talking freely with visiting relatives and resting in the sickbay (bedecked with a picture of Makarios).

245 Letter from N.E. Cox to Horace White, 7/1/57, PG11926/9; FO 953/1818.

246 Letter from Fletcher-Cooke to Cox, 21/8/56, PG11926/98; FO 953/1699.

247 This need was expressed at a meeting on 16/7/56 on Cyprus publicity held in the IPD, PG11926/41; FO 953/1695.

248 Letter from Fletcher-Cooke to Glass, 16/7/56, PG11926/44; FO 953/1695.

249 See a letter from N.E. Cox to Horace White, 11/12/56; the former was worried by the 'dearth of good publicity photos from Cyprus' but suggested that in Lady Harding's activities there was 'good scope for photography', PG11926/215; FO 953/1706.

250 No feature film tackled the Cyprus Emergency until 1965 when Ralph Thomas's *The High Bright Sun* was released (viewing copy held in the NFA). This Rank production was an adaptation by Ian Stuart Black of his novel of the same name (*The High Bright Sun*, Hutchinson, London, 1962). However, during the Emergency itself and in the years immediately after, the BBC had produced a number of television plays which fictionally dealt with aspects of the Cyprus situation; these included Troy Kennedy Martin's *Incident at Echo Six* (screened on 6/12/58), which examined the strains

experienced by young officers commanding troops in Cyprus and the same author's more controversial play about British Army interrogation methods, *The Interrogator* (screened on 22/12/61); BBC WAC scripts archive.

251 Letter from Smedley (CRO) to Millard (10 Downing Street), 18/6/56, PG11926/16; FO 953/1693.

252 See a telegram from Harding to Lennox-Boyd, 14/1/57, no. 70, and telegram no. 137 from Sir Harold Caccia (British Ambassador in Washington) to the Foreign Office, 25/1/57, PG11926/14; FO 953/1818.

253 Letter from Christopher to Hill, 10/11/58; CO 1027/317.

254 Minute from P.H.G. Wright to Major-General A.C. Shortt (WO), 23/12/58; CO 1027/137.

255 A Movietone item of 19/12/55, 'Cyprus Outrage' (no. 65441), for example, showed the scene in Ledra Street a few minutes after a 'terrorist outrage' had occurred. The camera showed scenes of confusion and destruction, playing on the emotive shot of a toyshop window shattered by bullet holes, and the commentary ended with the solemn warning that 'attacks like this underline the grim and hazardous conditions with which the serviceman in Cyprus is still confronted'.

256 See, for example, a Movietone item, 'Cyprus Bulletin', 19/1/56 (no. 65700), in which the 'British Tommies' were seen enjoying fish and chips (two of their 'three basic needs') in Nicosia.

257 For example, Movietone no. 67392, 'Cyprus, Terrorists on the Run' (21/6/56) and no. 69609, 'Operation Black Mac' (28/1/57); and Pathé no. 56-50, 'Cyprus Catastrophe' (21/6/56) and no. 56-51, 'Cyprus Fire' (25/6/56).

258 Movietone no. 73974, 'Cyprus Security Search' (27/5/58).

259 Movietone no. 68541, 'Operation Sparrowhawk' (15/10/56); here we see British soldiers helping old women and children, and befriending a small apple-eating Cypriot boy.

260 British Movietone no. 64968, 'Cyprus – Latest Dispatches' (27/10/55).

261 Mayes, *Cyprus and Makarios*, p. xi.

262 In answer to a Parliamentary Question put by Shinwell in March 1959, the Secretary of State for War (Soames) replied that fifty-seven officers and 1,340 of other ranks had been convicted by court martial since November 1955, with twenty-two officers and 353 others detained; extract from H.C. Debs, 11/3/59 in CO 926/882.

263 Foley, *Legacy of Strife*, p. 157.

Conclusion

There are several gaps in the literature on terrorism and the media, and on counter-insurgency more broadly, which this book may have started to fill. At one level, it addresses the inattention to historical background found in much writing on terrorism. Terrorism – even international terrorism – was not born in 1968. After all, Lehi had attacked targets beyond Palestine, in both Italy and Britain, during its campaign in the 1940s. Similarly, the perception that terrorism is essentially publicity-seeking, and consequently that any strategy for countering it must involve working with the mass communications media, has had greater longevity than is frequently supposed. Thus many of the concerns of policy-makers and the military in the period examined in this book (from 1944 to 1960) when confronted with what they regarded as terrorism, and many of the attempted remedies, have in fact been very similar to the dilemmas faced in (what is all too often seen as) the era of 'terrorism proper'. If this historical blind spot forms a weakness in the terrorism literature, a general criticism of the counter-insurgency genre is its inattention to the question of public opinion beyond the locus of the insurgency. It is generally accepted that 'winning hearts and minds' on the ground is one of the key constituents of a successful counter-insurgency strategy.[1] But the issue of how metropolitan governments and their militaries have attempted to legitimate the measures used to defeat colonial insurgencies in the eyes of international, and especially domestic, opinion has been neglected.

Why should this be so? Perhaps writers have tended to think, as Templer professed to, that it did not particularly matter what people in Britain thought about events in far-off colonies of which they knew little and cared even less. Crossman was undoubtedly right when he claimed that no election would be won or lost over Palestine – and the same could be said of each of the Emergencies examined. But to extrapolate from this that governments and their bureaucracies are consequently unconcerned about public perceptions of actions carried out in the name of the state – albeit in distant locations – would be misleading. What I hope this book has shown is that domestic public opinion *has* mattered: governments *do* wish to mediate how events are perceived, particularly when they believe their opponents are also contesting the same psychological territory.

Confronted with terrorism, government publicity staffs have faced intractable dilemmas. As we have seen in Palestine, Malaya, Cyprus, and to a lesser degree in Kenya, colonial officials believed that the terrorists were, in each case, aiming at people's hearts and minds, speaking not only to their own constituency but to wider international audiences. To cut off insurgent propaganda at source proved impracticable: underground printing presses enabled the pamphlet war to continue in each case, while attempts at jamming insurgent radio broadcasts also proved ineffective in Palestine and Cyprus. In each instance, the local vernacular press – often thought to be tendentious and a source (wittingly or otherwise) of psychological support to the 'terrorists', even if not under their direct control – was dealt with harshly, and subjected to rigorous censorship. But officials also faced the larger question of how to prevent the communications media from, as they saw it, playing the terrorists' game. Despite measures taken to influence reportage, we have seen that governments frequently conceptualized their position in the battle with the insurgents for media compliance as unwinnable. Government servants tended to assume that for the insurgents, just to have their existence and deeds reported was sufficient to represent a victory over the state they challenged. Terrorist deeds were themselves a form of propaganda, and the media, to some degree, unavoidably favoured the insurgents simply by reporting them. As Sir Thomas Lloyd remarked at the outset of the Malayan Emergency:

> The danger we fear is that, by the very fact of their continuing resistance against authority, men who were at the start no more than a band of thugs preying on the law-abiding members of the community may attract to themselves some of the glamour of national heroes. . . . The dividing line between the terrorist and the fighter for freedom is not always so clear in the minds of the outside world or to the people of the terrorists' own country as it seems to us.[2]

A widespread belief that part of the terrorist strategy is simply to keep their existence in the public eye has been encouraged by statements to this effect in the memoirs of Begin, Grivas and certain former Mau Mau members, as we have seen.

As with later British administrations, the tendency of those studied here to think that any reportage of terrorists' deeds was to their advantage generated a readiness to censor or suppress news of terrorism. We saw, for example, Sir Henry Gurney's frustration that the BBC's broadcasts on Malayan, as on Zionist, terrorism did the terrorist's 'job for him to his complete satisfaction'. Thus at times officials have wished for less news of terrorism to rectify the impression (as Gurney put it) that life was just a 'series of incidents'.[3] In the case of Makarios, Macmillan's government attempted to persuade the BBC to keep him from the small screen altogether. However, in each of the case studies contradictory impulses were at work. Recognizing that it could never be possible to cut off the 'oxygen of publicity' altogether, government publicists have generally put more effort into ensuring that terrorism was properly understood: that the insurgents' deeds were framed in a moral context which highlighted the illegitimacy of both the methods employed and the end to which they were directed. Thus Whitehall information staff, and their counterparts in the territories concerned, denigrated not only terrorism *per se* but sought to show that: a Zionist state would encroach on Arab rights, and unsettle the whole Middle East; Cyprus enjoined to Greece would similarly oppress the Turkish minority, while destabilizing NATO; Malaya could not be allowed to fall under the Communist rule of a minority ethnic group; or that a Mau Mau-dominated Kenya would mean the subjugation by one tribe of the others. Indeed, in the case of Palestine, officials thought initially that a surfeit of news about terrorism in the right quarters might be sufficient to stop Zionist terrorism in its tracks.

The government's dilemma in seeking to regulate, as far as possible, the level and tenor of reportage of terrorism was compounded by the fact that it could prove counter-productive to encourage too much domestic popular outrage against terrorism, as the Palestine case showed. Likewise, Macmillan's government faced the embarrassment of a retired general planning to have Makarios arrested for murder, using the goverment's own propaganda publications as evidence. If the insurgents did not seek to arouse sympathy in Britain for their cause so much as a groundswell of popular revulsion against lingering in a colony where the toll of lives was too great, then to emphasize the despicable nature of terrorism did not necessarily serve the government's cause. Yet in no case was the denigration of terrorism abandoned, because government publicists also had to demonstrate the legitimacy of their own actions, and highlighting the bankruptcy of the enemy's tactics was clearly central to this process. Thus an absence of news concerning acts of terrorism also held its dangers.

The reasons why influencing *British* opinion mattered in these various counter-insurgency campaigns varied, and they suggest that it is too simplistic to assume that governments are concerned only about public opinion on issues over which elections are directly fought. Colonial matters and decolonization did not have such powerful reverberations in Britain as in France. No individual British colony occupied the place in the nation's psyche that Algeria did in the French, and none of Britain's counter-insurgencies led to the toppling of a government as France's protracted struggle in North Africa did. Nevertheless, by the 1950s in Britain colonial policy was hotly contested between government and opposition. Thus, even if elections were not fought directly on colonial or foreign policy issues (after all, the Suez débâcle did not lead to the election of a Labour government following Eden's demise), governments may well have been anxious about an incremental erosion of public confidence in them should they appear to be handling colonial affairs maladroitly.

There were other reasons why governments attempted to influence hearts and minds at home. British opinion was at times thought capable of actually influencing the direction of the campaign within the colony: thus Attlee's government, for example, wanted the Zionist insurgents and their supporters (actual or potential) to realize that the British public – not just their government – condemned terrorist methods, and were determined not to surrender to intimidation. Such sentiments when expressed by Fleet Street formed a useful bulwark against the propaganda of the insurgents and their fellow travellers.

It certainly does not seem that governments ever encouraged ignorance in Britain of events in colonies, even if at times they may have wished that the media focused less exclusively on terrorism. Thus we saw in the case of Malaya, which in Britain was the least-reported conflict studied in this book, that Whitehall officials tried to *encourage* journalists to take an interest in the battle being fought in Malaya's jungles and rubber plantations. At least one Colonial Office member even contemplated 'something on the lines of the "Zinoviev letter"' to 'give that necessary jolt' which would stir the British people from their 'apathy over their colonial commitments'. Winning the hearts and minds of the indigenous population of Malaya required the latter to be reassured that 'although Britain was thousands of miles away, she was interested in their welfare'.[4]

Domestic and international power struggles also affected both how terrorism was presented and to whom. Cold War considerations permeated British governments' responses to all these insurgencies. Within Britain this resulted in trade union opinion forming a target of politicians' and publicists' attention. Certainly Attlee's administrations demonstrated concern that trade unionists, exposed as they were to Communist propaganda, were the section of the public most likely to be influenced by an alternative version of where legitimacy lay in colonial struggles. Thus the Foreign Office's anti-Communist Information Research Department played a considerable role in passing unattributable briefing material to trade unions via Transport House and the Labour Party's international department. In this instance, the Colonial and Foreign Offices felt it important not only to correct 'misunderstandings' on Malaya but to discredit Communist anti-imperialist propaganda more broadly. As the Colonial Office's N.D. Watson put it: 'If wrong information could be put about in this effective and widespread way on one occasion, the process could be repeated on others.'[5] The job of Whitehall propagandists was to ensure that the process was not. British governments were also sensitive to the effects which Communist (particularly Soviet) propaganda might have beyond the United Kingdom. Recognizing its appeal among growing number of newly independent states and peoples who aspired to that status, HMG had no wish to be seen, in any of these conflicts, to be putting down national liberation movements, or denying the right of self-determination. Showing that the terrorists lacked representative status was thus a recurring concern.[6]

As we have seen, the battle to de-legitimize opponents was waged partly through linguistic strategies. In each case, the importance which governments and insurgents attached to the process of labelling has become apparent. At the outset we queried whether governments have consciously sought to influence the language with which their opponents are described, and specifically whether the word 'terrorist' has been regarded as carrying a particular stigma. Although, as one might expect, both these questions could generally be answered in the affirmative, there have been notable occasions when the word 'terrorist' has been deliberately avoided. Thus in the case of Palestine we found that, precisely because they wished to signify the stigma attached to the type of violence employed by the Irgun and Lehi, the British military came to reject the word 'terrorist'. That term had, they felt, come to acquire undue glamour, and was to be replaced with words – like 'thug' or 'felon' – which better expressed the common criminality of the insurgents' deeds. In Malaya, members of the MRLA were officially 'bandits' for some years before becoming 'Communist Terrorists': partly, it will be recalled, on account of the insurance implications of giving 'bandits' a more threatening label, and partly because this appelation seemed to deflate the enemy's claim to represent a national liberation movement. When a change in terminology occurred, use of the word 'terrorists' was also intended to signify that a tougher approach to the MRLA was being adopted, as the Foreign Office had long been urging.

In the case of Malaya, the question of naming the enemy was also related to governmental debate over how far to acknowledge the insurgents' Communism, and whether or not to conjure up an international Communist conspiracy behind the 'banditry'. To portray the MCP as influenced by either the Chinese or the Soviet Communist Party (or both, or neither) carried local and international implications. While not wishing to suggest to the Malayan Chinese that the MCP was such a powerful international 'bandwagon' that they should leap on it, the government also wanted the propaganda line to serve the broader aims of encouraging a Sino-Soviet split, and of demonstrating to the United States that Britain was doing its fair share of containment in South East Asia. While in each Emergency (with the exception of Palestine, where the Zionist insurgents were portrayed as Fascistic rather than Communistic), government propagandists saw certain advantages in suggesting that 'terrorists' were also Communists, they have not always played on popular, particularly American, anti-Communism. With respect to Cyprus, for example, although the benefits of suggesting that EOKA was tainted with Communism were not lightly abandoned, not all Whitehall officials agreed that Britain should pander to Americans' desire to see a Red under every bed. Likewise, with respect to Mau Mau a debate ensued over whether to play on presumptions that Communists were involved in, or would seek to profit from, the insurgency. Indeed, disputes over the role of anti-Communist themes in the denigration of terrorism demonstrate clear fissures between Whitehall departments. The different approaches of the Colonial and Foreign Offices to propaganda are most clearly revealed in the clashes between Church House and the Foreign Office's Information Research Department: while the latter was prepared to stretch the facts in the service of the wider political cause, the Colonial Office was generally more scrupulous about evidence. The IRD's more cavalier attitude towards factual accuracy may partly be explained by the department's self-preservation instinct: its *raison d'être* was the existence of a 'Communist threat', and if the latter dried up, then presumably so too would the IRD. Some exaggeration of the threat was perhaps to be expected. Conceivably, one might also postulate that the IRD's ethos derived much more from the Political Warfare Executive's attitude towards 'facts' than the MOI's 'strategy of truth' in wartime. Many of the IRD's early personnel, including its first head, Ralph Murray, had been members of the PWE. In its black and grey activities especially, the PWE had tended to be less concerned about 'the truth' than its counterparts at either the BBC or the MOI, Sir Robert Bruce Lockhart (its head) regarding 'absolute or "straight" news' as a 'chimera' owing to 'personal factors and the limits of time and space'.[7] Fondness for various forms of black and covert activities did not evaporate at the end of the war, no doubt because, as Hugh Carleton Greene as aptly observed, they appeal 'to the small boy's heart which still beats under the black jacket or the be-ribboned tunic'.[8] A number of such men found a place to practise their skills in the IRD.

Even when Whitehall tried to suggest the contrary, the notion that Communists lay behind all anti-colonial unrest was taken up with alacrity by much of the British media and public, who feared that these largely invisible enemies might in fact be a fifth column for a more globally threatening foe. During each insurgency, there was much fevered looking for signs of Communist involvement from officials on the ground and the British press and public alike. Small details acquired undue significance: thus, for example, Baring's worried report to Lyttelton that a well-thumbed copy of *Teach Yourself Russian* had been found in a Kikuyu hut.[9] Representations of terrorism in popular culture were similarly keen to uncover Communist infiltration: from Ruark and Huxley's portrayal of Russian involvement in the planning of Mau Mau, to Diana Buttenshaw's thinly veiled fictional island of 'Sophos', where an unholy alliance of Communists and clerics had formed the 'Szit' movement, fighting for 'Halitos' with the Motherland.[10]

While government attempts at news management were not always successful where they ran against the news media's own preoccupations, the case studies are revealing of the ways in which Whitehall set about exerting influence. Reliance was largely placed on informal channels

265

of communication: pressure on Fleet Street, newsreel and television companies was exercised by discreet words in the appropriate ear. On the question of persuading the BBC not to interview Makarios, for example, Charles Hill made a telling reference to his customary 'informal chats' with the BBC's Harman Grisewood.[11] A subtle 'carrot and stick' system was operated, whereby 'helpful' editors were rewarded with privileged access to secret information, such as fuller details of the more depraved Mau Mau oaths, while others were denied it. Well-disposed papers were also amenable to Whitehall attempts to 'inspire' articles on aspects of the Emergencies which the government wished to publicize. In all the case studies, although the government produced its own publicity material (principally through the COI in the UK), the emphasis was primarily on news management, in London and, more importantly, at source in the territory concerned.

The case studies also reveal that the 'Whitehall way' was not always applied on the ground. There was much more heavy-handedness among colonial governments and the military in their dealings with the media. Indeed, a pattern is discernible from the examples of Malaya, Kenya and Cyprus: what had been an inadequate information office at the outset was overhauled (with varying speed), in tandem with the appointment of a tougher Governor or High Commissioner. Even where this 'supremo' was not himself a military man, the military were simultaneously given a higher profile in the counter-insurgency, and thus had greater powers over the release of news, and more contact with the media. Meanwhile, the colony requested appointment of a special public relations officer to look after presentation of news at the London end. On the ground, propaganda and psychological warfare were soon regarded as central to defeating insurgents – often without a real understanding of the limitations on what both could achieve. But the colonial governments and the military became increasingly defensive as accusations, in all cases, of brutality on the part of the security forces mounted. In each case, as the Colonial Office's P.R. Noakes put it, 'an extreme sensitivity to press criticism developed', which produced inappropriate measures to try to curb the unruly local and international press.[12]

Mediating the presentation of terrorism was thus never the whole story. Westminster, in conjunction with the colonial government, had to defend its own actions, and even Britain's very presence in the territory: where propaganda was employed to de-legitimize terrorism it was also used to project the positive British achievements in the contested colonies. The declaration of a State of Emergency inevitably drew attention to conditions in that colony, and to Britain's plans for its future once terrorism had been defeated. Government propagandists thus found that their work had to consist of a judicious mixture of positive and negative themes. As one recent analyst of the Northern Ireland Office's publicity output has written, HMG does not simply want, as is commonly assumed, images of senseless violence to predominate in the British public's perception of life in Northern Ireland: 'they also want "good news" coverage which does not automatically fit with the news values operated by many media outlets'.[13] The same could equally be said of these colonial insurgencies, although less effort was devoted to this work in Palestine. Elsewhere, however, the government flew in the face of the British media's news values to provide images of, for example, Lady Harding's charitable deed in Cyprus and Alan Lennox-Boyd's inspection tours of housing projects in Kenya.

There was not, then, always a complete identification of interest between government and media. Although the British media were generally keen to condemn terrorism as such (and doubtless would have done without Whitehall's promptings), sections of the British press, in particular, were not always so ready to laud the government's achievements in the colonies or to sanction certain methods of counter-insurgency. We have seen a recurrent concern lest 'black-and-tannery' reappear in various colonial settings – though this was more pronounced during some Emergencies than others. Over Malaya, perhaps because it was generally neglected by the British press and public alike, or possibly because the enemy in question were Communists, there was little visible concern at the use of head-hunting Dyaks, the pattern bombing of jungle areas, or Templer's collective punishments. But there was greater public, press and parliamentary unease over the way in which the campaign against Mau Mau was prosecuted, this despite the fact that no one – 'even of the sympathetic left' – in Britain, or the West generally, regarded Mau Mau as 'the plea of a nation-in-waiting'.[14] That voice of the Establishment *The Times* prided itself on acting as a moral conscience to the government over the conduct of the counter-insurgency in Kenya. Perhaps the Tory backbencher 'Cub' Alport was right when he wrote to his friend Michael Blundell that Conservative opinion was moving in an 'unexpectedly liberal direction' on the whole subject of race relations, which resulted in alarm at the number of Kikuyu being executed in Kenya.[15] What could have been more unexpected than Enoch Powell in July 1959 making a blistering attack on his own government over the Hola camp tragedy, in which he insisted that 'We cannot say, "We will have African standards in Africa, Asian standards in Asia and perhaps British standards here at home"'?[16]

The fact that the government did not always succeed in its attempts at news management raises the almost unanswerable question of the success of the propaganda effort sustained during each of these Emergencies. When such a question is posed, what sort of success are we trying to gauge, and how can it be measured? Generally, assessments made at the time of each insurgency were negative. In each one, criticisms were voiced that the government was neglecting propaganda, that it was failing to reach into the hearts and minds of the indigenous population, or that the colony's information services were disorganized. Some of this carping may have been justified: it did, in most cases, take some time to build up the local information staff, and they did not always remain long in post or establish sound working partnerships with the policy-makers. This suggests that Mockaitis's notion of a 'learning curve' via which Britain steadily learnt the precepts of successful counter-insurgency needs some adjustment, at least in the sphere of propaganda. Moreover, during each Emergency, propagandists felt hampered by a sense of alienation from the local population – a gulf which was psychological and cultural as much as linguistic. A recurrent doubt was expressed, as one Colonial Office official remarked with reference to the Malayan Communists, as to whether British propagandists had 'the technique to win the hearts and minds of chaps like this'.[17] If government information officers did not know who their enemy was in a literal sense – friend and foe often appearing indistinguishable on the ground – nor did they not know how the enemy thought, or how to address appeals to the indigenous populace as a whole. It is easy to conclude that the Chinese Malayans must have been puzzled by literally translated invocations to come 'off the fence'; or that leaflets 'with quotations from the House of Commons explaining why the West African solution was not suitable for Kenya's problems' – which Hugh Fraser MP found on a trip into a 'backward public lavatory in a backward area' of Kenya – probably found a different use from that intended.[18] Colonial officials and propagandists were of course right to regard their audiences as holding cultural values different from their own, even if many of their assumptions about the populations of these colonies were crudely racist. It is perhaps a peculiarity of certain Western states to regard, for example, killing for political motives in any situation other than a declared war as immoral. How were British propagandists to know whether or not their audiences thought the same? The answer lay in the recruitment of indigenous assistants (including surrendered terrorists like Lam Swee), and settlers who claimed to have authoritative insight into the mind-set of the colonized (most notably Louis Leakey in Kenya).[19] In the case of Palestine, however, officials appear to have judged that the idea of Zionism (and the perception of Britain's illegitimacy in the Holy Land) was too deeply entrenched to be susceptible to counter-propaganda.

Much of the contemporaneous criticism of Britain's propaganda effort during these insurgencies was based on ignorance of the actual extent of this work since so much of it, especially outside the territory itself, was carried on as undetectably as possible. Whitehall exhibited considerable squeamishness over being seen to be engaged in propaganda: the IRD's work was almost entirely secret, and British publicity material generally tried not to draw attention to itself as 'propaganda'. We have seen, too, that answers to Parliamentary Questions on Britain's propaganda often greatly underemphasized the actual extent of this work. Other criticisms of this type of activity were based on common misunderstandings about what propaganda can achieve and how it operates. Often, as Harold Evans remarked on the aftermath of the Suez débâcle, 'a failure in policy was being attributed to a failure in communication'.[20] Too many people, like Baring in Kenya, expected propaganda to work miracles in a vacuum, regardless of what politicians did. Many criticisms of propaganda were thus really attacks on government policy or the lack thereof. As we have seen, the propagandists themselves frequently expressed frustration at an absence of policy. For propaganda on any of these campaigns to have been really successful – if Tugwell is right that success is ultimately dependent on the government's having a clear and consistent message[21] – HMG would have needed a firm sense of purpose at outset. This felicitous state of affairs came closest to achievement in Malaya, where Templer was able to promise the indigenous population in 1952 that they would be independent in 1957. In reaching any conclusion, a measure of generosity seems due to both propagandists and policy-makers in each Emergency. While it is easy to condemn government vacillation, the conditions which allowed Templer's offer to be made in Malaya were not replicated elsewhere. In Malaya Britain had moderate Malay politicians groomed for leadership, but it took longer to realize in both Kenya and Cyprus that an 'arch-terrorist' would have to be moulded into this role. In the cases of Palestine and Cyprus, where various states were affected by, and thus attempted to influence, the settlement, choosing any one solution for the territory's future inevitably meant treading on some toes. In the late 1940s and 1950s, successive British governments were still feeling their way towards ending Britain's imperial commitments and calculating whose toes they could best afford to tread on, in the straitened post-war circumstances. It is thus not surprising that a clear policy on the future of contested colonies was often slow to emerge.

To sum up, then, British propaganda in what was peacetime at home was more widespread than one might imagine, though its precise extent is often frustratingly unknowable. It is to be hoped that the present government carries through its stated intent of opening the files of the IRD to public inspection. These would doubtless prove a salutary corrective to the notion that hearts and minds in the United Kingdom were not thought important during anticolonial struggles. The impact of propaganda is sufficiently hard to judge that it can be tempting to question 'did it make a difference?'. Although we cannot quantify the answer precisely, we should not abandon the endeavour. Perhaps one of the most illuminating aspects of any study of propaganda is to ascertain what governments *hoped* it would achieve, why they thought it necessary to persuade certain audiences, and how they alighted on particular messages. In each case study we have seen that governments have hoped to influence how the media reported terrorism in order that audiences both in Britain and beyond would perceive the illegitimacy of the insurgents' resort to violence.[22] While words alone were not thought sufficient to win battles, they were regarded as weapons which helped to shape perceptions of battles, of who deserved to win and lose, and how those battles ought to have been fought.

Notes

1   See Mockaitis, *British Counterinsurgency*, Charters, 'From Palestine to Northern Ireland', in Charters and Tugwell (eds), *Armies in Low-Intensity Conflict*, and Tugwell, 'Revolutionary Propaganda', *passim*.

2   Letter from Sir T. Lloyd to Sir Franklin Gimson (High Commissioner for Singapore) and Sir Alexander Newboult, 23/8/48; CO 537/3758.

3   Letter from Gurney to Higham, 25/4/50; CO 537/6579.

4   Report of a conversation between H.L. Brigstocke and A.J.W. Hockenhull (CO Specialist on Chinese Affairs), in a memo to Oliver Woods; *The Times* Archive, Malaysia file (1949-70).

5   Minute by N.D. Watson to J.D. Higham, 26/10/48; CO 537/5123.

6   The same point is made in Frank Furedi's recent volume, *Colonial Wars and the Politics of Third World Nationalism*, *passim*.

7   K. Young (ed.), *The Diaries of Sir Robert Bruce Lockhart*, vol. 2 *(1939—65)* (Macmillan, London, 1980), Introduction, p. 25.

8   H. Carleton Greene, *The Third Floor Front* (The Bodley Head, London, 1969), p. 26; cited by Wark, 'Coming In from the Cold', p. 70.

9   Telegram from Baring to Lyttelton, 29/4/53, no. 513; CO 822/454.

10 See Huxley's *A Thing to Love*, Ruark's *Something of Value* and Buttenshaw's *Violence in Paradise*.

11 Hill to Macmillan, 16/6/58; PREM 11/2226.

12 Minute by Noakes, 3/6/57; CO 926/880.

13 Miller, 'The Northern Ireland Information Service and the media', in Eldridge (ed.), *Getting the Message*, p. 98.

14 Berman and Lonsdale, 'The Moral Economy of Mau Mau', *Unhappy Valley*, Book 2, p. 279.

15 Letter from 'Cub' Alport to Blundell, 2/3/55, Blundell MSS, Box 3/2.

16 Extract from the House of Commons debate on the Hola Camp affair, on 27/7/59, in R. Collings (ed.), *Reflections of a Statesman: The Writings and Speeches of Enoch Powell* (Bellew, London, 1991), p. 206.

17 Minute by T.C. Jerrom, 1/1/53; CO 1022/46.

18 'Report of a Visit to Kenya, 17 Sept.–5 Oct. 1953, by Hon. H.C.P.J. Fraser MBE, MP'; CO 822/479.

19 On Leakey's role in advising the Kenya government on the workings of the 'Kikuyu mind', see B. Berman and J. Lonsdale, 'Louis Leakey's Mau Mau: A Study in the Politics of Knowledge', *History and Anthropology*, 5, ii (1991), 143–204.

20 Evans, *Downing Street Diary*, p. 13.

21 Tugwell, *Revolutionary Propaganda*, p. 328.

22 Furedi indeed suggests that British efforts to denigrate movements such as Mau Mau and the MRLA were remarkably successful, if one assesses their impact over a prolonged period. Why else, he asks, do people still regard Mau Mau as so evil? Thus his conclusion: 'Representing anti-colonial forces as not "genuine nationalists" in the emergencies and in other instances helps to reinforce the view that Britain

did not have to give way to public opinion in the colonies. The recasting of anti-colonial nationalism through decolonization represented for Britain at least a partial victory. . . . That is why its interpretation continues to prevail'; *Colonial Wars and the Politics of Third World Nationalism*, p. 273.

Bibliography

Unpublished Sources

Public Record Office, Kew, Surrey

CABINET PAPERS

CAB	21	Cabinet Committees, registered files
CAB	23	Cabinet Minutes, Dec. 1916–Sept. 1939
CAB	24	Cabinet Memoranda, Jan. 1915–Sept. 1939
CAB	27	Cabinet Committees
CAB	43	Cabinet Office, Irish Papers
CAB	65	War Cabinet, Minutes & Conclusions, 1939-1945
CAB	128	Cabinet Conclusions, 1945–61
CAB	129	Cabinet Memoranda, 1945–61
CAB	130	Cabinet Committees, *ad hoc* committees, 1945–61
CAB	134	Cabinet Committees, 1945–61

COLONIAL OFFICE PAPERS

CO	67	Cyprus, original correspondence
CO	68	Cyprus, Acts
CO	533	Kenya, original correspondence
CO	537	Supplementary correspondence
CO	717	Malaya, original correspondence
CO	733	Palestine, original correspondence
CO	822	East Africa, original correspondence
CO	825	Eastern, original correspondence
CO	866	Establishment, original correspondence
CO	875	Public relations and information, original correspondence
CO	926	Mediterranean, original correspondence
CO	935	Confidential print, Middle East
CO	967	Private office papers
CO	968	Defence, original correspondence
CO	1022	South East Asia Department, original correspondence
CO	1027	Information Department, original correspondence

DOMINIONS OFFICE PAPERS

DO 35   Dominions Office and Commonwealth Relations Office, original correspondence

FOREIGN OFFICE PAPERS

FO 371   General political correspondence
FO 421   Confidential print
FO 800   Private collections, ministers and officials, various
FO 930   Information files
FO 953   Foreign publicity
FO 973   Briefing background papers

HOME OFFICE PAPERS

HO 45   Registered papers
HO 144   Registered papers, supplementary
HO 189   International Conference on the Repression of Terrorism in Geneva, 1934–36

INFORMATION FILES

INF 1   Ministry of Information correspondence, 1936–46
INF 5   Crown Film Unit
INF 6   Film production documents
INF 12   Central Office of Information, registered files

PRIME MINISTER'S OFFICE PAPERS

PREM 1   Correspondence and papers, 1916–40
PREM 4   Confidential papers, 1939–46
PREM 8   Correspondence and papers, 1945–51
PREM 11   Correspondence and papers, 1951–64

WAR OFFICE PAPERS

WO 32   Registered files, general series
WO 35   Army records
WO 106   Military operations and intelligence records
WO 169   War diaries
WO 191   Campaigns
WO 193   Director of Military Operations, collation files
WO 216   Chief of Imperial General Staff papers
WO 236   Erskine Papers

WO 261   Quarterly historical reports
WO 275   Sixth Airborne Division, papers
WO 276   East Africa Command, papers
WO 282   General Officer Commanding, files
WO 291   Military operational research

Private Papers

IMPERIAL WAR MUSEUM, LONDON

General Sir George Erskine (Boxes 75/134/1 and 75/134/4)
Major Ian Gibb (Manuscript Memoir, 'A Walk in the Forest: Being an Account of a Junior Army Officer in SE Asia,1945–50')
Brigadier G.A. Rimbault (Box 91/32/1)
W.H. Thompson (Box 89/13/1, Manuscript Memoir, 'Only the Foothills')

THE TIMES ARCHIVE, LONDON

George Kinnear
Oliver Woods

RHODES HOUSE, OXFORD

Kenneth Blackburne (MSS Brit. Emp. s.460)
Michael Blundell (MSS Afr. s.746)
Arthur Creech Jones (MSS Brit. Emp. s.332)
General W. Hinde (MSS Afr. s.1580)
W.H. Ingrams (MSS Brit. Emp. s.425)
W.H. Thompson (MSS Afr. s.1534)

NATIONAL ARMY MUSEUM, LONDON

Sir Gerald Templer (7410-29, 8011-132, 8301-6)
Lord Harding of Petherton (8908-144-1, 8908-144-5, 8908-144-14, 8908-144-18, 8908-144-19)

Archives

BBC WRITTEN ARCHIVE CENTRE, CAVERSHAM, BERKSHIRE

Policy files : E1, E2, R28, R34, R51
Current affairs scripts

Television drama scripts

MASS-OBSERVATION ARCHIVE, Brotherton Library, Leeds University

Microfiche of the Tom Harrisson Mass-Observation Archive, University of Sussex

Unpublished Theses

David John Clark, 'The Colonial Police and Anti-terrorism: Bengal 1930–36, Palestine 1937–47, and Cyprus 1955–59' (PhD thesis, Oxford University, 1978)

Catherine J. Morris, '"With Malice Towards None": Publicity Considerations in the Formulation and Conduct of the Labour Government's Policy towards Palestine, 1945–47' (MPhil thesis, University of Leeds, 1989)

Maurice Tugwell, 'Revolutionary Propaganda and Possible Countermeasures' (PhD thesis, King's College, London, 1979)

Published Sources

Parliamentary Papers

'Palestine: A Statement of Policy', Cmd 6019 (1939)

'Report of the Anglo-American Commission of Inquiry Regarding the Problems of European Jewry and Palestine', Cmd 6808 (1946)

'Palestine: Statement of Information Relating to Acts of Violence', Cmd 6873 (1946)

'Report to the Secretary of State for the Colonies by the Parliamentary Delegation to Kenya, January 1954', Cmd 9081 (1954)

'East Africa Royal Commission (Dow) Report', Cmd 9475 (1955)

'Correspondence Exchanged between the Governor and Archbishop Makarios, March 1956', Cmd 9708 (1956)

'Documents Relating to the Death of Eleven Mau Mau Detainees at Hola Camp in Kenya', Cmnd 778 (1959)

F.D. Corfield, 'Historical Survey of the Origins and Growth of Mau Mau', Cmnd 1030 (1960)

Memoirs

'Avner', *Memoirs of an Assassin: Confessions of a Stern Gang Killer* (Anthony Blond, London, 1959)

William W. Baldwin, *Mau Mau Manhunt: The Adventures of the Only American Who Has Fought the Terrorists in Kenya* (E.P. Dutton, New York, 1957)

Donald L. Barnett and Karari Njama, *Mau Mau from Within: Autobiography and Analysis of Kenya's Peasant Revolt* (MacGibbon and Kee, London, 1966)

Menachem Begin, *The Revolt* (Nash Publishing, New York, 1977)

Sir Michael Blundell, *So Rough a Wind* (Weidenfeld and Nicolson, London, 1964)

Fenner Brockway, *Outside the Right: A Sequel to 'Inside the Left'* (George Allen and Unwin, London, 1963)

Fenner Brockway, *Towards Tomorrow: The Autobiography of Fenner Brockway* (Hart-Davis, MacGibbon, London, 1977)

Fenner Brockway, *Ninety-Eight Not Out* (Quartet Books, London, 1986)

James Cameron, *Point of Departure* (Oriel Press, Stocksfield, 1978)

Alexander Campbell, *The Heart of Africa* (Longmans, Green, London, 1954)

Michael Carver, *Out of Step: Memoirs of a Field Marshal* (Hutchinson, London, 1989)

Lord Chandos, *The Memoirs of Lord Chandos* (Readers Union, London, 1964)

F. Spencer Chapman, *The Jungle Is Neutral* (Chatto and Windus, London, 1949)

Winston Churchill, *My African Journey* (Hodder and Stoughton, London, 1908)

William Clark, *From Three Worlds* (Sidgwick and Jackson, London, 1986)

Geula Cohen, *Woman of Violence: Memoirs of a Young Terrorist, 1943–1948* (Rupert Hart-Davis, London, 1966)

Richard Crossman, *Palestine Mission: A Personal Record* (Hamish Hamilton, London, 1946)

Brian Crozier, *Free Agent. The Unseen War, 1941–91: The Autobiography of an International Activist* (HarperCollins, London, 1993)

Moshe Dayan, *Story of My Life* (Sphere Books, London, 1977)

Sefton Delmer, *Black Boomerang* (Secker and Warburg, London, 1962)

Michaela Denis, *Ride a Rhino* (Companion Book Club, London, 1959)

Eric Downton, *Wars without End* (Stoddart, Toronto, 1987)

Lawrence Durrell, *Bitter Lemons* (Faber and Faber, London, 1959)

Sir Anthony Eden, *Full Circle* (Cassell, London, 1960)

Robert Edwards, *Goodbye Fleet Street* (Coronet Books, London, 1989)

Harold Evans, *Downing Street Diary: The Macmillan Years 1957–1963* (Hodder and Stoughton, London, 1981)

Roy Farran, *Winged Dagger: Adventures on Special Service* (Collins, London, 1948)

Bernard Fergusson, *The Trumpet in the Hall, 1930–58* (Collins, London, 1970)

Charles Foley (ed.), *The Memoirs of General Grivas* (Longmans, London, 1964)

Sir Hugh Foot, *A Start In Freedom* (Hodder and Stoughton, London, 1964)

Sylvia Foot, *Emergency Exit* (Chatto and Windus, London, 1960)

Graham Greene, *Ways of Escape* (Penguin Books, London, 1981)

James Griffiths, *Pages from Memory* (J.M. Dent, London, 1969)

Harman Grisewood, *One Thing at a Time: An Autobiography* (Hutchinson, London, 1968)

General George Grivas-Dighenis, *Guerrilla Warfare and EOKA's Struggle: A Politico-Military Study* (Longmans, Green, London, 1964)

Sir John Gutch, *Colonial Servant* (self-published, 1987)

Thomas Hamilton, *Soldier Surgeon in Malaya* (Angus and Robertson, Sydney, 1957)

Bibliography

Gerald Hanley, *Warriors and Strangers* (Hamish Hamilton, London, 1971)

Jack Hawkins, *Anything for a Quiet Life* (Elm Tree Books, London, 1973)

Ian Henderson and Philip Goodhart, *The Hunt for Kimathi* (Pan Books, London, 1962)

Louis Heren, *Growing Up on 'The Times'* (Hamish Hamilton, London, 1978)

Lord Hill, *Behind the Screen: The Broadcasting Memoirs of Lord Hill of Luton* (Sidgwick and Jackson, London, 1974)

Elspeth Huxley, *The Flame Trees of Thika: Memories of an African Childhood* (Chatto and Windus, London, 1959)

Elspeth Huxley, *A New Earth: An Experiment in Colonialism* (Chatto and Windus, London, 1960)

Elspeth Huxley, *Out in the Midday Sun: My Kenya* (Penguin Books, London, 1987)

Douglas Hyde, *I Believed: The Autobiography of a Former British Communist* (Reprint Society, London, 1952)

Edmund Ions, *A Call to Arms: Interlude with the Military* (David and Charles, Newton Abbot, 1972)

Waruhiu Itote, *Mau Mau in Action* (Transafrica, Nairobi, 1979)

Bildad Kaggia, *The Roots of Freedom, 1921–1963* (East African Publishing House, Nairobi, 1975)

Josiah Mwangi Kariuki, *'Mau Mau' Detainee: The Account by a Kenya African of His Experiences in Detention Camps 1953–60* (Penguin Books, Harmondsworth, 1964)

Samuel Katz, *Days of Fire* (W.H. Allen, London, 1968)

Frank Kitson, *Gangs and Counter-gangs* (Faber and Faber, London, 1960)

Frank Kitson, *Bunch of Five* (Faber and Faber, London, 1977)

Arthur Koestler, *The Invisible Writing* (Collins with Hamish Hamilton, London, 1954)

Derek Lambert, *Just Like the Blitz: A Reporter's Notebook* (Hamish Hamilton, London, 1987)

Bernard Llewellyn, *With My Back to the East* (Travel Book Club, London, 1958)

The Diaries of Sir Robert Bruce Lockhart. vol. 2 (*1939–65*), ed. K. Young (Macmillan, London, 1980)

Iverach McDonald, *A Man of 'The Times': Talks and Travels in a Disrupted World* (Hamish Hamilton, London, 1976)

Malcolm MacDonald, *My Two Jungles* (Harrap, London, 1957)

Harold Macmillan, *Tides of Fortune* (Macmillan, London, 1969)

Richard Miers, *Shoot to Kill* (Faber and Faber, London, 1959)

Alasdair Milne, *D.-G. The Memoirs of a British Broadcaster* (Coronet Books, London, 1989)

Sir Philip Mitchell, *African Afterthoughts* (Hutchinson, London, 1954)

J.W.G. Moran, *The Camp across the River* (Peter Davies, London, 1961)

Ian Morrison, *Malayan Postscript* (Faber and Faber, London, 1942)

Kiboi Muriithi (with Peter Ndoria), *War in the Forest: The Autobiography of a Mau Mau Leader* (East African Publishing House, Nairobi, 1971)

Gerald Murphy, *Copper Mandarin: A Memoir* (Regency Press, London, 1984)

Ronnie Noble, *Shoot First! Assignments of a Newsreel Cameraman* (Harrap, London, 1955)

Victor Purcell, *The Memoirs of a Malayan Official* (Cassell, London, 1965)

Reflections of a Statesman: The Writings and Speeches of Enoch Powell, ed. R. Collings (Bellow, London, 1991)

J.C.W. Reith, *Into the Wind* (Hodder and Stoughton, London, 1949)

Donald Sinden, *A Touch of the Memoirs* (Futura, London, 1983)

Freya Stark, *Dust in the Lion's Paw: Autobiography 1939–1946* (Arrow Books, London, 1990)

Lam Swee, *My Accusation* (Malayan Government Printer, Kuala Lumpur, 1951)

Margaret Thatcher, *The Downing Street Years* (HarperCollins, London, 1993)

Penelope Tremayne, *Below the Tide* (Hutchinson, London, 1958)

Penelope Tremayne, *A Writer or Something* (Unwin Hyman, London, 1988)

Ashton Wade, *A Life on the Line* (Costello, Tunbridge Wells, 1988)

Joram Wamweya, *Freedom Fighter* (East African Publishing House, Nairobi, 1971)

Francis Williams, *Nothing So Strange* (Cassell, London, 1970)

Major R.D. Wilson, *Cordon and Search: With the Sixth Airborne Division in Palestine* (Gale and Polden, Aldershot, 1949)

Books

NON-FICTION

A. Odasuo Alali and Kenoye Kelvin Eke (eds), *Media Coverage of Terrorism: Methods of Diffusion* (SAGE Publications, Newbury Park, Calif., 1991)

Richard Aldrich (ed.), *British Intelligence, Strategy and the Cold War* (Routledge, London, 1992)

Yonah Alexander (ed.), *International Terrorism: National, Regional and Global Perspectives* (Praeger, New York, 1976)

Yonah Alexander and Alan O'Day (eds), *Terrorism in Ireland* (Croom Helm, London, 1984)

Yonah Alexander and R. Latter (eds), *Terrorism and the Media: Dilemmas for Government, Journalism and the Media* (Brassey's (US), Washington, 1990)

Yonah Alexander and Robert G. Picard, *In the Camera's Eye: News Coverage of Terrorist Events* (Brassey's (US), Washington, 1991)

Charles Allen, *The Savage Wars of Peace: Soldiers' Voices 1945–1989* (Futura, London, 1991)

David M. Anderson and David Killingray (eds), *Policing and Decolonisation: Politics, Nationalism and the Police, 1917–65* (Manchester University Press, Manchester, 1992)

Franz Ansprenger, *The Dissolution of the Colonial Empires* (Routledge, London, 1989)

M. Balfour, *Propaganda in War, 1939–1945* (Routledge and Kegan Paul, London, 1979)

280

Noel Barber, *The War of the Running Dogs: How Malaya Defeated the Communist Guerrillas 1948–60* (Fontana, London, 1972)

Dudley Barker, *Grivas: Portrait of a Terrorist* (The Cresset Press, London, 1959)

E. Barker, *The British between the Superpowers* (Macmillan, London, 1983)

Pat Barr, *Taming the Jungle: The Men Who Made British Malaya* (Readers Union, Newton Abbot, 1978)

J. Bowyer Bell, *Terror out of Zion: Irgun, Lehi, and the Palestine Underground, 1929–49* (St Martin's Press, New York, 1977)

Bruce Berman, *Control and Crisis in Colonial Kenya: The Dialectic of Domination* (James Currey, London, 1990)

Bruce Berman and John Lonsdale, *Unhappy Valley: Conflict in Kenya and Africa*. Book 2: *Violence and Ethnicity* (James Currey, London, 1992)

Nicholas Bethell, *The Palestine Triangle: The Struggle between the British, the Jews and the Arabs, 1935–48* (André Deutsch, London, 1979)

T.F.C. Bewes, *Kikuyu Conflict: Mau Mau and the Christian Witness* (Highway Press, London, 1953)

Roger Bolton, *Death on the Rock and Other Stories* (W.H. Allen, London, 1990)

Tom Bowden, *The Breakdown of Public Security: The Case of Ireland 1916–1921 and Palestine 1936–1939* (SAGE Publications, London, 1977)

D.G. Boyce, *Englishmen and Irish Troubles: British Public Opinion and the Making of Irish Policy, 1918–22* (Jonathan Cape, London, 1972)

Andrew Boyle, *Only the Wind Will Listen: Reith of the BBC* (Hutchinson, London, 1972)

J.A.C. Brown, *Techniques of Persuasion: From Propaganda to Brainwashing* (Penguin Books, Harmondsworth, 1963)

R. Buijtenhuis, *Mau Mau Twenty Years After: The Myth and the Survivors* (Mouton, The Hague, 1973)

Anthony M. Burton, *Urban Terrorism: Theory, Practice and Response* (Leo Cooper, London, 1975)

W. Byford-Jones, *Grivas and the Story of EOKA* (Robert Hale, London, 1959)

James Cameron, *What a Way to Run the Tribe: Selected Articles, 1948–67* (Macmillan, London, 1968)

Arthur Campbell, *Guerillas: A History and Analysis* (Arthur Barker, London, 1967)

Albert Camus, *The Rebel* (Penguin Books, London, 1971)

Michael Carver, *Harding of Petherton* (Weidenfeld and Nicolson, London, 1978)

Michael Carver, *War since 1945* (Weidenfeld and Nicolson, London, 1980)

Gerard Chaliand, *Terrorism: From Popular Struggle to Media Spectacle* (Saqi Books, London, 1987)

David Charters, *The British Army and Jewish Insurgency in Palestine, 1945–7* (Macmillan, London, 1989)

David Charters and Maurice Tugwell (eds), *Armies in Low-Intensity Conflict: A Comparative Analysis* (Brassey's, London, 1989)

Steve Chibnall, *Law-and-Order News: An Analysis of Crime Reporting in the British Press* (Tavistock, London, 1977)

Noam Chomsky, *The Culture of Terrorism* (Pluto Press, London, 1989)

Noam Chomsky, *Necessary Illusions: Thought Control in Democratic Societies* (Pluto Press, London, 1989)

Noam Chomsky, *Deterring Democracy* (Verso, London, 1991)

Sir Fife Clark, *The Central Office of Information* (George Allen and Unwin, London, 1970)

Anthony Clayton, *Counter-insurgency in Kenya, 1952–60: A Study of Military Operations against Mau Mau* (Transafrica, Nairobi, 1976)

John C. Clews, *Communist Propaganda Techniques* (Methuen, London, 1964)

Ray S. Cline and Yonah Alexander, *Terrorism as State-Sponsored Covert Warfare* (Hero Books, Fairfax, Va., 1896)

John Cloake, *Templer: Tiger of Malaya. The Life of Field Marshal Sir Gerald Templer* (Harrap, London, 1985)

Richard Clutterbuck, *Guerrillas and Terrorists* (Faber and Faber, London, 1977)

Richard Clutterbuck, *The Media and Political Violence* (Macmillan, Basingstoke, 1981)

Richard Clutterbuck (ed.), *The Future of Political Violence: Destabilisation, Disorder and Terrorism* (Macmillan, Basingstoke, 1986)

John Coates, *Suppressing Insurgency: An Analysis of the Malayan Emergency, 1948–54* (Westview Press, Boulder, Colo., 1992)

Helena Cobban, *The Palestine Liberation Organisation: People, Power and Politics* (Cambridge University Press, Cambridge, 1984)

Michael Cockerell *et al.*, *Sources Close to the Prime Minister: Inside the Hidden World of the News Manipulators* (Macmillan, Basingstoke, 1984)

Michael J. Cohen, *Palestine: Retreat from the Mandate* (Elek, London, 1978)

Michael J. Cohen, *Palestine and the Great Powers 1945–48* (Princeton University Press, Princeton, N.J., 1982)

Richard Collins, Peter Hennessy and David Walker, *Media, Culture and Society: A Critical Reader* (SAGE Publications, London, 1986)

Nancy Crawshaw, *The Cyprus Revolt: An Account of the Struggle for Union with Greece* (George Allen and Unwin, London, 1978)

Martha Crenshaw (ed.), *Terrorism, Legitimacy, and Power: The Consequences of Political Violence* (Wesleyan University Press, Middletown, Conn., 1983)

William Crofts, *Coercion or Persuasion: Propaganda in Britain after 1945* (Routledge, London, 1989)

Colin Cross, *The Fall of the British Empire 1918–1968* (Paladin, London, 1970)

Brian Crozier, *The Rebels: A Study of Post-war Insurrections* (Chatto and Windus, London, 1960)

Brian Crozier, *South-East Asia in Turmoil* (Penguin Books, Harmondsworth, 1965)

Charles Cruickshank, *The Fourth Arm: Psychological Warfare 1938–45* (Oxford University Press, Oxford, 1977)

Charles Cruickshank, *SOE in the Far East* (Oxford University Press, Oxford, 1983)

Donald Crummey (ed.), *Banditry, Rebellion and Social Protest in Africa* (James Currey, London, 1986)

Hugh Cudlipp, *Publish and Be Damned! The Astonishing Story of the 'Daily Mirror'* (Andrew Dakers, London, 1953)

James Curran and Vincent Porter, *British Cinema History* (Weidenfeld and Nicolson, London, 1983)

283

James Curran and Jean Seaton, *Power without Responsibility: The Press and Broadcasting in Britain* (Routledge, London, 4th ed., 1991)

Liz Curtis, *Ireland: The Propaganda War. The British Media and the Battle for Hearts and Minds* (Pluto Press, London, 1984)

John Darwin, *Britain and Decolonisation: The Retreat from Empire in the Post-war World* (Macmillan, Basingstoke, 1988)

Basil Davidson, *Africa in History: Themes and Outlines* (Paladin, London, 1987)

Ann Deighton, *Britain and the First Cold War* (Macmillan, Basingstoke, 1990)

Michael Dewar, *Brush Fire Wars: Minor Campaigns of the British Army since 1945* (Robert Hale, London, 1990)

Bethami A. Dobkin, *Tales of Terror: Television News and the Construction of the Terrorist Threat* (Praeger, New York, 1992)

Frances Donaldson, *The British Council: The First Fifty Years* (Jonathan Cape, London, 1984)

Leonard Doob, *Public Opinion and Propaganda* (Holt, New York, 1948)

Charles Douglas-Home, *Evelyn Baring: The Last Proconsul* (Collins, London, 1978)

Harry Eckstein (ed.), *Internal War: Problems and Approaches* (Free Press, New York, 1964)

Maurice Edelman, *Ben Gurion: A Political Biography* (Hodder and Stoughton, London, 1964)

Robert B. Edgerton, *Mau Mau: An African Crucible* (I.B. Tauris, London, 1990)

John Eldridge (ed.), *Getting the Message: News, Truth and Power* (Routledge, London, 1993)

Jacques Ellul, *Propaganda: The Formation of Men's Attitudes* (Vintage Books, New York, 1973)

Geoffrey Fairbairn, *Revolutionary Guerrilla Warfare: The Countryside Version* (Penguin, Harmondsworth, 1974)

Frantz Fanon, *The Wretched of the Earth* (Penguin Books, Harmondsworth, 1967)

Negley Farson, *Last Chance in Africa* (Victor Gollancz, London, 1949)

Paul Ferris, *Sir Huge: The Life of Huw Wheldon* (Michael Joseph, London, 1990)

Charles Foley, *Island in Revolt* (Longmans, London, 1962)

Charles Foley, *Legacy of Strife: Cyprus from Rebellion to Civil War* (Penguin Books, Harmondsworth, 1964)

Charles Foley and W.I. Scobie, *The Struggle for Cyprus* (Hoover Institution Press, Stanford, Calif., 1975)

R.G. Frey and Christopher W. Morris (eds), *Violence, Terrorism, and Justice* (Cambridge University Press, Cambridge, 1991)

Frank Furedi, *The Mau Mau War in Perspective* (James Currey, London, 1989)

Frank Furedi, *Colonial Wars and the Politics of Third World Nationalism* (I.B. Tauris, London, 1994)

G.H. Gallup, *The Gallup International Opinion Polls: Great Britain, 1937–1975.* Vol. 1: *1937–1964* (Random House, New York, 1976)

Conor Gearty, *Terror* (Faber and Faber, London, 1991)

Alexander George (ed.), *Western State Terrorism* (Polity Press, Cambridge, 1991)

Peter Golding, Graham Murdock and Philip Schlesinger (eds), *Communicating Politics: Mass Communications and the Political Process* (Leicester University Press, Leicester, 1986)

Celia Goodman (ed.), *Living with Koestler: Mamaine Koestler's Letters 1945–51* (Weidenfeld and Nicolson, London, 1985)

Patrick Gordon Walker, *The Commonwealth* (Mercury Books, London, 1965)

Anthony Gorst, Lewis Johnman and W. Scott Lucas (eds), *Contemporary British History 1931–1961: Politics and the Limits of Policy* (Pinter, London, 1991)

Sir Percival Griffiths, *Empire into Commonwealth* (Ernest Benn, London, 1969)

John Gunther, *Inside Africa* (Hamish Hamilton, London, 1955)

Fred Halliday, *The Making of the Second Cold War* (Verso, London, 2nd ed., 1986)

Edward S. Herman, *The Real Terror Network: Terror in Fact and Propaganda* (South End Press, Boston, 1982)

Edward S. Herman and Noam Chomsky, *Manufacturing Consent: The Political Economy of the Mass Media* (Pantheon Books, New York, 1988)

David Hirst, *The Gun and the Olive Branch: The Roots of Violence in the Middle East* (Faber and Faber, London, 1977)

E.J. Hobsbawm, *Bandits* (Penguin Books, Harmondsworth, 1972)

Ted Honderich, *Violence for Equality: Inquiries in Political Philosophy* (Routledge, London, 3rd ed., 1989)

Alan Hooper *The Military and the Media* (Gower, Aldershot, 1982)

Edward Horne, *A Job Well Done, Being a History of the Palestine Police Force, 1920–1948* (Palestine Police Old Comrades Benevolent Association, Leigh-on-Sea, Essex, 1982)

Ellic Howe, *The Black Game: British Subversive Operations against the Germans during the Second World War* (Queen Anne Press/Futura, London, 1982)

Stephen Howe, *Anticolonialism in British Politics: The Left and the End of Empire 1918–1964* (Clarendon Press, Oxford, 1993)

A.J. Hughes, *East Africa: The Search for Unity. Kenya, Tanganyika, Uganda, and Zanzibar* (Penguin Books, Harmondsworth, 1963)

J.C. Hurewitz, *The Struggle for Palestine* (Schocken Books, New York, 1976)

Elspeth Huxley (ed.), *Nine Faces of Kenya: An Anthology* (Harvill, London, 1991)

Elspeth Huxley and Margery Perham, *Race and Politics in Kenya* (Faber and Faber, London, 1956)

Albert M. Hyamson, *Palestine under the Mandate, 1920–1948* (Methuen, London, 1950)

Leontios Ierodiakonou, *The Cyprus Question* (Almqvist and Wiksell, Stockholm, 1971)

Peter Janke with Richard Sim, *Guerrilla and Terrorist Organisations: A World Directory and Bibliography* (Harvester, Brighton, 1983)

Keith Jeffery and Peter Hennessy, *States of Emergency: British Governments and Strikebreaking since 1919* (Routledge and Kegan Paul, London, 1983)

Martin Jones, *Failure in Palestine: British and United States Policy after the Second World War* (Mansell, London, 1986)

Garth S. Jowett and Victoria O'Donnell, *Propaganda and Persuasion* (SAGE Publications, Newbury Park, Calif., 2nd ed., 1992)

Charles W. Kegley, Jr (ed.), *International Terrorism: Characteristics, Causes, Controls* (St Martin's Press, New York, 1990)

Sam Keen, *Faces of the Enemy: Reflections of the Hostile Imagination* (Harper and Row, San Francisco, 1986)

Frank Kitson, *Warfare as a Whole* (Faber and Faber, London, 1987)

Frank Kitson, *Low Intensity Operations: Subversion, Insurgency, Peace-Keeping* (Faber and Faber, London, 1991)

Phillip Knightley, *The First Casualty. From the Crimea to the Falklands: The War Correspondent as Hero, Propagandist, and Myth Maker* (Pan Books, London, 1989)

Arthur Koestler, *Promise and Fulfilment: Palestine 1917–1949* (Papermac, London 1983)

Stephen Koss, *The Rise and Fall of the Political Press in Britain* (Fontana Press, London, 1990)

Brian Lapping, *End of Empire* (Granada, London, 1985)

Walter Laqueur (ed.), *The Israel–Arab Reader* (Penguin Books, London, 1970)

Walter Laqueur, *Terrorism* (Weidenfeld and Nicolson, London, 1977)

Walter Laqueur and Yonah Alexander (eds), *The Terrorist Reader: A Historical Anthology* (Meridian, New York, 1987)

Anthony Lavers, *The Kikuyu Who Fight Mau Mau* (Eagle Press, Nairobi, 1955)

L.S.B. Leakey, *Mau Mau and the Kikuyu* (Methuen, London, 1952)

L.S.B. Leakey, *Defeating Mau Mau* (Methuen, London, 1954)

Ione Leigh, *In the Shadow of the Mau Mau* (W.H. Allen, London, 1954)

Captain P.S. Le Geyt, *Makarios in Exile* (Anagennisis Press, Nicosia, 1961)

Marius Livingston *et al.*, *International Terrorism in the Contemporary World* (Greenwood Press, Westport, Conn., 1978)

Juliet Lodge (ed.), *Terrorism: A Challenge to the State* (Martin Robertson, Oxford, 1981)

W.R. Louis and R.W. Stookey (eds), *The End of the Palestine Mandate* (I.B. Tauris, London, 1986)

J.N. McHugh, *Anatomy of Communist Propaganda July 1948–December 1949* (Malayan Government Printer, Kuala Lumpur, 1950)

A.J. Mackenzie, *Propaganda Boom* (Right Book Club, London 1938)

John M. MacKenzie, *Propaganda and Empire: The Manipulation of British*

Public Opinion, 1880–1960 (Manchester University Press, Manchester, 1984)

John M. MacKenzie (ed.), *Imperialism and Popular Culture* (Manchester University Press, Manchester, 1986)

Gerald McKnight, *The Mind of the Terrorist* (Michael Joseph, London, 1974)

Ian McLaine, *Ministry of Morale: Home Front Morale and the Ministry of Information in World War II* (George Allen and Unwin, London, 1979)

Brian McNair, *Images of the Enemy: Reporting the New Cold War* (Routledge, London, 1988)

Fred Majdalany, *State of Emergency: The Full Story of Mau Mau* (Longmans, London, 1962)

Sir Robert Marett, *Through the Back Door: An Inside View of Britain's Overseas Information Services* (Pergamon Press, Oxford, 1968)

Lester Markel *et al.*, *Public Opinion and Foreign Policy* (Harper Brothers, New York, 1949)

David Maughan-Brown, *Land, Freedom and Fiction: History and Ideology in Kenya* (Zed Books, London, 1985)

Annabelle May and Kathryn Rowan (eds), *Inside Information: British Government and the Media* (Constable, London, 1982)

Stanley Mayes, *Cyprus and Makarios* (Putnam, London, 1960)

Stanley Mayes, *Makarios: A Biography* (Macmillan, Basingstoke, 1981)

Abraham H. Miller (ed.), *Terrorism, the Media and the Law* (Transnational, New York, 1982)

David Miller, *Don't Mention the War: Northern Ireland, Propaganda and the Media* (Pluto Press, London, 1994)

Thomas R. Mockaitis, *British Counterinsurgency, 1919–60* (Macmillan, Basingstoke, 1990)

Wolfgang J. Mommsen and Gerhard Hirschfeld (eds), *Social Protest, Violence and Terror in Nineteenth- and Twentieth-Century Europe* (Macmillan, Basingstoke, 1982)

Elizabeth Monroe, *Britain's Moment in the Middle East, 1914–1956* (Methuen, London, 1965)

Eric Moonman (ed.), *The Violent Society* (Frank Cass, London, 1987)

Shaikshwar Nath, *Terrorism in India* (National Publishing House, New Delhi, 1980)

Benjamin Netanyahu (ed.), *Terrorism: How the West Can Win* (Avon Books, New York, 1987)

Edgar O'Ballance, *Terrorism in the 1980s* (Arms and Armour Press, London, 1989)

Conor Cruise O'Brien, *Passion and Cunning: Essays on Nationalism, Terrorism and Revolution* (Simon and Schuster, New York, 1989)

Marjorie Ogilvy-Webb, *The Government Explains: A Study of the Information Services* (George Allen and Unwin, London, 1965)

Major J.B. Oldfield, *The Green Howards in Malaya* (Gale and Polden, Aldershot, 1953)

Noel O'Sullivan (ed.), *Terrorism, Ideology, and Revolution: The Origins of Modern Political Violence* (Wheatsheaf Books, Brighton, 1986)

Ritchie Ovendale, *Britain, the United States, and the End of the Palestine Mandate, 1942–48* (Boydell Press, Woodbridge, Suffolk, 1989)

Ritchie Ovendale, *The Origins of the Arab–Israeli Wars* (Longman, London, 2nd ed., 1992)

Julian Paget, *Counter-insurgency Campaigning* (Faber and Faber, London, 1967)

David L. Paletz and Alex P. Schmid (eds), *Terrorism and the Media* (SAGE Publications, Newbury Park, Calif., 1992)

Albert Parry, *Terrorism from Robespierre to Arafat* (Vanguard Press, New York, 1976)

Peter Partner, *Arab Voices: The BBC Arabic Service 1938–1988* (BBC, London, 1988)

Margery Perham, *The Colonial Reckoning. The Reith Lectures: 1961* (Collins, London, 1963)

Jan Nederveen Pieterse, *White on Black: Images of Africa and Blacks in Western Popular Culture* (Yale University Press, New Haven, 1992)

Tom Pocock, *East and West of Suez* (The Bodley Head, London, 1986)

Nicholas Pronay and Derek Spring (eds), *Propaganda, Politics and Film, 1918–45* Macmillan, London, 1982)

Nicholas Pronay and Keith Wilson (eds), *The Political Re-education of Germany and Her Allies after World War II* (Croom Helm, London, 1985)

Victor Purcell, *Malaya: Communist or Free?* (Victor Gollancz, London, 1954)

Lucian W. Pye, *Guerrilla Communism in Malaya: Its Social and Political Meaning* (Princeton University Press, Princeton, N.J., 1956)

Terence H. Qualter, *Opinion Control in the Democracies* (Macmillan, London, 1985)

D.H. Rawcliffe, *The Struggle for Kenya* (Victor Gollancz, London, 1954)

John Reddaway, *Burdened with Cyprus: The British Connection* (Weidenfeld and Nicolson, London, 1986)

Walter Reich (ed.), *Origins of Terrorism: Psychologies, Ideologies, Theologies, States of Mind* (Cambridge University Press, Cambridge, 1990)

Jeffrey Richards, *Visions of Yesterday* (Routledge and Kegan Paul, London, 1973)

General Sir Charles Richardson, *From Churchill's Secret Circle to the BBC: The Biography of Lieutenant-General Sir Ian Jacob* (Brassey's (UK), London, 1991)

Anthony H. Richmond, *The Colour Problem: A Study of Racial Relations* (Penguin Books, Harmondsworth, 1961)

C.H. Rolph, *Kingsley: The Life, Letters and Diaries of Kingsley Martin* (Victor Gollancz, London, 1973)

Carl G. Rosberg, Jr and John Nottingham, *The Myth of 'Mau Mau': Nationalism in Kenya* (Praeger, New York, 1966)

Trevor Royle, *War Report: The War Correspondent's View of Battle from the Crimea to the Falklands* (Grafton Books, London, 1989)

Philip Schlesinger, *Putting 'Reality' Together: BBC News* (Methuen, London, 1987)

Philip Schlesinger, *Media, State and Nation: Political Violence and Collective Identities* (SAGE Publications, London, 1991)

Philip Schlesinger, Graham Murdock and Philip Elliott, *Televising 'Terrorism': Political Violence in Popular Culture* (Comedia, London, 1983)

A.P. Schmid and J. de Graaf, *Violence as Communication: Insurgent Terrorism and the Western News Media* (SAGE Publications, London, 1982)

A.P. Schmid and A.J. Jongman, *Political Terrorism: A New Guide to Actors, Authors, Concepts, Data Bases, Theories and Literature* (North-Holland Publishing, Amsterdam, 2nd ed., 1988)

Stephen Segallar, *Invisible Armies: Terrorism into the 1990s* (Harcourt Brace Jovanovich, Orlando, Fla., 1987)

Colin Seymour-Ure, *The British Press and Broadcasting since 1945* (Basil Blackwell, Oxford, 1991)

J. Shaw, E. Gueritz and A.E. Younger (eds), *Ten Years of Terrorism: Collected Views* (Royal United Services Institute, London, 1979)

Anthony Short, *The Communist Insurrection in Malaya 1948–1960* (Frederick Muller, London, 1975)

K.R.M. Short, *The Dynamite War: Irish-American Bombers in Victorian Britain* (Gill and Macmillan, Dublin, 1979)

Christopher Simpson, *Science of Coercion: Communication Research and Psychological Warfare 1945–60* (Oxford University Press, Oxford, 1994)

Michael Sissons and Philip French (eds), *The Age of Austerity* (Oxford University Press, Oxford, 1986)

Robert O. Slater and Michael Stohl (eds), *Current Perspectives on International Terrorism* (Macmillan, Basingstoke, 1988)

Bradley Smith, *The Shadow Warriors: OSS and the Origins of the CIA* (André Deutsch, London, 1983)

Justin Davis Smith, *The Attlee and Churchill Administrations and Industrial Unrest 1945–55: A Study in Consensus* (Pinter, London, 1990)

David Stafford, *Britain and European Resistance, 1940–1945: A Survey of the Special Operations Executive, with Documents* (Macmillan, Basingstoke, 1980)

Henry Stanhope, *The Soldiers: An Anatomy of the British Army* (Hamish Hamilton, London, 1979)

M.R. Stenson, *Industrial Conflict in Malaya: Prelude to the Communist Revolt of 1948* (Oxford University Press, London, 1970)

Robert Stephens, *Cyprus: A Place of Arms. Power Politics and Ethnic Conflict in the Eastern Mediterranean* (Pall Mall Press, London, 1966)

Claire Sterling, *The Terror Network: The Secret War of International Terrorism* (Weidenfeld and Nicolson, London, 1981)

C.T. Stoneham, *Mau Mau* (Museum Press, London, 1953)

C.T. Stoneham, *Out of Barbarism* (Museum Press, London, 1955)

Richard Stubbs, *Hearts and Minds in Guerrilla Warfare: The Malayan Emergency, 1948–60* (Oxford University Press, Oxford, 1989)

Christopher Sykes, *Crossroads to Israel* (Indiana University Press, Bloomington, 1973)

Robert Taber, *The War of the Flea: A Study of Guerrilla Warfare Theory and Practice* (Paladin, St Albans, 1970)

Philip M. Taylor, *Munitions of the Mind: War Propaganda from the Ancient World to the Nuclear Age* (Patrick Stephens, Wellingborough, 1990)

Bibliography

Robert Thompson, *Defeating Communist Insurgency: Experiences from Malaya and Vietnam* (Chatto and Windus, London, 1966)

David Throup, *Economic and Social Origins of Mau Mau, 1945–53* (James Currey, London, 1987)

Charles Townshend, *The British Campaign in Ireland 1919–21: The Development of Political and Military Policies* (Oxford University Press, Oxford, 1975)

Charles Townshend, *Political Violence in Ireland: Government and Resistance since 1848* (Clarendon Press, Oxford, 1983)

Charles Townshend, *Britain's Civil Wars: Counterinsurgency in the Twentieth Century* (Faber and Faber, London, 1986)

Michael Tracey, *A Variety of Lives: A Biography of Sir Hugh Greene* (The Bodley Head, London, 1983)

Paul Virilio, *War and Cinema: The Logistics of Perception* (Verso, London, 1989)

Eugene V. Walter, *Terror and Resistance: A Study of Political Violence with Case Studies of Some Primitive African Communities* (Oxford University Press, Oxford, 1969)

Michael Walzer, *Just and Unjust Wars: A Moral Argument with Historical Illustrations* (Basic Books, New York, 2nd ed., 1992)

Grant Wardlaw, *Political Terrorism: Theory, Tactics, and Counter-measures* (Cambridge University Press, Cambridge, 2nd ed., 1989)

Martin Warner and Roger Crisp (eds), *Terrorism, Protest and Power* (Edward Elgar, Aldershot, 1990)

Peter Weiler, *British Labour and the Cold War* (Stanford University Press, Stanford, Calif., 1988)

Paul Wilkinson (ed.), *British Perspectives on Terrorism* (George Allen and Unwin, London, 1981)

Paul Wilkinson, *Terrorism and the Liberal State* (New York University Press, New York, 2nd ed., 1986)

Paul Wilkinson and Alasdair M. Stewart, *Contemporary Research on Terrorism* (Aberdeen University Press, Aberdeen, 1987)

Francis Williams, *Press, Parliament and People* (William Heinemann, London, 1946)

Francis Williams, *Ernest Bevin: Portrait of a Great Englishman* (Hutchinson, London, 1952)

Colin Wills, *Who Killed Kenya?* (Dennis Dobson, London, 1953)

Christopher Wilson, *Before the Dawn in Kenya: An Authentic Account of Life in East Africa When It Was under African Rule* (English Press, Nairobi, 1952)

Sir Richard Winstedt, *Malaya and Its History* (Hutchinson's University Library, London, no date)

J. Wright, *Terrorist Propaganda* (Macmillan, Basingstoke, 1991)

Woodrow Wyatt, *Southwards from China: A Survey of South East Asia since 1945* (Hodder and Stoughton, London, 1952)

Peter R. Young (ed.), *Defence and the Media in Time of Limited War* (Frank Cass, London, 1992)

FICTION

John Appleby, *The Bad Summer* (Hodder and Stoughton, London, 1958)

Noel Barber, *Tanamera: A Novel of Singapore* (Coronet Books, London, 1989)

Ian Stuart Black, *The High Bright Sun* (Hutchinson, London, 1961)

Pierre Boulle, *Sacrilege in Malaya* (Fontana Books, London, 1961)

Robert Buckner, *Sigrid and the Sergeant* (Heinemann, London, 1958)

Robert Buckner, *Tiger by the Tail* (Heinemann, London, 1960)

Anthony Burgess, *Malayan Trilogy: Time for a Tiger; The Enemy in the Blanket; Beds in the East* (Pan Books, London, 1964)

Diana Buttenshaw, *Violence in Paradise* (Hodder and Stoughton, London, 1957)

Arthur Campbell, *Jungle Green* (George Allen and Unwin, London, 1953)

Joseph Conrad, *Heart of Darkness* (Penguin Books, London, 1985)

Stephen Cook, *Empire Born* (Hodder and Stoughton, London, 1986)

S.C. George, *Planter's Wife* (Jarrolds, London, 1951)

Katherine Gordon, *Cheetah* (Hodder and Stoughton, London, 1986)

Millicent Gordon, *African Dawn* (Avon Books, New York, 1989)

Joel Gross, *This Year in Jerusalem* (Piatkus, Loughton, Essex, 1984)

Han Suyin *And The Rain My Drink* (Jonathan Cape, London, 1956)

Bibliography

Gerald Hanley, *The Consul at Sunset* (Reprint Society, London, 1952)

M. Harding, *Mask of Friendship* (Collins, London, 1956)

Douglas Hurd and Andrew Osmond, *The Smile on the Face of the Tiger* (Collins, London, 1969)

Elspeth Huxley, *A Thing to Love* (Chatto and Windus, London, 1954)

Arthur Koestler, *Thieves in the Night* (Hutchinson, London, 1965)

Daniel Nash, *My Son Is in the Mountains* (Jonathan Cape, London, 1955)

Daniel Nash, *Not Yours the Island* (Jonathan Cape, London, 1956)

Daniel Nash, *Stay the Execution* (Jonathan Cape, London, 1957)

Ngugi wa Thiong'o, *Petals of Blood* (Heinemann, London, 1977)

Ngugi wa Thiong'o, *A Grain of Wheat* (Heinemann, Oxford, 1986)

Ngugi wa Thiong'o, *Matigari* (Heinemann, Oxford, 1989)

Simon Raven, *The Feathers of Death* (Anthony Blond, London, 1959)

V.S. Reid, *The Leopard* (Heinemann, London, 1980)

Robert Ruark, *Something of Value* (Doubleday, Garden City, New York, 1955)

Robert Ruark, *Uhuru* (Hamish Hamilton, London, 1962)

Richard St Barbe Baker, *Kabongo: The Story of a Kikuyu Chief* (George Ronald, Oxford, 1955)

C.T. Stoneham, *The Dongoi Killer* (Museum Press, London, 1952)

C.T. Stoneham, *Kenya Mystery* (Museum Press, London, 1954)

Leslie Thomas, *The Virgin Soldiers* (Penguin Books, London, 1991)

W.B. Thomas, *The Touch of Pitch* (Allan Wingate, London, 1956)

James Ramsey Ullman, *Windom's Way* (Fontana Books, London, 1956)

David Unwin, *The Governor's Wife* (Michael Joseph, London, 1954)

Leon Uris, *Exodus* (Corgi Books, London, 1972)

Tom Wolfe, *Radical Chic and Mau-Mauing the Flak Catchers* (Cardinal/Sphere, London, 1989)

Susan Yorke, *Agency House, Malaya* (Macfadden-Bartell, New York, 1969)

Articles

David Anderson, 'Policing and Communal Conflict: The Cyprus Emergency, 1954-60', *Journal of Imperial and Commonwealth History*, 21, iii (Sept. 1993), 177–207

Caroline Anstey, 'The Projection of British Socialism: Foreign Office Publicity and American Opinion, 1945–50', *Journal of Contemporary History*, 19 (1984), 417–51

Anthony Arblaster, 'What Is Violence?', *Socialist Register* (1975), 224–49

J. Bowyer Bell, 'Trends on Terror: The Analysis of Political Violence', *World Politics*, 19, iii (April 1977), 476–88

Bruce Berman and John Lonsdale, 'Louis Leakey's Mau Mau: A Study in the Politics of Knowledge', *History and Anthropology*, 5, ii (1991), 143–204

Y.S. Brenner, 'The "Stern Gang" 1940–48', *Middle Eastern Studies*, 2, i (Oct. 1965), 2–30

Susan Carruthers, 'Two Faces of 1950s Terrorism: The Film Presentation of Mau Mau and the Malayan Emergency', *Small Wars and Insurgencies*, 6(1) (Spring 1995), 17–44.

David Charters, 'British Intelligence in the Palestine Campaign', *Intelligence and National Security*, 6, i, (Jan. 1991), 115–40

Patrick Clawson, 'Why We Need More But Better Coverage of Terrorism', *Orbis*, 27, (Winter 1987), 701–10

A.S. Cleary, 'The Myth of Mau Mau in its International Context', *African Affairs*, 89, 355 (April 1990), 227–45

Frederick Cooper, 'Mau Mau and the Discourses of Decolonization', *Journal of African History*, 29 (1988), 313–20

Martha Crenshaw, 'An Organisational Approach to the Analysis of Political Terrorism', *Orbis*, 29, iii (Fall 1985), 465–89

Gerald Cromer, '"In the Mirror of the Past": The Use of History in the Justification of Terrorism', *Terrorism and Political Violence*, 3, iv (1991), 164–78

Sir Alan Cunningham, 'Palestine: The Last Days of the Mandate', *International Affairs*, 24 (1948), 481–90

Richard Dyer, 'White', *Screen*, 29, iv (Autumn 1988), 44–64

R. Fletcher, 'British Propaganda since World War Two: A Case Study', *Media, Culture and Society*, 4, (1982), 97–109

295

Frank Furedi, 'Britain's Colonial Emergencies and the Invisible Nationalists', *Journal of Historical Sociology*, 2, iii (Sept. 1989), 240–64

Frank Furedi, 'Britain's Colonial Wars: Playing the Ethnic Card', *Journal of Commonwealth and Comparative Politics*, 28 (March 1990), 70–89

Frank Furedi, 'Creating a Breathing Space: The Political Management of Colonial Emergencies', *Journal of Imperial and Commonwealth History*, 21, iii (Sept. 1993), 89–106

L.F.E. Goldie, 'Profile of a Terrorist: Distinguishing Freedom Fighters from Terrorists', *Syracuse Journal of International Law and Commerce*, 14 (Winter 1987), 125–39

Maia Green, 'Mau Mau Oathing Rituals and Political Ideology in Kenya: A Re-analysis', *Africa*, 60, i (1990), 69–87

H.C. Greisman, 'Social Meanings of Terrorism: Reification, Violence and Social Control', *Contemporary Crises*, 1 (1977), 303–18

Evanthis Hatzivassiliou, 'Blocking *Enosis*: Britain and the Cyprus Question, March–December 1956', *Journal of Imperial and Commonwealth History*, 19, ii (1991), 247–63

Randall W. Heather, 'Intelligence and Counter-Insurgency in Kenya, 1952–56', *Intelligence and National Security*, 5, iii (July 1990), 57–83

Jenny Hocking, 'Orthodox Theories of "Terrorism": The Power of Politicised Terminology', *Politics*, 19, ii (Nov. 1984), 103–10

Robert Holland, 'Never, Never Land: British Colonial Policy and the Roots of Violence in Cyprus, 1950–54', *Journal of Imperial and Commonwealth History*, 21, iii (Sept. 1993), 148–76

Ze'ev Iviansky, 'Individual Terror: Concept and Typology', *Journal of Contemporary History*, 12 (1977), 43–63

Sir Geoffrey Jackson, 'Terrorism and the News Media', *Terrorism and Political Violence*, 2, iv (Winter 1990), 521–8

Brian Jenkins, 'New Modes of Conflict', *Orbis*, 28, i (Spring 1984), 5–16

Walter Laqueur, 'Reflections on Terrorism', *Foreign Affairs*, 65, i (1986), 86–100

John Lonsdale, 'Mau Maus of the Mind: Making Mau Mau and Remaking Kenya', *Journal of African History*, 31 (1990), 393–421

Captain Michael T. McEwen, 'Psychological Operations against Terrorism: The Unused Weapon', *Military Review*, 66 (Jan. 1986), 59–67

Bili Melman, 'The Terrorist in Fiction', *Journal of Contemporary History*, 15 (1980), 559–76

Ray Merrick, 'The Russia Committee of the British Foreign Office and the Cold War, 1946–47', *Journal of Contemporary History*, 20 (1985), 453–68

Ralph Miliband and Marcel Liebman, 'Reflections on Anti-Communism', *Socialist Register* (1984), 1–22

Thomas R. Mockaitis, 'Minimum Force, British Counter-insurgency and the Mau Mau Rebellion: A Reply', *Small Wars and Insurgencies*, 3, i (Autumn 1992), 87–9

John Newsinger, 'A Counter-insurgency Tale: Kitson in Kenya', *Race and Class*, 31, iv (1990), 62–72

John Newsinger, 'Minimum Force, British Counter-insurgency and the Mau Mau Rebellion', *Small Wars and Insurgencies*, 3, i (Spring 1992), 47–57.

Robert Oakley, 'International Terrorism', *Foreign Affairs*, 65, i (1987), 611–29

Ritchie Ovendale, 'The Palestine Policy of the British Labour Government 1945–1946', *International Affairs*, 55, iii (July 1979), 409–31

Ritchie Ovendale, 'The Palestine Policy of the British Labour Government 1947: The Decision to Withdraw', *International Affairs*, 56, i (Jan. 1980), 73–93

Ritchie Ovendale, 'Britain, the United States and the Cold War in South-East Asia 1949-1950', *International Affairs*, 58, iii (July 1982), 447–64

Guillaume Parmentier, 'The British Press in the Suez Crisis', *Historical Journal*, 23, ii (1980), 435–48

Christopher Pyle, 'Defining Terrorism', *Foreign Policy*, 64 (Fall 1986), 63–78

David Rapoport, 'The International World as Some Terrorists Have Seen It: A Look at a Century of Memoirs', *Journal of Strategic Studies*, 10 (1987), 32–58

Mary Shannon, 'Rehabilitating the Kikuyu', *African Affairs*, 54, 214 (1955), 129–37

H. Smith, 'The BBC Television Newsreel and the Korean War', *Historical Journal of Film, Radio and Television*, 8, iii (1988), 227–52

L. Smith, 'Covert British Propaganda: The Information Research Department, 1947–77', *Millennium: Journal of International Studies*, 9, i (1980), 67–83

R. Smith, 'A Climate of Opinion: British Officials and the Development of British Soviet Policy, 1945–7', *International Affairs*, 64 (1988), 631–47

Abraham D. Sofaer, 'Terrorism and the Law', *Foreign Affairs*, 64, v (1986), 901–22

A.J. Stockwell, 'Colonial Planning during World War Two: The Case of Malaya', *Journal of Imperial and Commonwealth History*, 2, iii (May 1974), 333–51

A.J. Stockwell, 'British Imperial Policy and Decolonization in Malaya, 1942–52', *Journal of Imperial and Commonwealth History*, 13, i (Oct. 1984), 68–87

A.J. Stockwell, 'Insurgency and Decolonisation during the Malayan Emergency', *Journal of Commonwealth and Comparative Politics*, 25, i (March 1987), 71–81

A.J. Stockwell, '"A Widespread and Long-Concocted Plot to Overthrow Government in Malaya"? The Origins of the Malayan Emergency', *Journal of Imperial and Commonwealth History*, 21, iii (Sept. 1993), 66–88

Charles Townshend, 'The Irish Republican Army and the Development of Guerrilla Warfare, 1916–1921', *English Historical Review*, 94 (1979), 318–45

W. Walk, 'Coming in from the Cold: British Propaganda and Red Army Defectors, 1945–1952', *International History Review*, 9, i (Feb. 1987), 48–72

Everett L. Wheeler, 'Terrorism and Military Theory: An Historical Perspective', *Terrorism and Political Violence*, 3 (Summer 1991), 6–33

Reg Whitaker, 'Fighting the Cold War on the Home Front: America, Britain, Australia and Canada', *Socialist Register* (1984), 23–67

Luise White, 'Separating the Men from the Boys: Constructions of Gender, Sexuality, and Terrorism in Central Kenya, 1939–1959', *International Journal of African Historical Studies*, 23, i (1990), 1–25

Pamphlets

Anon., *The Kenya Picture* (Government Printer, Nairobi, undated though with a foreword by General Erskine dated 5/1/54)

Anon., *The Mau Mau in Kenya* (foreword by Granville Roberts) (Hutchinson, London, 1954)

Anon., *Truce? Diary of Principal Internal Security Incidents in Cyprus from 14th March 1957 to 31st March 1958* (Government of Cyprus, Nicosia, 1958)

Philip Bolsover, *Kenya: What Are the Facts?* (Communist Party of Great Britain, London, 1953)

J.H. Brimmell, *A Short History of the Malayan Communist Party* (Donald Moore, Singapore, 1956)

J.C. Carothers, *The Psychology of Mau Mau* (Government Printer, Nairobi, 1954)

Central Office of Information, *The Fight against Communist Terrorism in Malaya* (HMSO, London, 1953)

Richard Francis, *What Price Free Speech?* (A paper given by the Director of News and Current Affairs of the BBC to the Law Society Conference in Coventry, 27 February 1982)(BBC Publications, London, 1982)

Glasgow University Media Group, *Speak No Evil: The British Broadcasting Ban, the Media and the Conflict in Ireland* (unpublished report, 1990)

Maurice Hayes, *Conflict Research*, (University of Ulster, Centre for the Study of Conflict, Occasional Paper No.2, 1990)

William McGurn, *Terrorist or Freedom Fighter? The Cost of Confusion* (Institute for European Defence & Strategic Studies, Occasional Paper No. 25, London, 1987)

Harry Pollitt, *Malaya: Stop the War!* (Communist Party of Great Britain, London, 1952)

Wilton Park Papers, *Terrorism and the Media: Ethical and Practical Dilemmas for Government, Journalists and Public* (Wilton Park Conference No. 316, 11–15 January 1988)

Newspapers

BRITISH LIBRARY, NEWSPAPER SECTION, COLINDALE, LONDON

Daily Express	*Listener*
Daily Herald	*New Statesman and Nation*
Daily Mail	*Picture Post*
Daily Mirror	*Radio Times*
Daily Telegraph	*Spectator*
Daily Worker	*Tribune*
Evening Standard	
Manchester Guardian	
News Chronicle	
Observer	
Reynolds News	
Sunday Despatch	
Sunday Express	
Sunday Times	
The Times	

Film Sources

Feature Films

The High, Bright Sun (Rank, 1965, dir. Ralph Thomas)
Men of Two Worlds (Ealing, 1946, dir. Thorold Dickinson)
The Planter's Wife (Pinnacle, 1952, dir. Ken Annakin)
Simba (Rank, 1955, dir. Brian Desmond Hurst)
Something of Value (MGM, 1957, dir. Richard Brooks)
West of Zanzibar (Ealing, 1954, dir. Harry Watt)

Pressbooks, cuttings and production materials for *The Planter's Wife,* *Simba* and *Safari* (Columbia, 1956, dir. Terence Young) were also viewed at the National Film Archive, London

Documentaries

Operation Malaya (1953, dir. David MacDonald; viewing copy in NFA)
COI 690, *1955, The Year in Malaya* (IWM)
COI 694, *The Knife* (1955, IWM)
COI 837, *Malaya Speaks* (1955, IWM)
'End of Empire' Series, Channel 4, first screened 1985
'Palestine' Series, Thames TV, first screened 1978

Newsreels

All remaining items on Palestine (1944–47), Malaya (1948–60), Kenya (1952–60) and Cyprus (1955–60) were viewed at the following archives:

British Movietone, Denham, Uxbridge, Middlesex

British Pathé News Library, Pinewood Studios, Iver Heath, Bucks

Gaumont-British and Paramount material at Visnews Library, Reuters Television Ltd., London

Index

Index

Index